VOLUME FIFTY ONE

ADVANCES IN CHILD DEVELOPMENT AND BEHAVIOR

Equity and Justice in Developmental Science: Implications for Young People, Families, and Communities

ADVANCES IN CHILD DEVELOPMENT AND BEHAVIOR

Series Editor

JANETTE B. BENSON
Morgridge College of Education,
Department of Psychology,
University of Denver,
Denver, Colorado, USA

VOLUME FIFTY ONE

ADVANCES IN CHILD DEVELOPMENT AND BEHAVIOR

Equity and Justice in Developmental Science: Implications for Young People, Families, and Communities

Edited by

STACEY S. HORN

Department of Educational Psychology, College of Education, University of Illinois at Chicago, USA

MARTIN D. RUCK

Department of Psychology, The Graduate Center, City University of New York, USA

LYNN S. LIBEN

Department of Psychology, The Pennsylvania State University, USA

ELSEVIER

AMSTERDAM • BOSTON • HEIDELBERG • LONDON
NEW YORK • OXFORD • PARIS • SAN DIEGO
SAN FRANCISCO • SINGAPORE • SYDNEY • TOKYO

Academic Press is an imprint of Elsevier

Academic Press is an imprint of Elsevier
50 Hampshire Street, 5th Floor, Cambridge, MA 02139, United States
525 B Street, Suite 1800, San Diego, CA 92101-4495, United States
The Boulevard, Langford Lane, Kidlington, Oxford OX5 1GB, United Kingdom
125 London Wall, London, EC2Y 5AS, United Kingdom

First edition 2016

ISBN: 978-0-12-801896-5
ISSN: 0065-2407 (Series)

For information on all Academic Press publications
visit our website at https://www.elsevier.com/

Publisher: Zoe Kruze
Acquisition Editor: Kirsten Shankland
Editorial Project Manager: Hannah Colford
Production Project Manager: Radhakrishnan Lakshmanan
Cover Designer: Maria Inês Cruz

Typeset by SPi Global, India

CONTENTS

CONTRIBUTORS

Daniela Aldoney
University of Maryland, College Park, College Park, MD, United States

Jiwoon Bae
University of North Carolina at Chapel Hill, Chapel Hill, NC, United States

Donte L. Bernard
University of North Carolina at Chapel Hill, Chapel Hill, NC, United States

Rebecca S. Bigler
University of Texas at Austin, Austin, TX, United States

Janelle T. Billingsley
North Carolina Central University, Durham, NC, United States

Stacia Bourne
University of Utah, Salt Lake City, UT, United States

Rachel Byington
School of Human Ecology, University of Wisconsin-Madison, Madison, WI, United States

Natasha Cabrera
University of Maryland, College Park, College Park, MD, United States

Shelby Cooley
Community Center for Education Results, Seattle, WA, United States

Juan Del Toro
New York University, New York, NY, United States

Laura Elenbaas
University of Maryland, College Park, MD, United States

Constance A. Flanagan
School of Human Ecology, University of Wisconsin-Madison, Madison, WI, United States

Erika Fountain
Georgetown University, Washington, DC, United States

Erin Gallay
School of Human Ecology, University of Wisconsin-Madison, Madison, WI, United States

Kristin Henning
Georgetown University School of Law, Washington, DC, United States

Diane L. Hughes
New York University, New York, NY, United States

Melanie Killen
University of Maryland, College Park, MD, United States

Silvia H. Koller
Instituto de Psicologia, Universidade Federal do Rio Grande do Sul, Porto Alegre, Brazil

Catherine Kuhns
University of Maryland, College Park, College Park, MD, United States

Jenessa L. Malin
University of Maryland, College Park, College Park, MD, United States

Frosso Motti-Stefanidi
National and Kapodistrian University of Athens, Athens, Greece

Enrique W. Neblett Jr.
University of North Carolina at Chapel Hill, Chapel Hill, NC, United States

Anne Petersen
CHGD, University of Michigan, Ann Arbor; Global Philanthropy Alliance, St. Joseph, MI, United States

John M. Rohrbach
University of Texas at Austin, Austin, TX, United States

Allison Sambo
School of Human Ecology, University of Wisconsin-Madison, Madison, WI, United States

Kiara L. Sanchez
Rice University, Houston, TX, United States

Effua E. Sosoo
University of North Carolina at Chapel Hill, Chapel Hill, NC, United States

Suman Verma
Panjab University, Chandigarh, India

Cecilia Wainryb
University of Utah, Salt Lake City, UT, United States

Jon Alexander Watford
New York University, New York, NY, United States

Mackenzie D.M. Whipps
New York University, New York, NY, United States

Henry A. Willis
University of North Carolina at Chapel Hill, Chapel Hill, NC, United States

Jennifer L. Woolard
Georgetown University, Washington, DC, United States

Hirokazu Yoshikawa
New York University, New York, NY, United States

PREFACE

This is the second volume in the *Advances in Child Development and Behavior* series addressed to *Equity and Justice in Developmental Science*. Collectively, the two volumes address a wide range of conceptual, methodological, and contextual issues relevant to equity and justice for and rights of children and youth. The chapters in the first volume of the set focused primarily on conceptual and methodological issues; the chapters in the current volume focus on the implications of equity and justice for young people, their families, and their communities.[1]

The current volume begins with several chapters focusing on issues related to ethnic-racial socialization, ethnic-racial identity, and discrimination experiences. In Chapter 1, Hughes, Alexander Watford, and Toro first provide a comprehensive review of developmental knowledge regarding these three constructs and how they are both stressors and resources in the lives of ethnic-minority youth. They argue that these constructs represent interdependent, mutually defining phenomena. Given this interdependence, the authors also argue that these constructs must be studied using an ecological/transactional perspective. This perspective allows for a better understanding of setting-level features that produce and reproduce these ethnic-racial phenomena and affect development. Finally, using ecological/transactional frameworks of human development, the authors provide examples of the independent and interdependent ways in which these ethnic-racial dynamics play out in, and are affected by four proximal contexts: families, peer groups, schools, and neighborhoods.

In Chapter 2, Neblett, Sosoo, Willis, Bernard, Bae, and Billingsley also examine racial identity, racial socialization, and discrimination. They focus on the benefits of using person-centered approaches (PCAs), rather than variable-centered approaches, to study racialized experiences in diverse populations of youth. They argue that PCAs allow for more nuanced understandings of how racial and ethnic processes affect young people and provide insight into the factors that help young people navigate racism in their everyday lives. In addition, they review studies that employ PCA methods to study the relationships among racial identity, racial socialization, and

[1] For a summary of the origins and development of this two-volume set, as well as overviews of the individual chapters in the first volume, please see the earlier *Preface* reprinted below.

racialized experiences in African American youth. Finally, they consider the challenges and limitations of PCAs for better understanding diverse intragroup experiences among African American (and other racial and ethnic-minority youth).

In Chapter 3, Cabrera, Kuhns, Malin, and Aldoney explore racial socialization within ethnic-majority and ethnic-minority families. First, they identify and compare the ethnic-racial socialization practices and beliefs of ethnic-minority and ethnic-majority groups focusing on racial cognitions and parental socialization practices. Second, they examine the impact of these practices on young people's abilities to form intergroup friendships. In addition, they review gaps in the literature related to preparing young people to interact with others in an increasingly diverse world, and outline a research agenda for moving this work forward.

In Chapter 4, Cooley, Elenbaas, and Killen focus on intergroup social exclusion as a form of prejudice. They introduce their integrative social reasoning developmental model as a way to understand past research on intergroup social exclusion and to identify critical areas in need of further investigation. They present three areas of research related to children's social inclusion and exclusion decisions: intergroup contact and friendship, peer group norms, and messages from parents and teachers. Based on their review of these three areas of research, they argue that children's intergroup social exclusion involves an interplay of moral reasoning and intergroup attitudes. Finally, they argue that developmental science has a responsibility to better understand the factors that impact children's capacity to resist bias, prejudice, and negative intergroup attitudes and engage in inclusion and the just treatment of others.

In Chapter 5, Bigler, Rohrbach, and Sanchez examine interracial peer encounters by exploring how intergroup contact leads to more positive intergroup attitudes. They first review the historical research on intergroup contact and then identify limitations of this work for conceptualizing and articulating how contact leads to positive intergroup attitudes among children. They propose a new conceptual model—General Intergroup Friendship Theory (GIFT)—aimed at articulating this developmental pathway. Included in the theory are three component processes said to lead to positive intergroup attitudes: intergroup contact, intergroup interaction, and intergroup friendship, of which the last is critical for moving from intergroup contact to positive intergroup attitudes. They argue that GIFT also provides a framework for understanding pathways to positive intergroup attitudes in varied social groups (e.g., gender, religion, sexual orientation).

In Chapter 6, Woolard, Henning, and Fountain investigate the US juvenile justice system and its implications for equity and justice. They outline the various steps involved in the juvenile justice process for individuals. Noting the significant impact that plea bargaining has on equitable and just treatment within the justice system, the authors focus on this aspect of the judicial process and outline the two conditions that must be met for a plea bargain to be legal. Next, they review the literature regarding the factors that contribute to adolescents having (or not having) the knowledge they need to navigate the plea bargaining process. Finally, they examine how the aspects of the plea bargaining process are affected by procedural justice, paternalism, and coercion and the implications these have for equity and justice, particularly for the most marginalized young people within the juvenile justice system.

In Chapter 7, Flanagan, Byington, Gallay, and Sambo introduce the idea of the environmental commons, a term that refers to the use, conservation, and sustainability of natural resources as critical to equity and justice for human development. They discuss involvement in the environmental commons as a human right that has been impacted by globalization, privatization, and poverty. Then they investigate youth civic participation and youth advocacy through an examination of young peoples' participation within the environmental commons. Drawing on Bandura's notion of moral disengagement and Prillentensky's social justice framework, the authors discuss challenges to engaging individuals in environmental justice campaigns and suggest conditions needed to foster this engagement. Finally, they review research that presents critical strategies and experiences in childhood that lead to engagement in the commons.

In Chapter 8, Whipps and Yoshikawa explore the experiences of young people in mixed-status immigrant families. These are families in which children have resident or legal citizen status but one or more parent is undocumented. Whipps and Yoshikawa review the prevalence of these families within the United States, and developmental constraints and risks faced by children in these families. They present several challenges that researchers and practitioners face when studying and working with these families to foster more positive developmental outcomes for young people. In their analysis, they argue that researchers should employ Prillentensky's social justice framework when theorizing about, designing, conducting, and disseminating research on mixed-status immigrant families in order to increase the relevance and usefulness of the research and to enhance equity and justice for these highly marginalized families.

In Chapter 9, Wainryb and Bourne examine the impact that conditions and contexts of war have on developmental ecologies and pathways for young people. They begin their chapter by reviewing the array of inequities faced by war-exposed youth including limited access to services, familial and community disruption, and exposure to trauma. They next argue that war creates not only inequities of the sort listed above but also that the conditions and context of war alter the developmental pathways available to young people and thereby profoundly affect opportunities for healthy development. Finally, Wainryb and Bourne argue that developmental science has an obligation to work to better understand the developmental inequities produced by civil conflict, violence, and war even if it cannot yet provide the tools needed to correct them.

In the final chapter, Petersen, Koller, Motti-Stefanidi, and Verma examine issues of equity and justice at the global level and explicate the ways that globalization, population growth, and poverty create developmental inequities and unjust developmental circumstances, particularly for children and youth in the majority world. They argue that the structural challenges (e.g., poverty, civil war) related to growing up in majority world contexts must be addressed by global and national governmental bodies in order to slow and reverse developmental disparities in these contexts. Finally, the authors highlight some examples of strong, emerging programs effective in supporting and developing the strengths of children and youth within the majority world. They conclude with a discussion of the types of support necessary from both the minority and majority worlds that would further strengthen developmental opportunities for young people and enable them to become leaders of a more just, equitable world.

In sum, the chapters in this volume take an in-depth look at equity and justice in developmental science across several diverse contexts at both the proximal and distal levels. As in the earlier volume in this two-set series, the chapters cover a diverse array of developmental phenomena and diverse populations. This volume adds to the theoretical and methodological focus of the earlier volume by specifically addressing *implications* of equity and justice for development, as well as by highlighting approaches for fostering more equitable developmental outcomes for children and adolescents. Individually and collectively, the chapters in these two volumes contribute to developmental research and to promoting more equitable and just contexts in which youth can develop.

Several organizations and people contributed in important ways to the development of this volume. First, we would like to thank the Society for Research in Child Development (SRCD) for supporting efforts to increase attention to equity and justice within developmental science. We would also like to thank the W. T. Grant Foundation, especially Adam Gamoran, for its support of an SRCD Presidential Preconference in March 2015 that helped to shape this two-volume set on equity and justice in developmental science. The staff at Elsevier provided support and encouragement throughout the production of these volumes. In addition to Elsevier staff thanked in the earlier volume, we here add our thanks to Hannah Colford and Radhakrishnan Lakshmanan for their work on the current volume. Finally, we express our gratitude to the chapter authors for their important contributions to this volume and their dedication to improving the lives of children and adolescents.

Young peoples' developmental opportunities are shaped by the world around them. When inequities and injustices exist, developmental pathways become constrained in ways that impact opportunities for developmental thriving. As developmental scientists, we have an ethical responsibility to better understand (in)equity and (in)justice and their effects on development in childhood and adolescence. The chapters in Volumes 50 and 51 of the *Advances in Child Development and Behavior* series begin to do this. We hope that these two volumes serve as a catalyst and a roadmap for developmental scientists to continue this important work.

Stacey S. Horn
Department of Educational Psychology
University of Illinois at Chicago

Martin D. Ruck
Department of Psychology
The Graduate Center
City University of New York

Lynn S. Liben
Department of Psychology
The Pennsylvania State University

PREFACE TO VOLUME 50

At about the time we began working on the preface to these two volumes—*Equity and Justice in Developmental Sciences*—white supremacists in Minneapolis opened fire on a Black Lives Matter protest, injuring five protesters; in Chicago, a videotape that showed a white police officer repeatedly shooting a 14-year-old African-American boy was released to the public (after a year-long cover-up); ISIS terrorists launched bomb attacks in crowded public places in both Beirut and Paris killing and injuring hundreds of civilians; and Syrian refugees fleeing civil war and ethnic cleansing were being turned away from some countries across the globe. In contrast to these negative events, several countries across the globe have implemented laws that support the rights of lesbian and gay couples to legally marry, have made significant advances to reduce childhood poverty, and have established mechanisms to halt the spread of HIV/AIDS throughout the population, especially among children. These events represent only a small sample of issues related to equity and justice that individuals, families, and communities across the globe encounter in the course of their daily lives.

We live in a world in which equity and justice not only impact the health, development, and well-being of young people but also structure the global (and local) environments in which young people live, learn, and grow. Issues related to the distribution of resources; access to health care, education, sustainable food, and water sources; and climate change significantly impact the physical and psychological development of children and youth. In addition, migration across countries; increased ethnic diversity within countries; intergroup conflict; and bias related to such factors as race, ethnicity, religion, and sexual orientation have profound implications for young peoples' social relationships and everyday experiences in families, schools, and communities.

Developmental scientists have an ethical responsibility to advance understanding of how inequality and injustice affect the development of young people, as well as to study, advocate for, and design more equitable and just practices, policies, contexts, and institutions for children and youth. Issues related to equity and justice are found in many areas of developmental science and have been studied by researchers from various disciplines that include social psychology, education, sociology, anthropology, cognitive science, and developmental psychology. Given this diversity, the corpus of research on equity and justice within developmental science often lacks coherence. These two volumes in the *Advances in Child Development and Behavior* series are intended to help bring greater coherence and integration to the developmental study of equity and justice.

The volumes represent an important outcome of work that began in 2011 when the Society for Research in Child Development (SRCD) established a taskforce to consider the role of diversity, broadly defined, in developmental research and the field of developmental science. The initial taskforce was comprised of members from diverse disciplines who studied various aspects of diversity. It recommended that SRCD establish a standing committee on equity and justice, a recommendation that was accepted by the organization's Governing Council. The inaugural Committee on Equity and Justice authored the following mission statement, which continues to undergird the committee's work:

> *Equity and justice are goals for healthy child development and are increasingly a focus of research in developmental science. The need for addressing issues of equity and justice has become especially apparent as the world becomes increasingly global, and as children are living in ever more heterogeneous communities. Reflecting the importance of the topic for scientific inquiry, the SRCD Committee on Equity and Justice has as its mission to: 1) promote the importance and legitimacy of national, international, and interdisciplinary scientific scholarship on topics related to equity and justice in childhood and adolescence; 2) enhance efforts to build coherence and to foster conceptual advances within and across the varied approaches to research on equity and justice; and 3) foster the dissemination and implementation of findings that bear on programs and policies related to equity and justice at both national and international levels.*

Since its establishment in 2012, the Committee on Equity and Justice has been instrumental in proposing, organizing, and implementing activities within the field. Among these have been symposia at SRCD biennial meetings, a stand-alone research conference, a special section of *Child Development*, and a meeting of researchers and practitioners held as a Presidential SRCD Biennial Preconference. It was in the context of these activities that the idea emerged to assemble two volumes on equity and justice for the *Advances in Child Development and Behavior* series. These volumes build on the energy and momentum from the SRCD-based activities and from related conversations and meetings during the last several years.

We have divided chapters between the two volumes so that Volume 1 addresses primarily *Theoretical and Methodological Issues* and Volume 2 addresses primarily *Implications for Diverse Young People, Families, and Communities.*

We have included chapters that cover a diverse (although not exhaustive) collection of phenomena (e.g., intergroup relations, discrimination, access to resources, political violence) and a diverse (although again, not exhaustive) collection of populations. Taken together, the chapters in these volumes thus touch on a broad range of developmental work related to equity and justice, with individual chapters providing in-depth coverage of illustrative areas within this field.

Volume 1 begins with a chapter by Turiel, Chung, and Carr that provides historical perspectives on the ways in which struggles for equal rights and social justice have been represented (or not) in developmental science over the past several decades. The authors argue that psychological research often fails to address issues of equity and justice due to a tendency to reduce complex psychological phenomenon to measureable incremental units. Further, they argue that this focus fails to consider the complex psychological processes involved in how individuals confront and make decisions about situations involving social welfare, justice, and rights both in their interpersonal interactions and in the broader society. Finally, they discuss contextual factors that affect understanding and judgments of equity and justice in daily life.

In Chapter 2, Ghavami, Katsiaficas, and Rogers focus on how using intersectional models to study equity and justice in childhood and adolescence can advance developmental science by increasing our understanding of how multiple social identities (e.g., gender, race, and sexual orientation) intersect to impact development. They review research on intersectional social identities across three distinct developmental periods, focusing on three psychological domains or phenomenon—racial/ethnic identity and socialization, intergroup relations, and political and civic engagement. They conclude by discussing the implications of using an intersectional approach to the study of equity and justice for research, policy, and practice.

The next three chapters in the volume focus on how specific aspects of human diversity impact, often differentially, children and youth's experiences of equity and justice and their opportunities for developmental thriving. First, Keating (Chapter 3) examines the importance of a developmental approach to social disparities in developmental health research. In particular, Keating examines the concept of the social gradient as it relates to the link between disparities in social circumstances (social inequality) and disparities in developmental health. Next, he outlines how core biodevelopmental mechanisms lead to disparities in development that yield social disadvantage in both the short term and across the life course. Keating argues that countries with steep social gradients (i.e., high social inequality) have populations with more negative developmental health outcomes. He concludes by arguing that population-level social inequality results from specific and deliberate choices made by nation states, and that developmental health disparities could be remedied by making choices that lead to lower levels of social inequality.

Focusing specifically on gender, Brown and Stone (Chapter 4) review recent research on how sexism impacts development and thriving across gender categories. They document the prevalence of five distinct forms of sexism and discuss the implications of each of these for young peoples' developmental health and well-being. The five forms of sexism include stereotypes and discrimination against boys related to school behavior and disparate school discipline; stereotypes and discrimination against girls related to science, mathematics, technology, and engineering; stereotypes and discrimination in sports; gendered peer harassment; and sexualized gender stereotypes. They discuss how these forms of sexism intersect in ways that lead to inequity and injustice for children and adolescents.

Next, Snapp, Russell, Arredonda, and Skiba (Chapter 5) address the politics and processes of inclusion of LGBTQ youth in developmental and educational research. They suggest that tensions between—on the one hand—LGBTQ students' rights to participation and recognition, and—on the other hand—students' rights to protection and privacy impact the inclusion of sexual orientation and gender identity (SOGI) in data collection efforts in national, state, and local research. In addition, they argue that due to bias and discrimination, the right to protection and privacy from being forced to disclose one's sexual orientation or gender identity is critical to protecting the health and well-being of young people. However, they also argue that *not* providing safe opportunities for young people to participate fully in research also harms young people by rendering their educational experiences invisible. They conclude by providing recommendations for navigating this tension so that educational research can be more SOGI-inclusive.

The final three chapters of this volume focus specifically on methodological issues and strategies for improving research on equity and justice in developmental science. Rivas-Drake, Guillaume, and Camacho (Chapter 6) focus on strategies for recruiting and retaining ethnic and racial minority populations into developmental research as these populations are currently underrepresented in and underserved by current developmental research. The authors focus on three critical themes related to recruiting and retaining ethnic and racial minority populations: trust, researcher identity and insider/

outsider status, and responsibility. They highlight ways in which developmental scientists who attend to these themes provide far richer and much-needed opportunities to conduct research with these underserved populations.

Relatedly, in Chapter 7, Ozer focuses specifically on the value of youth-led participatory action research (YPAR). This approach provides an important strategy for recruiting and retaining underserved populations within developmental research and, in addition, offers a mechanism for promoting equity and positive development among young people who are marginalized through systemic oppression, discrimination, and racism. Similar to intersectional and community-based participatory approaches to research, this cutting-edge YPAR approach provides a context in which participants play a collaborative role in the developmental research endeavor.

In the final chapter of this volume, Mistry, White, Chow, Griffin, and Nenadal (Chapter 8) focus on mixed-methods research as a way to advance equity and justice in developmental science. They review and discuss the limitations of mono-method approaches (qualitative or quantitative) and delineate how mixed-methods research provides opportunities to overcome those limits. Using examples from available research on conceptions of social inequality, they highlight opportunities, strategies, and challenges in using mixed-methods approaches to advance research on equity and justice in the developmental sciences.

In sum, the chapters in this volume cover a wide range of theoretical, conceptual, and methodological dimensions of developmental research focused on equity and justice. In addition, they focus on diverse populations as well as on diverse developmental phenomena. The conceptual and empirical work reviewed makes the case that equity and justice issues are critical to consider when conceptualizing, designing, conducting, interpreting, and applying developmental research. Although the chapters are broad in scope, even these only begin to scratch the surface of developmental research on equity and justice. In Volume 2, we extend coverage with chapters focused more directly on the implications of developmental scholarship for youth, families, and communities. Chapters in Volume 2 focus on diverse contexts of development such as peer groups, families, juvenile justice, immigration, political violence, and the majority world. In addition, they focus on developmental phenomena related to equity and justice such as racism, discrimination, racial resilience, ethnic–racial socialization, resource allocation, and intergroup contact.

This series would not have been possible without the vision and efforts of many people. We are grateful to SRCD, particularly to Lonnie Sherrod, Executive Director, and to the members of the Governing Council more generally, for supporting and encouraging so many SRCD initiatives related to equity and justice. Their intellectual and financial support has been essential for moving the field forward. We are also grateful to the many colleagues who have been involved with the Committee on Equity and Justice since its inception. They have been responsible for extending and clarifying our own thinking as well as for enriching the field more broadly. We also appreciate Janette Benson's recognition of the importance of the topics of equity and justice in developmental science, and her willingness to commit two volumes of the *Advances in Child Development and Behavior* series to these topics. The Elsevier staff provided essential support, guidance, and encouragement along the way. In particular, we thank Sarah Lay, Zoe Kruze, and Malathi Samayan for all their expertise and patience in bringing these volumes to completion.

Of course, no edited book comes to fruition without the intellectual contributions and hard work of the chapter authors. We express our gratitude to them all for their exciting and strong scholarly contributions. We are also grateful for their deep commitment to advancing equity and justice in the lives of children and youth. We look forward to seeing the impact of their ideas, frameworks, and insights in the years ahead.

Stacey S. Horn
Department of Educational Psychology
University of Illinois at Chicago

Martin D. Ruck
Department of Psychology
The Graduate Center
City University of New York

Lynn S. Liben
Department of Psychology
The Pennsylvania State University

CHAPTER ONE

A Transactional/Ecological Perspective on Ethnic–Racial Identity, Socialization, and Discrimination

Diane L. Hughes[1], Jon Alexander Watford, Juan Del Toro
New York University, New York, NY, United States
[1]Corresponding author: e-mail address: diane.hughes@nyu.edu

Contents

Abstract

We first review current literature on three ethnic–racial dynamics that are considered to be resources and stressors in the lives of ethnic-minority youth: ethnic–racial identity, socialization, and discrimination. Next, we propose that a more contextualized view of these ethnic–racial dynamics reveals that they are interdependent, inseparable, and mutually defining and that an ecological/transactional perspective on these ethnic–racial dynamics shifts researchers' gaze from studying them as individual-level processes to studying the features of settings that produce them. We describe what is known about how identity, socialization, and discrimination occur in four microsystems—families, peers, schools, and neighborhoods—and argue that focusing on specific characteristics of these microsystems in which particular types of identity, socialization, and discrimination processes cooccur would be informative.

Equity and Justice in Developmental Science: Implications for Young People, Families, and Communities (S.S. Horn, M.D. Ruck & L.S. Liben, Eds.)
Advances in Child Development and Behavior (J.B. Benson, Series Ed.), Vol. 51
ISSN 0065-2407 http://dx.doi.org/10.1016/bs.acdb.2016.05.001

1. INTRODUCTION

Babies Jane, Janice, John, and Jamal are born in the same hospital, same day, same hour. Their parents have much in common as well. They could all be college educated or they could all be high school dropouts. They could be lawyers, or artists, or sanitation workers, or unemployed. They could live and love in any corner of the United States. But they will experience distinctly different realities. Why? Jane and John were born with pinkish skin tones, whereas Janice's and Jamal's are shades of brown. Other than family, few people will call attention to their skin color, although they will naturally notice it, as all of us do. The children will be told that it does not matter but they will see and feel that it does. Thus, all four will come to attach some level of meaning to their skin color. They will come to associate it with belonging to an "ethnic" or "racial" group. They will develop ideas about how connected they feel to others like them and will develop positive or negative feelings about their group as a whole. They will gain knowledge about how others view their group and about how societal rewards, penalties, stressors, resources, equity, and justice are distributed accordingly. In sum, as these babies grow, they will accumulate a wealth of "racial knowledge."

Before proceeding further, it is important to clarify our terminology. We recognize that "race" only minimally identifies biologically or genetically distinct groups and is largely socially constructed. However, race continues to have powerful meaning in the United States, such that the processes of enacting and learning race remain relevant to many youth of color, especially those whom are subject to others' ascriptive racial designations (Nagel, 1994; Penuel & Wertsch, 1995). The concept of "ethnicity"—which is more often represented as chosen, malleable, and fluid (Nagel, 1994)—designates groups of people with shared and intergenerationally transmitted values, language, and traditions. Historically, the term "race" has primarily been used in studies of US-born Blacks and Whites, whereas the term "ethnic" has been used more broadly across multiple groups (Hughes et al., 2006; Umaña-Taylor, O'Donnell, et al., 2014; Umaña-Taylor, Quintana, et al., 2014). We use the hyphenated term ethnic–racial, reflecting our belief that both are important in shaping youths' identity processes, the messages they are given and receive, and their discrimination experiences.

However, for purposes of brevity, we use the term "racial knowledge" to refer to children's understanding of themselves as ethnic–racial group members, their attitudes toward their own and other groups, and their understandings of racial hierarchies, systems of social stratification, as well as associated processes of prejudice and discrimination (Hughes & Chen, 1999).

Developmental scientists and other scholars have studied children's developing racial knowledge and the forces that shape it over the life course from multiple perspectives and across multiple stages of development. In the social cognition literature, for example, scholars have sought to identify cognitive precursors to race awareness among young children—including labeling, identification, and constancy (e.g., Katz, 2003). Research on children's racial attitudes has examined the early underpinnings and manifestations of young children's prejudice, particularly their in-group preference and out-group bias (Bigler & Liben, 2006). Studies of middle childhood have examined the dynamics of children's peer relations including intergroup processes (McGuire, Rutland, & Nesdale, 2015; Palmer, Rutland, & Cameron, 2015), cross-race friendships (McGlothlin & Killen, 2010; Rowley, Burchinal, Roberts, & Zeisel, 2008), stereotype knowledge (McKown & Strambler, 2009; Verkuyten & Kinket, 2000), and children's reasoning and moral judgments about race-based social inclusion and exclusion (Hitti, Mulvey, Rutland, Abrams, & Killen, 2014; Killen, Henning, Kelly, Crystal, & Ruck, 2007). Each of these literatures has contributed critical pieces of information about youth's developing racial knowledge.

Although studies exist across multiple developmental stages, adolescence is a critical period during which youths' racial knowledge becomes more complex and gains developmental import, due to cognitive advances as well as individual- and setting-level changes that occur during this developmental stage (Brown & Bigler, 2005). In particular, it is during adolescence that youth develop capacities for abstract and metacognitive thought. These capacities permit them to engage in social comparison processes in which they appraise their own experiences relative to others' experiences and to recognize structures and regularities in larger systems. Thus, adolescents can evaluate the meaning of ethnicity–race and their own group membership in more sophisticated ways than can younger children. In addition, adolescents' self-concept and identity become increasingly salient as they seek to define themselves as individuals and as members of social groups.

As adolescents spend more time with their peers, a new source of information becomes available for exploring what ethnicity–race means to them. At the level of settings, the combination of adolescents' physical maturation and their increasing independence, especially during junior high school, may mean that they are more likely to encounter people who judge and interact with them based on predominant ethnic–racial stereotypes, which can include viewing them as threatening and menacing (Way, Hernández, Rogers, & Hughes, 2013). Thus, adolescence is a period during which racial knowledge becomes more intricate, due both to changes occurring within adolescents and to changes occurring in how others perceive and relate to them.

Empirical research on ethnic–racial dynamics during adolescence has focused primarily on three constructs: ethnic–racial identity, ethnic–racial socialization, and ethnic–racial discrimination. Ethnic–racial identity refers both to individuals' beliefs and attitudes about their ethnic–racial group, including beliefs about others' views, and to the processes by which these beliefs and attitudes develop (Umaña-Taylor, O'Donnell, et al., 2014; Umaña-Taylor, Quintana, et al., 2014). Ethnic–racial socialization consists of behaviors, practices, and social regularities that communicate information and worldviews about race and ethnicity to children (Hughes, Del Toro, Rarick, & Way, 2015). Ethnic–racial discrimination refers broadly to unfair or differential treatment on the basis of ethnicity–race (Brown & Bigler, 2005). Over the past decade and a half, the number of studies on ethnic–racial identity, socialization, and discrimination has increased exponentially due to the fact that these concepts are highly relevant to a US youth population that is more ethnically and racially diverse than at any prior point in US history. A search in PsycINFO using ethnic or racial as keywords combined with identity, socialization, or discrimination (peer-reviewed articles; children or adolescents as limits) indicated that of 720 of 926 empirical articles on ethnic–racial identity had been published since the year 2000, as had 250 of 282 total articles on ethnic–racial socialization, and 238 of 264 articles on ethnic–racial discrimination. Fortunately, growth in these research literatures has been accompanied by conceptual and methodological advances that have substantially deepened our understanding of how identity, socialization, and discrimination operate as well as for whom and under which conditions (see chapter "Racism, Racial Resilience, and African American Youth Development: Person-Centered Analysis as a Tool to Promote Equity and Justice" by Neblett et al., this volume). Despite this growth, there are two limitations of the existing literature that we address in this chapter. First, scholars have, understandably, approached the concepts of identity, socialization, and discrimination as separate entities that can be studied independently. We propose, instead, that these phenomena are interdependent, cooccurring—indeed mutually defining—elements of a system of racial knowledge that youth configure, reconfigure, and act upon. Second, scholars have focused too narrowly on adolescents' ethnic–racial identity, socialization, and discrimination as person-level processes, with insufficient attention to identifying characteristics of the contexts in which they are embedded. As a result of this person-level focus, empirical studies have produced limited information about setting-level levers for change that might more fully support and promote positive outcomes among youth. Recognizing the dynamic interdependence of identity, socialization, and discrimination across multiple ecological environments shifts researchers' gaze toward setting-level, rather than individual-level, change to promote youths' positive development.

Accordingly, our goals in this chapter are twofold. First, we provide a broad overview of the literature on adolescents' ethnic–racial identity, socialization, and discrimination experiences, establishing the significance of these processes for adolescents. In particular, for each of these concepts, we highlight conceptual and empirical advances including inclusion of multiple ethnic–racial groups, multidimensional conceptualization and assessment of constructs, attention to developmental change, and examination of consequences across multiple developmental domains. We also discuss empirical findings regarding relationships between these ethnic–racial phenomena. Second, drawing on Bronfenbrenner's (1979) bioecological model, Altman and Rogoff's (1987) transactional worldview, and sociocultural approaches to identity (Moje & Martinez, 2007; Penuel & Wertsch, 1995), we describe how ethnic–racial identity, socialization, and discrimination are mutually defining and inseparable processes deeply rooted in the microsystems in which youth operate—including family, peer group, school, and neighborhood. Notably, because racial knowledge is acquired and enacted at all levels of the ecological environment, our focus on microsystems is only a first step toward elaborating an ecological/transactional perspective. We suggest that, in order to more fully understand the interplay between these ethnic–racial dynamics and adolescents' positive development, researchers need to move beyond individual-level frameworks to identify the characteristics of settings in which particular types of identities, socialization experiences, and discrimination experiences coexist to influence development.

2. ETHNIC–RACIAL IDENTITY

Among the most widely recognized tasks adolescents face is that of coming to terms with who they want to be and how they fit into existing social groups and settings. This identity seeking process involves trying on and discarding multiple identities while weighing values, goals, and behaviors in relation to the various roles they might adopt across life contexts. Identity development includes resolution of personal identities—representations of who the self is as distinct from others—and of social identities—representations of who the self is based on membership in social categories and groups. All people develop a portfolio of identities that emerge to greater or lesser extents in a given moment depending on the situation they are in and the audience they are facing (Nagel, 1994). Moreover, identities are subject to ascriptive processes in which others shape, reinforce, and sometimes constrain who one is permitted to be (Penuel & Wertsch, 1995). Both personal and social identities affect how individuals appraise their world and their social and psychological experiences across time and across settings.

Ethnic–racial identities are key components of adolescents' social identities. They are especially salient for ethnic–racial minority youth who must reconcile their group membership with their awareness of stereotypes and expectations that others hold about their group (Tajfel & Turner, 1986; Way et al., 2013). To date, the literature on ethnic–racial identity has been concerned with two primary components—one focused on *how* identities develop and a second focused on its evaluative components (Umaña-Taylor, O'Donnell, et al., 2014; Umaña-Taylor, Quintana, et al., 2014).

Drawing on ego-identity frameworks, scholars studying processes of ethnic–racial identity development contend that it is a stage-like phenomenon in which the meaning of ethnicity–race is initially unexamined (Phinney, 1993). Identity development involves an active search for information about the meaning of group membership followed by identity resolution, which ideally includes commitment to and affirmation of one's ethnic–racial group. Some stage models incorporate a stimulus for identity exploration, termed an "encounter" in Cross's Nigrescence model (Cross, 2005). Studies locate the period of intense exploration in late adolescence and early adulthood (French, Seidman, & Allen, 2006; Yip, Seaton, & Sellers, 2006). For instance, Yip et al. (2006) compared the identity statuses of African American adolescents, college students, and adults, using cluster profiles derived from Phinney's (1993) proposed stages of identity development. In this study, 42% of adolescents were in the moratorium stage, characterized by active exploration of their ethnicity–race, compared to about 25% of college students or adults. Fewer than one in three adolescents were characterized as being in the achieved status, characterized by an active commitment to the meaning of their ethnicity–race based on intensive exploration, compared with about one-half of college students or adults. In a study of adolescent mothers, Umaña-Taylor and colleagues reported that identity exploration increased over 5 years among those who were 15 years of age or younger at the initial assessment but not among those who were older. Both younger and older adolescent mothers increased in identity resolution and affirmation over time (Umaña-Taylor, Updegraff, Jahromi, & Zeiders, 2015).

Studies of the evaluative components of ethnic–racial identity are rooted in Sellers and colleagues' widely adopted multidimensional conceptualization of identity (Sellers, Smith, Shelton, Rowley, & Chavous, 1998) which distinguishes the importance of ethnicity–race to one's self-definition (termed centrality), the importance of identity at a particular moment (termed salience); one's own evaluations of one's group (termed private regard); one's evaluations of others' views of one's group (termed public regard); and the content of one's beliefs about how one should behave as a group member (termed ideology). Distinguishing components of ethnic–racial identity has facilitated critical insights regarding how identities vary across groups and have developmental import. For example, although most studies report relatively high private regard among all adolescents, Chinese youth report lower private regard relative to youth from other ethnic–racial-groups (Fuligni, Witkow, & Garcia, 2005; Rivas-Drake, Hughes, & Way, 2008), whereas Latino youth (especially Puerto Rican youth) report high private regard relative to youth from other ethnic–racial groups (French, Seidman, Allen, & Aber, 2000; Rivas-Drake et al., 2008). Some comparative studies have found that ethnicity–race is more central to African American youths' self-concepts, compared to those of Latino youth (Altschul, Oyserman, & Bybee, 2006). Finally, African American youth report lower public regard compared to youth from other ethnic–racial backgrounds (Altschul et al., 2006; Rivas-Drake, Hughes, & Way, 2009b). As we shall describe, centrality, private regard, and public regard are also differentially associated with adolescents' well-being.

Recent longitudinal studies have documented change over time in these identity components, underscoring that ethnic–racial identities are configured and reconfigured in accordance with shifts in youths' contexts and experiences. French et al. (2006), in a study of adolescents followed over the transitions from elementary to middle school and from middle to high school, found that increases in private regard were most pronounced immediately following school transitions. The authors suggested that, upon entering new environments, adolescents must learn to navigate new ethnic–racial dynamics. This navigation process provides additional information about the meaning of ethnicity–race and, thus, can result in shifts in adolescents' identity, socialization, and discrimination experiences. Indeed, studies in which adolescents remain in the same setting have found stability in private regard over time (Greene, Way, & Pahl, 2006; Ho & Graham, 2008; Hughes, Way, & Rivas-Drake, 2011; Kiang, Witkow, & Champagne, 2013).

Adolescents' ideas about others' views of their ethnic–racial group (public regard) also change over time. Several studies suggest that Black and Latino adolescents become increasingly aware of others' negative views about their group during middle and high school (Altschul et al., 2006; Ho & Graham, 2008; Hughes, McGill, Ford, & Tubbs, 2011; Hughes, Way, et al., 2011). As with private regard, decreases in public regard probably reflect shifts in racial knowledge that are based on adolescents' experiences across settings. Consistent with this idea, Seaton, Yip, and Sellers (2009), in a 3-year longitudinal study among African American adolescents, found that public regard decreased only among those who had experienced discrimination. Moreover, in contrast to a decline in public regard among African American, Dominican, and Puerto Rican adolescents, Hughes, McGill, et al. (2011) and Hughes, Way, et al. (2011) found that public regard increased among Chinese adolescents. In light of youths' astute awareness of ethnic–racial stereotypes (Way et al., 2013), Chinese youth may increasingly learn positive stereotypes about their group from teachers, peers, and other adults.

The past decade of studies has also documented relationships between components of ethnic–racial identity and a broad range of socioemotional, academic, and behavioral outcomes among adolescents. For instance, adolescents who report more attachment and belonging to their ethnic–racial group also report more positive self-concepts (Phinney, 1993; Umaña-Taylor, Vargas-Chanes, Garcia, & Gonzales-Backen, 2008) and more favorable academic adjustment (Oyserman, Bybee, & Terry, 2003). More identity exploration has been associated with higher self-esteem (Umaña-Taylor, Yazedjian, & Bámaca-Gómez, 2004). More positive private regard has also been associated with higher self-esteem (Lee & Yoo, 2004), greater psychological well-being (Sellers, Copeland-Linder, Martin, & Lewis, 2006; Wong, Eccles, & Sameroff, 2003), higher academic efficacy and grades (Fuligni et al., 2005; Wong et al., 2003), and lower perceived stress (Sellers et al., 2006). Public regard, though studied less often, has been associated with more positive academic motivation (Chavous et al., 2003; Rivas-Drake, 2011), fewer depressive symptoms (Rivas-Drake et al., 2008), and fewer somatic symptoms (Rivas-Drake, Hughes, & Way, 2009a; Rivas-Drake et al., 2009b).

In sum, the growing literature on adolescents' ethnic–racial identities provides substantial evidence that such identities are critical resources that can enhance adolescents' development and well-being. Advances in conceptualization and methodology, including coverage of adolescents from multiple ethnic–racial groups, expansion of the dimensions of identity of interest, attention to change over time, and examination of adaptation in multiple developmental domains, have each contributed substantially to researchers' understanding of how and under what conditions ethnic–racial identities operate.

3. ETHNIC–RACIAL SOCIALIZATION

In ethnically and racially stratified societies such as the United States, the socialization process inevitably includes messages to children about ethnicity–race. Adolescents' learning about ethnicity–race—and their resulting racial knowledge—takes place in every segment of youths' environment as their interactions and observations yield information about which ethnic–racial groups are valued, smart, beautiful, dangerous, disruptive, rich, and so forth—and which are not. Ethnic–racial socialization shapes the meaning adolescents ascribe to their ethnic–racial group membership, adolescents' expectations about experiences they may have as group members, their knowledge of the history and values associated with being a group member, their sense of group belonging and pride, and their beliefs about how others view and treat various groups. Importantly, adolescents are not passive recipients of such messages, but instead initiate and select the messages they internalize (Hughes & Chen, 1999).

In conceptual and empirical work, researchers have focused primarily on the role that parents play in children's ethnic–racial socialization (Priest et al., 2014). Exceptions include a handful of studies on how youth learn ethnicity–race in neighborhood contexts (Moje & Martinez, 2007; Winkler, 2012) and in schools (Aldana & Byrd, 2015; Byrd, 2015;

Hurd, 2008; Kao, 2000; Lewis, 2003; Pollock, 2004). As the central node of young children's lives, parents' attitudes, values, and behaviors are especially salient in transmitting information and perspectives to youth about ethnicity–race. Until recently, the majority of this research and theoretical writing focused on African Americans—a group that historically has been at the bottom of the racial hierarchy in terms of access to privileges and economic resources (e.g., Peters & Massey, 1983; Spencer, 1983; Tatum, 1987). Growth in the ethnic–racial socialization literature within the past decade has involved expansion of the concept to multiple ethnic–racial minority and immigrant groups including Mexican (Derlan, Umaña-Taylor, Updegraff, & Jahromi, 2015), Korean (Seol, Yoo, Lee, Park, & Kyeong, 2015), Chinese (Huynh & Fuligni, 2010), and White (Hagerman, 2014) parents or adolescents.

Recent studies of ethnic–racial socialization have also used a more differentiated conceptualization of the process relative to earlier studies in which ethnic–racial socialization was assessed in unidimensional terms. With this differentiation, researchers acknowledge that parents vary in what they choose to teach their children about ethnicity–race. Some parents teach group differences, discrimination, and disadvantage; others teach history, culture, and traditions; others emphasize the value of diversity and egalitarian perspectives; still others do some combination or all of these. In our work, we have utilized a fourfold conceptualization that distinguishes (a) messages that promote ethnic pride and transmit knowledge about cultural history and heritage (termed cultural socialization); (b) messages intended to prepare children to adapt to and operate within a racialized world, including exposure to prejudice and discrimination (termed preparation for bias); (c) messages emphasizing diversity and racial equality (termed egalitarianism); and (d) cautions and warnings to children about other ethnic groups (termed promotion of mistrust). Neblett and colleagues represent parents' ethnic–racial socialization using person centered rather than variable centered approaches, distinguishing profiles such as "multifaceted," "unengaged," "high positive," and "low salience" (see chapter "Racism, Racial Resilience, and African American Youth Development: Person-Centered Analysis as a Tool to Promote Equity and Justice" by Neblett et al., this volume; for alternative conceptualizations, see Bentley-Edwards & Stevenson, 2016; Stevenson, McNeil, Herrero-Taylor, & Davis, 2005).

The advantage of a multidimensional assessment is that it yields more precise information about what is communicated and by whom, enabling researchers to ask more useful questions about its antecedents and consequences. In our studies across diverse samples, over 90% of participants report messages about egalitarianism (Hughes et al., 2015) and the overwhelming majority report cultural socialization as well (Hughes & Chen, 1999). Few parents report promotion of mistrust, regardless of ethnicity (Hughes et al., 2006). However, preparation for bias is far more common among African American parents than among parents from other ethnic–racial minority groups, whereas ethnic–racial group differences in cultural socialization and egalitarianism are small and often nonsignificant (Hughes, 2003; Hughes et al., 2006). In addition, preparation for bias and promotion of mistrust are more sensitive than is cultural socialization to parents' subjective experiences of ethnic–racial discrimination across multiple contexts (Hughes, 2003; Hughes & Chen, 1997) and to their own and their children's perceptions of children's unfair treatment, especially from adults (Hughes & Johnson, 2001).

Scholars also increasingly recognize that ethnic–racial socialization is a dynamic process that varies across development. For example, parents tend not to engage in certain ethnic–racial socialization practices with young children, especially discussions about bias and intergroup relations, given that younger children have only a rudimentary understanding of the concept of ethnicity–race (Katz, 2003). In other words, parents' guesses about children's readiness to understand ethnic–racial issues are well synchronized with children's actual racial knowledge. Consistent with this idea, our longitudinal data indicate linear increases in preparation for bias between 11 and 14 years of age, especially for boys, albeit stability over time in cultural socialization (Hughes, Hagelskamp, Del Toro, Shrout, & Way, 2010). Other studies suggest this pattern as well (Hughes, 2003; Hughes & Chen, 1997; McHale et al., 2006). As with other ethnic–racial identity processes, change in ethnic–racial socialization is unlikely to be organic. More likely, it is a function of changes in situations, experiences and interactions across time and contexts alongside shifts in parents' understanding of children's knowledge and children's developmental readiness to hear ethnic–racial socialization messages. Research on what changes, when, and for whom is sorely needed.

Finally, a growing number of studies have examined the consequences of parents' ethnic–racial socialization for youth. Most of these studies have focused on cultural socialization and preparation for bias. Cultural socialization has consistently been associated concurrently and longitudinally with more favorable adjustment including higher self-esteem (Mohanty, Keokse, & Sales, 2007; Rivas-Drake et al., 2009b), higher academic engagement and performance (Oyserman et al., 2003), fewer behavior problems (Caughy & Owen, 2014; Johnston, Swim, Saltsman, Deater-Deckard, &

Petrill, 2007), and fewer depressive symptoms (Umaña-Taylor, O'Donnell, et al., 2014; Umaña-Taylor, Quintana, et al., 2014). Empirical findings regarding preparation for bias have been mixed, with some documenting that preparation for bias is associated with more favorable self-beliefs, behavioral adjustment, and academic adjustment and other studies documenting that it is associated with less favorable self-beliefs, behavioral, and academic outcomes (Hughes et al., 2006). In a recent study, we found that adolescents who reported moderate preparation for bias evidenced less steep declines in self-esteem and less steep increases in symptomatology compared to adolescents who reported very low or very high preparation for bias (Hughes, Del Toro, & Way, 2016).

A handful of studies have examined egalitarianism in relation to youth outcomes, although there are too few of them to draw integrative conclusions. For example, Neblett and colleagues found that egalitarianism was associated with African American adolescents' academic curiosity, although not with their academic persistence or grades (Neblett, Philip, Cogburn, & Sellers, 2006) and with fewer problem behaviors and greater well-being (Neblett, Banks, Cooper, & Smalls-Glover, 2013). In our work, White adolescents who received more egalitarian messages—according to their own and their mothers' reports—evidenced less socioemotional competence in their cross-race friendships as compared to their same-race friendships, consistent with findings in the literature on the limitations of color-bind ideologies (Hughes et al., 2015). Mandara (2006) found that boys whose parents instilled passive or race-less messages performed less well academically than did parents imparting cultural pride messages.

To summarize, studies of parents' ethnic–racial socialization suggest that such socialization is a critical component of parenting, especially in ethnic–racial minority families. As with research on ethnic–racial identity, conceptual and methodological expansions and improvements have contributed substantially to researchers' understanding of how such socialization operates. Studies indicate that the frequency and content of ethnic–racial socialization messages vary across ethnic–racial groups and across development. In addition, dimensions of ethnic–racial socialization differentially predict adolescents' development and well-being.

4. ETHNIC–RACIAL DISCRIMINATION

Exposure to ethnic–racial discrimination is a common part of many youths' experiences, especially among youth of color. Indeed, studies find that most youth report exposure to discrimination when directly asked.

For example, in a daily diary study of African American youth, Seaton and Douglass (2014) found that 97% reported at least one experience of discrimination over a 2-week period. The 2-week average was 26 discriminatory events, or 2.5 events per day. Huynh and Fuligni (2010) reported that two-thirds of Latino, Asian American, and European American high school-aged adolescents reported having experienced discrimination from adults or peers. About 12% of this sample reported at least one incident of discrimination within a 14-day period. In the later study, even low levels of discrimination predicted a range of academic and psychosocial outcomes.

Recently, as in the identity and socialization literatures, studies of adolescents' discrimination experiences have advanced from assessing discrimination as a unidimensional construct to distinguishing different types and sources of discrimination. Multidimensional assessment has enabled researchers to obtain a more nuanced perspective on who experiences discrimination and, in particular, on how its nature differs for boys vs girls and for youth of varied ethnic–racial backgrounds. The recent distinction between discrimination from adults vs peers has been especially informative in this regard. African American and Latino adolescents report more frequent discrimination from adults in the community (storeowners, police), whereas Asian youth report more frequent discrimination from peers (Fisher, Wallace, & Fenton, 2000; Greene et al., 2006; Rivas-Drake et al., 2008). Adult vs peer discrimination has also been associated with different sorts of developmental outcomes (Benner & Graham, 2013) as we shall discuss momentarily. Hughes, Del Toro, Harding, Way, and Rarick (2016) further distinguished discrimination from school vs nonschool adults, as well as implicit vs explicit types of peer discrimination, with significant ethnic–racial and gender differences in initial levels of discrimination and in trajectories of change over time. Thus, multidimensional assessment has provided more nuanced insights into the nature and frequency of youths' discrimination experiences.

Recent studies have also examined how adolescents' discrimination experiences change over repeated assessments, with the expectation that adolescents' exposure to discrimination may become more frequent as adolescents get older because of increased awareness of discrimination, increased autonomy from parents, and increased mobility from their local environments. Generally, however, empirical findings have not always supported this expectation. Most studies report stability or declines over time in perceived discrimination from peers (Bellmore, Nishina, You, & Ma, 2012; Niwa, Way, & Hughes, 2014; White, Zeiders, Knight, Roosa, & Tein, 2014). Hughes et al. (2016) reported average linear increases in discrimination from peers during middle school but average declines following the transition to high school. Among studies of discrimination from adults, Niwa et al. (2014) found stability in youths' reports of discrimination from adults in middle school and Greene et al. (2006) reported an increase (at trend level) in perceived discrimination from adults in high school. A few studies have reported increases in discrimination, assessed unidimensionally, in middle and high school (Benner & Graham, 2011; Brody et al., 2006; Martin et al., 2011). Thus, further exploration is needed to determine the conditions under which increases or decreases in perceived discrimination are more likely.

As with other ethnic–racial constructs, adolescents' perceptions of discrimination have been associated with an array of socioemotional, academic, and behavioral indicators. Across multiple ethnic–racial groups, perceived discrimination has been associated with less favorable academic motivation, engagement, and performance (e.g., Benner & Kim, 2009; Huynh & Fuligni, 2010); disidentification with school (Schmader, Major, & Gramzow, 2001); higher anxiety and depression (Greene et al., 2006; Simons et al., 2002; Way, Muhkerjee, & Hughes, 2008); and lower quality of relationships with peers, adults, and the school community (Liang, Alvarez, Juang, & Liang, 2007; Osterman, 2000). Adam et al. (2015) recently finding that cumulative discrimination experiences assessed during adolescence contributed to differences in African American and White adults' diurnal cortisol patterns more so than did contemporary discrimination experiences suggests long-term deleterious consequences of discrimination. Further, Benner and Graham's (2013) study suggests specificity in relationships between varied sources of discrimination and youth adjustment. In their study, only peer discrimination predicted psychological adjustment, only school discrimination predicted academic performance, and only societal discrimination predicted public regard.

In sum, numerous studies over the past decade or so have contributed to researchers' knowledge about the frequency with which adolescents experience discrimination, the nature and source of such discrimination, possible changes in exposure to discrimination over time (although findings across studies vary considerably here), and associations between discrimination and well-being across important developmental domains. It is apparent by now that ethnic–racial discrimination is a salient experience during adolescence, especially for ethnic–racial minority youth. More importantly, ethnic–racial discrimination is an important source of stress and distress that warrants further inquiry and further action.

5. INTERRELATIONSHIPS AMONG ETHNIC–RACIAL IDENTITY, SOCIALIZATION, AND DISCRIMINATION

As suggested already, scholars have recognized that identity, socialization, and discrimination are interrelated in complex ways. Studies documenting direct, mediated, moderated, and reciprocal relationships are numerous. Although most studies of these interrelationships have been cross-sectional, longitudinal studies have, in most cases, also supported researchers' hypothesized causal pathways.

Among the clearest linkages is that between socialization and identity. Adolescents whose parents place a greater emphasis on socializing cultural knowledge and pride report that their ethnicity is more important to them and have more positive feelings about their ethnic group (Chavous, Rivas, Green, & Helaire, 2002; González, Umaña-Taylor, & Bámaca, 2006; Rivas-Drake et al., 2009a, 2009b). Adolescents who report more preparation for bias from their parents also report lower public regard (Rivas-Drake et al., 2009a, 2009b).

Relationships between identity components and discrimination have been documented as well. Adolescents reporting more frequent discrimination experiences also report more identity exploration (Pahl & Way, 2006; Umaña-Taylor & Guimond, 2012), higher ethnic–racial identity centrality (Umaña-Taylor & Guimond, 2012), and lower private and public regard (Rivas-Drake et al., 2009a, 2009b). However, adolescents are also more likely to expect discrimination when race is more central to their self-concepts (Neblett, Shelton, & Sellers, 2004; Rowley et al., 2008) or when they are more active in exploring their ethnic–racial identity (Pahl & Way, 2006), suggesting bidirectional relationships between identity and discrimination.

Studies have also examined ethnic–racial socialization as both a predictor and an outcome of discrimination. Hughes and Johnson (2001) found that children's reports of more frequent unfair treatment due to race predicted parents' reports of their preparation for bias messages. In Hughes et al. (2010), using autoregressive latent trajectory analysis over three waves of data, there were bidirectional longitudinal relationships between youths' discrimination and preparation for bias, suggesting that parents' preparation for bias may occur in reaction to youths' discrimination experiences but may also predispose youth to expect more discrimination.

Finally, studies have found that both identity and socialization enable youth to cope with discrimination. The negative relationships between discrimination and indicators of poorer youth adjustment are attenuated in the presence of multiple identity components including centrality, private regard, and public regard (Fuller-Rowell et al., 2012; Sellers et al., 2006). Both cultural socialization and preparation for bias have been found to attenuate these relationships as well (Burt, Simons, & Gibbons, 2012; Wang & Huguley, 2012). Others have found that ethnic–racial socialization, assessed unidimensionally, is associated with reduced distress from discrimination (Leslie, Smith, Hrapczynski, & Riley, 2013) and strategies for coping with discrimination (Scott, 2003).

5.1 Summary

Thus far, we have provided a broad overview of current knowledge regarding ethnic–racial identity, socialization, and discrimination. Each is an important mechanism through which youth act upon, negotiate, acquire, and reconfigure racial knowledge. Deeper understanding of these phenomena has been facilitated by conceptual and methodological approaches including investigating multiple ethnic–racial groups, use of multidimensional conceptualizations and assessment tools, and longitudinal designs that permit investigation of temporal patterning. We also described literature on interrelationships between these concepts, of which there are many. The literature to date suggests that strong and positive ethnic–racial identities are assets for youth, facilitating positive self-beliefs and enhanced functioning across critical developmental domains. Ethnic–racial socialization can either promote or impede positive adaptation, depending on the nature of messages transmitted and received. Discrimination experiences challenge youths' academic, psychological, socioemotional, and physical well-being.

Based on existing findings, researchers could conceivably generate infinite additional questions regarding the conditions under which and for whom the aforementioned relationships hold and the mechanisms through which they operate. Continued growth in these literatures would undoubtedly reinforce researchers' current understandings. In our view, however, inquiries that extend what we already know to a broader range of outcomes and conditions would only yield incremental gains in the field's comprehension of ethnic–racial phenomena. To more fully understand their role in adolescents' lives, we need to know more about how they unfold in day-to-day settings and social interactions, as these are where racialized structures, ideologies, and social regularities reside. New theoretical and methodological approaches that shift our gaze from the adolescent to the setting are needed to complement existing approaches.

6. CONCEPTUALIZING ECOLOGICAL/TRANSACTIONAL PERSPECTIVES ON YOUTHS' RACIAL KNOWLEDGE

The late Urie Bronfenbrenner's proposal that development takes place in the context of increasingly complex nested structures is by now one of the most widely embraced ideas in developmental science. Bronfenbrenner (1979) argued that approaches that have overlapping and embedded settings at the forefront enable us to represent individuals' lives in the way they actually live them, rather than as parsed into what Barker (1968) calls "behavioral tesserae," or "fragments of behavior that are created or selected by the investigator ... in accordance with his scientific aims" (pp. 4 and 5). Accordingly, increased attention to identifying setting characteristics that accompany particular types of ethnic–racial identity, socialization, and discrimination may enable researchers to identify adaptive and troublesome features of settings, rather than of individuals, to support youths' positive development. An ecological/transactional perspective points toward settings as the fundamental unit of analysis.

What is a setting? Perhaps the simplest and most common conception is a distinctive, physically and temporally bounded environment, such as a classroom or an afterschool program (Livert et al., 2002). However, settings may also be situations or networks such as families, peer groups, or mutual help organizations that have no physical or spatial location but nevertheless exist as entities within which individuals are embedded. In Bronfenbrenner's (1979) bioecological model, settings most proximal to the child are those in which the child participates directly and are called "microsystems." Among the most salient microsystems for adolescents are family, peers, schools, and neighborhoods. As noted earlier, elaborating how ethnic–racial identity, socialization, and discrimination unfold in these microsystems is only an initial step toward an ecological/transactional perspective, as processes at the more distal levels of the ecological environment (exosystem, mesosystem, chronosystem, and macrosystem) are likely operative as well.

The usefulness of an ecological/transactional framework for pursuing further understanding of adolescents' ethnic–racial knowledge is based, first and foremost, on recognition that ethnic–racial dynamics are operative in every setting within racialized social systems (Lewis, 2003). Family events, school hallways, cafeteria lunch tables, neighborhood playgrounds, basketball courts, peer networks, churches, and parks all function—to greater or lesser extents—as racial spaces in which specific norms, regularities, rules, behavior patterns, and associated meaning structures reside. Youth act upon and acquire racial knowledge in each of these spaces. Identities—rather than being constituted solely by internal beliefs, attitudes, and orientations that reside within the person—are performed or produced in time- and space-bound situations that include other social actors and audiences (Moje & Martinez, 2007). Others' reflections, observations, and judgments are integral to these enactments, as identities require validation from and can be constrained by members of a cultural community (Penuel & Wertsch, 1995). Adolescents' ethnic–racial socialization occurs in these settings through the explicit, implicit, deliberate, unintended, verbal, and nonverbal processes in which socializing agents engage (Hughes & Chen, 1999), including episodes of discrimination. Such socialization also occurs through more elusive mechanisms in which socializers transfer an "interpretive logic" about ethnicity–race, or a "generalized orientation that guides children's assessment and management of situations" (Applegate, Burleson, & Delia, 1992, p. 8). To quote Omi and Winant (1994): "Everybody learns some combination, some version, of the rules of racial classification and of her own racial identity, often without teaching or conscious inculcation" (p. 30). Thus, adolescents' ethnic–racial identity, socialization, and discrimination experiences are enveloped in settings.

To which features of settings should we attend? Drawing from Bronfenbrenner (1979), settings have role relationships and interpersonal structures, alongside physical and structural features, that function as demands and affordances for behavioral, psychological, and social processes. In Moos and Lemke's (1983) framework, policies and programs, physical and architectural features, aggregate characteristics or attitudes of setting participants (termed suprapersonal characteristics) and features of the social climate, including social relationships and social interactions, each communicate setting demands and affordances. Sarason's (1982) concept of *behavioral regularities*—patterns of behavior that are repeated across time and settings—and Seidman's (1988) concept of *social regularities*—social roles, social interactions, and social relationships that are repeated across time and settings—each describes extra-individual-level setting dynamics that are consequential for setting participants. In accordance with transactional worldviews (Altman & Rogoff, 1987), these extra-individual-level characteristics and psychological/social processes coexist as intrinsic and inseparable parts of the whole that are defined by and define one another. Importantly, transactional representations of phenomena stand in contrast to worldviews that Altman and Rogoff identify as being interactional—emphasizing cause–effect and typically linear relationships between phenomena—or organismic—emphasizing holistic units but viewing unit parts as separable, albeit intricately connected. Thus, the key contribution of such a transactional worldview is the idea that the ethnic–racial dynamics of focus here—identity, socialization, and discrimination—are often overlapping and indistinguishable components of ethnic–racial dynamics that occur at the extra-individual level.

In the remainder of this chapter, we suggest ways in which identity, socialization, and discrimination are mutually defining and inseparable in the context of four relevant microsystems: families, peer groups, schools, and neighborhoods. We provide examples of studies in which setting characteristics or situations have been the focal unit of analysis. The study of holistic units provides a different lens for constructing ethnic–racial identity, socialization, and discrimination as inherently inseparable and may allow for new ideas and principles pertaining to adolescents' experiences across contexts.

6.1 Families

The family is a primary context for adolescents' identity, socialization, and discrimination experiences. Adolescents explore, construct, display, and reconstruct their ethnic–racial identities within family settings (Awokoya, 2012; Tatum, 2004). They receive a multitude of ethnic–racial socialization messages from family members and through family practices (Hughes et al., 2006). They observe, hear about, talk about, and try to make sense of the dynamics of discrimination within family contexts (Juang & Syed, 2014). To date, because most of our knowledge about these processes comes from survey based cross-sectional studies, researchers have limited insight into how socialization processes unfold naturally in the course of families' daily activities or about extra-individual-level family characteristics that shape them.

In line with a transactional worldview, the conceptual boundaries that researchers draw between identity, socialization, and discrimination become especially blurred within the family context. The sense of "we-ness" that constitutes identification with a family also includes identification with a cultural, ethnic, and racial heritage. Moreover, the family settings in which ethnicity–race is salient—those in which identities are explored and affirmed and in which centrality, private regard, and public regard emerge—are also crucial instances of ethnic–racial socialization. Family gatherings, celebrations, and cultural holidays, for example, can serve as identity triggers, providing clues as to what it "means" to be an ethnic–racial group member (Hughes et al., 2008). However, these family situations also serve as instantiations of youths' ethnic–racial identity (Phinney, 1993). Practices that are deeply rooted in families' daily routines, for example, cooking ethnic food, listening to ethnic music, and arranging artifacts in the home (Hughes et al., 2008), are components of cultural socialization but are also situations in which youth construct ethnicity–race as central to their self-definitions and in which they develop positive ethnic–racial regard. Situations in which adolescents discuss or are exposed to discrimination within family contexts are also situations in which adolescents construct their sense of public regard for their group. In fact, for some researchers, ethnic–racial identity includes awareness of discrimination as a defining identity component (Oyserman, Brickman, & Rhodes, 2007). Instances of discrimination, as relived in families, also constitute a significant source of youths' ethnic–racial socialization. Thus, not only are identity, socialization, and discrimination interrelated within family contexts but they are inseparable and mutually defining.

Notably, existing empirical studies have rarely captured the many types of family transactions that are relevant to adolescents' ethnic–racial identity, socialization, and discrimination experiences. For instance, much of what adolescents learn occurs through what Boykin and Toms (1985) refer to as "cultural motifs" that are largely invisible to parents and other family members but are displayed in a "consistent, persistent, and enduring fashion" (p. 42) unaccompanied by directives or imperatives to learn them. A grandmother is driving with her granddaughter through an urban poor predominantly Black and Latino neighborhood and utters a snide remark about the residents' lifestyles. A Mexican parent warns his teenage son to "be careful" as he is leaving to run an errand in a White neighborhood. A family is having a large catered dinner party, and all of the other guests are the same race as the family. Adolescents enact and acquire ethnic–racial knowledge in each of these situations, such that identity, socialization, and discrimination processes are simultaneously manifest.

Only a handful of studies focus either conceptually or analytically on family-level characteristics or situations as the unit of analysis for understanding adolescents' ethnic–racial experiences. Illustratively, Tatum (2004), based on interviews with African American adolescents attending predominantly White schools, categorized families as being race-conscious, race-neutral, or class conscious/race avoidant. Adolescent interviews were analyzed in terms of varied ethnic–racial identity, socialization, and discrimination processes that were emergent in these distinct family types. For instance, adolescents who described race-conscious family contexts also manifested a clear sense of their ethnic–racial identity, including ethnic–racial pride and a keen awareness of discrimination. Adolescents in class conscious/race avoidant family contexts described numerous struggles and feelings of alienation from family and peers in establishing ethnic–racial identity, especially as these pertained to situations in which they felt ethnically racially distinctive or discriminated against. Notably, although adolescents served as informants, the focal unit for analysis was the family as a whole. The conceptualization of relevant family-level characteristics included history of contact with other African Americans, neighborhood, and school ethnic composition, embeddedness in African American networks, organizations, and institutions, and physical/architectural features of the home including art, music, and artifacts, as well as family members' racial attitudes. Adolescents' ethnic–racial identity, socialization, and discrimination experiences were inseparable from the larger family context in which they were embedded.

As another example, we used parents' and adolescents' stories about situations in which ethnic–racial socialization occurred as the unit of analyses for learning about adolescents' identity, socialization, and discrimination experiences across multiple contexts. Based on interviews with ethnically diverse adolescents and caregivers at three assessment points (6th, 8th, and 11th grade), stories were defined as narrative accounts of specific situations in which coders identified a beginning, middle, and end. We coded story features such as the stimulus for discussion, the physical location (e.g., home, family celebration, car, grocery store, hospital), who was present, who initiated the conversation, adolescents' roles, and length of episode alongside indicators of emergent identity, socialization, and discrimination processes. These analyses made clear that ethnic–racial socialization episodes were quite often about identity as well, and often initiated in response to a discrimination experience. In particular, cultural socialization and favorable private regard and exploration tended to cooccur in descriptions of holiday, religious and birthday celebrations. Evidence of low public regard, preparation for bias, and discrimination experiences often cooccurred in these situations as well.

In sum, a focus on family-level characteristics or situations as the unit of analysis for understanding ethnic–racial dynamics in adolescents' lives provides a perspective within which viewers are better able to see the interrelated and mutually defining interdependence of adolescents' identity, socialization, and discrimination experiences. Descriptively, a focus on situations or settings provides an up close view of characteristics of family contexts in which particular types of ethnic–racial dynamics are most likely to emerge.

6.2 Peers

As children approach adolescence, they spend less time with their families and more time with their friends and classmates (Brown, 2004). Consequently, peer groups are important contexts for adolescents' ethnic–racial identity, socialization, and discrimination experiences. As within families, adolescents explore, construct, and enact their ethnic–racial identities in the course of their everyday interactions with their peers (Nasir, McLaughlin, & Jones, 2009). Peers are also key agents of ethnic–racial socialization (Hughes, McGill, et al., 2011; Wang, Benner, & Kim, 2015) and, as described earlier, are frequently the perpetrators of adolescents' ethnic–racial discrimination experiences (Fisher et al., 2000; Greene et al., 2006; Pahl & Way, 2006; Wong et al., 2003). Among peers, as in other contexts, identity formation and enactment, socialization, and discrimination are intimately linked and mutually defining. For instance, situations involving ethnic–racial discrimination or teasing are also situations in which adolescents' peers socialize ethnicity–race. In the context of discrimination, an adolescent's identity is made salient and becomes more central to self-definition whereas their conceptions of others' views of their group (public regard) are internalized and possibly reconfigured (Douglass, Mirpuri, English, & Yip, 2015).

The dynamic interrelatedness of identity, socialization, and discrimination is especially evident in the few studies in which peer groups have been the unit of analysis. For instance, in a 2-year ethnography, Kromidas (2012) analyzed "linguistic crossings"—situations in which youth appropriate the language and behavioral styles of an ethnic–racial group of which they are not a member—as the unit of analysis. In navigating the goals, rules, normative expectations, and behaviors that were emergent in such crossings, youth were regularly enacting particular identities, learning the boundaries of ethnic–racial groupings, and navigating the rules of and protocols for social inclusion and exclusion in the course of these everyday interactions with peers. In Douglass et al. (2015), stories of racial teasing and discrimination were the unit of analysis. The authors coded contextual features such as the relational context of youths' ethnic–racial experiences

(18% involved nonfriends or strangers; 82% involved close peers or friends), whether reference to humor, joking, or teasing was evident (76% of the time), and whether the interaction invoked explicit ethnic–racial stereotypes (present in 55% of situations). Findings indicated that discrimination stories were rarely only about discrimination, per se, but were about identity performances and ethnic–racial learning as well.

These examples aside, researchers currently know less about characteristics of peer contexts in which dynamics of ethnicity–race emerge than about identity, socialization, and discrimination as person-level processes. In quantitative studies, the most commonly examined characteristic, to date, has been ethnic–racial heterogeneity of peer groups, typically operationalized as same-race vs intergroup contact. For example, contact with same-ethnic peers has been associated with increased exploration and belonging (Kiang & Fuligni, 2009; Phinney, Romero, Nava, & Huang, 2001), increased private regard (Yip, Douglass, & Shelton, 2013), and with change in identity status over time (Yip, Seaton, & Sellers, 2010). Moreover, perceived peer support for ethnic–racial identity has been associated with more favorable ethnic identity processes in studies using quantitative (Kiang, Harter, & Whitesell, 2007) and qualitative (DeCuir-Gunby, Martin, & Cooper, 2012) methods. In this regard, DeCuir-Gunby et al. (2012) described how African American students attending a predominantly White school relied on each other to recognize, make meaning of, and respond to discrimination experiences and to affirm their identities as they transitioned from school to neighborhood contexts. Thus, as measured at the individual level, same-race peer interactions serve an important role in the development of positive ethnic–racial identities, but these developmental processes are also tightly interwoven with adolescents' ethnic–racial learning and their discrimination experiences.

Peer contexts not only support adolescents' ethnic–racial experiences but also inform and constrain them, based largely on images about ethnic–racial groups that peer group members collectively hold. Kao (2000), in a focus group study of students in two ethnically racially mixed Chicago high schools, documented that Black, Asian, and Latino adolescents articulated clear stereotypes that linked ethnicity–race to academic ability and other skills and preferences. These stereotypes resulted in segregated peer groups, segregated extracurricular activity participation and racially distinct ideas about possible selves. Qualitative studies have also described the prevalence of ethnic–racial stereotypes within peer groups as well as adolescents' resistance to such stereotypes as critical components of racialization processes and ethnic–racial identity making during adolescence (Awokoya, 2012; DeCuir-Gunby et al., 2012; Kromidas, 2012; Lewis, 2003; Pollock, 2004; Tatum, 2004; Way et al., 2013). Thus, the mutually defining coexistence of identity, socialization, and discrimination is especially evident in shared stereotypes and preconceived notions of ethnic–racial authenticity that are emergent within peer contexts.

Peer contexts are also characterized by descriptive and injunctive norms—both setting-level constructs—that take form as standards for behavior that peers expect of other peer group members. In some peer contexts "race talk" and ethnic–racial teasing are accepted and expected (Douglass et al., 2015; Kromidas, 2012), whereas in other peer contexts youth have learned to avoid any mention of ethnicity–race. In some peer contexts, negative attitudes regarding out-groups are prevalent and made explicit whereas in others such attitudes are noticeably absent. Adolescents' ethnic–racial identity, socialization, and discrimination experiences are embedded in peer contexts that operate according to these varied norms. For instance, adolescents may be reluctant to associate with other-race peers not because of their own ethnic–racial preferences but because of peers' expectations. In both DeCuir-Gunby et al. (2012) and Tatum's (2004) interviews, African American adolescents noted that their African American peers directed racial epithets and accusations of nonauthenticity at them when they did not sit at the "Black table" in the lunchroom. Peer norms also shape youths' ethnic–racial attitudes. Increases in same-race peers' positive and negative attitudes toward other groups' predict increases in adolescents' own positive and negative views (van Zalk, Kerr, Van Zalk, & Stattin, 2013). Peer intergroup contact affects youths' attitudes toward out-groups by way of changing youths' perceptions of in-group norms (De Tezanos-Pinto, Bratt, & Brown, 2010).

Thus, adolescents operate in peer contexts in which they enact particular types of identities, learn particular types of lessons about ethnicity–race, and have particular types of ethnic–racial experiences—some of which involve discrimination. Relevant extra-individual-level characteristics of peer contexts include ethnic–racial homogeneity vs heterogeneity, aggregate attitudes about what it means to be a particular ethnic–racial group member, shared stereotypes, aggregate identity attitudes, norms around intergroup vs intragroup contact, and the prevalence of and appropriateness of "race talk," each of which are closely interwoven with adolescents' ethnic–racial identities, ethnic–racial learning, and ethnic–racial discrimination experiences.

6.3 Schools

In a 2004 article, Pollock noted the following: "U.S. schools are particular places where people both distribute opportunities along racial lines and form identities in racial terms. Indeed, schools are key sites where U.S. young people and adults—in a striking institutional choreography—actually make each other racial" (p. 32). In accordance with this perspective, countless ethnographies and quantitative studies in psychology, sociology, anthropology, and education have examined ethnic–racial dynamics within school contexts, including processes of identity construction (e.g., Hurd, 2008; Maslak, 2008; Nasir et al., 2009), the nature of "race talk" among teachers, administrators, and students (e.g., Anagnostopoulos, Everett, & Carey, 2013; Pollock, 2004), boundary crossing, inclusion, and exclusion (Lewis, 2003), and the implications of multicultural curricular materials and school programming for youths' self-beliefs, ethnic–racial identities, and intergroup relations (Gonzalez, Eades, & Supple, 2014; Maslak, 2008). Studies within psychology and education have also examined differential student–teacher relationships, teacher's expectations, and school disciplinary practices favoring White and Asian students relative to Black and Latino students (Skiba, Michael, Nardo, & Peterson, 2002). The literature in each of these areas is quite large, underscoring researchers' awareness that schools and classrooms serve as primary settings for youths' identity construction and enactment (Lewis, 2003), their ethnic–racial socialization experiences (Aldana & Byrd, 2015; Hughes, McGill, et al., 2011; Hughes, Way, et al., 2011), and their discrimination experiences (Benner & Graham, 2013).

As in the family context, the boundaries between ethnic–racial identity, socialization, and discrimination become especially blurred within school contexts. For instance, "social regularities" (Seidman, 1988) at the school level such as race differentials in ability group placement (Kearns, Ford, & Linney, 2005) or school disciplinary practices (Skiba et al., 2002) elicit particular types of ethnic–racial identities, send important messages about ethnicity–race, and involve differential treatment and discrimination. In Ferguson's (2000) ethnography of school disciplinary practices, the author illustrates how the confluence of school physical, social, and spatial features converged to promote African American boys' tendency to take up identities as "trouble makers" and to be vastly over represented in "the punishing room." Specifically, Ferguson recorded the location and physical layout of "the punishing room" where disciplinary consequences were enacted alongside teachers', parents', peers', and counselors' acceptance of and expectations for disruptive behaviors among African American boys. She also examined school policy and programming in addition to student–teacher and student–student interactions. Nasir et al. (2009) similarly illustrated how school-level characteristics served as demands and affordances for two distinct types of African American identities among students in a predominantly African American low achieving high school. For some students, being Black meant holding deep knowledge of and respect for Black history and culture. These students held "race-conscious and socially aware" identities. The school provided them with higher than average academic standards; programming, resources, and spaces in the library and college counseling office to support college attainment; and leadership roles in the school. Race-conscious and socially aware students gave and received support for academic success from their peers and occupied school spaces such as the library and the guidance office. For other students, being Black meant being a "gangsta" or a "thug." The school offered them little in the way of academic content, held low expectations for their academic work, and provided them with no information about college or requirements for graduation. These students enacted and received reinforcement for "street savvy" Black identities in unmonitored school hallways and gyms where they gambled and smoked marijuana during school hours with little adult intervention.

School social regularities such as those identified in Ferguson (2000) and Nasir et al. (2009) occur in accordance with multiple setting demands and affordances that emanate from structural and physical features of the context, school policies, programs, and curricular materials and goals, as well as interpersonal transactions. In turn, setting participants draw meaning from such regularities and, in Pollock's (2004) words, "make each other racial." Racial group differences that are evident in these regularities come to be seen as natural and expected, and as stemming from inherent racial differences in academic ability, effort, or importance.

Researchers investigating ethnic–racial identity, socialization, and discrimination have not completely ignored school-level characteristics, of course. However, the school-level characteristics that have been examined the most are school or classroom ethnic–racial composition and diversity. This is a "suprapersonal" setting feature within Moos and Lemke's (1983) framework, operationalized primarily through school record data. Scholars have emphasized that school-level ethnic–racial composition of settings determines adolescents' opportunity to interact with same- vs cross-race peers as well as the nature of demands students face in navigating stereotypes and intergroup relations (Yip et al., 2010). In schools in which the student body is more ethnically racially diverse, students perceive more discrimination and a less positive school racial climate overall (Benner & Graham, 2013; Seaton & Yip, 2009). Where the teaching staff is more ethnically racially diverse; however, students report less discrimination (Seaton & Yip, 2009). School diversity has also been associated specifically with ethnic–racial identity processes in several studies. In Umaña-Taylor and Fine (2004), Latino students in schools with fewer Latinos reported more positive ethnic identities. In French et al. (2000), adolescents who transitioned into high schools that were more ethnically diverse than were the middle schools they had attended reported changes in private regard and identity exploration.

More proximal than aggregate student and staff demographic characteristics, a handful of studies have assessed the overall racial climate of schools. The few measures of school racial climate that exist include items regarding student voice, equitable treatment from teachers and staff, and inclusive curricular materials (Brand, Felner, Seitsinger, Burns, & Bolton, 2008; Brand, Felner, Shim, Seitsinger, & Dumas, 2003; Mattison & Aber, 2007). Ethnic–racial minority students in schools that teachers and other students rate as having a more favorable racial climate report significantly better academic, behavioral, and socioemotional adjustment (Brand et al., 2003, 2008). Benner, Crosnoe, and Eccles (2015) reported that adolescents attending schools in which the average student perceived more prejudice in the school had lower grades but not less attachment to school. Byrd and Chavous (2011) found that students' perceptions of the teacher and peer racial climate, as well as their perceptions of teacher and peer discrimination, were related to students' centrality, private regard, and public regard, albeit in complex ways.

In sum, schools are settings in which adolescents construct and reconstruct their identities, receive implicit, and explicit messages about ethnicity–race, and experience discrimination of varied types from varied sources. These ethnic–racial dynamics are also manifest through a confluence of setting demands and affordances. The latter are evident in multiple aspects of the school context including student–student and student–teacher relationships, disciplinary policies and practices, curricula, and ability tracking, each of which contribute to the overall racial climate of the school. These aspects of the school often create qualitatively different academic spaces for students of varied ethnic–racial backgrounds. Although school officials rarely discuss these qualitative differences in school experiences with students, students nevertheless perceive and make meaning of them, with important consequences for students' academic and psychosocial outcomes.

6.4 Neighborhoods

Families, peer groups, and schools are nested within neighborhoods, which are more distal than the former but nevertheless constitute a critical context for youths' ethnic–racial identity, socialization, and discrimination. In ways similar to schools and peer groups, neighborhoods provide a local site at which adolescents navigate the constantly shifting terrain of race in everyday life (Kromidas, 2012). Youth construct and enact their identities based on their day-to-day interactions in the physical spaces of neighborhoods such as stores, gas stations, parks, street corners, and front stoops. Especially in ethnic enclaves, community resources and cultural spaces within neighborhoods also provide youth with opportunities to interact with others of their same ethnic group in positive contexts and to learn about their history, language, and culture in ways that influence positive constructions of their ethnic identity. Youth also acquire racial knowledge through interpersonal transactions that take place in neighborhood settings, including both those they observe and those they experience. They also acquire it as they gain exposure to highly visible and racialized sociostructural patterns in the United States, including poverty and segregation. Indeed, both Moje and Martinez (2007) and Winkler (2012) argue that youth learn ethnicity–race the most when they travel to other neighborhoods, seeing the wider world beyond their own. As with other contexts, identity, socialization, and discrimination experiences are simultaneously manifest in varied neighborhood contexts.

Certainly, scholars have recognized the importance of neighborhood features in shaping youths' ethnic–racial identities, what they learn about ethnicity–race, and their discrimination experiences. In a study of African American families of mixed SES, Smith, Atkins, and Connell (2003) found that having more college-educated neighbors was linked to children's diminished perceptions of racial barriers, whereas more residential stability predicted greater interracial distrust. In Oyserman and Yoon (2009), adolescents who lived in more segregated census tracts evidenced lower racial–ethnic connectedness, awareness of racism, and embedded achievement. Similarly, Bennett (2006) and Supple, Ghazarian, Frabutt, Plunkett, and Sands (2006) found that youth who perceived greater neighborhood risk reported less racial pride and belonging. In several studies, parents in ethnically racially mixed neighborhoods have been found to express more concern about possible discrimination for their children and, in turn, offer more ethnic–racial socialization that is focused on discrimination (Stevenson et al., 2005; Thornton, Chatters, Taylor, & Allen, 1990) compared to their counterparts in less diverse neighborhoods. Caughy, Nettles, O'Campo, and Lohrfink (2006) found that parents living in predominantly African American neighborhoods, which were characterized by greater physical/social disorder and greater fear of retaliation or victimization, were more likely to transmit preparation for bias and promotion of mistrust of messages than were parents residing in mixed neighborhoods. Parents in neighborhoods high in collective efficacy and cohesion were more likely to report ethnic–racial pride messages. In Benner and Graham (2013), youth living in neighborhoods with more ethnic–racial minorities reported more signs of racism in the neighborhoods, which in turn predicted more frequent reports of societal racism and greater racial awareness. Thus, the literature suggests linkages between structural and social process features of neighborhoods and ethnic–racial stressors and supports in adolescents' lives.

Two ethnographies highlight the importance of specific features of adolescents' neighborhoods and of contrasts between features of their own neighborhoods and other neighborhoods to which they travel, pointing scholars toward macrostructural influences on adolescents' ethnic–racial identity, socialization, and discrimination experiences. Although consideration of macrostructural influences is beyond our scope, it seems worthwhile to mention these findings briefly. Moje and Martinez (2007) introduced the concepts of "home fronts" and "contact zones" to mark the contrast between Latino adolescents' experiences in their own vs other neighborhoods. Home fronts were physical and cultural spaces that shaped and promoted adolescents' positive ethnic–racial identities. They provided opportunities for Latino youth to engage intergenerationally with older ethnic–racial group members and provided youth with ethnic–racial identity tool kits that included Spanish language abilities, knowledge of traditions, music, history, and cultural values. Contact zones were spaces youth encountered as they traversed surrounding communities. Youths' awareness of how racism and discrimination work was often generated in these contact zones as youth noticed how others in the world responded to them based on their social class, race, and language. Moje and Martinez (2007) argued that neighborhoods are not only racialized and racially coded; they also shape racial ascriptions that take place within them. Illustratively, youth often felt that others made assumptions about their worthiness or behaviors (based on their ethnicity–race and social class) in outside neighborhoods that others in their own neighborhood did not make. Thus, neighborhood contexts can operate to support youths' ethnic–racial identities, sending positive messages about their group and providing safe spaces but can also operate to undermine youths' identities, transmitting clear messages that promote low public regard by way of extant stereotypes and discrimination experiences.

Winkler (2010), in a study of African American youth, similarly found that youth most palpably recognized how their neighborhoods shaped their experiences when they moved from one place to another. In particular, youth became aware of limits on how they were permitted to act and behave in neighborhoods outside of their own. Travel to other communities and cities shed light on structural racism as youth noted differences in resources, poverty, crime, drugs, and physical neglect across neighborhoods. Thus, Winkler (2010) argued that "place" communicates influential and enduring messages about ethnicity–race, influencing youths' ideas about ethnically or racially ascribed behaviors, racial boundaries, racial hostility, and ultimately, about racial equity and justice.

In sum, then, ethnic–racial dynamics in neighborhoods—as in other contexts—contain demands and affordances through which youth learn and enact their identities, receive numerous messages about ethnicity–race, and experience and observe ethnic–racial stereotypes and discrimination. Although structural neighborhood features have been examined—most notably neighborhood ethnic–racial composition—scholars need more information about the mechanisms through which ethnic–racial dynamics within neighborhoods shape youths' understanding ethnicity–race and of themselves as ethnic–racial group members as well as how these dynamics support or undermine youths' well-being.

7. SUMMARY AND CONCLUSIONS

In this chapter, we focused on three ethnic–racial dynamics that are resources and stressors in the lives of youth: ethnic–racial identity, socialization, and discrimination. Over the past two decades, the literature examining these phenomena has increased exponentially. Thus, there is substantial empirical information about ethnic–racial group differences in these stressors and supports, about their multidimensionality, and about their consequences for youths' well-being and development. Indeed, in each area, the literature theoretically and methodologically has become much more sophisticated.

Although researchers' knowledge has increased substantially, studies have overwhelmingly examined ethnic–racial identity, socialization, and discrimination as individual-level constructs. When context has been studied, researchers have paid more attention to what Bronfenbrenner (1979) calls "social address" concepts such as ethnic composition of peer groups, neighborhoods, and schools. Social address approaches inform us about aggregate or suprapersonal features of settings but fail to provide an up close view of the processes in these settings that are consequential for youth.

We proposed that a more contextualized view of these ethnic–racial dynamics underscores the fact that they are interdependent, inseparable, and mutually defining, consistent with Altman and Rogoff's (1987) transactional world view. For instance, private regard cooccurs with socialization messages that communicate heritage and ethnic pride and positive intergroup relationships. Low public regard tends to emerge in situations where there is intergroup conflict or anxiety about being with nonethnic group members and in situations where there is discrimination or regularities that suggest that one group is better than the other. Ethnicity becomes central and salient to youth in situations where either there is an emphasis on cultural history and heritage and in situations characterized by discrimination—that is, in situations in which youth receive messages about positive or negative aspects of their group.

An ecological/transactional perspective on ethnic–racial identity, socialization, and discrimination shifts researchers' gaze from studying these ethnic–racial dynamics as individual-level processes to studying the features of settings that produce them. Ultimately, support for the positive development of youth requires change in setting-level features, rather than in individual-level phenomena. Although youths' identities, their socialization experiences, and their discrimination experiences clearly have import, researchers need to know much more than we currently do about characteristics of families, peer groups, school and classroom environments, and neighborhoods that produce them.

As a start, we have sought to provide initial thoughts about setting-level characteristics that are likely to matter and to describe studies that have incorporated setting-level constructs.

Within families, such characteristics include participation in identity-relevant activities, cultural motifs (Boykin & Toms, 1985) relevant to ethnicity–race, family friendship networks, the ethnic–racial composition of friendship networks, and physical/architectural features of the home. Within peer groups, extra-individual characteristics obviously include ethnic–racial heterogeneity vs homogeneity, as has been studied already, but also include peer descriptive and injunctive norms around intergroup relationships, shared stereotypes, aggregate identity attitudes, and the prevalence and nature of "race talk." School-level ethnic–racial composition and school racial climate—constituted by ethnic–racial dynamics emanating from student–student and student–teacher dynamics, school policies and programming, ethnically or racially charged social regularities, and physical/architectural support for diversity—are setting-level features that produce certain types of identity, socialization, and discrimination experiences as well. Finally, at the neighborhood level, dynamics such as the availability of intergenerational and programmatic supports for identity; aggregate ethnic–racial attitudes, and contrasts between structural and social features of one's residential neighborhood and other neighborhoods to which one travels matter for what youth learn about ethnicity–race and how they experience it.

To conclude, we have argued that the existing literature has reached the point where continued focus on adolescents' identity, socialization, and discrimination experiences at the individual level will yield only incremental usable knowledge. Researchers need to move toward analyses of the coproduction of these ethnic–racial dynamics at the level of the settings in which adolescents participate.

REFERENCES

Adam, E. K., Heissel, J. A., Zeiders, K. H., Richeson, J. A., Ross, E. C., Ehrlich, K. B., … Peck, S. C. (2015). Developmental histories of perceived racial discrimination and diurnal cortisol profiles in adulthood: A 20-year prospective study. *Psychoneuroendocrinology*, *62*, 279–291. http://dx.doi.org/10.1016/j.psyneuen.2015.08.018.

Aldana, A., & Byrd, C. M. (2015). School ethnic–racial socialization: Learning about race and ethnicity among African American students. *The Urban Review*, *47*(3), 563–576. http://dx.doi.org/10.1007/s11256-014-0319-0.

Altman, I., & Rogoff, B. (1987). World views in psychology: Trait, interactional, organismic, and transactional perspectives. In D. Stools & I. Altman (Eds.), *Handbook of environmental psychology* (pp. 7–40). New York, NY: Wiley.

Altschul, I., Oyserman, D., & Bybee, D. (2006). Racial-ethnic identity in mid-adolescence: Content and change as predictors of academic achievement. *Child Development*, *77*(5), 1155–1169. http://dx.doi.org/10.1111/j.1467-8624.2006.00926.x.

Anagnostopoulos, D., Everett, S., & Carey, C. (2013). 'Of course we're supposed to move on, but then you still got people who are not over those historical wounds': Cultural memory and US youth's race talk. *Discourse & Society*, *24*(2), 163–185.

Applegate, J. L., Burleson, B. R., & Delia, J. G. (1992). Reflection-enhancing parenting as an antecedent to children's social-cognitive and communicative development. In I. E. Sigel, A. V. McGillicuddy-DeLisi, & J. J. Goodnow (Eds.), *Parental belief systems: The psychological consequences for children* (2nd ed., pp. 3–39). Hillsdale, NJ: Lawrence Erlbaum Associates.

Awokoya, J. T. (2012). Identity constructions and negotiations among 1.5- and second-generation Nigerians: The impact of family, school, and peer contexts. *Harvard Educational Review*, *82*(2), 255–281.

Barker, R. G. (1968). *Ecological psychology: Concepts and methods for studying the environment of human behavior*. Stanford, CA: Stanford University Press.

Bellmore, A., Nishina, A., You, J., & Ma, T. L. (2012). School context protective factors against peer ethnic discrimination across the high school years. *American Journal of Community Psychology, 49*(1–2), 98–111. http://dx.doi.org/10.1007/s10464-011-9443-0.

Benner, A. D., Crosnoe, R., & Eccles, J. S. (2015). Schools, peers, and prejudice in adolescence. *Journal of Research on Adolescence, 25*, 173–188. http://dx.doi.org/10.1111/jora.12106.

Benner, A. D., & Graham, S. (2011). Latino adolescents' experiences of discrimination across high school: Correlates and influences on educational outcomes. *Child Development, 82*, 508–519. http://dx.doi.org/10.1111/j.1467-8624.2010.01524.x.

Benner, A. D., & Graham, S. (2013). The antecedents and consequences of racial/ethnic discrimination during adolescence: Does the source of discrimination matter? *Developmental Psychology, 49*, 1602–1613. http://dx.doi.org/10.1037/a0030557.

Benner, A. D., & Kim, S. Y. (2009). Experiences of discrimination among Chinese American adolescents and the consequences for socioemotional and academic development. *Developmental Psychology, 45*, 1682–1694. http://dx.doi.org/10.1037/a0016119.

Bennett, M. D., Jr. (2006). Culture and context: A study of neighborhood effects on racial socialization and ethnic identity content in a sample of African American adolescents. *Journal of Black Psychology, 32*(4), 479–500. http://dx.doi.org/10.1177/0095798406292470.

Bentley-Edwards, K. L., & Stevenson, H. C., Jr. (2016). The multidimensionality of racial/ethnic socialization: Scale construction for the Cultural and Racial Experiences of Socialization (CARES). *Journal of Child and Family Studies, 25*(1), 96–108. http://dx.doi.org/10.1007/s10826-015-0214-7.

Bigler, R. S., & Liben, L. S. (2006). A developmental intergroup theory of social stereotypes and prejudice. In R. V. Kail (Ed.), *Advances in child development and behavior: Vol. 34* (pp. 39–89). San Diego, CA: Elsevier Academic Press.

Boykin, A. W., & Toms, F. D. (1985). Black child socialization: A conceptual framework. In H. P. McAdoo & J. L. McAdoo (Eds.), *Black children: Social, educational, and parental environments* (pp. 33–51). Thousand Oaks, CA: Sage Publications.

Brand, S., Felner, R. D., Seitsinger, A., Burns, A., & Bolton, N. (2008). A large scale study of the assessment of the social environment of middle and secondary schools: The validity and utility of teachers' ratings of school climate, cultural pluralism, and safety problems for understanding school effects and school improvement. *Journal of School Psychology, 46*(5), 507–535. http://dx.doi.org/10.1016/j.jsp.2007.12.001.

Brand, S., Felner, R., Shim, M., Seitsinger, A., & Dumas, T. (2003). Middle school improvement and reform: Development and validation of a school-level assessment of climate, cultural pluralism, and school safety. *Journal of Educational Psychology, 95*(3), 570–588. http://dx.doi.org/10.1037/0022-0663.95.3.570.

Brody, G. H., Chen, Y. F., Murry, V. M., Ge, X., Simons, R. L., Gibbons, F. X., & Cutrona, C. E. (2006). Perceived discrimination and the adjustment of African American youths: A five-year longitudinal analysis with contextual moderation effects. *Child Development, 77*(5), 1170–1189. http://dx.doi.org/10.1111/j.1467-8624.2006.00927.x.

Bronfenbrenner, U. (1979). *The ecology of human development: Experiments by design and nature.* Cambridge, MA: Harvard University Press.

Brown, B. B. (2004). Adolescents' relationships with peers. In R. M. Lerner & L. Steinberg (Eds.), *Handbook of adolescent psychology* (2nd ed., pp. 363–394). Hoboken, NJ: John Wiley & Sons Inc.

Brown, C. S., & Bigler, R. S. (2005). Children's perceptions of discrimination: A developmental model. *Child Development, 76*(3), 533–553. http://dx.doi.org/10.1111/j.1467-8624.2005.00862.x.

Burt, C. H., Simons, R. L., & Gibbons, F. X. (2012). Racial discrimination, ethnic-racial socialization, and crime: A micro-sociological model of risk and resilience. *American Sociological Review, 77*(4), 648–677. http://dx.doi.org/10.1177/0003122412448648.

Byrd, C. M. (2015). The associations of intergroup interactions and school racial socialization with academic motivation. *The Journal of Educational Research, 108*(1), 10–21.
Byrd, C. M., & Chavous, T. (2011). Racial identity, school racial climate, and school intrinsic motivation among African American youth: The importance of person–context congruence. *Journal of Research on Adolescence, 21*(4), 849–860.
Caughy, M. O. B., Nettles, S. M., O'Campo, P. J., & Lohrfink, K. F. (2006). Neighborhood matters: Racial socialization of African American children. *Child Development, 77*(5), 1220–1236. http://dx.doi.org/10.1111/j.1467-8624.2006.00930.x.
Caughy, M. O. B., & Owen, M. T. (2014). Cultural socialization and school readiness of African American and Latino preschoolers. *Cultural Diversity and Ethnic Minority Psychology, 21*(3), 391–399. http://dx.doi.org/10.1037/a0037928.
Chavous, T. M., Bernat, D., Schmeelk-Cone, K., Caldwell, C., KohnWood, L. P., & Zimmerman, M. A. (2003). Racial identity and academic attainment among African American adolescents. *Child Development, 74*(4), 1076–1091. http://dx.doi.org/10.1111/1467-8624.00593.
Chavous, T. M., Rivas, D., Green, L. C., & Helaire, L. (2002). The roles of student background, perceptions of ethnic fit and racial identification in the academic adjustment of African Americans at a predominantly White university. *Journal of Black Psychology, 28*(3), 234–260.
Cross, W. E., Jr. (2005). Ethnicity, race, and identity. In T. S. Weisner (Ed.), *Discovering successful pathways in children's development: Mixed methods in the study of childhood and family life* (pp. 171–182). Chicago, IL: University of Chicago Press.
DeCuir-Gunby, J. T., Martin, P. P., & Cooper, S. M. (2012). African American students in private, independent schools: Parents and school influences on racial identity development. *The Urban Review, 44*(1), 113–132. http://dx.doi.org/10.1007/s11256-011-0178-x.
Derlan, C. L., Umaña-Taylor, A. J., Updegraff, K. A., & Jahromi, L. B. (2015). Mothers' characteristics as predictors of adolescents' ethnic–racial identity: An examination of Mexican-Origin teen mothers. *Cultural Diversity and Ethnic Minority Psychology*, 1–7. http://dx.doi.org/10.1037/cdp0000072.
De Tezanos-Pinto, P., Bratt, C., & Brown, R. (2010). What will the others think? In-group norms as a mediator of the effects of intergroup contact. *British Journal of Social Psychology, 49*, 507–523. http://dx.doi.org/10.1348/014466609X471020.
Douglass, S., Mirpuri, S., English, D., & Yip, T. (2015). They were just making jokes: Ethnic/racial teasing and discrimination among adolescents. *Cultural Diversity and Ethnic Minority Psychology, 22*(1), 69–82. http://dx.doi.org/10.1037/cdp0000041.
Ferguson, A. A. (2000). *Bad boys*. Ann Arbor, MI: University of Michigan Press.
Fisher, C. B., Wallace, S. A., & Fenton, R. E. (2000). Discrimination distress during adolescence. *Journal of Youth and Adolescence, 29*(6), 679–695. http://dx.doi.org/10.1023/A:1026455906512.
French, S. E., Seidman, E., & Allen, L. (2006). The development of ethnic identity during adolescence. *Developmental Psychology, 42*(1), 1–10. http://dx.doi.org/10.1037/0012-1649.42.1.1.
French, S. E., Seidman, E., Allen, L., & Aber, J. L. (2000). Racial/ethnic identity, congruence with the social context, and the transition to high school. *Journal of Adolescent Research, 15*, 587–602. http://dx.doi.org/10.1177/0743558400155004.
Fuligni, A. J., Witkow, M., & Garcia, C. (2005). Ethnic identity and the academic adjustment of adolescents from Mexican, Chinese, and European backgrounds. *Developmental Psychology, 41*(5), 799. http://dx.doi.org/10.1037/0012-1649.41.5.799.
Fuller-Rowell, T. E., Cogburn, C. D., Brodish, A. B., Peck, S. C., Malanchuk, O., & Eccles, J. S. (2012). Racial discrimination and substance use: Longitudinal associations and identity moderators. *Journal of Behavioral Medicine, 35*(6), 581–590. http://dx.doi.org/10.1007/s10865-011-9388-7.

Gonzalez, L. M., Eades, M. P., & Supple, A. J. (2014). School community engaging with immigrant youth: Incorporating personal/social development and ethnic identity development. *School Community Journal, 24*(1), 99–117.
González, A. G., Umaña-Taylor, A. J., & Bámaca, M. Y. (2006). Familial ethnic socialization among adolescents of Latino and European descent: Do Latina mothers exert the most influence? *Journal of Family Issues, 27*(2), 184–207. http://dx.doi.org/10.1177/0192513X05279987.
Greene, M. L., Way, N., & Pahl, K. (2006). Trajectories of perceived adult and peer discrimination among Black, Latino, and Asian American adolescents: Patterns and psychological correlates. *Developmental Psychology, 42*(2), 218–236. http://dx.doi.org/10.1037/0012-1649.42.2.218.
Hagerman, M. A. (2014). White families and race: Colour-blind and colour-conscious approaches to white racial socialization. *Ethnic and Racial Studies, 37*(14), 2598–2614. http://dx.doi.org/10.1080/01419870.2013.848289.
Hitti, A., Mulvey, K. L., Rutland, A., Abrams, D., & Killen, M. (2014). When is it okay to exclude a member of the ingroup? Children's and adolescents' social reasoning. *Social Development, 23*(3), 451–469. http://dx.doi.org/10.1111/sode.12047.
Ho, A., & Graham, S. (2008). Ethnic identity development in Latina/o early adolescents. In *Poster presented at the biennial meeting of the society for research on adolescence, Chicago, IL.*
Hughes, D. (2003). Correlates of African American and Latino parents' messages to children about ethnicity and race: A comparative study of racial socialization. *American Journal of Community Psychology, 31*, 15–33. http://dx.doi.org/10.1023/A:1023066418688.
Hughes, D. L., & Chen, L. (1997). When and what parents tell children about race: An examination of race-related socialization among African American families. *Applied Developmental Science, 1*, 200–214. http://dx.doi.org/10.1207/s1532480xads0104_4.
Hughes, D. L., & Chen, L. (1999). The nature of parents' race-related communications to children: A developmental perspective. In L. Balter & C. S. Tamis-LeMonda (Eds.), *Child psychology: A handbook of contemporary issues* (1st ed., pp. 467–490). New York, NY: Psychology Press.
Hughes, D., Del Toro, J., Harding, J. F., Way, N, & Rarick, J. (2016). Trajectories of sources and types of discrimination across early and middle adolescence predicting academic, psychological and behavioral outcomes. *Child Development.*
Hughes, D., Del Toro, J., Rarick, J., & Way, N. (2015). Liberty and justice for all: When and how parents teach egalitarian views to their children. In L. Balter & C. Tamis-LeMonda (Eds.), *Child psychology: A handbook of contemporary issues* (3rd ed., pp. 401–422). New York, NY: Psychology Press.
Hughes, D. L., Del Toro, J., & Way, N. (2016). *Either too much honey or too big a stick: The impact of moderate preparation for bias on youth development.* Manuscript in progress.
Hughes, D., Hagelskamp, C., Del Toro, J., Shrout, P., & Way, N. (2010). *Reciprocity in longitudinal relationships between ethnic-racial socialization, discrimination, and ethnic-identity: Autoregressive latent trajectory analysis.* (unpublished manuscript).
Hughes, D., & Johnson, D. (2001). Correlates in children's experiences of parents' racial socialization behaviors. *Journal of Marriage and Family, 63*, 981–995. http://dx.doi.org/10.1111/j.1741-3737.2001.00981.x.
Hughes, D. L., McGill, R. K., Ford, K. R., & Tubbs, C. (2011). Black youths' academic success: The contribution of racial socialization from parents, peers, and schools. In N. Hill, T. L. Mann, & H. E. Fitzgerald (Eds.), *Development and context, prevention and social policy:* (Vols. 1 and 2). *African American children and mental health* (pp. 95–124). Santa Barbara, CA: Praeger/ABC-CLIO.
Hughes, D., Rivas, D., Foust, M., Hagelskamp, C., Gersick, S., & Way, N. (2008). How to catch a moonbeam: A mixed-methods approach to understanding ethnic socialization processes in ethnically diverse families. In S. M. Quintana & C. McKown

(Eds.), *Handbook of race, racism, and the developing child* (pp. 226–277). Hoboken, NJ: John Wiley & Sons Inc.

Hughes, D., Rodriguez, J., Smith, E. P., Johnson, D. J., Stevenson, H. C., & Spicer, P. (2006). Parents' ethnic-racial socialization practices: A review of research and directions for future study. *Developmental Psychology, 42*, 747–770. http://dx.doi.org/10.1037/0012-1649.42.5.747.

Hughes, D., Way, N., & Rivas-Drake, D. (2011). Stability and change in private and public ethnic regard among African American, Puerto Rican, Dominican, and Chinese American early adolescents. *Journal of Research on Adolescence, 21*(4), 861–870. http://dx.doi.org/10.1111/j.1532-7795.2011.00744.x.

Hurd, C. A. (2008). Cinco de Mayo, normative Whiteness, and the marginalization of Mexican-descent students. *Anthropology & Education Quarterly, 39*, 293–313. http://dx.doi.org/10.1111/j.1548-1492.2008.00023.x.

Huynh, V. W., & Fuligni, A. J. (2010). Discrimination hurts: The academic, psychological, and physical well-being of adolescents. *Journal of Research on Adolescence, 20*(4), 916–941. http://dx.doi.org/10.1111/j.1532-7795.2010.00670.x.

Johnston, K. E., Swim, J. K., Saltsman, B. M., Deater-Deckard, K., & Petrill, S. A. (2007). Mothers' racial, ethnic, and cultural socialization of transracially adopted Asian children. *Family Relations, 56*(4), 390–402. http://dx.doi.org/10.1111/j.1741-3729.2007.00468.x.

Juang, L. P., & Syed, M. (2014). Sharing stories of discrimination with parents. *Journal of Adolescence, 37*, 303–312. http://dx.doi.org/10.1016/j.adolescence.2014.02.004.

Kao, G. (2000). Group images and possible selves among adolescents: Linking stereotypes to expectations by race and ethnicity. *Sociological Forum, 15*(3), 407–430. Kluwer Academic Publishers-Plenum Publishers.

Katz, P. A. (2003). Racists or tolerant multiculturalists? How do they begin? *American Psychologist, 58*(11), 897b. http://dx.doi.org/10.1037/0003-066X.58.11.897b.

Kearns, T., Ford, L., & Linney, J. A. (2005). African American student representation in special education programs. *The Journal of Negro Education, 74*, 297–310.

Kiang, L., & Fuligni, A. J. (2009). Ethnic identity in context: Variations in ethnic exploration and belonging within parent, same-ethnic peer, and different-ethnic peer relationships. *Journal of Youth and Adolescence, 38*, 732–743. http://dx.doi.org/10.1007/s10964-008-9278-7.

Kiang, L., Harter, S., & Whitesell, N. R. (2007). Relational expression of ethnic identity in Chinese Americans. *Journal of Social and Personal Relationships, 24*, 277–296. http://dx.doi.org/10.1177/0265407507075414.

Kiang, L., Witkow, M. R., & Champagne, M. C. (2013). Normative changes in ethnic and American identities and links with adjustment among Asian American adolescents. *Developmental Psychology, 49*(9), 1713. http://dx.doi.org/10.1037/a0030840.

Killen, M., Henning, A., Kelly, M. C., Crystal, D., & Ruck, M. (2007). Evaluations of interracial peer encounters by majority and minority US children and adolescents. *International Journal of Behavioral Development, 31*(5), 491–500. http://dx.doi.org/10.1177/0165025407081478.

Kromidas, M. (2012). Affiliation or appropriation? Crossing and the politics of race among children in New York City. *Childhood: A Global Journal of Child Research, 19*, 317–331. http://dx.doi.org/10.1177/0907568212441036.

Lee, R. M., & Yoo, H. C. (2004). Structure and measurement of ethnic identity for Asian American college students. *Journal of Counseling Psychology, 51*(2), 263. http://dx.doi.org/10.1037/0022-0167.51.2.263.

Leslie, L. A., Smith, J. R., Hrapczynski, K. M., & Riley, D. (2013). Racial socialization in transracial adoptive families: Does it help adolescents deal with discrimination stress? *Family Relations, 62*(1), 72–81. http://dx.doi.org/10.1111/j.1741-3729.2012.00744.x.

Lewis, A. E. (2003). Everyday race-making: Navigating racial boundaries in schools. *American Behavioral Scientist*, *47*, 283–305. http://dx.doi.org/10.1177/0002764203256188.
Liang, C. T., Alvarez, A. N., Juang, L. P., & Liang, M. X. (2007). The role of coping in the relationship between perceived racism and racism-related stress for Asian Americans: Gender differences. *Journal of Counseling Psychology*, *54*(2), 132. http://dx.doi.org/10.1037/1948-1985.S.1.56.
Livert, D., & Hughes, D. L. (2002). The ecological paradigm: Persons in settings. In T. A. Revenson, A. R. D'Augelli, S. E. French, D. L. Hughes, D. Livert, E. Seidman, M. Shinn, & H. Yoshikawa (Eds.), *A quarter century of community psychology: Readings from the American Journal of Community Psychology* (pp. 51–63). New York, NY: Kluwer Academic/Plenum Publishers.
Mandara, J. (2006). The impact of family functioning on African American males' academic achievement: A review and clarification of the empirical literature. *Teachers College Record*, *108*, 206–223. http://dx.doi.org/10.1111/j.1467-9620.2006.00648.x.
Martin, M. J., McCarthy, B., Conger, R. D., Gibbons, F. X., Simons, R. L., Cutrona, C. E., & Brody, G. H. (2011). The enduring significance of racism: Discrimination and delinquency among black American youth. *Journal of Research on Adolescence*, *21*(3), 662–676. http://dx.doi.org/10.1111/j.1532-7795.2010.00699.x.
Maslak, M. A. (2008). School as a site of Tibetan ethnic identity construction in India? Results from a content analysis of textbooks and Delphi study of teachers' perceptions. *Educational Review*, *60*(1), 85–106. http://dx.doi.org/10.1080/00131910701794671.
Mattison, E., & Aber, M. S. (2007). Closing the achievement gap: The association of racial climate with achievement and behavioral outcomes. *American Journal of Community Psychology*, *40*(1–2), 1–12. http://dx.doi.org/10.1007/s10464-007-9128-x.
McGlothlin, H., & Killen, M. (2010). How social experience is related to children's intergroup attitudes. *European Journal of Social Psychology*, *40*, 625–634. http://dx.doi.org/10.1002/ejsp.733.
McGuire, L., Rutland, A., & Nesdale, D. (2015). Peer group norms and accountability moderate the effect of school norms on children's intergroup attitudes. *Child Development*, *86*, 1290–1297. http://dx.doi.org/10.1111/cdev.12388.
McHale, S. M., Crouter, A. C., Kim, J. Y., Burton, L. M., Davis, K. D., Dotterer, A. M., & Swanson, D. P. (2006). Mothers' and fathers' racial socialization in African American families: Implications for youth. *Child Development*, 77(5), 1387–1402. http://dx.doi.org/10.1111/j.1467-8624.2006.00942.x.
McKown, C., & Strambler, M. J. (2009). Developmental antecedents and social and academic consequences of stereotype-consciousness in middle childhood. *Child Development*, *80*(6), 1643–1659. http://dx.doi.org/10.1111/j.1467-8624.2009.01359.x.
Mohanty, J., Keokse, G., & Sales, E. (2007). Family cultural socialization, ethnic identity, and self-esteem: Web-based survey of international adult adoptees. *Journal of Ethnic and Cultural Diversity in Social Work*, *15*(3–4), 153–172. http://dx.doi.org/10.1300/J051v15n03_07.
Moje, E. B., & Martinez, M. (2007). The role of peers, families, and ethnic-identity enactments in educational persistence and achievement of Latino and Latina youths. In A. J. Fuligni (Ed.), *Contesting stereotypes and creating identities: Social categories, social identities, and educational participation* (pp. 209–238). New York: Russell Sage Foundation.
Moos, R. H., & Lemke, S. (1983). Assessing and improving ecological settings. In E. Seidman (Ed.), *Handbook of social intervention* (pp. 147–163). Beverly Hills: Sage.
Nagel, J. (1994). Constructing ethnicity: Creating and recreating ethnic identity and culture. *Social Problems*, *41*, 152–176. http://dx.doi.org/10.1525/sp.1994.41.1.03x0430n.
Nasir, N. I. S., McLaughlin, M. W., & Jones, A. (2009). What does it mean to be African American? Constructions of race and academic identity in an urban public high school. *American Educational Research Journal*, *46*(1), 73–114. http://dx.doi.org/10.3102/0002831208323279.

Neblett, E. W., Jr., Banks, K. H., Cooper, S. M., & Smalls-Glover, C. (2013). Racial identity mediates the association between ethnic-racial socialization and depressive symptoms. *Cultural Diversity and Ethnic Minority Psychology*, *19*(2), 200. http://dx.doi.org/10.1037/a0032205.

Neblett, E. W., Philip, C. L., Cogburn, C. D., & Sellers, R. M. (2006). African American adolescents' discrimination experiences and academic achievement: Racial socialization as a cultural compensatory and protective factor. *Journal of Black psychology*, *32*(2), 199–218. http://dx.doi.org/10.1177/0095798406287072.

Neblett, E. W., Shelton, N. J., & Sellers, R. M. (2004). The role of racial identity in managing daily racial hassles. In G. Philogene (Ed.), *Racial identity in context: The legacy of Kenneth B. Clark* (pp. 77–90). Washington, DC: American Psychological Association. http://dx.doi.org/10.1037/10812-005.

Niwa, E. Y., Way, N., & Hughes, D. L. (2014). Trajectories of ethnic-racial discrimination among ethnically diverse early adolescents: Associations with psychological and social adjustment. *Child Development*, *85*(6), 2339–2354.

Omi, M., & Winant, H. (1994). *Racial formation in the United States: From the 1960s to the 1990s*. New York, NY: Routledge.

Osterman, K. F. (2000). Students' need for belonging in the school community. *Review of Educational Research*, *70*(3), 323–367. http://dx.doi.org/10.2307/1170786.

Oyserman, D., Brickman, D., & Rhodes, M. (2007). Racial-ethnic identity in adolescence: Content and consequences for African American and Latino and Latina youth. In A. J. Fuligni (Ed.), *Contesting stereotypes and creating identities: Social categories, identities and educational participation* (pp. 91–114). New York, NY: Russell-Sage.

Oyserman, D., Bybee, D., & Terry, K. (2003). Gendered racial identity and involvement with school. *Self and Identity*, *2*(4), 307–324. http://dx.doi.org/10.1080/714050250.

Oyserman, D., & Yoon, K.-I. (2009). Neighborhood effects on racial-ethnic identity: The undermining role of segregation. *Race and Social Problems*, *1*, 67–76. http://dx.doi.org/10.1007/s12552-009-9007-1.

Pahl, K., & Way, N. (2006). Longitudinal trajectories of ethnic identity among urban Black and Latino adolescents. *Child Development*, 77(5), 1403–1415. http://dx.doi.org/10.1111/j.1467-8624.2006.00943.x.

Palmer, S. B., Rutland, A., & Cameron, L. (2015). The development of bystander intentions and social-moral reasoning about intergroup verbal aggression. *British Journal of Developmental Psychology*, *33*, 419–433. http://dx.doi.org/10.1111/bjdp.12092.

Penuel, W. R., & Wertsch, J. V. (1995). Dynamics of negation in the identity politics of cultural other and cultural self. *Culture & Psychology*, *1*(3), 343–359. http://dx.doi.org/10.1177/1354067X9513002.

Peters, M. F., & Massey, G. (1983). Mundane extreme environmental stress in family stress theories: The case of Black families in White America. *Marriage & Family Review*, *6*(1–2), 193–218. http://dx.doi.org/10.1300/J002v06n01_10.

Phinney, J. S. (1993). A three-stage model of ethnic identity development in adolescence. In M. E. Bernal & G. P. Knight (Eds.), *Ethnic identity: Formation and transmission among Hispanics and other minorities* (pp. 61–79). Albany, NY: SUNY Press.

Phinney, J. S., Romero, I., Nava, M., & Huang, D. (2001). The role of language, parents, and peers in ethnic identity among adolescents in immigrant families. *Journal of Youth and Adolescence*, *30*, 135–153. http://dx.doi.org/10.1023/A:1010389607319.

Pollock, M. (2004). Race bending: "mixed" youth practicing strategic racialization in California. *Anthropology & Education Quarterly*, *35*(1), 30–52. http://dx.doi.org/10.1525/aeq.2004.35.1.30.

Priest, N., Walton, J., White, F., Kowal, E., Baker, A., & Paradies, Y. (2014). Understanding the complexities of ethnic-racial socialization processes for both minority and majority groups: A 30-year systematic review. *International Journal of Intercultural Relations*, *43*, 139–155.

Rivas-Drake, D. (2011). Ethnic-racial socialization and adjustment among Latino college students: The mediating roles of ethnic centrality, public regard, and perceived barriers to opportunity. *Journal of Youth and Adolescence, 40*(5), 606–619. http://dx.doi.org/10.1007/s10964-010-9564-z.

Rivas-Drake, D., Hughes, D., & Way, N. (2008). A closer look at peer discrimination, ethnic identity, and psychological well-being among urban Chinese American sixth graders. *Journal of Youth and Adolescence, 37*(1), 12–21. http://dx.doi.org/10.1007/s10964-007-9227-x.

Rivas-Drake, D., Hughes, D., & Way, N. (2009a). A preliminary analysis of associations among ethnic racial socialization, ethnic discrimination, and ethnic identity among urban sixth graders. *Journal of Research on Adolescence, 19*(3), 558–584. http://dx.doi.org/10.1111/j.1532-7795.2009.00607.x.

Rivas-Drake, D., Hughes, D., & Way, N. (2009b). Public ethnic regard and perceived socio-economic stratification: Associations with well-being among Dominican and Black American youth. *The Journal of Early Adolescence, 29*(1), 122–141. http://dx.doi.org/10.1177/0272431608324479.

Rowley, S. J., Burchinal, M. R., Roberts, J. E., & Zeisel, S. A. (2008). Racial identity, social context, and race-related social cognition in African Americans during middle childhood. *Developmental Psychology, 44*, 1537–1546. http://dx.doi.org/10.1037/a0013349.

Sarason, S. B. (1982). *The culture of the school and the problem of change*. Boston, MA: Allyn & Bacon.

Schmader, T., Major, B., & Gramzow, R. H. (2001). Coping with ethnic stereotypes in the academic domain: Perceived injustice and psychological disengagement. *Journal of Social Issues, 57*(1), 93–111. http://dx.doi.org/10.1111/0022-4537.00203.

Scott, L. D. (2003). The relation of racial identity and racial socialization to coping with discrimination among African American adolescents. *Journal of Black Studies, 33*(4), 520–538. http://dx.doi.org/10.1177/0021934702250035.

Seaton, E. K., & Douglass, S. (2014). School diversity and racial discrimination among African-American adolescents. *Cultural Diversity and Ethnic Minority Psychology, 20*(2), 156. http://dx.doi.org/10.1037/a0035322.

Seaton, E. K., & Yip, T. (2009). School and neighborhood contexts, perceptions of racial discrimination, and psychological well-being among African American adolescents. *Journal of Youth and Adolescence, 38*(2), 153–163. http://dx.doi.org/10.1007/s10964-008-9356-x.

Seaton, E. K., Yip, T., & Sellers, R. M. (2009). A longitudinal examination of racial identity and racial discrimination among African American adolescents. *Child Development, 80*(2), 406–417. http://dx.doi.org/10.1111/j.1467-8624.2009.01268.x.

Seidman, E. (1988). Back to the future, community psychology: Unfolding a theory of social intervention. *American Journal of Community Psychology, 16*(1), 3–24. http://dx.doi.org/10.1007/BF00906069.

Sellers, R. M., Copeland-Linder, N., Martin, P. P., & Lewis, R. H. (2006). Racial identity matters: The relationship between racial discrimination and psychological functioning in African American adolescents. *Journal of Research on Adolescence, 16*(2), 187–216. http://dx.doi.org/10.1111/j.1532-7795.2006.00128.x.

Sellers, R. M., Smith, M. A., Shelton, J. N., Rowley, S. A., & Chavous, T. M. (1998). Multidimensional model of racial identity: A reconceptualization of African American racial identity. *Personality and Social Psychology Review, 2*(1), 18–39. http://dx.doi.org/10.1207/s15327957pspr0201_2.

Seol, K. O., Yoo, H. C., Lee, R. M., Park, J. E., & Kyeong, Y. (2015). Racial and ethnic socialization as moderators of racial discrimination and school adjustment of adopted and nonadopted Korean American adolescents. *Journal of Counseling Psychology, 63*(3), 294–306. http://dx.doi.org/10.1037/cou0000120.

Simons, R. L., Murry, V., McLoyd, V., Lin, K. H., Cutrona, C., & Conger, R. D. (2002). Discrimination, crime, ethnic identity, and parenting as correlates of depressive symptoms among African American children: A multilevel analysis. *Development and Psychopathology*, *14*(2), 371–393. http://dx.doi.org/10.1017/S0954579402002109.

Skiba, R. J., Michael, R. S., Nardo, A. C., & Peterson, R. L. (2002). The color of discipline: Sources of racial and gender disproportionality in school punishment. *The Urban Review*, *34*(4), 317–342. http://dx.doi.org/10.1023/A:1021320817372.

Smith, E. P., Atkins, J., & Connell, C. M. (2003). Family, school, and community factors and relationships to racial–ethnic attitudes and academic achievement. *American Journal of Community Psychology*, *32*(1–2), 159–173. http://dx.doi.org/10.1023/A:1025663311100.

Spencer, M. B. (1983). Children's cultural values and parental child rearing strategies. *Developmental Review*, *3*(4), 351–370. http://dx.doi.org/10.1016/0273-2297(83)90020-5.

Stevenson, H. C., McNeil, J. D., Herrero-Taylor, T., & Davis, G. Y. (2005). Influence of perceived neighborhood diversity and racism experience on the racial socialization of Black youth. *Journal of Black Psychology*, *31*(3), 273–290. http://dx.doi.org/10.1177/0095798405278453.

Supple, A. J., Ghazarian, S. R., Frabutt, J. M., Plunkett, S. W., & Sands, T. (2006). Contextual influences on Latino adolescent ethnic identity and academic outcomes. *Child Development*, 77(5), 1427–1433. http://dx.doi.org/10.1111/j.1467-8624.2006.00945.x.

Tajfel, H., & Turner, J. C. (1986). The social identity theory of intergroup behaviour. In S. Worchel & W. G. Austin (Eds.), *Psychology of intergroup relations* (2nd ed., pp. 7–24). Chicago: Nelson-Hall.

Tatum, B. D. (1987). *Assimilation blues: Black families in a white community*. New York, NY: Greenwood Press.

Tatum, B. D. (2004). Family life and school experience: Factors in the racial identity development of Black youth in White communities. *Journal of Social Issues*, *60*, 117–135. http://dx.doi.org/10.1111/j.0022-4537.2004.00102.x.

Thornton, M. C., Chatters, L. M., Taylor, R. J., & Allen, W. R. (1990). Sociodemographic and environmental correlates of racial socialization by Black parents. *Child Development*, *61*(2), 401–409. http://dx.doi.org/10.2307/1131101.

Umaña-Taylor, A. J., & Fine, M. A. (2004). Examining ethnic identity among Mexican-origin adolescents living in the United States. *Hispanic Journal of Behavioral Sciences*, *26*(1), 36–59. http://dx.doi.org/10.1177/0739986303262143.

Umaña-Taylor, A. J., & Guimond, A. B. (2012). A longitudinal examination of parenting behaviors and perceived discrimination predicting Latino adolescents' ethnic identity. *Journal of Latina/o Psychology*, *1*(S), 14–35. http://dx.doi.org/10.1037/2168-1678.1.S.14.

Umaña-Taylor, A. J., O'Donnell, M., Knight, G. P., Roosa, M. W., Berkel, C., & Nair, R. (2014). Mexican-origin early adolescents' ethnic socialization, ethnic identity, and psychosocial functioning. *The Counseling Psychologist*, *42*(2), 170–200. http://dx.doi.org/10.1177/0011000013477903.

Umaña-Taylor, A. J., Quintana, S. M., Lee, R. M., Cross, W. E., Rivas-Drake, D., Schwartz, S. J., … Seaton, E. (2014). Ethnic and racial identity during adolescence and into young adulthood: An integrated conceptualization. *Child Development*, *85*(1), 21–39. http://dx.doi.org/10.1111/cdev.12196.

Umaña-Taylor, A. J., Updegraff, K. A., Jahromi, L. B., & Zeiders, K. H. (2015). Trajectories of ethnic–racial identity and autonomy among Mexican-origin adolescent mothers in the United States. *Child Development*, *86*(6), 2034–2050. http://dx.doi.org/10.1111/cdev.12444.

Umaña-Taylor, A. J., Vargas-Chanes, D., Garcia, C. D., & Gonzales-Backen, M. (2008). A longitudinal examination of Latino adolescents' ethnic identity, coping with discrimination, and self-esteem. *The Journal of Early Adolescence*, *28*(1), 16–50. http://dx.doi.org/10.1177/0272431607308666.

Umaña-Taylor, A. J., Yazedjian, A., & Bámaca-Gómez, M. (2004). Developing the ethnic identity scale using Eriksonian and social identity perspectives. *Identity: An International Journal of Theory and Research*, *4*(1), 9–38. http://dx.doi.org/10.1207/S1532706XID0401_2.

van Zalk, M. H. W., Kerr, M., Van Zalk, N., & Stattin, H. (2013). Xenophobia and tolerance toward immigrants in adolescence: Cross-influence processes within friendships. *Journal of Abnormal Child Psychology*, *41*(4), 627–639. http://dx.doi.org/10.1007/s10802-012-9694-8.

Verkuyten, M., & Kinket, B. (2000). Social distances in a multi ethnic society: The ethnic hierarchy among Dutch preadolescents. *Social Psychology Quarterly*, *63*(1), 75–85. http://dx.doi.org/10.2307/2695882.

Wang, Y., Benner, A. D., & Kim, S. Y. (2015). The Cultural Socialization Scale: Assessing family and peer socialization toward heritage and mainstream cultures. *Psychological Assessment*, *27*(4), 1452–1462. http://dx.doi.org/10.1037/pas0000136.

Wang, M. T., & Huguley, J. P. (2012). Parental racial socialization as a moderator of the effects of racial discrimination on educational success among African American adolescents. *Child Development*, *83*(5), 1716–1731. http://dx.doi.org/10.1111/j.1467-8624.2012.01808.x.

Way, N., Hernández, M. G., Rogers, L. O., & Hughes, D. L. (2013). "I'm not going to become no rapper": Stereotypes as a context of ethnic and racial identity development. *Journal of Adolescent Research*, *28*(4), 407–430.

Way, N., Muhkerjee, P., & Hughes, D. (2008). *The source, type, and consequences of perceived discrimination among urban middle school students*. Chicago, IL: Presentation at the Society for Research on Adolescence.

White, R. M. B., Zeiders, K. H., Knight, G. P., Roosa, M. W., & Tein, J. Y. (2014). Mexican origin youths' trajectories of perceived peer discrimination from middle childhood to adolescence: Variation by neighborhood ethnic concentration. *Journal of Youth and Adolescence*, *43*, 1700–1714. http://dx.doi.org/10.1007/s10964-014-0098-7.

Winkler, E. N. (2010). "I learn being black from everywhere I go": Color blindness, travel, and the formation of racial attitudes among African American adolescents, Sociological Studies of Children and Youth. *Children and youth speak for themselves*, Vol. 13, 423–453. Emerald Group Publishing.

Winkler, E. (2012). *Learning race, learning place: Shaping racial identities and ideas in African American childhoods*. New Brunswick, NJ and London: Rutgers University Press.

Wong, C. A., Eccles, J. S., & Sameroff, A. (2003). The influence of ethnic discrimination and ethnic identification on African American adolescents' school and socioemotional adjustment. *Journal of Personality*, *71*(6), 1197–1232. http://dx.doi.org/10.1111/1467-6494.7106012.

Yip, T., Douglass, S., & Shelton, J. N. (2013). Daily intragroup contact in diverse settings: Implications for Asian adolescents' ethnic identity. *Child Development*, *84*(4), 1425–1441. http://dx.doi.org/10.1111/cdev.12038.

Yip, T., Seaton, E. K., & Sellers, R. M. (2006). African American racial identity across the lifespan: Identity status, identity content, and depressive symptoms. *Child Development*, 77(5), 1504–1517. http://dx.doi.org/10.1111/j.1467-8624.2006.00950.x.

Yip, T., Seaton, E. K., & Sellers, R. M. (2010). Interracial and intraracial contact, school-level diversity, and change in racial identity status among African American adolescents. *Child Development*, *81*(5), 1431–1444. http://dx.doi.org/10.1111/j.1467-8624.2010.01483.x.

CHAPTER TWO

Racism, Racial Resilience, and African American Youth Development: Person-Centered Analysis as a Tool to Promote Equity and Justice

Enrique W. Neblett Jr.*,[1], Effua E. Sosoo*, Henry A. Willis*, Donte L. Bernard*, Jiwoon Bae*, Janelle T. Billingsley†
*University of North Carolina at Chapel Hill, Chapel Hill, NC, United States
†North Carolina Central University, Durham, NC, United States
[1]Corresponding author: e-mail address: eneblett@unc.edu

Contents

Abstract

Racism constitutes a significant risk to the healthy development of African American youth. Fortunately, however, not all youth who experience racism evidence negative developmental outcomes. In this chapter, we examine person-centered analysis (PCA)—a quantitative technique that investigates how variables combine across individuals—as a useful tool for elucidating racial and ethnic protective processes that mitigate the negative impact of racism. We review recent studies employing PCA in examinations of racial identity, racial socialization, and other race-related experiences, as well as how these constructs correlate with and impact African American youth

Equity and Justice in Developmental Science: Implications for Young People, Families, and Communities (S.S. Horn, M.D. Ruck & L.S. Liben, Eds.)
Advances in Child Development and Behavior (J.B. Benson, Series Ed.), Vol. 51
ISSN 0065-2407 http://dx.doi.org/10.1016/bs.acdb.2016.05.004

development. We also consider challenges and limitations of PCA and conclude with a discussion of future research and how PCA might be used to promote equity and justice for African American and other racial and ethnic minority youth who experience racism.

1. INTRODUCTION

Laquan McDonald. Aiyana Jones. Michael Brown. Dajerria Becton. Tamir Rice. Rekia Boyd. Trayvon Martin. Jordan Davis. Kalief Browder. John Crawford. Each name arguably invokes an experience of racial injustice suffered by an African American child, adolescent, or young adult in the US criminal justice system. Evidence suggests that racism and other forms of systemic oppression constitute significant risks to the healthy development of Black and other racial and ethnic minority youth in the United States (Jones & Neblett, 2016; Neblett, Rivas-Drake, & Umaña-Taylor, 2012). Yet, not all youth who undergo racism and racial injustice experience negative developmental outcomes. What factors account for individual differences in responses to racial discrimination experienced by African American youth? What tools can developmental scientists use to better understand how youth of color negotiate experiences of racial adversity?

In this chapter, we consider person-centered analysis (PCA)—a quantitative technique that investigates how variables combine across individuals—as a promising analytic tool for elucidating racial and ethnic protective processes that mitigate the negative impact of racism for African American children, adolescents, and young adults. The chapter begins with a review of background literature and makes a case for the use of PCA in increasing our understanding of racial and ethnic resilience in African American and other racial and ethnic minority youth. Next, we review several recent studies employing PCA to examine the relations between racism, racial identity, racial socialization, and Black youth development. Finally, we conclude with caveats and considerations as well as ideas for new research collaborations and future research that will build the field of equity and justice research in developmental science and alleviate the personal suffering of youth who experience racism.

2. BACKGROUND

Racism refers broadly to differential, unequal treatment that privileges one racial group over another. In his classic text, *Prejudice and Racism*, Jones (1972) argued that racism was a transformation of prejudice, which he defined as "negative attitudes toward a person or group based upon a social comparison process in which the individual's own group is taken as the positive point of reference" (p. 3). According to Jones, racism is characterized by "the exercise of power against a racial group defined as inferior by individuals and institutions with the intentional or unintentional support of the entire culture" (p. 117) and can manifest itself in three forms: individual racism, institutional racism, or cultural racism. *Individual racism*, commonly referred to as racial discrimination, consists of behaviors that reinforce the "inferiorization" of one racial group, believed to be superior, over another group. *Institutional racism* reflects the conscious or inadvertent institutionalization of prejudice that through the practices of institutions impinges upon the rights and access of particular racial groups. Finally, *cultural racism* consists of cultural manifestations (e.g., via images, ideas, symbols, and language), suggesting the superiority of one group's cultural heritage over another.

Consistent with seminal theories of racial and ethnic minority youth development (García Coll et al., 1996; Spencer, 2006), empirical evidence suggests a link between individual racism and a host of unfavorable developmental outcomes in racial and ethnic minority youth. In a recent systematic review examining relationships between reported racial discrimination and child and youth health (aged 12–18 years), Priest et al. (2013) reported statistically significant associations between individual racism and negative mental health outcomes (e.g., depression, anxiety, behavior problems, pregnancy/birth outcomes) in a majority of studies. However, not all youth who report individual racism evidence negative outcomes. Over the years, a growing number of studies have highlighted racial, ethnic, and culturally relevant experiences that mitigate the relationship between racism and negative developmental outcomes (Neblett et al., 2008; Sellers, Copeland-Linder, Martin, & Lewis, 2006; Wong, Eccles, & Sameroff, 2003). Two of the most prominent influences, particularly during adolescence and the transition to adulthood, include *racial* and *ethnic identity*—the personal significance and meaning of race and/or ethnicity to an individual (Sellers, Smith, Shelton, Rowley, & Chavous, 1998)—and *racial socialization*—explicit and nonexplicit transmission of parents' attitudes and beliefs about the significance and meaning of race (Hughes et al., 2006).

2.1 Racial and Ethnic Identity

Racial identity and ethnic identity are terms that refer broadly to how individuals define themselves with respect to race and/or ethnicity. Arroyo and

Zigler (1995) defined *racial identity* as "attempts to balance racial group membership needs and personal desires for positive relations with the larger society" (p. 903). Sellers et al. (1998) defined racial identity as the personal significance and meaning of race to one's self-concept. While earlier models of racial identity construed racial identity as a unidimensional construct (see Marks, Setttles, Cooke, Morgan, & Sellers, 2004), several leading racial and ethnic identity scholars have made the case for conceptualizing racial and ethnic identity as multidimensional constructs (Allen, Thornton, & Watkins, 1992; Demo & Hughes, 1990; Phinney & Ong, 2007; Sanders-Thompson, 1995; Sellers et al., 1998).

Three of the most commonly cited multidimensional models of racial identity include Cross' revised Nigrescence model, Phinney's (1989) multigroup model of ethnic identity, and Sellers' Multidimensional Model of Racial Identity (MMRI; Sellers et al., 1998). In his revised identity model, Cross (1991, 1995) asserted that racial identity consisted of diverse attitudes reflecting: a stronger connection to being American as opposed to being Black (*assimilation*); acceptance of negative stereotypes about Blacks (*miseducation*), intense self-loathing because of one's Black identity (*self-hatred*); anti-White responses to the dominant culture in the United States; adherence to African-centered values (*Afrocentricity*); and Black self-acceptance and willingness to engage with other cultural groups (*multiculturalist inclusive*). Phinney and Ong (2007) defined *ethnic identity* as a multidimensional construct that consists of a sense of belonging or connectedness to an ethnic group defined by one's cultural heritage including values, traditions, and language (*commitment*), and a process of learning about one's group (*exploration*). Finally, in one of the most widely recognized multidimensional models of racial identity, Sellers and colleagues' (1998) MMRI argued that racial identity is comprised of the personal significance and meaning of race as indexed by: the relevance of one's race in a particular moment (*salience*); the extent to which individuals normatively define themselves as Black (*centrality*); individuals' feelings toward African Americans and feelings about being African American (*private regard*); individuals' beliefs about how others view African Americans (*public regard*); beliefs about the uniqueness of being Black (*nationalist*); beliefs about the similarities between the oppression that African Americans face and that of other groups (*oppressed minority*); emphasis on the similarities between African Americans and the rest of American society (*assimilationist*); and beliefs about similarities among all humans (*humanist*). The reader wishing a more detailed treatment of multidimensional models of racial identity should refer to Marks et al. (2004).

2.2 Racial Socialization

Racial socialization refers to the process by which race-related messages about the meaning of race and racism are transmitted by parents intergenerationally (Neblett et al., 2008) and is thought to be one of the most critical developmental processes for African American youth (García Coll et al., 1996; Neblett et al., 2012). Like racial and ethnic identity, scholars have conceptualized racial socialization as a multidimensional construct consisting of various kinds of parental messages, activities, and behaviors (Bowman & Howard, 1985; Boykin & Toms, 1985; Hughes et al., 2006; Stevenson, 1994). Among the most commonly noted in the literature are messages that: teach children about their racial–ethnic heritage and history and promote racial pride (*racial pride/cultural socialization*); highlight the existence of inequalities between groups and prepare youth to cope with discrimination (*racial barriers/preparation for bias*); emphasize individual character traits such as hard work over racial or ethnic group membership (*egalitarianism*); focus on the necessity of individual excellence and the development of positive character traits (*self-development*); promote feelings of individual worth within the broader context of the child's race or ethnicity (*self-worth messages*); emphasize negative characteristics associated with being African American (*negative messages*); convey distrust in interracial communications (*promotion of mistrust*); engage in race-related activities and behaviors (e.g., buying African American literature and art) (*socialization behaviors*); and avoid mention of issues pertaining to race or ethnicity (*silence about race*) (Hughes et al., 2006; Lesane-Brown, Scottham, Nguyên, & Sellers, 2006; Neblett et al., 2012). Together, these multiple aspects of racial socialization are thought to combine to provide African American and other racial and ethnic minority youth with a view of both the significance and meaning of race (and ethnicity) in US society.

3. PCA AS A TOOL IN RESILIENCE RESEARCH WITH AFRICAN AMERICAN YOUTH

To date, the majority of studies examining racial and ethnic identity, racial socialization, and youth development have employed variable-centered analytic approaches to study the ways in which racial and ethnic identity and racial socialization act as resilience factors for Black youth. These approaches focus on the relationship between specific variables or dimensions of racial or ethnic identity and socialization and specific outcomes after controlling for the influence of other dimensions. These approaches, however, are not without limitations. As we have noted, many racial identity scholars characterize racial identity as a multidimensional construct (e.g., Cross, 1991; Phinney & Ong, 2007; Sanders-Thompson, 1991, 1995; Sellers et al., 1998), and failure to employ analytic approaches that treat racial identity as a multidimensional whole may inadequately model racial identity as it is theorized to exist and as it occurs in nature. In the case of racial socialization messages, parents usually instill a variety of different messages about race and ethnicity, and it is the confluence of different messages that combine to shape the child's views of the significance and meaning of race. One might imagine that a child who solely receives messages that highlight the existence of racial inequality might evidence different outcomes than a child who, in conjunction with such warnings, also receives a number of racial pride messages. The former may possess a racial worldview that emphasizes a sense of inferiority as a result of being African American, while the latter may be informed of danger but also equipped with feelings of possibilities (Neblett et al., 2008).

Person-centered analyses represent an alternative analytic strategy that can account for the complexity of multidimensional constructs such as ethnic identity and racial socialization and their impact on development. PCA has been primarily conducted using two specific analytic techniques: *k*-means iterative cluster analysis (also referred to as hierarchical cluster analysis) and latent profile analysis (LPA). In *k*-means cluster analysis, an algorithm is used to partition observations or data points into a smaller number of theoretically homogeneous groups. Variables are standardized and various statistical criteria (e.g., agglomeration schedule coefficients) are used in conjunction with a graphic representing the arrangement of possible cluster groups (also known as a dendrogram) to determine the number of clusters that best fits the data (see Chavous et al., 2003 for an example of this approach). LPA is a model-based extension of traditional *k*-means clustering that uses more formal statistical criteria for selecting the best cluster solution (Madgison & Vermunt, 2004). In this approach, statistical software is used to generate indices for a predetermined number of cluster models. Model fit and comparisons are assessed using the likelihood ratio chi-squared statistic (L^2) in conjunction with the Bayesian information criterion (BIC), an index of model fit and parsimony, to identify the optimal cluster or profile solution. Typically, a model with the largest association between the indicators explained (or greatest reduction in L^2) and the lowest BIC value is preferred. Both *k*-means cluster analysis and

LPA are used to examine the extent to which multiple observations, data points, or dimensions group together in theoretically meaningfully ways.

4. PCA IN RACIAL AND ETHNIC RESILIENCE RESEARCH: RESEARCH EXAMPLES

With increasing awareness of the incongruence between the multidimensional conceptualization of racial resilience factors and variable-centered approaches which focus on specific variables, a growing number of studies have adopted a person-centered approach to study racial resilience in African American youth. These studies typically: (1) identify unique patterns or combinations of dimensions or characteristics across persons or individuals; and (2) investigate how dimensions or characteristics combine across individuals and correlate with or shape developmental outcomes. In the sections that follow, we summarize studies that examine patterns of racial and ethnic identity, racial socialization, and in some cases, hybrid studies that examine patterns of racial and ethnic identity, racial socialization, and/or other critical determinants of Black youth development (see Table 1). Our focus in this chapter is on Black children, adolescents, and young adults; however, we acknowledge that similar work also has been done with other racial and ethnic minority youth (e.g., Gillen-O'Neel et al., 2015) and may prove useful in understanding racial and ethnic resilience in youth of color.

4.1 Racial and Ethnic Identity

How might the personal significance and meaning of race or ethnicity aid African American youth in negotiating race-related adversity and other forms of systemic oppression? Studies employing person-centered analyses to examine racial and ethnic identity as resilience factors have focused on broad developmental outcomes that include academic and psychosocial outcomes such as academic achievement, academic valuing, and psychological well-being. In one such study, Harris and Marsh (2010) used profile analysis to investigate whether adopting a raceless identity or persona (i.e., discounting one's race to "circumvent the stigma attached to being Black and to achieve vertical mobility"; Fordham, 1988, p. 59) leads to better educational outcomes such as school achievement and high educational aspirations for Black high school students than does a nonraceless identity. Prior work has suggested that Blacks who aspire to maintain academic success and achieve upward socioeconomic mobility feel pressured to adopt

Table 1 Studies That Utilized Person-Centered Analysis to Examine Racial Identity, Racial Socialization, and Hybrid Race-Related and Parenting Variables

Study	Sample Size	Design	Independent Variable	Outcome Variable	Findings
1. Racial identity					
Harris and Marsh (2010)	629 Adolescents	Longitudinal	Raceless perspective	Educational outcomes	Race Neutral cluster showed lower achievement and educational aspirations
Chavous et al. (2003)	606 AA adolescents	Longitudinal	Racial identity	Academic outcomes	Alienated cluster showed less interest in school, inconsistent attendance, and low college attendance
Shelvin, Rivadeneyra, and Zimmerman (2014)	190 AA children	Cross-sectional	Knowledge of specific racial stereotypes and Black identity profiles	Stereotype threat vulnerability	Racial identity profiles moderated the effect of stereotype threat
Worrell, Andretta, and Woodland (2014)	477 AA adolescents	Cross-sectional	Racial identity (CRIS and Nigrescence profiles)	Psychological functioning	Individuals with Conflicted-Self-Hatred profiles reported higher scores on 4 syndromes and sydrome scores more likely to be in the clinically significant range
Yip, Seaton, and Sellers (2006)	940 AA adolescents, college students, and adults	Cross-sectional	Ethnic identity (Phinney's ethnic identity statuses)	Depressive symptoms	Achieved status linked with higher racial centrality and private regard and lower depressive symptoms

Seaton, Scottham, and Sellers (2006)	224 AA adolescents	Longitudinal	Ethnic identity (Phinney's ethnic identity statuses)	Psychological well-being	Individuals in the more advanced racial identity statuses had higher levels of psychological well-being
Seaton (2009)	322 AA adolescents	Cross-sectional	Racial identity	Psychological well-being	Racial identity profiles moderated the discrimination-depressive symptoms link
2. Racial socialization					
Cooper, Smalls-Glover, Neblett, and Banks (2015)	166 AA fathers	Cross-sectional	Father and child sociodemographic characteristics	Racial socialization profiles	No support for relationship between father characteristics and racial socialization profile membership No child age-related variation in fathers' racial socialization practices Racial socialization profile membership varied by child gender
White-Johnson, Ford, and Sellers (2010)	212 AA mothers	Cross-sectional	Mother and child demographic factors Mother and child race-related experiences Mothers' racial identity	Parental racial socialization messages	No differences in child age or gender across different racial socialization profiles; mothers in Multifaceted profile reported higher levels of education

Continued

Table 1 Studies That Utilized Person-Centered Analysis to Examine Racial Identity, Racial Socialization, and Hybrid Race-Related and Parenting Variables—cont'd

Study	Sample Size	Design	Independent Variable	Outcome Variable	Findings
					No profile differences in child racial discrimination experiences; mothers in the Multifaceted profile experienced significantly more racial discrimination and reported more racial socialization during their own childhoods Mothers in the Multifaceted profile held racial identity attitudes that were consistent with the messages they conveyed to their children
Caughy, Nettles, and Lima (2011)	218 AA parents	Cross-sectional	Racial socialization	Child cognitive/behavioral outcomes	Profiles linked with gender and neighborhood characteristics; also predict internalizing behaviors and cognitive performance
Neblett et al. (2008)	361 AA adolescents	Longitudinal	Racial socialization	Psychological adjustment	Profiles act as resilience and vulnerability factors in discrimination-adjustment link

3. Hybrid person-centered studies					
Smalls (2010)	94 AA youth (ages 11–14)	Cross-sectional	Racial socialization and adolescents' feelings toward their mothers' parenting	Youth engagement	Profiles associated with academic and task engagement
Smalls and Cooper (2012)	125 AA adolescents (ages 10–14)	Cross-sectional	Racial group regard and barrier socialization	Gender	Girls more likely High Engagement-Race Salient; boys more likely Low Engagement-Non-Salient
Dunbar, Perry, Cavanaugh, and Leerkes (2015)	192 AA young adults (ages 18–24)	Cross-sectional	Racial and emotion socialization	Emotional adaptation	Young adults whose mothers fit the cultural-supportive profile or the moderate bias preparation profile had lower levels of depressive symptoms than young adults whose mothers fit the high bias preparation profile No relationship between mothers' socialization and young adults' anger expression

Continued

Table 1 Studies That Utilized Person-Centered Analysis to Examine Racial Identity, Racial Socialization, and Hybrid Race-Related and Parenting Variables—cont'd

Study	Sample Size	Design	Independent Variable	Outcome Variable	Findings
Richardson et al. (2015)	491 AA adolescents	Longitudinal	Experiences of racial discrimination and parental messages about preparation for racial bias	Racial identity	8th grade discrimination/parent messages clusters were associated with 11th grade racial identity cluster membership; boys experiencing more frequent discrimination but fewer parental coping messages were overrepresented in the racial identity cluster characterized by low centrality, low private regard, and average public regard in 11th grade

AA, African American.

a raceless identity because achievement is perceived as a "White" domain that is antithetical to Black culture.

A sample of 629 adolescents was drawn from the Maryland Adolescent Development In Context Study (MADICS), a longitudinal research project examining the psychological causes of behavior and developmental trajectories during adolescence. In this study, the authors created five profiles on the basis of individuals' responses to two pairs of items that assessed feelings of similarity (e.g., "I have a strong attachment to other Black people") and dissimilarity (e.g., "Being Black has little to do with how I feel about myself") to other Blacks: (1) *Race Neutral or Raceless* (did not affirm either measure); (2) *Race Similar* (affirmed similarity measure but not dissimilarity measure); (3) *Race Dissimilar* (affirmed dissimilarity measures but not similarity measure); (4) *Race Ambivalent* (affirmed both similarity and dissimilarity measures); and (5) *Mild Ambivalent* (all other possible combinations).

The results indicated that Blacks in the *Race Neutral* profile did not have higher achievement than those in other profiles. Those in the *Race Neutral* profile demonstrated lower achievement and educational aspirations, attributed less value to school, and were more detached from school than Blacks in the *Ambivalent* and *Similar* profiles. Aside from demonstrating that the results were inconsistent with the racelessness perspective, this analysis illustrates how responses to items comprising similarity and dissimilarity dimensions of racial identity might be used to identify different combinations of responses and how those messages might account for individual differences in academic outcomes.

In another study of academic developmental outcomes, Chavous and colleagues (2003) used PCA to explore the relationships between racial identity, educational beliefs, and academic performance outcomes for African American adolescents. Whereas the study by Harris and Marsh (2010) focused on group affiliation (as indexed by similarity/dissimilarity to one's racial group), Chavous et al. (2003) operationalized racial identity using three dimensions of Sellers' MMRI: racial centrality, private regard, and public regard. Participants were 606 African American 17-year-old adolescents participating in a longitudinal study of academic and social development. Educational beliefs (school relevance, school efficacy, and school importance), racial identity (racial centrality, private regard, and public regard), and school outcomes (school status and GPA) were obtained. Using *k*-means iterative cluster analysis, four profiles of racial identity variables were identified. On the basis of standardized racial identity scores, students characterized by high race centrality (i.e., personal significance and meaning of race), high private regard (i.e., positive feelings about African Americans and being African American), and low public regard (beliefs that others do not see Blacks favorably) were labeled as *Buffering/Defensive*; those with low centrality, high private regard, and low public regard were labeled *as Low Connectedness/High Affinity*; those with higher than average scores on all three identity variables were labeled as *Idealized*; and those with lower than average scores on all three variables were labeled as *Alienated*.

Results indicated that the *Alienated* group showed less interest in school than the *Buffering/Defensive* and *Idealized* identity groups, had a higher percentage of students not attending school consistently, and had the lowest percentage of students attending college. Overall, the findings indicated that high centrality, high private regard, and high public regard were related to more positive academic beliefs, and youth who had a positive societal view about African Americans demonstrated stronger school attachment. At the same time, it is important to note that the *Buffering/Defensive* group (which had lower public regard) fared better than the *Alienated* group, suggesting that low public regard *in combination* with high centrality and high private regard might also serve a protective function. These results reveal some intricacy in youths' conceptualization of racial identity in that the two patterns to emerge were not simply high or low racial identity. Whereas some students demonstrated high centrality and private regard, they differed in terms of their views of how they believed others saw African Americans (i.e., public regard). Similarly two profile groups had lower centrality and public regard but differed with regard to levels of private regard (*Low Connectedness* vs *Alienated*). With the use of PCA, we are able to obtain a richer depiction of the different constellations of identity that may account for individual differences in academic performance among Black youth.

Building on these examples, Shelvin et al. (2014) examined whether the knowledge of specific racial stereotypes and racial identity profiles would influence vulnerability to stereotypes. Stereotype threat, the threat of confirming a negative stereotype about one's group, has been found to have a detrimental effect on one's performance (Steele & Aronson, 1995). However, little work has examined individual differences that affect susceptibility to this threat. In this study, participants were 190 African American children ranging from 10 to 12 years old. Participants completed the Stereotype Awareness Task (SAT), a prompt that asked children to list all the stereotypes they knew about Black people. The Multidimensional Inventory of Black Identity—Teen (MIBI-t), which operationalizes the MMRI described earlier, was also administered to measure multiple aspects or dimensions of

Black racial identity, specifically centrality, private regard, public regard, and ideology (individuals' beliefs about how Blacks should act). A second testing session occurred 2 weeks later to weaken the connection between the SAT and the stereotype threat paradigm. During the second session, children were randomly assigned to either the neutral or experimental conditions. All participants were administered a challenging language arts test, but only those in the experimental condition were told that the test was a measure of intelligence and that the scores of Black and White children would be compared.

Results indicated that children in the experimental condition obtained lower scores on the language test compared to those in the neutral condition. Furthermore, racial identity profiles moderated the stereotype threat effect. Shelvin and colleagues attempted to use the racial identity categories delineated by Chavous et al. (2003), but notably, a third of their participants did not fit into those groupings. Using hierarchical cluster analysis, six racial identity profiles were identified: *Marginalized*, *Assimilators*, *Ethnically Diffuse*, *High Connected*, *Low Connected/High Affinity*, and *Idealized*. The only profiles to show the stereotype threat effect were individuals who viewed being Black as important to their identity (*High Connected*) and individuals who had neither strong connection to Black or ethnic minority culture, nor an overly strong desire to assimilate into majority culture (*Marginalized*). These findings not only suggest having a strong identity to a stereotyped group may make that stereotype particularly threatening under threat conditions, but also highlight two very different profiles (e.g., *High Connected* and *Marginalized*) that may act as vulnerability factors in the context of stereotype threat.

A second group of studies examines racial or ethnic identity profiles in the context of clinical and developmental outcomes such as psychiatric symptomatology and psychological well-being. Using Cross' (1991) revised racial identity model as a point of departure, Worrell et al. (2014) employed PCA to examine racial identity profiles and psychological functioning in an adolescent sample. The investigators first examined the internal consistency and structural validity of the Cross Racial Identity Scale (CRIS), which operationalized Cross' revised Nigrescence model. The CRIS assesses six dimensions or subscales of racial identity including: (1) a preference for a national or American identity (assimilation); (2) acceptance of the negative stereotypes about African Americans (miseducation); (3) self-loathing because of one's Black identity (self-hatred); (4) a strong, negative emotional response to the dominant culture in the United States (anti-White);

(5) beliefs that African Americans should live by Afrocentric principles (Afrocentric); and (6) Black self-acceptance and a willingness to engage with other cultural groups (multiculturalist/inclusive). Worrell and colleagues also examined whether the Nigrescence racial identity profiles identified in college-age populations generalize to at-risk adolescent samples and the extent to which the observed clusters varied in psychological functioning.

Participants were 477 African American adolescents (12–19 years old) who had been arrested in a city in the mid-Atlantic. Participants completed the CRIS and the Conners Comprehensive Behavior-Rating Scales—Self-Report (CBRS—SR), a self-report index of mental health. This measure assessed several disorders in the Diagnostic and Statistical Manual of Mental Disorders (DSM-IV): major depressive episode, manic episode, generalized anxiety disorder, and obsessive compulsive disorder.

CRIS scores were shown to be psychometrically sound, and *k*-means iterative cluster analysis yielded five profiles. These included *Miseducation-Pro-Black* (high miseducated and Afrocentricity scores), *Conflicted-Self-Hatred* (high self-hatred in combination with elevated assimilation, miseducation, and Afrocentricity), *Multiculturalist* (high multiculturalist inclusive scores), *Low Race Salience* (low scores across all CRIS subscales), and *Conflicted-Anti-White* (elevated Self-Hatred, Afrocentricity, and Anti-White scores). Youth in different clusters also varied with regard to their psychological functioning. Specifically, individuals in the *Conflicted-Self-Hatred* profile had higher syndrome scores than individuals in the *Conflicted-Anti-White*, *Multiculturalist*, and *Low Race Salience* profiles. *Conflicted-Anti-White* adolescents also reported higher syndrome scores than *Low Race Salience* adolescents. *Conflicted-Self-Hatred* attitudes had the most negative correlates and were also associated with higher scores on internalizing problems, implying that this group might benefit from psychotherapeutic interventions.

In an application of Phinney and Ong's (2007) multigroup ethnic identity framework, Yip et al. (2006) investigated the four ethnic identity stages associated with the commitment and exploration dimensions of ethnic identity (described above). Briefly, individuals in the *Diffused* status have not committed to an identity and have not begun to explore their identity. Individuals in the *Foreclosed* status have committed to an identity, but have based their decision on the opinions of others rather than their own personal exploration. Individuals in *Moratorium* status are exploring, but have not committed to an identity. Those in the *Achieved* stage have committed to an identity after exploring what that identity means. Using *k*-means cluster analysis, Yip and colleagues sought to determine (1) whether the distribution of the statuses (as indexed by patterns of exploration and commitment) varied across developmental periods; (2) whether individuals across statuses differed with regard to the personal significance and meaning they attribute to race (i.e., racial identity as defined by Sellers et al., 1998); and (3) whether there were any differences across statuses in psychological functioning.

Participants were 940 African Americans in three developmental periods: adolescents (13–17 years old), college students (18–23 years old), and adults (27–78 years old). They completed items from the Multigroup Ethnic Identity Measure (MEIM) to measure the extent to which individuals were searching for information about their racial group (exploration subscale) and the degree to which they have committed to membership in their racial group (commitment subscale). The Multidimensional Inventory of Black Identity—Short (MIBI-S) was used to assess the racial centrality, private regard, public regard, nationalist, minority, assimilation, and humanist dimensions of racial identity.

Yip et al. (2006) found all four identity statuses within the three age groups. However, developmental period influenced the distribution of individuals across the statuses: 27% of adolescents, 47% of college students, and 56% of adults were classified as *Achieved*. Specifically, *Achieved* status was the modal status for the college students and adults, while *Moratorium* was the modal status for adolescents. In terms of racial identity, individuals in the *Achieved* status (high exploration and commitment) had more positive esteem for being African American (private regard) and were more likely to ascribe significance and importance to their Black identity (centrality). In contrast, those who had neither explored nor committed to their identity (i.e., *Diffused*) were lower in centrality. Lastly, the association between identity statuses and depressive symptoms only emerged within the college student sample: individuals with *Diffused* identities reported higher levels of depressive symptoms than those with *Achieved* identities. Unique contributions of this study include landscaping how different combinations of exploration and commitment levels may evolve over the course of development, as well as demonstrating how the different patterns of ethnic identity relate to: (1) personal views about the significance and meaning of race; and (2) psychological functioning and depressive symptoms, in particular.

In a study similar to that of Yip et al. (2006), Seaton et al. (2006) examined Phinney's ethnic identity model solely with adolescents. They investigated whether adolescents progressed through the statuses in a manner consistent with the progression by prior ethnic identity models (i.e., *Diffused* to *Foreclosed* to *Moratorium*, etc.) and whether specific statuses were associated with higher or lower levels of psychological well-being. Participants were 224 African American adolescents aged 11–17 who completed the first two waves of a 3-year longitudinal study. As in the study by Yip et al. (2006), participants were administered the MEIM to assess ethnic identity.

Hierarchical cluster analyses revealed four profiles that corresponded to *Diffused*, *Foreclosed*, *Moratorium*, and *Achieved* identity statuses. Seventy-two percent of the sample demonstrated a pattern of identity progression consistent with that suggested by Martin and Marcia (1966) and Phinney (1989). Thirty-three percent demonstrated progression from less mature to more mature statuses, 39% remained stable in their racial identity statuses (of these, 55% remained in the *Achieved* or *Foreclosed*), and 28% changed in ways that are inconsistent with the identity formation model (they showed regression).

Support was also found for the proposition that individuals in more advanced racial identity statuses (e.g., *Achieved*) have higher levels of psychological well-being. Specifically, individuals in the *Achieved* status showed more positive well-being outcomes than individuals in the *Diffused* status at both time points. Individuals in the *Foreclosed* status also showed more positive well-being outcomes than individuals in the *Diffused* status. These fine-grained analyses in which *Achieved* and *Foreclosed* individuals fair better in terms of well-being than the *Diffused* group would not be possible with a unidimensional or traditional variable-centered analysis that focuses on one dimension controlling for the others.

In the same way that Shelvin and colleagues examined racial identity profiles as resilience factors in the context of stereotype vulnerability, Seaton (2009) examined whether racial identity profiles might buffer the association between multiple types of racial discrimination and psychological well-being. Participants were 322 African American adolescents (13–18 years old) who completed measures of racial identity (MIBI-S), perceptions of racial discrimination (The Index of Race-Related Stress), self-esteem (The Rosenberg Self-Esteem Scale), and depressive symptoms (CES-D).

Hierarchical cluster analyses replicated three of the four racial identity profiles identified by Chavous et al. (2003): Buffering/Defensive, Alienated, and Idealized groups. Seaton (2009) found that perceptions of collective/institutional racism were linked to decreased self-esteem and increased depressive symptoms, while perceptions of individual racism were linked to increased depressive symptoms. In contrast, perceptions of cultural racism were not linked to self-esteem and depressive symptoms. Racial identity profiles moderated the relation between perceptions of racial discrimination and levels of depressive symptoms. Specifically, higher levels of individual racism were related to higher depressive symptoms for *Alienated* youth, but unrelated to depressive symptoms for *Buffering/Defensive* and *Idealized* youth.

4.1.2 Summary

Although far from exhaustive, the studies included in our review provide an illustration of how PCA has been used to examine racial identity profiles as they relate to academic and psychosocial outcomes and also how racial identity profiles may act as resilience factors in the context of racism-related stress experiences such as racial discrimination and stereotype threat. Studies reveal several different patterns of racial identity dimensions, and these combinations or patterns moderated the association between racial discrimination and stereotype threat and educational and psychological outcomes. The value in these approaches is that they provide a fuller picture of racial identity than a unidimensional approach is able to provide. As noted in some cases (e.g., Chavous et al., 2003), individuals might score very similarly on one or more dimensions of racial identity but exhibit very different developmental outcomes as a function of how those dimensions combine with other dimensions of racial identity. Conversely, individuals might evidence dissimilar profiles but display similar outcomes (e.g., *High Connected* and *Marginalized* in the context of stereotype threat; Shelvin et al., 2014). Taken together, these studies corroborate theory regarding the multidimensional nature of racial identity, demonstrate significant heterogeneity with regard to how Black youth define their group and personal identities, and add depth to our understanding of how racial identity correlates with important developmental outcomes.

4.2 Racial Socialization

In the aftermath of several recent police shootings involving Black youth (e.g., Michael Brown, Trayvon Martin, Tamir Rice), some have asserted that parental teachings and admonitions about race might play an important role in decreasing the likelihood of negative and sometimes deadly consequences. Could it be that particular combinations or patterns of racial socialization activities might mitigate the detrimental impact of social inequality and injustice that some Black youth face as a result of racism and other systemic forms of oppression? In an effort to better understand the variety inherent in racial socialization practices that might prepare youth to cope with race-related adversity, many researchers have also used person-centered analytic approaches to determine how these activities converge to create unique racial socialization profiles. As a result of these efforts, empirical studies have uncovered factors that contribute to the racial socialization practices of parents, as well as how these practices ultimately go on to affect the development of African American adolescents. Studies range from descriptive to correlational studies that link profiles to outcomes. In this section, we begin with a review of more descriptive studies and then progress to increasingly complex correlational and longitudinal studies examining racial socialization as a resilience factor.

In a recent investigation of African American fathers, Cooper et al. (2015) investigated how racial socialization practices and profiles may vary across fathers' and children's demographics. The researchers hypothesized that there would be variation in African American fathers' racial socialization patterns and expected profiles to differ by fathers' demographics, such as age, marital status, and education, as well as child characteristics, such as age and gender. The study included 166 African American fathers (average age of 32.2) of adolescents (average age of 12.6) who resided in a midsized city in the Southeast United States.

Using LPA, Cooper et al. (2015) identified profiles among five racial socialization dimensions within their sample of Black fathers (racial pride, racial barriers, egalitarian messages, negative messages, self-development messages, behavioral messages). These included: *Infrequent Racial Socializers*, *Negative Racial Socializers*, *Positive Racial Socializers*, *Low Race Salience Socializers*, and *Race Salience Socializers*. *Positive Racial Socializers* were fathers who conveyed above average scores on all socialization messages with the exception of negative messages (below sample mean). This profile represented the largest profile group (38%) in the sample. The second largest profile group (37%), *Low Race Salience*, referred to those fathers who did not overtly address racial barriers or promote awareness of cultural pride and communicated more moderate levels of messages emphasizing self-development. Both the *Race Salient* profile (ones with greater frequencies of practices that highlight racial and cultural awareness as well as negative socialization messages) and the *Negative Racial Socializer* profile (ones with greater frequencies of negative racial socialization messages) represented a relatively small proportion of fathers (both ~8.5%). The smallest profile (8%) identified was the *Infrequent Racial Socializers*, and they fell well below the average on all racial socialization dimensions.

Surprisingly, no profile differences emerged with respect to father characteristics, such as age, educational level, or marital status, and child age; however, results indicated that racial socialization patterns varied as a function of child gender. For example, fathers with sons exhibited *Low Race Salience* socialization patterns, whereas fathers with daughters conveyed more racially explicit racial socialization messages. Accordingly, fathers of daughters were less likely to be represented in the *Infrequent Racial Socialization* profile and had a higher representation in the *Race Salience* profile. These results provide some insight into which *combinations* of messages parents are likely to use with their sons and daughters as opposed to typical examinations of gender differences that have focused on single messages in isolation (e.g., racial pride messages, racial barrier messages).

Racial socialization profiles have also been shown to vary among African American mothers. Using a person-centered profile approach, White-Johnson et al. (2010) investigated the racial socialization practices of African American mothers. The aim of their study was twofold. First, using LPA, they aimed to identify patterns in mothers' reports of racial pride messages, racial barrier messages, egalitarian messages, self-worth messages, negative messages, and racial socialization behaviors. Next, their study also aimed to determine whether the profiles of racial socialization practices differed based on mother and child demographic background characteristics, mother and child racial experiences, and mother racial identity attitudes.

The researchers obtained data from the first wave of a 3-year cross-sequential study of race and psychosocial adjustment in African American adolescents and their primary caregivers in a Midwestern city. Of the households contacted to participate, only the 212 dyads in which the primary caregiver was both the child's mother and self-reported as an African American were included in their analyses. The mothers' ages ranged from 29 to 57 years, and the adolescents' ages ranged from 11 to 17 years.

The results indicated that there were three racial socialization profiles among their sample of African American mothers: the *Multifaceted*, *Low Race Salience*, and *Unengaged* profiles. The *Multifaceted* profile transmitted the highest number of socialization messages overall, with the exception of self-worth and negative messages. Mothers in the *Multifaceted* profile reported racial socialization activities that conveyed a positive view of African American culture and history, while at the same time identifying obstacles their children would face as a result of their racial status. For mothers with a *Low Race Salience profile*, egalitarian and self-worth messages were the most common socialization themes communicated. Mothers in this profile also used a racial socialization strategy that de-emphasized the importance of race in the lives of their children and instead focused on the individual worth of the child. On the other hand, mothers in the *Unengaged* profile communicated few racial socialization messages to their children relative to mothers in the other two profiles, with the exception of communicating relatively higher negative messages about being African American.

Unlike several previous studies, White-Johnson et al. (2010) found no significant differences in adolescent background demographics, such as age or gender, across the *Multifaceted*, *Low Race Salience*, and *Unengaged* profiles. However, there were profile differences in the mothers' background demographics, specifically with regard to level of education attainment. Mothers in the *Multifaceted* profile reported higher levels of education than mothers in the *Low Race Salience* and *Unengaged* profiles. These data provide vital information about the determinants of particular combinations of beneficial messages and also might be useful in providing important information for psychoeducational approaches to racial socialization for mothers from diverse socioeconomic backgrounds.

White-Johnson et al. (2010) also examined the extent to which profiles correlated with child racial discrimination experiences. There were no profile differences in child racial discrimination experiences; however, mothers who reported conveying more racial barrier messages had children who also reported more frequent experiences of racial discrimination. Also, there were significant racial socialization profile differences in mothers' experiences with discrimination. For example, mothers in the *Multifaceted* profile experienced significantly more racial discrimination than those in the *Unengaged* profile. Furthermore, this study also highlighted the multigenerational impact of racial socialization. Mothers who transmitted more racial socialization messages to their children overall (*Multifaceted* profile) reported more racial socialization during their own childhood, whereas individuals who received less racial socialization as children were disconnected from the racial socialization process (*Unengaged* profile) with their own children.

Finally, White-Johnson et al. (2010) also examined the link between the observed racial socialization profiles and racial identity attitudes. Mothers in the *Multifaceted* profile attributed greater personal significance to being Black and generally felt positively toward other African Americans while believing that other groups held less positive attitudes toward them. Mothers with a *Low Race Salience* profile had similar attitudes, but endorsed less positive views/attitudes toward other African Americans. Mothers with an *Unengaged* profile reported lower levels of racial centrality as compared to the other groups. Together, these results indicate heterogeneity in socialization practices across African American mothers while also highlighting important demographic and psychosocial correlates of African American maternal racial socialization.

In addition to demographic and racial identity correlates of racial socialization, racial socialization profiles can also play a role in the psychological adjustment of African American children and adolescents. In a study of the contexts, correlates, and outcomes associated with racial socialization profiles, Caughy et al. (2011) first examined whether or not they could identify distinct groups of parents who varied according to the content of their racial socialization messages across a variety of domains. Second, they aimed to see if such groups were distinguishable by any demographic, child, or neighborhood characteristics. Finally, they investigated if racial socialization profiles were differentially associated with child cognitive and/or behavioral outcomes.

Using self-report and observational data on racial socialization from 218 African American parents of young children from Baltimore city neighborhoods, Caughy et al. (2011) employed LPA to identify four distinct racial socialization profiles: *Silence About Race* group (did not endorse any of the socialization messages with low scores on Afrocentric home environment), *Cultural Socialization Emphasis* group (average scores for cultural pride higher than other racial socialization messages), *Coping Emphasis/Cultural Socialization* group (includes all messages but attenuated messages regarding promotion of mistrust), and a *Balanced* approach group (similarly elevated cultural pride and preparation for bias scores with relatively higher promotion of mistrust messages compared to the other groups). Their findings revealed that most of the parents fell into the *Balanced* approach group, whereas the least common profile was *Silence About Race.* Furthermore, *Silence About Race* and the *Balanced* approach were more common among parents of boys than girls, whereas *Cultural Socialization Emphasis* was more common among parents of girls than boys. They also found that *Silence About Race* was less common in neighborhoods with high levels of negative social climate, and that a combination of messages referring to cultural socialization, preparation for discrimination, and promotion of mistrust was more common in neighborhoods with high community involvement. It is interesting to note that while there were group differences in profiles as a function of the gender of the child, there were no significant mean differences for individual socialization scores for boys vs girls. In this case, the use of a person-centered profile information yields important information about gender differences that otherwise would not be detected with a variable-centered approach.

Finally, the study by Caughy et al. (2011) indicated that problem behaviors, specifically internalizing behaviors such as anxiety and depression, were higher for children whose parents were in the *Balanced* and *Cultural Socialization* groups as compared with the *Coping Emphasis/Cultural Socialization* group (which had lower promotion of mistrust messages relative to the *Balanced* group). Moreover, although there were no main effect differences in cognitive outcomes associated with the various racial socialization profile groups, differences did arise as a function of the gender of the child. For girls, an emphasis on cultural socialization (i.e., the *Cultural Socialization Emphasis* profile) was associated with higher cognitive scores, whereas a combination of cultural socialization, coping with discrimination, and promotion of mistrust (i.e., the *Balanced* profile) was associated with lower cognitive scores compared to other approaches. This unique study makes several contributions. In addition to documenting diverse patterns of racial socialization, the study documents which combinations of messages correlate with gender, neighborhood, and even cognitive outcomes. Of note, racial barrier and cultural socialization messages appear to have protective qualities, but the net effect depends on the presence or absence of other (e.g., promotion of mistrust) messages. The observed patterns lay the foundation for not only understanding racial socialization processes more complexly, but also theory building regarding racial socialization and its influences on individual responses to racism-related stress as a function of individual (e.g., gender) and contextual factors (e.g., neighborhood climate).

In one of the few studies to date to examine racial socialization profiles as resilience factors in the context of individual racism and psychological adjustment over time, Neblett and colleagues (2008) examined the relations between racial discrimination experiences, patterns of racial socialization practices, and changes in psychological adjustment. The study included 361 self-identified African American adolescents in grades 7 through 11 from 11 middle and high schools in a public school district in a Midwestern city. Using LPA, results indicated four patterns of child-reported racial socialization experiences within the sample: *High Positive*, *Moderate Positive*, *Low Frequency*, and *Moderate Negative*. The two largest clusters, the *High Positive* and the *Moderate Positive*, emphasized positive messages such as racial pride and self-worth along with messages that emphasize the barriers that African Americans are likely to face. These two clusters were very similar but differed in the overall frequency of messages, and these two groups also reported receiving egalitarian messages. The third cluster, *Low Frequency*, were those who reported receiving the fewest messages (but with average self-worth messages) and engaging in the least amount of racial socialization activities. The final cluster, *Moderate Negative*, were those that received a pattern of racial socialization in which they more frequently received negative messages about African Americans relative to others in the sample.

Adolescents who experienced *High Positive* patterns of racial socialization reported the most positive psychological adjustment outcomes (lower depressive symptoms and perceived stress and higher well-being), whereas adolescents in the *Low Frequency* and *Moderate Negative* racial socialization clusters reported the least favorable outcomes. Of note, children in the latter two groups were indistinguishable with respect to their psychological adjustment. Again, this kind of comparison between different combinations of messages would not be possible in the independent examination of individual socialization messages.

Racial discrimination was associated with higher levels of depressive symptoms, more perceived stress, and lower levels of psychological well-being. However, certain racial socialization profiles moderated these effects. For example, adolescents who were in the *Moderate Negative* socialization cluster demonstrated increased vulnerability to problem behaviors relative to the other groups when experiencing discrimination, while *High Positive* racial socialization attenuated the impact of racial discrimination on perceived stress and problem behaviors. In contrast to a variable-centered approach, which would focus on one racial socialization moderator at a time, the use of PCA in this study allowed the investigators to understand how different patterns of messages (e.g., racial pride coupled with barrier messages) might act as resilience or even vulnerability factors (e.g., a pattern of negative messages) in the context of African American youths' experiences with racial discrimination.

4.2.1 Summary

Overall, the summarized research provides evidence that a person-oriented profile analytic approach is an effective method for exploring the heterogeneity of racial socialization practices in African American families and their impact on the well-being of adolescents. As with the racial identity studies, finding revealed that racial socialization is multidimensional, and characterizing it as simply "high" or "low" would fail to capture the unique patterning and levels of various messages. The number of studies to examine demographic and race-related correlates of the racial socialization profiles (e.g., child and caregiver gender, racial discrimination experiences) provides important insights about the dynamic nature of racial socialization, and it is noteworthy that in some cases, the conclusions drawn about the relations between demographic variables (e.g., gender) and race-related experiences (e.g., racial discrimination) and racial socialization varied as a function of whether one employed a variable-centered or person-centered approach (Caughy et al., 2011; White-Johnson et al., 2010). Taken together, the use of PCA in the examination of racial socialization as a resilience factor has the potential to not only elucidate the diverse ways in which parents teach their children about the significance and meaning of race but also suggest ways in which context shapes racial socialization outcomes with implications for practice and interventions with diverse Black youth and their families.

5. HYBRID PERSON-CENTERED STUDIES

Whereas the majority of studies employing a person-centered approach focus on patterns of dimensions within a construct (e.g., racial identity or racial socialization but not both), a few recent studies examine patterns of racial identity and racial socialization or patterns of racial identity and racial socialization in conjunction with other constructs suggested by developmental theory to influence youth outcomes. For example, Smalls (2010) used PCA to investigate the combined effects of racial socialization and aspects of the mother–child relationship as they related to academic engagement outcomes. In this investigation, 94 self-identified African American youth between the ages of the 11 and 14 completed surveys assessing indices of maternal racial socialization (i.e., racial pride and racial barrier messages), parenting styles, climate of the mother–child relationship, and engagement (i.e., persistence and academic engagement).

The results from this study revealed three unique patterns of reports of racial socialization messages and parenting styles: *Cultural Affective-Race Salient* (low on child-centered parenting, average on positive climate parenting, and above average frequencies of racial pride and barrier socialization), *Low Affective-Nonsalient* (low on both racial socialization message and positive climate parenting, but average on child-centered parenting), and *Traditional Affective-Race Salient* (high on both racial messages and both components of affective relationship quality). Participants in the *Traditional Affective-Race Salient* group reported the highest academic and task engagement, in contrast to participants in the *Low Affective-Nonsalient* cluster, who reported the lowest frequencies of racial socialization and lowest levels of overall engagement. The findings from this study illustrate that although the presence of racial socialization messages is important, it is critical to consider the family context from which these messages emanate.

Expanding on the Smalls (2010) study, Smalls and Cooper (2012) used LPA to investigate gendered patterns in the clustering of private regard (racial identity), barrier socialization messages, grades, and behavioral engagement (i.e., academic effort and motivation behaviors). One hundred twenty-five self-identified African American youth in the 6th through the 8th grade (10–14 years old) completed surveys assessing racial barrier socialization, private regard, grades, and behavioral academic achievement.

LPA yielded two unique clusters of identity, socialization, grades, and engagement: a *High Engagement-Race Salient* cluster, categorized by scores above the sample mean on private regard, barrier socialization, grades, and engagement; and a *Low Engagement-Non-Salient* cluster categorized by scores below the sample mean on all four variables. Youth that were in the *High Engagement-Race Salient* cluster reported higher private regard and socialization; however, it is important to note that private regard and barrier socialization were not statistically different between the two clusters. With respect to gender differences, girls were nearly twice as likely to belong to the *High Engagement-Race Salient* cluster, while boys had greater representation (though more balanced) in the *Low Engagement-Non-Salient* cluster. This study provides one of the few examples of studies that combine multiple constructs (e.g., identity, socialization, grades, engagement) to identify patterns across individuals.

In another study advancing the work of Smalls (2010) and Smalls and Cooper (2012), Dunbar et al. (2015) investigated the extent to which profiles of maternal and paternal racial and emotional socialization practices varied as a function of family income and child gender, as well as how these profiles were associated with child emotional adaptation. One hundred ninety-two African American young adults who ranged in age from 18 to 24 years were recruited from classrooms and locations on a college campus (e.g., the university student center food court) to participate in this study. After providing consent, participants completed measures of parental racial socialization, parental emotional socialization, depressive symptoms, and anger symptoms.

On the basis of LPA conducted with cultural socialization, preparation for bias, promotion of mistrust, supportive responses (e.g., encouragement), and nonsupportive responses (e.g., punishment), Dunbar et al. (2015) identified four unique profiles of youth-reported maternal racial and emotional socialization practices. The first profile identified was labeled

Cultural-Supportive and was characterized by the highest levels of cultural socialization endorsement and supportive responses to negative emotions compared with all the other profiles, moderate levels of preparation for bias and nonsupportive responses, and low levels of promotion of mistrust. The second profile, identified as *Low Engaged*, was characterized by low levels of endorsement across all socialization constructs. The third cluster was labeled *Moderate Bias Preparation* and was characterized by moderate levels of socialization across constructs with scores above the mean on preparation for bias, promotion of mistrust, and nonsupportive responses and scores near the mean on cultural socialization and supportive responses. The final cluster was named *High Bias Preparation* and was characterized by moderate levels of cultural socialization, high levels of preparation for bias, the highest levels of promotion of mistrust compared with all other profiles, and scores below the mean on supportive responses and above the mean on nonsupportive responses.

In contrast to the maternal profiles, analyses revealed three unique paternal profiles of emotional and racial socialization practices. The first cluster was labeled *Multifaceted* and was characterized by moderate levels on four of the five socialization constructs, with low levels of promotion of mistrust. A *Low Engaged* cluster was also identified for paternal emotional and racial socialization practices. This cluster was characterized by low scores across all socialization constructs, similar to the *Low Engaged* cluster discussed for paternal reports of socialization. The third and final cluster was labeled *High Bias Preparation* and was identified by its moderate levels of cultural socialization, high levels of preparation for bias, and the highest levels of promotion of mistrust. The authors found that males were more likely than females to have mothers who fit the *High Bias Preparation* profile than any other maternal profile. In addition, individuals with higher family income were more likely to have mothers who fit the *Cultural-Supportive* profile compared with the *Moderate Bias* preparation profile and fathers who fit the *Multifaceted* profile compared with the *Low Engaged* profile.

With respect to emotional adaptation, young adults whose mothers fit the *Cultural-Supportive* profile or the *Moderate Bias Preparation* profile had lower levels of depressive symptoms than young adults whose mothers fit the *High Bias Preparation* profile. Interestingly, mothers' socialization was not related to young adults' anger expression. However, young adults whose fathers fit the *Multifaceted* profile had marginally lower levels of anger expression than young adults whose fathers fell within the *Low Engaged* profile. Taken together, these results illustrate the importance of considering the ways in which racial socialization practices combine with supportive and nonsupportive parenting responses to emotions. Furthermore, this study sheds light on ways in which psychosocial factors such as gender and income may impact the type of racial and emotional socialization messages youth may receive and how these messages pattern together. Although the analysis does not tell us why there is a correlation, the findings lay the foundation for future research to examine how particular combinations of socialization experiences, in context, might lead to particular outcomes.

One last example of a hybrid person-centered study includes a recent examination of patterns of racial discrimination and racial socialization experiences. Richardson et al. (2015) examined the associations between youth racial identity and two types of environmental feedback: racial discrimination and parental racial socialization. Participants were 491 African American adolescents from a large public school district participating in the MADICS study. Racial discrimination was measured with the Classroom/Teacher and Peer discrimination scale. Parental Bias Preparation Messages were measured with the Proactive Responses to Discrimination Scale. All measures were obtained during participants' 8th and 11th grade years.

Cluster analyses resulted in four profiles of adolescents experiencing racial discrimination and parental discrimination coping messages: *High Discrimination/Average* parent messages, *Average discrimination/Average* parent messages, *Low Discrimination/Low* parent messages, and *Low Discrimination/High* parent messages. *High Discrimination/Average* parent messages was the largest cluster, and boys were overrepresented in this group. In contrast, girls were overrepresented in the *Low Discrimination/High* parent messages cluster.

Richardson and colleagues also examined associations of adolescents' racial discrimination and parent messages in 8th grade with *profiles* of adolescents' 11th grade racial identity (as measured by the centrality, public regard, and private regard subscales of the MIBI-t). Three profiles were identified across centrality, private regard, and public regard racial identity variables. The *Idealized* cluster was characterized by high levels of racial centrality, private regard (positive feelings about African Americans and being African American), and public regard (i.e., individuals felt others viewed Blacks favorably). The *Detached* cluster was characterized by low racial centrality, low private regard, and moderate public regard. The *Buffering/Defensive* cluster was characterized by high group connectedness and racial pride. Adolescents that were in *High Discrimination/Average* parent messages cluster in 8th grade were less represented in the *Idealized* racial identity cluster in 11th grade. Boys in this cluster in 8th grade were more likely represented in the *Detached* cluster in 11th grade. The hypothesis that youth who receive more proactive coping messages from parents (*Low Discrimination/High* parent messages) would feel more positive about their identities was not supported. Instead, analyses indicated that boys in *High Discrimination* and girls in *Average Discrimination* clusters in 8th grade had greater representation in the *Detached* racial identity cluster in 11th grade, but this was not the case for adolescents with low experiences of discrimination. Overall, the results indicated that boys experience more frequent discrimination than girls but receive fewer coping messages, suggesting the importance of considering the context of gender in adolescents' racial discrimination experiences and parental racial socialization. Furthermore, adolescents who reported experiencing more discrimination and average coping support were less likely to have positive feelings toward their racial identity. This study is perhaps the only of its kind in its hybrid examination of discrimination experiences and racial socialization messages as predictors of racial identity profiles.

5.1 Summary

Developmental theory (e.g., García Coll et al., 1996) has warranted further exploration into the ways in which racial identity and racial socialization work in tandem with other developmental correlates (e.g., academic engagement, racial discrimination experiences) to influence a variety of outcomes among African American youth. As evidenced by this section, the hybrid approach can highlight the complex interplay among racial identity, racial socialization, and other psychosocial factors. For example, some studies using this approach illustrate that racial socialization and racial identity messages can interact with aspects of the parent–child relationships (e.g., climate) to influence academic outcomes. In addition, studies have applied this technique to illustrate that racial and emotional socialization patterns may differ as a function of family income, and child and parent gender to differentially impact psychological and adaptive outcomes. The hybrid approach has also been used to explore how racial socialization and racial discrimination patterns work in conjunction to predict racial identity profiles. In some cases, the observed patterns yielded profiles that were high or low across the board on the dimensions clustered, but in several studies, investigators observed patterns characterized by low, moderate, and high levels of clustered variables, which would seem to make the case for the diverse and multidimensional nature of these constructs. In sum, the innovative hybrid approach sheds light on the multifaceted ways (i.e., patterns) in which identity, diverse socialization experiences (racial and emotional), and racial discrimination experiences co-occur to impact African American youth, in ways that other variable-centered analytic techniques cannot.

6. CHALLENGES AND CONSIDERATIONS

Our review provides a glimpse into some of the creative ways in which person-centered analyses have been used to examine individual differences in developmental outcomes as a function of race-related attitudes, beliefs, and experiences (e.g., racial identity, socialization, racial discrimination). However, the use of PCA is not without its own challenges and limitations. First, when cluster or latent profile analytic techniques are used to identify profiles or clusters within individuals, the approach is probably best thought of as a data reduction device in which a theoretically infinite number of patterns are summarized in terms of a smaller number of clusters or latent profiles. In essence, one might think of profiles or clusters as landmarks in the multivariate space of observed variables that permit investigators to navigate around the space and describe salient individual group differences. To be clear, PCA does not identify all the possible combinations that exist and, in fact, the combinations and patterns obtained are shaped by the observed variables selected for analysis and the source characteristics and contexts of the data. While in many cases similar clusters were observed in diverse samples, there were also cases where cluster groups observed in one study were not replicated in another. Failed replication of some clusters may illustrate the sensitivity of the clusters to the data input and reminds us of the variability that exists within clusters. While PCA may help to identify generalities and similarities among individuals on characteristics on the observed variables, it cannot possibly provide extensive information about how individuals' experiences and other dimensions not captured by the cluster (which may in turn influence outcomes) differ within clusters.

In addition to thinking about PCA as a tool for making sense of patterns in the data (and not as a tool for definitely identifying all patterns that exist), several considerations are important to take into account at each stage of the research process. First, the investigator must make careful choices about which observed variables to include when conducting PCA. If a model contains seven dimensions of racial identity (e.g., Sellers et al.'s MMRI), should all seven dimensions be included in the profiles, or would it be best to use theory to guide which dimensions are analyzed? Both approaches have been employed with advantages and disadvantages. It is true that including all of the dimensions may more accurately reflect the construct as it occurs in nature, but as we discuss below, the more dimensions included in a cluster, the more challenging it can be to interpret or make sense of group differences that emerge.

Second, in the data analytic phase of person-centered analyses, naming the clusters and profiles can be a challenging enterprise. We are frequently asked at conference presentations for the best approach, and our usual reply is that naming clusters is at best an imprecise science. We have reviewed some studies that name clusters on the basis of raw average subdimension scores, others that rely exclusively on standardized means and others that employ some combination of the two. We favor this latter approach as relying solely on one or the other could lead to faulty conclusions. We have seen cases where investigators have used standardized patterns where individual subscales are described as high or low, which may be true relative to the sample mean, but when the raw means are examined what appears low relative to the sample average may be high in an absolute sense and vice versa. The naming of the clusters can become even more challenging the more dimensions one includes in the analysis. With several dimensions making up a profile, how can one accurately capture the most salient dimensions or patterns of dimensions within the profile as a whole? In our own work, we have highlighted dimensions that approach or are plus or minus one standard deviation below the mean in naming clusters, but this approach is not foolproof and should still be conducted in conjunction with consideration of the raw score means.

Third, the interpretation of cluster differences can also be difficult. When one cluster is different from another with regard to a developmental outcome or moderates the association between variables, or predicts future cluster membership, what does this mean? Interpretation of the clusters can be even more difficult to comprehend the more dimensions that comprise the profile. What particular dimensions or combination of dimensions are most responsible for differences across groups? Careful study of the obtained profiles is required. In our own work, we note statistically significant differences in subdimensions between profiles that are differentially associated with developmental outcomes. For example, if one profile demonstrates more positive adjustment or psychological well-being, we pay close attention to statistical differences between those groups on the dimensions that comprise the profile groups. In this way, it may be possible to determine the key combinations of factors that may be most influential in accounting for differences in responses to racism and other race-related forms of oppression.

7. FUTURE DIRECTIONS

Despite the aforementioned challenges inherent in the use of PCA, we believe there is still great value in the use of this approach for the study of racial resilience in African American and other racial and ethnic minority youth who experience racism. As we seek to determine how person-centered approaches to racism, racial resilience, and youth development might promote equity and justice, several directives are indicated. First, there is great promise in the hybrid approach (combining multiple constructs to identify profiles) adopted by several recent studies. This approach, even more so than focusing solely on multiple dimensions of one construct, may help us to better model and approximate the complex interaction between individuals and context that takes place in reality. Neither identity nor socialization is a sole determinant of youths' developmental outcomes; instead it is the confluence of these racial resilience factors with several other determinants of development that together shape youth trajectories. Future research should continue to not only identify multidimensional multi-construct profiles across academic and psychosocial domains, but also use the associations between demographics and other contextual variables to generate hypotheses about mediational pathways that can subsequently be tested and used to inform theory. At the same time, investigators will need to be prudent and thoughtful about (and use theory to guide) what dimensions make sense to examine together.

Second, to the extent possible, we call for the use of multidimensional person-centered approaches with nationally representative data. As we have hinted above, the diverse identity, socialization, and hybrid profiles identified to date may be specific to the geographic regions and other contextual characteristics of the samples that have been used in the studies reviewed. The use of rigorous person-centered analytic techniques with survey instruments possessing strong psychometric properties for the constructs of interest may help to build confidence in the profiles that have emerged to date. Along these lines, it will be critical for federal and foundation dollars to continue to fund longitudinal research and proposals that examine racial and ethnic minority youth on a national (or even multinational) scale.

A final consideration in our treatment of racial resilience, equity, and justice is the need for more studies that examine not only individual racism but also institutional and cultural racism and other forms of systemic oppression. Of the studies reviewed, only Seaton (2009) examined different kinds of racism. However given our emphasis on the multidimensionality of race-related constructs, we would be remiss to not consider different patterns of racism experiences and racism as a multidimensional construct. One important future direction will be to consider how person-centered approaches might be used to examine how combinations of risk and resilience factors and other critical developmental processes may mitigate the experience of significant structural and system level variables that African American youth experience such as socioeconomic status, under-resourced schools, and segregated communities with higher crime rates and more limited social services.

8. CONCLUSION

African American and other racial and ethnic minority youth in the United States arguably bear the disproportionate brunt of inequality and injustice, which can often lead to negative developmental outcomes. Yet there is hope. In this chapter, we have explored the use of person-centered analyses as an approach to studying the racial and ethnic resilience of African American youth in the context of racism experiences and youth development. We argued that person-centered analyses may confer several advantages over traditional variable-centered approaches to the research topic, and reflect developmental processes in a more ecologically valid manner, and we provided several examples of how investigators have used this approach in recent work. While there are several inherent challenges to the approach, PCA represents a vital and important tool in the promotion of equity and justice for racial and ethnic minority youth. Studies of racism, resilience, and development must now move beyond the exclusive focus on individual racism to examine the multidimensional nature of racism as it affects youth of color while we also use the approach to capture the complexity and multidimensionality of resilience and vulnerability processes of youth who experience racism. In charting the patterns of protective factors and characteristics and their underlying mechanisms, we will take several important steps forward as we translate research into dissemination efforts. These endeavors will inform the public, lay the foundation for social advocacy and political reform, and improve equity and justice for African American, racial and ethnic minority youth, and all youth in the United States.

REFERENCES

Allen, R. L., Thornton, M. C., & Watkins, S. C. (1992). An African American racial belief system and social structural relationships: A test of invariance. *National Journal of Sociology, 6*(2), 157–186.

Arroyo, C. G., & Zigler, E. (1995). Racial identity, academic achievement, and the psychological well-being of economically disadvantaged adolescents. *Journal of Personality and Social Psychology, 69*(5), 903–914. http://doi.org/10.1037/0022-3514.69.5.903.

Bowman, P. J., & Howard, C. (1985). Race-related socialization, motivation, and academic achievement: A study of Black youths in three-generation families. *Journal of the American Academy of Child Psychiatry, 24*(2), 134–141.

Boykin, A. W., & Toms, F. D. (1985). Black child socialization: A conceptual framework. In H. P. McAdoo & J. L. McAdoo (Eds.), *Black children: Social, educational, and parental environments* (pp. 33–51). Thousand Oaks, CA: SAGE Publications.

Caughy, M. O., Nettles, S. M., & Lima, J. (2011). Profiles of racial socialization among African American parents: Correlates, context, and outcome. *Journal of Child and Family Studies, 20*(4), 491–502. http://doi.org/10.1007/s10826-010-9416-1.

Chavous, T. M., Bernat, D. H., Schmeelk-Cone, K., Caldwell, C. H., Kohn-Wood, L., & Zimmerman, M. A. (2003). Racial identity and academic attainment among African American adolescents. *Child Development, 74*(4), 1076–1090. http://doi.org/10.1111/1467-8624.00593.

Cooper, S. M., Smalls-Glover, C., Neblett, E. W., & Banks, K. H. (2015). Racial socialization practices among African American fathers: A profile-oriented approach. *Psychology of Men & Masculinity, 16*(1), 11–22. http://doi.org/10.1037/a0035654.

Cross, W. E. J. (1991). *Shades of black: Diversity in African-American identity*. Philadelphia, PA: Temple University Press.

Cross, W. E., Jr. (1995). The psychology of nigrescence: Revising the Cross model. In J. G. Ponterotto, J. M. Casas, L. A. Suzuki, & C. M. Alexander (Eds.), *Handbook of multicultural counseling* (pp. 93–122). Thousand Oaks, CA: Sage Publications.

Demo, D. H., & Hughes, M. (1990). Socialization and racial identity among Black Americans. *Social Psychology Quarterly, 53*(4), 364–374. http://doi.org/10.2307/2786741.

Dunbar, A. S., Perry, N. B., Cavanaugh, A. M., & Leerkes, E. M. (2015). African American parents' racial and emotion socialization profiles and young adults' emotional adaptation. *Cultural Diversity and Ethnic Minority Psychology, 21*(3), 409–419. http://doi.org/10.1037/a0037546.

Fordham, S. (1988). Racelessness as a factor in Black students' school success: Pragmatic strategy or pyrrhic victory? *Harvard Educational Review, 58*, 54–84.

García Coll, C., Lamberty, G., Jenkins, R., McAdoo, H. P., Crnic, K., Waskik, B. H., et al. (1996). An integrative model for the study of developmental competencies in minority children. *Child Development, 67*(5), 1891–1914. http://doi.org/10.2307/1131600.

Gillen-O'Neel, C., Mistry, R. S., Brown, C. S., Rodriguez, V. C., White, E. S., & Chow, K. A. (2015). Not excluded from analyses: Ethnic and racial meanings and identification among multiethnic/racial early adolescents. *Journal of Adolescent Research, 30*(2), 143–179. http://doi.org/10.1177/0743558414560626.

Harris, A. L., & Marsh, K. (2010). Is a raceless identity an effective strategy for academic success among Blacks? *Social Science Quarterly, 91*(5), 1242–1263. http://doi.org/10.1111/j.1540-6237.2010.00730.x.

Hughes, D., Rodriguez, J., Smith, E. P., Johnson, D. J., Stevenson, H. C., & Spicer, P. (2006). Parents' ethnic-racial socialization practices: A review of research and directions

for future study. *Developmental Psychology, 42*(5), 747–770. http://doi.org/10.1037/0012-1649.42.5.747.
Jones, J. M. (1972). *Prejudice and racism*. Reading, MA: Addison-Wesley Pub. Co.
Jones, S. C. T., & Neblett, E. W. (2016). Future directions in research on racism-related stress and racial-ethnic protective factors for Black youth. *Journal of Clinical Child & Adolescent Psychology*. Advance online publication. http://dx.doi.org/10.1080/15374416.2016.1146991.
Lesane-Brown, C. L., Scottham, K. M., Nguyên, H. X., & Sellers, R. M. (2006). *The racial socialization questionnaire—teen (RSQ-t): A new measure for use with African American adolescents*. Unpublished manuscript.
Madgison, J., & Vermunt, J. (2004). Latent class models. In D. W. Kaplan (Ed.), *The Sage handbook of quantitative methodology for the social sciences* (pp. 176–198). Thousand Oaks, CA: Sage Publications.
Marks, B., Setttles, I. H., Cooke, D. Y., Morgan, L., & Sellers, R. M. (2004). African American racial identity: A review of contemporary models and measures. In R. L. Jones (Ed.), *Black psychology* (4th ed., pp. 383–404). Hampton, VA: Cobb & Henry.
Martin, P. P., & Marcia, J. E. (1966). Development and validation of ego-identity status. *Journal of Personality and Social Psychology, 3*(5), 551–558. http://doi.org/10.1037/h0023281.
Neblett, E. W., Jr., Rivas-Drake, D., & Umaña-Taylor, A. J. (2012). The promise of racial and ethnic protective factors in promoting ethnic minority youth development. *Child Development Perspectives, 6*(3), 295–303. http://doi.org/10.1111/j.1750-8606.2012.00239.x.
Neblett, E. W., Jr., White, R. L., Ford, K. R., Philip, C. L., Nguyên, H. X., & Sellers, R. M. (2008). Patterns of racial socialization and psychological adjustment: Can parental communications about race reduce the impact of racial discrimination? *Journal of Research on Adolescence, 18*(3), 477–515. http://doi.org/10.1111/j.1532-7795.2008.00568.x.
Phinney, J. (1989). Stages of ethnic identity development in minority group adolescents. *Journal of Early Adolescence, 9*, 34–49.
Phinney, J. S., & Ong, A. D. (2007). Conceptualization and measurement of ethnic identity: Current status and future directions. *Journal of Counseling Psychology, 54*(3), 271–281. http://doi.org/10.1037/0022-0167.54.3.271.
Priest, N., Paradies, Y., Trenerry, B., Truong, M., Karlsen, S., & Kelly, Y. (2013). A systematic review of studies examining the relationship between reported racism and health and wellbeing for children and young people. *Social Science & Medicine, 95*, 115–127. http://doi.org/10.1016/j.socscimed.2012.11.031.
Richardson, B. L., Macon, T. A., Mustafaa, F. N., Bogan, E. D., Cole-Lewis, Y., & Chavous, T. M. (2015). Associations of racial discrimination and parental discrimination coping messages with African American adolescent racial identity. *Journal of Youth and Adolescence, 44*(6), 1301–1317. http://doi.org/10.1007/s10964-014-0196-6.
Sanders-Thompson, V. (1991). African American race consciousness and racial identification. *The Western Journal of Black Studies, 15*(3), 154–158.
Sanders-Thompson, V. L. (1995). The multidimensional structure of racial identification. *Journal of Research in Personality, 29*(2), 208–222.
Seaton, E. K. (2009). Perceived racial discrimination and racial identity profiles among African American adolescents. *Cultural Diversity and Ethnic Minority Psychology, 15*(2), 137–144. http://doi.org/10.1037/a0015506.
Seaton, E. K., Scottham, K. M., & Sellers, R. M. (2006). The status model of racial identity development in African American adolescents: Evidence of structure, trajectories, and well-being. *Child Development, 77*(5), 1416–1426. http://doi.org/10.1111/j.1467-8624.2006.00944.x.
Sellers, R. M., Copeland-Linder, N., Martin, P. P., & Lewis, R. L. (2006). Racial identity matters: The relationship between racial discrimination and psychological functioning in

African American adolescents. *Journal of Research on Adolescence, 16*(2), 187–216. http://doi.org/10.1111/j.1532-7795.2006.00128.x.
Sellers, R. M., Smith, M. A., Shelton, J. N., Rowley, S. A. J., & Chavous, T. M. (1998). Multidimensional model of racial identity: A reconceptualization of African American racial identity. *Personality and Social Psychology Review, 2*(1), 18–39. http://doi.org/10.1207/s15327957pspr0201_2.
Shelvin, K. H., Rivadeneyra, R., & Zimmerman, C. (2014). Stereotype threat in African American children: The role of Black identity and stereotype awareness. *Revue Internationale de Psychologie Sociale, 27*(3–4), 175–204.
Smalls, C. (2010). Effects of mothers' racial socialization and relationship quality on African American youth's school engagement: A profile approach. *Cultural Diversity and Ethnic Minority Psychology, 16*(4), 476–484. http://doi.org/10.1037/a0020653.
Smalls, C., & Cooper, S. M. (2012). Racial group regard, barrier socialization, and African American adolescents' engagement: Patterns and processes by gender. *Journal of Adolescence, 35*(4), 887–897. http://doi.org/10.1016/j.adolescence.2011.12.007.
Spencer, M. B. (2006). Phenomenology and ecological system theory: Development of diverse groups. In W. Damon & R. Lerner (Eds.), *Handbook of child psychology: Vol. 1* (6th ed., pp. 829–893). New York, NY: Wiley.
Steele, C. M., & Aronson, J. (1995). Stereotype threat and the intellectual test performance of African Americans. *Journal of Personality and Social Psychology, 69*(5), 797–811. http://doi.org/10.1037/0022-3514.69.5.797.
Stevenson, H. C. (1994). Validation of the scale of racial socialization for African American adolescents: Steps toward multidimensionality. *The Journal of Black Psychology, 20*(4), 445–468. http://dx.doi.org/10.1177/00957984940204005.
White-Johnson, R. L., Ford, K. R., & Sellers, R. M. (2010). Parental racial socialization profiles: Association with demographic factors, racial discrimination, childhood socialization, and racial identity. *Cultural Diversity and Ethnic Minority Psychology, 16*(2), 237–247. http://doi.org/10.1037/a0016111.
Wong, C. A., Eccles, J. S., & Sameroff, A. (2003). The influence of ethnic discrimination and ethnic identification on African American adolescents' school and socioemotional adjustment. *Journal of Personality, 71*(6), 1197–1232. http://doi.org/10.1111/1467-6494.7106012.
Worrell, F. C., Andretta, J. R., & Woodland, M. H. (2014). Cross racial identity scale (CRIS) scores and profiles in African American adolescents involved with the juvenile justice system. *Journal of Counseling Psychology, 61*(4), 570–580. http://doi.org/10.1037/cou0000041.
Yip, T., Seaton, E. K., & Sellers, R. M. (2006). African American racial identity across the lifespan: Identity status, identity content, and depressive symptoms. *Child Development, 77*(5), 1504–1517. http://doi.org/10.1111/j.1467-8624.2006.00950.

CHAPTER THREE

Helping Children Navigate a Diverse World: Parents' Contributions

Natasha Cabrera[1], Catherine Kuhns, Jenessa L. Malin, Daniela Aldoney
University of Maryland, College Park, College Park, MD, United States
[1]Corresponding author: e-mail address: ncabrera@umd.edu

Contents

Abstract

We review the existing literature on how parents prepare their children to navigate an increasingly diverse world. In particular, we focus much of our attention on the ethnic–racial socialization practices and beliefs of ethnic minority and majority groups, as this area of the field is currently the most expounded. We begin by exploring the current and future demographic characteristics of the United States to better contextualize research on social justice by developmental scientists. We then review the theoretical frameworks typically used to guide this body of research. Next we examine ethnic minority parents' ethnic–racial socialization practices and discuss their implications. We then consider ethnic majority parents' ethnic–racial socialization practices. Finally we address gaps in the current literature and offer directions for future research. Taken together, this small body of literature is critical to understanding how children are socialized about diversity.

Equity and Justice in Developmental Science: Implications for Young People, Families, and Communities (S.S. Horn, M.D. Ruck & L.S. Liben, Eds.)
Advances in Child Development and Behavior (J.B. Benson, Series Ed.), Vol. 51
ISSN 0065-2407 http://dx.doi.org/10.1016/bs.acdb.2016.05.002

Population projections from the US Census Bureau suggest that by the end of this decade no single racial or ethnic group will constitute a majority of children under 18 years (US Census Bureau, 2012). Such dramatic demographic change has implications for all facets of development, but in particular social development. Compared to previous decades, children in the United States today are more likely than ever to grow up in heterogeneous, as opposed to homogeneous, environments and to meet people from diverse cultural groups. It is also likely that children are exposed to negative stereotypes about ethnic minority children in the United States as well as about children from a wide array of countries and cultures. This diversity is likely to go beyond race and ethnicity, to encompass religion, sexual orientation, language, and other identifying characteristics.

How do children develop the skills they need to understand and get along with others who may be different from them? Children learn to get along with others and form friendships and relationships by interacting with peers, teachers, and caregivers in their most proximal environments—home and school/child care. Because parents are the most proximal and influential socializing agents for children, the focus of this chapter is on the strategies that parents use to prepare children to navigate increasingly diverse social and cultural contexts. For purposes of this chapter, children who are able to successfully navigate diverse contexts are those who can form intergroup relationships and friendships and exhibit less prejudice toward others.

We organize this chapter into five sections. First, we begin with a brief review of the increasing diversity in the United States. Second, we discuss theories illuminating how parents may help their children navigate these diverse contexts. In Sections 3 and 4, we review the strategies parents use to help prepare their children to navigate a diverse world, starting with the strategies of ethnic minority parents use and then contrasting these with the strategies of ethnic majority parents. Finally, we discuss gaps in this literature and avenues for future direction. Overall, we provide an illustrative review of existing theoretical frameworks and empirical evidence focused on how parents rear their children in an increasingly diverse world.

1. GROWING UP IN A DIVERSE WORLD

Before discussing the particular strategies parents use to help children navigate an increasingly diverse world, it is fitting to provide a demographic picture of the socially diverse context in which children are reared in the United States. America's under-18 population is racially and ethnically more diverse than it has ever been. In the decade between 2002 and 2012, the number of White students enrolled in public elementary and secondary schools decreased from 28.6 million (59% of public school enrollments) to 25.4 million (51%). In contrast, the number of Latino students enrolled during this period increased from 8.6 million (18%) to 12.1 million students (24%; Kena et al., 2015). A closer look at the nation's ethnic composition reveals a rich representation of multiple ethnic and racial groups. In 2012, the racial and ethnic composition of K–12 students in public schools included: 54% non-Latino White, 22% Latino, 15% Black, 5% Asian, 1% Native Hawaiian/Pacific Islander, and 1% American Indian/Alaska Native. Additionally, 2% of students reported two or more races (Bitterman, Gray, & Goldring, 2013). By the year 2044, over 50% of the US population will belong to a minority group (defined as any group other than non-Latino White; US Census Bureau, 2015). To add to this diversity, there is also an increasing number of multiracial births in the United States (Pew Research Center, 2015). According to the projections from the US Census Bureau, the multiracial population will triple by 2060 (Pew Research Center, 2015). These statistics highlight increasing diversity that will bring not only opportunities for learning and enrichment but also challenges associated with understanding and getting along with others.

What are the implications of this increasing diversity for children's social development? For children, this increased diversity means that they will have more opportunities to come into contact and interact with children from diverse ethnic, religious, and socioeconomic backgrounds in various settings, formally or informally, including public spaces, schools, and neighborhoods. Although these opportunities expose children to different positive cultural experiences, they also expose them to unfamiliar situations that can trigger implicit and explicit biases (McGlothlin & Killen, 2010). According to the US Department of Justice, roughly 19% of all hate crimes occur in school and over 50% of these are racially motivated, with 66% motivated by anti-Black bias and 21% by anti-White bias (Sandholtz, Langton, & Planty, 2013). Although these statistics do not speak to motive, parents need to equip children with the social skills, beliefs, and expectations that can foster positive interactions and friendships with a diverse group of peers.

2. HELPING CHILDREN NAVIGATE DIVERSE CONTEXTS

How do parents prepare their children to be part of such a diverse society? Parents and other caregivers provide children with the social experiences they need to learn about themselves and others. These experiences can result in the formation of long-lasting bonds and relationships (Ainsworth & Bowlby, 1991) with parents and peers (Cox & Paley, 1997) in socially and culturally appropriate ways (Weisner, 2002). Thus, socialization begins in the home where children learn socially and culturally appropriate values and behaviors that enable them to be socially competent and act as members of a social group (Grusec & Hastings, 2014; Maccoby, 1992; Maccoby & Martin, 1983). Typically, researchers define social competence as the ability to integrate thoughts, feelings, emotions, and behaviors to achieve interpersonal goals valued within a particular sociocultural context while at the same time maintaining personal relationships with others (Rubin & Rose-Krasnor, 1992; Shaffer, Burt, Obradović, Herbers, & Masten, 2009). Children who are socially competent display particular behaviors that suggest a certain set of values (e.g., social justice, responsibility), positive self-identity (e.g., sense of competence, worth), interpersonal skills (e.g., maintains friendly relationships, resolves conflicts, expresses emotions), self-regulation (e.g., controls impulses, delays gratification), planning and decision making (e.g., follows directions, makes choices), and cultural competence (e.g., ability to interact effectively with people of varying ethnic backgrounds) (McCay & Keyes, 2001). That is, a socially competent child is someone who has the capacity to successfully navigate a diverse social context.

Many parents aspire to have children who get along with peers, including peers from differing cultures or who have different belief systems. Parents might be able to attain this goal by encouraging the facilitation and development of cross-race friendships, decreasing their own levels of bias and prejudice, and increasing intergroup contact. According to *intergroup contact theory*, contact with members of other groups is required to reduce prejudice and discrimination (Crystal, Killen, & Ruck, 2008; Thijs & Verkuyten, 2008; Tropp & Prenovost, 2008). Another way to promote intergroup friendships is to recognize the reasons why children might both exclude and include others within a particular social context (Tajfel & Turner, 1986). Drawing from *social identity theory*, individuals derive a sense of self-worth from their group membership, and are therefore inclined to compare their group favorably with others. By interacting with peers from a different ethnic–racial group, for example, children may promote positive attitudes toward the out-group, which can result in a reduction in discrimination (Edmonds & Killen, 2009). The evidence based on these theoretical frameworks is very convincing: peer interactions that reflect intergroup and extensive positive contact are catalytic to the formation of high-quality friendships, increase cross-group friendships, and decrease prejudice, racial bias, and discriminatory behavior (see chapters "Children's Intergroup Relations and Attitudes" by Bigler et al. and "Social Exclusion Based on Group Membership Is a Form of Prejudice" by Cooley et al., this volume; Crystal et al., 2008; Jugert, Noack, & Rutland, 2011; McGlothlin & Killen, 2006; Tajfel & Turner, 1986; Tropp & Pettigrew, 2005).

Despite the general consensus that increased contact with peers from different ethnic and socioeconomic backgrounds is a central benchmark to efforts that reduce racial segregation and prejudice (Rutland & Killen, 2015), there is surprisingly little empirical research on the strategies parents use at home to get their children socially ready for diverse school contexts. We were unable to find any studies that provide empirical support for the idea that parental support of intergroup contact results in less discriminatory behavior by the child. One can argue that parents who choose public schools where children are likely to encounter a broad swath of American diversity are implicitly sending a message to their children that diversity is important and it matters for their development. However, there is little empirical evidence that this is the case (Schneider & Buckley, 2002), and even if parents were intentional about school choice, the social and economic segregation of schools makes it difficult to discern whether such parental choice indeed results in less prejudice and more tolerance (Dessel, 2010). There is, however, a strong literature on intergroup contact in school settings, demonstrating that children benefit when teachers promote positive intergroup contact (Cameron, Rutland, & Brown, 2007). Understanding parents' role in increasing positive peer contact with members of "out-groups" can also bolster school efforts to integrate schools in a meaningful way (Rutland, Killen, & Abrams, 2010). The dearth of research on the strategies parents use to expose children to diversity and increase positive intergroup contact may reflect different parents' priorities. A large literature suggests that parents spend a lot of time and energy in activities and related experiences to ensure their children succeed academically (Epstein, 1991; Parcel & Dufur, 2001; Reynolds, 1992; Schaub, 2010). This alternative area of research—parents' role in their children's intergroup contact and relationships—seems ripe for future investigation and attention (Binder et al., 2009; Dhont, Van Hiel, De Bolle, & Roets, 2012; Feddes, Noack, & Rutland, 2009).

Although we found no studies specifically focused on how parents encourage intergroup friendships, there is an extensive literature on parents' ethnic–racial socialization practices, including determinants and consequences for children's development. Racial and ethnic socialization typically refers to the way parents transmit information, attitudes, and ideas about race and ethnicity. That is, what are the messages about race and ethnicity that both ethnic minority and majority parents tell their children (Brown, Tanner-Smith, Lesane-Brown, & Ezell, 2007; Hughes et al., 2006; Knight, Bernal, Garza, Cota, & Ocampo, 1993; Umaña-Taylor, Alfaro, Bámaca, & Guimond, 2009). Given the rapidly changing demographic landscape of the United States, such socialization practices are important and needed as they prepare children to understand how others might perceive them and, consequently, how others might engage and interact with them. Although these approaches do not explicitly focus on promoting increased intergroup relationships and reducing prejudice, we review this literature because it has important implications for understanding the challenges children might have in navigating a diverse social context. How children interact in diverse contexts and how successfully they navigate these contexts might depend on their understanding of both their own and others' racial and ethnic identities, cultural values and prejudices, as well as the prejudice and discrimination they may expect to face throughout their lifetimes. In the following sections we review research on the approaches parents use to ethnically and racially socialize their children. To do so, we differentiate between the practices used by ethnic minority and ethnic majority parents.

3. ETHNIC MINORITY PARENTS' ETHNIC–RACIAL SOCIALIZATION PRACTICES

Teaching ethnic minority children about their heritage has implications for the development of a strong sense of self and identity, important ingredients for the formation of positive social relationships with peers (Kiang & Fuligni, 2009; Wills et al., 2007). Historically, the term *racial socialization* has been used to understand the strategies Black parents use to teach their children about racism and maintain self-esteem and ethnic pride (Boykin & Toms, 1985; Murry & Brody, 2002; Peters, 2002). Often looked at as the primary medium for transmission of cultural practices and beliefs for African American families, racial socialization includes both parents' desire to help their children develop a positive racial self-concept while also providing them with strategies to cope when faced with discrimination and racism (Rodriguez, McKay, & Bannon, 2008). Likewise, the term *ethnic socialization*, which originated in experiences of immigrant Asian, Latino, and in some cases African and Caribbean populations, has been used to describe research that examines how parents teach their children about their country of origin. Research on ethnic socialization has typically focused on ethnic identity development, cultural retention, and in-group affiliation (Knight et al., 1993; Quintana & Vera, 1999; Umaña-Taylor, Zeiders, & Updegraff, 2013). Despite the differing origins of these constructs, there is conceptual overlap between them. Hughes et al. (2006) proposed merging the two terms into one: *ethnic–racial socialization* to refer to the process through which children learn about racism and ethnic diversity. Ethnic–racial socialization includes parents' verbal and nonverbal messages about the meaning and significance of race and ethnicity, group membership and identity, racial and ethnic stratification, and intergroup and intragroup contacts. Still, today much of the research in the United States uses the term racial socialization when examining African Americans, while the term ethnic socialization is used in research on multiple ethnic groups (Hughes et al., 2006). For purposes of this chapter, we adopt Hughes' term of ethnic–racial socialization, but in describing specific research findings, we use the terms preferred by researchers of those studies.

What do racial/ethnic minority parents teach their children about their own race/ethnicity, as well as how to relate to others from different races/ethnicities? According to Hughes et al. (2006), it is through four mechanisms: messages of cultural socialization, preparation for bias, promotion of mistrust, and mainstream socialization that children learn beliefs, values, and expectations that help them navigate a diverse world, or at least help them understand who they are. In the following sections, we will highlight the various types of ethnic–racial socialization practices, family-level predictors of ethnic–racial socialization, and the link between ethnic–racial socialization practices and child outcomes.

3.1 Ethnic–Racial Socialization Practices

3.1.1 Cultural Socialization

Cultural socialization refers to parental practices that teach children about their own race and ethnic heritage, cultural customs, and traditions. Examples of cultural socialization practices include talking about history or historical figures, reading culturally relevant books, celebrating cultural holidays, and encouraging children to use their native language. Parents are more likely to engage in discussions of cultural socialization than any other form of ethnic–racial socialization (e.g., preparation for bias, promotion of mistrust; Caughy, O'Campo, Randolph, & Nickerson, 2002; Hughes & Chen, 1999). In studies of Black families, the percentage of parents who report using cultural socialization ranges from 33% (Marshall, 1995) to 80% or more (Coard, Wallace, Stevenson, & Brotman, 2004). Phinney and Chavira (1995) found that, on average, Japanese parents report that roughly 66% of their ethnic–racial socialization practices were cultural socialization message, while Dominican, Mexican, and Puerto Rican parents reported that cultural socialization messages comprised 85% of their ethnic–racial socialization practices (Hughes, 2003). The emphasis on cultural socialization also increased if parents perceived more discrimination themselves or if they had a strong ethnic identity (Hughes, 2003).

3.1.2 Preparation for Bias

Ethnic minority families also use various ethnic–racial socialization messages to prepare their children for discrimination by others. *Preparation for bias* refers to parents' aim to increase children's awareness of discrimination and provide them with coping strategies they can use when it occurs. This construct is typically measured by asking parents to report whether they have ever told their children that others might treat them badly because of their race or ethnicity. Studies of Black families show that between 67% and 90% of parents report preparing even their young children for bias (Caughy et al., 2002; Coard et al., 2004; Hughes, 2003; Hughes & Chen, 1999). Black parents are more likely than other parents to report preparation for bias as a parenting technique, perhaps because of the historical relevance and unique nature of discrimination many Black people in the United States experience (Hughes, 2003). Although this strategy teaches children to be prepared for discrimination by others, its exclusive emphasis on bias and discrimination may have the unintended consequence of isolating members of the outgroup (Biafora, Taylor, Warheit, & Zimmerman, 1993; Biafora, Warheit, Zimmerman, & Gil, 1993; Stevenson, 1997). This may reduce positive intergroup contact or leave racial/ethnic minority children feeling wary of interethnic friendships. This is an important area for future research.

3.1.3 Promotion of Mistrust

Another way ethnic minority parents teach their children about the potential for discrimination and to be wary of interracial interactions is by *promoting mistrust* (Hughes et al., 2006). This approach is distinct from preparation for bias in that it includes no messages about coping strategies, though it can include warnings about discrimination/bias (Hughes et al., 2006). Promotion of mistrust is difficult to accurately measure, in part because it tends to undermine the promotion of positive race relations and it is probably least common among parents. A study of socioeconomically diverse, urban Black parents and their children revealed that the majority of parents incorporated racial socialization messages routinely as part of their parenting, with messages regarding cultural pride occurring more frequently than messages regarding promotion of mistrust (Caughy et al., 2002). While the implications of parents promoting messages of mistrust for children's intergroup friendships are understudied, it seems reasonable to suspect that such messages would lead to fewer instances of intergroup contact and a wariness on behalf of the children receiving those messages to engage with the ethnic groups such messages were directed toward.

3.1.4 *Mainstream Socialization*

Parents also encourage children to develop the skills and characteristics that are necessary to thrive in the mainstream or dominant culture and orient them away from their native culture. Strategies that promote a color-blind approach teach children that they should not notice race in their interactions with others, and it is more prevalent among majority White parents than minority parents (e.g., Hamm, 2001); this issue will be discussed later in this chapter. A potential negative outcome of mainstream socialization messages is that it might encourage assimilation into dominant culture perhaps at the cost of ethnic pride (Phinney, Horenczyk, Liebkind, & Vedder, 2001). Aside from a study examining parents' beliefs and practices around cross-ethnic friendships in focus groups (Hamm, 2001), we found no research suggesting that this approach encourages cross-ethnic friendships with children from other ethnic minority groups.

3.2 Correlates of Ethnic Minority Parents' Ethnic–Racial Socialization Practices

In this section we briefly discuss the family-level predictors that explain variation in how minority parents socialize their children on issues of race and ethnicity as well as discuss the literature that links socialization practices to children's outcomes.

3.2.1 *Family-Level Predictors of Ethnic–Racial Socialization*

Parents' ethnic–racial socialization practices are grounded in their own beliefs and attitudes about ethnicity and race and are a salient aspect of child rearing among ethnic minority families. This is particularly true among Black mothers with higher levels of education (White-Johnson, Ford, & Sellers, 2010) and those with a strong sense of their own racial and cultural identities (Romero, Cuéllar, & Roberts, 2000; Scottham & Smalls, 2009; Thomas & Speight, 1999). A small-scale study of middle-class Black mothers and fathers revealed that parents' internalization of their own racial identity was positively associated with their use of racial socialization practices (Thomas & Speight, 1999). Moreover, almost all parents (96%) in the sample believed it was important to engage in racial socialization practices with their children. However, parents varied in why it was important to teach their children about race or ethnicity. Parents most commonly reported that they engaged in these practices because of the presence of racism (21%), to prepare their children for challenges (18%), and to teach their children to function effectively in society (11%). Parents most commonly talked with their children about achievement (26%), racial pride (19%), and overcoming racism (13%; Thomas & Speight, 1999).

Romero et al. (2000) examined correlates of parents' cultural socialization practices among a sample of college-enrolled Mexican-origin mothers and fathers and found that parents with stronger Mexican cultural identities reported engaging in more Latino cultural socialization practices than parents with weaker Mexican cultural identities. Low-acculturated parents reported engaging in more Latino cultural socialization practices and US cultural socialization practices than high-acculturated parents. In another study, Hughes (2003) conducted a comparative cross-sectional study on ethnic identity in a sample of economically diverse Black, Puerto Rican, and Dominican American mothers or fathers with children 6–17 years old and found that parents who perceived more discrimination engaged in more ethnic/cultural socialization practices. However, this association was stronger for Black and Dominican American parents than for Puerto Rican parents. For Dominican and Puerto Rican American parents, ethnic identity was a stronger predictor of preparation for bias than it was for Black parents. Further, these associations were stronger for parents of older (10–17) than for parents of younger children (6–9), suggesting that parents may view younger children as being too young to be burdened with issues of ethnicity and discrimination.

More recently, Scottham and Smalls (2009) examined the association between Black mothers' racial identity and their racial socialization practices with their middle- and high-school-aged children. Based on mothers' reports of dimensions of racial identity, including private regard (i.e., affect toward group membership), public regard (i.e., perception of how non-group members perceive group members), and centrality (i.e., importance of their race to their self-concept). Using cluster analysis four distinct profiles of racial identity emerged: buffering defensive (i.e., high centrality and private regard but low public regard), idealized (high centrality, private regard, and public regard), low affiliation (low centrality and private regard, but mid-level public regard), and moderate (mid-level on centrality, private regard, and public regard). The findings revealed that mothers in the buffering defensive cluster communicated more racial pride messages to their children than mothers in the moderate- and low-affiliation clusters. They also found that mothers in both the buffering defensive and idealized clusters reported more frequently engaging with their children in activities related to Black culture than mothers in the moderate- and low-affiliation clusters.

Children's individual characteristics also influence the ethnic–racial socialization practices their parents use with them. For example, ethnic minority parents seem to adjust their messages of race and ethnicity depending on their children's age and gender. Research suggests that younger children receive fewer messages regarding race, especially preparation for bias or communication about discrimination, compared to older children partly because parents believe a certain level of cognitive maturity is required before children can handle discussions about race or ethnicity (Caughy et al., 2002; Hughes, 2003; Hughes & Chen, 1997). In contrast, older children, and especially boys, hear more preparation for bias messages. Because racial/ethnic minority boys are often viewed as threatening and report more discrimination compared to racial/ethnic minority girls (Stevenson, Cameron, Herrero-Taylor, & Davis, 2002), parents target more messages about ethnicity and race to their sons than their daughters (Fischer & Shaw, 1999; Stevenson et al., 2002).

In our study of Latino immigrant parents and their 2-year-old children, FAMILIA, most mothers and fathers (68% and 78%, respectively) reported that it was important to talk to their child about their culture. On average, mothers and fathers felt that discussions of culture and heritage should begin around age 4. Even so, most parents in our study (67% of mothers and 78% of fathers) answered *no* to the question "Do you think your child knows s/he is from your country of origin?" and most parents (80%) responded *never* to the question "In the last year, how many times did you prepare your child for discrimination?" However, there was variability suggesting that some parents begin engaging in cultural socialization practices prior to toddlerhood in order to prepare their children for bias and protect them from negative stereotypes (Hughes et al., 2006). These emerging findings highlight the need for additional research in early childhood that seeks to identify when ethnic–racial socialization begins.

3.2.2 Links to Child Outcomes

As expected, we found no empirical evidence that the various ways in which parents engage in ethnic–racial socialization with their children results in less prejudice toward others and more intergroup contact. There is, however, a substantive body of work examining the link to other child outcomes, notably socioemotional and academic outcomes (Banerjee, Harrell, & Johnson, 2011). While a comprehensive review of that literature is outside the scope of this chapter, we highlight a few studies that have shown that parents' ethnic–racial socialization practices are associated with children's social and academic outcomes. For example, a study of socioeconomically diverse, urban Black parents and their children revealed that parents who emphasized socialization messages of racial pride had children with fewer reported behavior problems (Caughy et al., 2002). Studies with older children have found that not only is cultural pride (i.e., parents telling children to be proud of their race or ethnicity) directly associated with academic adjustment (e.g., effort at school), especially when it is delivered in a democratic way, but it also buffers the impact of racial discrimination on adolescents' academic achievement (Cooper & Smalls, 2010). However, some research has suggested that not all ethnic–racial socialization practices have positive influences on children's development. For example, there is some research showing that promotion of mistrust is negatively associated with children's social competence (Tran & Lee, 2010) and positively associated with depressive symptoms (Liu & Lau, 2013). Further, Friend, Hunter, and Fletcher (2011) found that there was a differential association between preparation for bias and academic achievement for fifth grade boys and girls. Specifically, boys who received more preparation for bias messages were more likely to have higher grade point averages, whereas girls who received more preparation for bias messages were more likely to have lower grade point averages. The authors hypothesize that by receiving more preparation for bias messages from their parents, boys may have been better equipped to cope with racism, while girls may have perceived the preparation for bias messages as overwhelmingly negative.

Overall, the above review points to several clear conclusions. First, ethnic–racial socialization practices do not implicitly include messages of empathy, respect for diversity, and the importance of relating to others from diverse cultural groups. They are exclusively focused on strengthening the positive view of one's cultural heritage rather than strengthening positive views about the heritage and culture of others. It is unclear whether having a strong sense of self-concept and having a strong sense of ethnic identity is enough to be able to interact positively with others from the out-group. Second, the body of research on this issue has primarily focused on older children and on mothers; thus the way parents teach about race and ethnicity to young children (0–3) as well as the contributions of fathers remains unknown. Third, the intersection of parental socialization messages of promotion of mistrust, preparation for bias, and interethnic friendships is a vastly understudied area, and research is needed to uncover how such socialization messages influence children's peer relationships. Fourth, the study of mainstream socialization messages on behalf of parents is an important direction for future research with ethnic minority families. It is unclear if ethnic minority parents engage in these practices and if they do what their impact is on children's development. Finally, it is still unclear if ethnic–racial socialization practices impact children's prejudicial attitudes, beliefs, and actions in diverse social contexts. Longitudinal research that includes measures of children's peer interactions in contexts outside of the home could provide valuable insight as to how such practices influence children's developing schemas of race and ethnicity.

4. ETHNIC MAJORITY PARENTS' ETHNIC–RACIAL SOCIALIZATION PRACTICES

How do *ethnic majority* families socialize their children on issues about race and ethnicity? This is an important question because all children in the United States increasingly live in racially, ethnically, and economically diverse communities, and thus it is important to understand whether majority children are encouraged to have intergroup friendships and reduced bias and stereotypes as well as what messages they hear about race and ethnicity.

4.1 Ethnic–Racial Socialization Practices

Our search of the literature revealed that in contrast to the ethnic–racial socialization practices of ethnic minority families, ethnic majority families have generally adopted a color-blind approach that is rooted in the belief that acknowledging race issues is paramount to sensitizing children to racial differences and promoting prejudice (Pahlke, Bigler, & Suizzo, 2012). That is, ethnic majority parents feel it is best not to engage in explicit ethnic–racial socialization practices in order to promote an egalitarian viewpoint. The overwhelming consensus from research with ethnic majority parents is that they either do not engage in racial or ethnic socialization practices with their children or when they do they endorse a color-blind socialization approach that emphasizes that all individuals are equal and neglects to highlight differences across racial or ethnic groups (Pahlke et al., 2012; Samuels, 2009). A qualitative study of multiracial adults who were raised from infancy by White middle-class adoptive parents revealed that most participating adoptive parents did not discuss race with their children or engage in racial socialization strategies (e.g., preparation for bias; Samuels, 2009). Another small-scale study examined a booksharing interaction between highly educated White mothers and their 4- to 5-year-old children. The book included ethnically and racially diverse characters. Yet, the findings revealed that most of the participating mothers did not mention race, ethnicity, diversity, or intergroup contact while reading with their children (Pahlke et al., 2012). However, mothers who had more cross-race friendships had children with lower levels of racial bias than children of mothers who had fewer cross-race friendships. For example, Lee, Grotevant, Hellerstedt, Gunnar, and Minnesota International Adaption Project Team (2006) conducted a large-scale study of White middle-class parents with 5- to 13-year-old internationally adopted children. The authors found that the White parents in the study had relatively low scores on color-blind racial attitudes and relatively high scores on racialization parenting beliefs. These findings stand in contrast to the aforementioned studies, which suggested the majority of White parents endorsed a color-blind approach. Thus, these findings are likely specific to White parents who have adopted an international child. The authors also explored the pathways from a color-blind approach to racial socialization practices. That is, they found that parents who endorsed a color-blind approach engaged in fewer racial socialization practices with their children because they felt that engaging in those practices was less important.

The color-blind approach may also suggest that some parents do not value cross-race or interethnic friendships for their children or the view these friendships as a priority. In a small-scale qualitative study of Black and White families aiming to understand parents' perspectives on their children's cross-ethnic peer relations, Hamm (2001) found that White parents overwhelmingly supported the notion of a color-blind approach (i.e., encouraged their children not to notice race or ethnicity). When pressed further, they stated that a goal was to have their child have contact with peers from different ethnic groups, but they also remained ambivalent about the significance of cross-ethnic relationships. Most parents admitted their children were developing in ethnically and racially homogenous areas but did not feel it was their responsibility to broaden their children's contact with children from diverse groups.

Overall, the evidence that White and other ethnic–racial majority parents use color-blind approaches to socialize their children about race is based on small samples, descriptive data, and is not methodologically rigorous. Thus, generalizations from this work are tentative at best.

4.2 Correlates of Ethnic Majority Parents' Ethnic–Racial Socialization Practices

The limited research on ethnic majority families has largely not explored within group variability to understand family-level correlates of ethnic majority parents' socialization practices. The literature has also largely ignored its implications for children's development. However, one line of research has focused on transmission of prejudice as a means of examining how parents socialize their children to get along, or not get along, with others. This stands in contrast to the aforementioned literature with ethnic/racial minority families, which emphasized the importance of ethnic–racial socialization for children's academic and social outcomes.

A growing body of research shows that ethnic majority children learn prejudicial attitudes from their parents. Sinclair, Dunn, and Lowery (2005) studied a White sample of parents and their fourth and fifth grade children and found that parents' prejudice and children's implicit and explicit bias (i.e., children had to assign positive and negative adjectives to pictures of a White boy and a Black boy) were positively associated but only when children strongly identified with their parents (e.g., how much they cared about making their parent proud). In contrast, when children did not identify with their parents, parents' prejudice was negatively associated with children's explicit bias. Similarly, a small-scale study of White Italian mothers, fathers, and their kindergarteners found that parents' explicit racial bias was not related to children's racial attitudes (Castelli, Zogmaister, & Tomelleri, 2009). However, the authors found that mothers' (but not fathers') implicit racial bias was a significant predictor of children's racial attitudes (i.e., assigning a positive or negative trait to a picture of a white and a black boy). In a similar study based on a differential effects model that mothers and fathers have different spheres of influence on their children, O'Bryan, Fishbein, and Ritchey (2004) found that while mothers primarily influenced their adolescents' HIV/AIDS, racial, and overweight prejudices, fathers were the primary influence on their adolescents' sex-role stereotyping and homosexual prejudice.

These studies are suggestive but fall short of explaining why and how parents' prejudice influences their children's attitudes. Furthermore, research on ethnic majority families and their socialization practices regarding beliefs and values of diversity and social justice is greatly understudied. Future research is needed that specifically explores the mechanism by which prejudice is transmitted from parent to child among ethnic majority families. Moreover, it would be important to understand the association between parental prejudice or use of the color-blind approach and children's opportunities for intergroup contact, which might be the mechanism by which parents' prejudice may influence children's developmental outcomes.

5. GAPS IN THE LITERATURE AND FUTURE DIRECTIONS

As discussed throughout this chapter, there are considerable gaps in the literature with regard to the role that parents play in socializing children to get along with diverse others, increase intergroup contact, and reduce prejudice. First, there is a scarcity of research focused on the strategies both ethnic majority and minority parents provide their children with to navigate an increasingly diverse world. A wealth of research focuses on diversity in the school setting, and numerous school-based interventions target increasing tolerance, respect, empathy, and diversity starting in elementary school. Given that parents are highly influential on their children's development, the lack of research on parenting strategies to increase intergroup contact is surprising and paves the road for a rich research agenda. Perhaps because schools take initiative in promoting empathy, tolerance, and respect, parents leave such tough discussions and subject matter at the hands of the school and teachers. Parents may expect that children will learn to navigate social interactions with diverse peers by themselves, and do not feel the need to discuss such topics at home. Indeed, as the demographic makeup of the United States continues to change so rapidly, parents' own experiences with diversity as children may not mirror their children's experiences with diversity. Moreover, ecological views of development suggest that microsystems such as the home and school are the most important contexts for development. Understanding how both school and home contribute to the development of intergroup attitudes and behaviors seems a pressing imperative. As the diversity of the United States continues to increase, such efforts to understand the independent and combined influence of parents and teachers should dominate the research agenda on this topic.

Second, there is a lack of research that focuses on parent's ethnic–racial socialization strategies in early childhood. Children's early socialization has important implications for their later development. While some research suggests that parents may assume children are too young to engage in discussions about race, it may be that parents are communicating about race and respect in more nuanced ways that are geared toward younger children. Future research should address how both ethnic minority and majority parents teach their young children about tolerance, diversity, and respect, and more closely examine the ways in which they choose to engage in such lessons.

Third, most research on diversity has highlighted racial or ethnic diversity. There is a dearth of research on how parents socialize children to get along with children from diverse out-groups. There are multiple sources for potential exclusion based on gender, nationality, immigrant status, and sexual orientation, thus efforts to achieve equity and justice need to move beyond the specific, albeit important, context of race and ethnicity. Research is clearly needed to understand what parents do at home to prepare children to navigate a socially, culturally, and diverse and complex world and produce a new generation of socially just and responsible individuals.

Finally, the research on parents has primarily focused on mothers' socialization practices. Thus, there is a lack of research on how fathers transmit messages about ethnicity, tolerance, and respect. Previous research suggests that fathers contribute to their children's development in unique ways, and there is no reason to assume that fathers transmit the same messages about tolerance, diversity, and respect that mothers do. Understanding how mothers and fathers' values, goals, and practices relate to raising a socially just child would lay the foundation for a more ecological view of children's development. This is an open empirical question that should be further explored.

As children develop they begin to differentiate themselves from others. Children learn to navigate this increasing diversity not only from teachers and peers but also from parents. Children's interactions with their parents present timely opportunities to develop social justice competencies (e.g., appreciating diversity, rejecting discrimination, and prejudicial attitudes). Thus, an important next step is to develop interventions that go beyond the school and childcare settings and include parents. Parents, like educators, face the challenge of preparing children to live in a diverse world in which some groups have greater societal benefits than others. Parents may take a color-blind approach (primarily seen with ethnic–racial majority parents) or a promotion of mistrust approach (primarily seen with ethnic–racial minority parents). Both strategies do not give families opportunities to integrate diversity into their daily life and engage in discussions about discrimination and prejudice. It is essential that researchers further examine children's social interactions with their parents in order to understand how children develop their perceptions of others. Growing this literature has vast implications for intervention and prevention programs.

ACKNOWLEDGMENT

We are thankful to Melanie Killen for excellent feedback on earlier drafts of this manuscript.

REFERENCES

Ainsworth, M. S., & Bowlby, J. (1991). An ethological approach to personality development. *American Psychologist, 46*, 333–341.

Banerjee, M., Harrell, Z. T., & Johnson, D. J. (2011). Racial/ethnic socialization and parental involvement in education as predictors of cognitive ability and achievement in African American children. *Journal of Youth and Adolescence, 40*, 595–605.

Biafora, F. A., Taylor, D. L., Warheit, G. J., & Zimmerman, R. S. (1993). Cultural mistrust and racial awareness among ethnically diverse Black adolescent boys. *The Journal of Black Psychology, 19*, 266–281.

Biafora, F. A., Warheit, G. J., Zimmerman, R. S., & Gil, A. G. (1993). Racial mistrust and deviant behaviors among ethnically diverse Black adolescent boys. *Journal of Applied Social Psychology, 23*, 891–910.

Binder, J., Brown, R., Zagefka, H., Funke, F., Kessler, T., Mummendey, A., ... Leyens, J. P. (2009). Does contact reduce prejudice or does prejudice reduce contact? A longitudinal test of the contact hypothesis among majority and minority groups in three European countries. *Journal of Personality and Social Psychology, 96*, 843–856.

Bitterman, A., Gray, L., & Goldring, R. (2013). *Characteristics of public and private elementary and secondary schools in the United States: Results from the 2011–12 schools and staffing survey (NCES 2013–312)*. Washington, DC: U.S. Department of Education, National Center for Education Statistics. Retrieved from, http://nces.ed.gov/pubsearch.

Boykin, A. W., & Toms, F. D. (1985). Black child socialization: A conceptual framework. In H. P. McAdoo & J. L. McAdoo (Eds.), *Black children: Social, educational, and parental environments* (pp. 33–51). Newbury Park, CA: Sage.

Brown, T. N., Tanner-Smith, E. E., Lesane-Brown, C. L., & Ezell, M. E. (2007). Child, parent, and situational correlates of familial ethnic/race socialization. *Journal of Marriage and Family, 69*, 14–25.

Cameron, L., Rutland, A., & Brown, R. (2007). Promoting children's positive intergroup attitudes towards stigmatized groups: Extended contact and multiple classification skills training. *International Journal of Behavioral Development, 31*, 454–466.

Castelli, L., Zogmaister, C., & Tomelleri, S. (2009). The transmission of racial attitudes within the family. *Developmental Psychology, 45*, 586–591.

Caughy, M. O., O'Campo, P. J., Randolph, S. M., & Nickerson, K. (2002). The influence of racial socialization practices on the cognitive and behavioral competence of African American preschoolers. *Child Development, 73*, 1611–1625.

Coard, S. I., Wallace, S. A., Stevenson, H. C., Jr., & Brotman, L. M. (2004). Towards culturally relevant preventive interventions: The consideration of racial socialization in parent training with African American families. *Journal of Child and Family Studies, 13*, 277–293.

Cooper, S. M., & Smalls, C. (2010). Culturally distinctive and academic socialization: Direct and interactive relationships with African American adolescents' academic adjustment. *Journal of Youth and Adolescence, 39*, 199–212.

Cox, M. J., & Paley, B. (1997). Families as systems. *Annual Review of Psychology, 48*, 243–267.
Crystal, D., Killen, M., & Ruck, M. (2008). It is who you know that counts: Intergroup contact and judgments about race-based exclusion. *British Journal of Developmental Psychology, 26*, 51–70.
Dessel, A. (2010). Prejudice in schools: Promotion of an inclusive culture and climate. *Education and Urban Society, 42*, 407–429.
Dhont, K., Van Hiel, A., De Bolle, M., & Roets, A. (2012). Longitudinal intergroup contact effects on prejudice using self- and observer-reports. *British Journal of Social Psychology, 51*, 221–238.
Edmonds, C., & Killen, M. (2009). Do adolescents' perceptions of parental racial attitudes relate to their intergroup contact and cross-race relationships? *Group Processes and Intergroup Relations, 12*, 5–21.
Epstein, J. L. (1991). Effects on student achievement of teachers' practices of parent involvement. In *Annual meeting of the American Educational Research Association*: Elsevier Science/JAI Press.
Feddes, A. R., Noack, P., & Rutland, A. (2009). Direct and extended friendship effects on minority and majority children's interethnic attitudes: A longitudinal study. *Child Development, 80*, 377–390.
Fischer, A. R., & Shaw, C. M. (1999). African Americans' mental health and perceptions of racist discrimination: The moderating effects of racial socialization experiences and self-esteem. *Journal of Counseling Psychology, 46*, 395.
Friend, B. C. A., Hunter, A. G., & Fletcher, A. C. (2011). Parental racial socialization and the academic achievement of African American children: A cultural-ecological approach. *Journal of African American Studies, 15*, 40–57.
Grusec, J. E., & Hastings, P. D. (Eds.), (2014). *Handbook of socialization: Theory and research*. New York, NY: Guilford Publications.
Hamm, J. (2001). Barriers and bridges to positive cross-ethnic relations: African American and White parent socialization beliefs and practices. *Youth and Society, 33*, 62–98.
Hughes, D. (2003). Correlates of African American and Latino parents' messages to children about ethnicity and race: A comparative study of racial socialization. *American Journal of Community Psychology, 31*, 15–33.
Hughes, D., & Chen, L. (1997). When and what parents tell children about race: An examination of race-related socialization among African American families. *Applied Developmental Science, 1*, 200–214.
Hughes, D., & Chen, L. (1999). The nature of parents' race-related communications to children: A developmental perspective. In L. Balter & C. S. Tamis-Lemonda (Eds.), *Child psychology: A handbook of contemporary issues* (pp. 467–490). Philadelphia: Psychology Press.
Hughes, D., Rodriguez, J., Smith, E. P., Johnson, D. J., Stevenson, H. C., & Spicer, P. (2006). Parents' ethnic-racial socialization practices: A review of research and directions for future study. *Developmental Psychology, 42*, 747–770.
Jugert, P., Noack, P., & Rutland, A. (2011). Friendship preferences among German and Turkish preadolescents. *Child Development, 82*, 812–829.
Kena, G., Musu-Gillette, L., Robinson, J., Wang, X., Rathbun, A., Zhang, J., ... Dunlop Velez, E. (2015). *The condition of education 2015 (NCES 2015-144)*. Washington, DC: U.S. Department of Education, National Center for Education Statistics. Retrieved from, http://nces.ed.gov/pubsearch.
Kiang, L., & Fuligni, A. J. (2009). Ethnic identity in context: Variations in ethnic exploration and belonging within parent, same-ethnic peer, and different-ethnic peer relationships. *Journal of Youth and Adolescence, 38*, 732–743.
Knight, G. P., Bernal, M. E., Garza, C. A., Cota, M. K., & Ocampo, K. A. (1993). Family socialization and the ethnic identity of Mexican-American children. *Journal of Cross-Cultural Psychology, 24*, 99–114.

Lee, R. M., Grotevant, H. D., Hellerstedt, W. L., Gunnar, M. R., & Minnesota International Adaption Project Team. (2006). Cultural socialization in families with internationally adopted children. *Journal of Family Psychology: JFP: Journal of the Division of Family Psychology of the American Psychological Association (Division 43)*, *20*, 571–580.

Liu, L. L., & Lau, A. S. (2013). Teaching about race/ethnicity and racism matters: An examination of how perceived ethnic racial socialization processes are associated with depression symptoms. *Cultural Diversity and Ethnic Minority Psychology*, *19*, 383.

Maccoby, E. E. (1992). The role of parents in the socialization of children: An historical overview. *Developmental Psychology*, *28*, 1006–1017.

Maccoby, E. E., & Martin, J. A. (1983). Socialization in the context of the family: Parent-child interaction. In P. H. Mussen (Series Ed.) & E. M. Hetherington (Vol. Ed.), *Handbook of child psychology: Vol. 4. Socialization, personality, and social development*. New York: Wiley.

Marshall, S. (1995). Ethnic socialization of African American children: Implications for parenting, identity development, and academic achievement. *Journal of Youth and Adolescence*, *24*, 377–396.

McCay, L. O., & Keyes, D. W. (2001). Developing social competence in the inclusive primary classroom. *Childhood Education*, *78*, 70–78.

McGlothlin, H., & Killen, M. (2006). Intergroup attitudes of European American children attending ethnically homogeneous schools. *Child Development*, *77*, 1375–1386.

McGlothlin, H., & Killen, M. (2010). How social experience is related to children's intergroup attitudes. *European Journal of Social Psychology*, *40*, 625–634.

Murry, V. M., & Brody, G. H. (2002). Racial socialization processes in single-mother families: Linking maternal racial identity, parenting, and racial socialization in rural, single-mother families with child self worth and self-regulation. In H. P. McAdoo (Ed.), *Black children: Social, educational, and parental environments* (pp. 97–115). Thousand Oaks, CA: Sage.

O'Bryan, M., Fishbein, H. D., & Ritchey, P. N. (2004). Intergenerational transmission of prejudice, sex role stereotyping, and intolerance. *Adolescence*, *39*, 407–426.

Pahlke, E., Bigler, R. S., & Suizzo, M. A. (2012). Relations between colorblind socialization and children's racial bias: Evidence from European American mothers and their preschool children. *Child Development*, *83*, 1164–1179.

Parcel, T. L., & Dufur, M. J. (2001). Capital at home and at school: Effects on student achievement. *Social Forces*, *79*, 881–911.

Peters, M. F. (2002). Racial socialization of young Black children. In H. P. McAdoo (Ed.), *Black children: Social, educational, and parental environments* (2nd ed., pp. 57–72). Thousand Oaks, CA: Sage.

Pew Research Center. (2015). *Multiracial in America: Proud, diverse and growing in numbers*. Washington, DC.

Phinney, J. S., & Chavira, V. (1995). Parental ethnic socialization and adolescent coping with problems related to ethnicity. *Journal of Research on Adolescence*, *5*, 31–54.

Phinney, J. S., Horenczyk, G., Liebkind, K., & Vedder, P. (2001). Ethnic identity, immigration, and well-being: An interactional perspective. *Journal of Social Issues*, *57*, 493–510.

Quintana, S. M., & Vera, E. M. (1999). Mexican American children's ethnic identity, understanding of ethnic prejudice, and parental ethnic socialization. *Hispanic Journal of Behavioral Sciences*, *21*, 387–404.

Reynolds, A. J. (1992). Comparing measures of parent involvement and their effects on academic achievement. *Early Childhood Research Quarterly*, *7*, 441–462.

Rodriguez, J., McKay, M. M., & Bannon, W. M. (2008). The role of racial socialization in relation to parenting practices and youth behavior: An exploratory analysis. *Social Work in Mental Health*, *6*, 30–54.

Romero, A. J., Cuéllar, I., & Roberts, R. E. (2000). Ethnocultural variables and attitudes toward cultural socialization of children. *Journal of Community Psychology*, *28*, 79–89.
Rubin, K. H., & Rose-Krasnor, L. (1992). Interpersonal problem solving and social competence in children. In *Handbook of social development* (pp. 283–323). New York: Springer.
Rutland, A., & Killen, M. (2015). A developmental science approach to reducing prejudice and social exclusion: Intergroup processes, social-cognitive development, and moral reasoning. *Social Issues and Policy Review*, *9*, 121–154.
Rutland, A., Killen, M., & Abrams, D. (2010). A new social-cognitive developmental perspective on prejudice the interplay between morality and group identity. *Perspectives on Psychological Science*, *5*, 279–291.
Samuels, G. M. (2009). "Being raised by white people": Navigating racial difference among adopted multiracial adults. *Journal of Marriage and Family*, *71*, 80–94.
Sandholtz, N., Langton, L., & Planty, M. (2013). Hate crime victimization, 2003–2011. *US Department of Justice*.
Schaub, M. (2010). Parenting for cognitive development from 1950 to 2000 the institutionalization of mass education and the social construction of parenting in the United States. *Sociology of Education*, *83*, 46–66.
Schneider, M., & Buckley, J. (2002). What do parents want from schools? Evidence from the Internet. *Educational Evaluation and Policy Analysis*, *24*, 133–144.
Scottham, K. M., & Smalls, C. P. (2009). Unpacking racial socialization: Considering female African American primary caregivers' racial identity. *Journal of Marriage and Family*, *71*, 807–818.
Shaffer, A., Burt, K. B., Obradović, J., Herbers, J. E., & Masten, A. S. (2009). Intergenerational continuity in parenting quality: The mediating role of social competence. *Developmental Psychology*, *45*, 1227.
Sinclair, S., Dunn, E., & Lowery, B. (2005). The relationship between parental racial attitudes and children's implicit prejudice. *Journal of Experimental Social Psychology*, *41*, 283–289.
Stevenson, H. C. (1997). Managing anger: Protective, proactive, or adaptive racial socialization identity profiles and African-American manhood development. *Journal of Prevention and Intervention in the Community*, *16*, 35–61.
Stevenson, H. J., Cameron, R., Herrero-Taylor, T., & Davis, G. Y. (2002). Development of the teenager experience of racial socialization scale: Correlates of race-related socialization frequency from the perspective of Black youth. *The Journal of Black Psychology*, *28*, 84–106.
Tajfel, H., & Turner, J. C. (1986). The social identity theory of inter-group behavior. In S. Worchel & W. Austin (Eds.), *Psychology of intergroup relations* (pp. 7–24). Chicago: Nelson Hall.
Thijs, J., & Verkuyten, M. (2008). Peer victimization and academic achievement in a multiethnic sample: The role of perceived academic self-efficacy. *Journal of Educational Psychology*, *100*, 754.
Thomas, A. J., & Speight, S. L. (1999). Racial identity and racial socialization attitudes of African American parents. *The Journal of Black Psychology*, *25*, 152–170.
Tran, A. G., & Lee, R. M. (2010). Perceived ethnic–racial socialization, ethnic identity, and social competence among Asian American late adolescents. *Cultural Diversity and Ethnic Minority Psychology*, *16*, 169.
Tropp, L. R., & Pettigrew, T. F. (2005). Relationships between intergroup contact and prejudice among minority and majority status groups. *Psychological Science*, *16*, 951–957.
Tropp, L. R., & Prenovost, M. A. (2008). The role of intergroup contact in prediction children's interethnic attitudes: Evidence from meta-analytic and field studies. In S. R. Levy & M. Killen (Eds.), *Intergroup attitudes and relations in childhood through adulthood* (pp. 236–248). Oxford, UK: Oxford University Press.

US Census Bureau. (2012). *U.S. Census Bureau projections show a slower growing, older, more diverse nation a half century from now.* Retrieved from, http://www.census.gov/newsroom/releases/archives/population/cb12-243.html.

US Census Bureau. (2015). *Projections of the size and composition of the U.S. population: 2014 to 2060* (Report No. P25-1143). Retrieved from, https://www.census.gov/library/publications/2015/demo/p25-1143.html.

Umaña-Taylor, A. J., Alfaro, E. C., Bámaca, M. Y., & Guimond, A. B. (2009). The central role of family socialization in Latino adolescents' cultural orientation. *Journal of Marriage and Family, 71*, 46–60.

Umaña-Taylor, A. J., Zeiders, K. H., & Updegraff, K. A. (2013). Family ethnic socialization and ethnic identity: A family-driven, youth-driven, or reciprocal process? *Journal of Family Psychology, 27*, 137–146.

Weisner, T. S. (2002). Ecocultural pathways, family values, and parenting. *Parenting, 2*, 325–334.

White-Johnson, R. L., Ford, K. R., & Sellers, R. M. (2010). Parental racial socialization profiles: Association with demographic factors, racial discrimination, childhood socialization, and racial identity. *Cultural Diversity and Ethnic Minority Psychology, 16*, 237–247.

Wills, T. A., Murry, V. M., Brody, G. H., Gibbons, F. X., Gerrard, M., Walker, C., & Ainette, M. G. (2007). Ethnic pride and self-control related to protective and risk factors: Test of the theoretical model for the strong African American families program. *Health Psychology, 26*, 50.

CHAPTER FOUR

Social Exclusion Based on Group Membership is a Form of Prejudice

Shelby Cooley*, Laura Elenbaas[†], Melanie Killen[†,1]
*Community Center for Education Results, Seattle, WA, United States
[†]University of Maryland, College Park, MD, United States
[1]Corresponding author: e-mail address: mkillen@umd.edu

Contents

Abstract

Children around the world are affected by bias, prejudice, and discrimination. In this chapter, we argue that intergroup social exclusion—exclusion of peers on the basis of group membership—is a form of prejudice. As such, research efforts should be directed at uncovering the negative intergroup attitudes that sustain these behaviors,

Equity and Justice in Developmental Science: Implications for Young People, Families, and Communities (S.S. Horn, M.D. Ruck & L.S. Liben, Eds.)
Advances in Child Development and Behavior (J.B. Benson, Series Ed.), Vol. 51
ISSN 0065-2407 http://dx.doi.org/10.1016/bs.acdb.2016.04.004

and encouraging the development of children's capacity to resist biases in favor of inclusion and just treatment of others. In order to interpret what is known about intergroup social exclusion in childhood, as well as identify compelling issues for current investigation, we introduce our integrative social reasoning developmental model, which emphasizes how children weigh moral and social concerns in everyday peer contexts. This chapter emphasizes three areas of research that have contributed to understanding social inclusion and exclusion decisions in childhood which include the roles of: (1) intergroup contact and friendship, (2) peer group norms, and (3) messages from parents and teachers. While providing a background on the state of research to date, this chapter also pinpoints recent work, shedding new light on the complex interplay of moral reasoning and intergroup attitudes in children's inclusion and exclusion decisions.

1. INTERGROUP SOCIAL EXCLUSION AS A FORM OF PREJUDICE

Children around the world are affected by bias, prejudice, and discrimination (Killen, Rutland, & Ruck, 2011). National and international policies on child well-being focus on promoting the rights of all children regardless of religion, nationality, race, gender, sexual orientation, or (dis)ability. Unfortunately, exclusion on the basis of group memberships like these is a common experience in children's social lives (Killen & Rutland, 2011). While many laws have changed to promote freedom from prejudicial attitudes and behaviors, the psychological attitudes that reflect discriminatory and biased viewpoints are still ubiquitous in our society (Verkuyten, 2011). In fact, social exclusion in childhood and adolescence is not limited to issues of large-scale inequalities in access to resources and opportunities for certain social groups. Many children regularly face exclusion from peer groups in everyday life due to stereotypes, biases, and prejudice that children themselves hold, and perpetuate, in their peer world. Thus, understanding the origins of these attitudes is essential for promoting change.

This is important because children who are excluded by peers due to their social group membership are at risk for negative psychological outcomes. For example, children and adolescents who are the targets of prejudice and discrimination, including exclusion, report elevated rates of anxiety, depression, and substance abuse, as well as decreased academic motivation (Douglass, Yip, & Shelton, 2014; Neblett, White, Philip, Nguyên, & Sellers, 2008; Seaton, Yip, Morgan-Lopez, & Sellers, 2012). Though most research has focused on the detrimental impact of exclusion on children who are the targets of prejudicial attitudes, in fact, children who reject friendships with others because of their own biases and stereotypes also face negative consequences. Positive participation in diverse social groups has both individual and societal benefits, as it promotes academic success and productive work experiences in adulthood (Rubin, Bukowski, & Parker, 2006; Tatum, 2003; Wilson & Rodkin, 2011).

Social exclusion is harmful, both for children who are excluded and for children who perpetuate stereotypes and biases through daily interactions. In this chapter, we argue that intergroup social exclusion—or social exclusion on the basis of group membership—is a form of prejudice. As such, research efforts should be directed at uncovering the negative intergroup attitudes that sustain these behaviors, as well as highlighting children's capacity to resist biases in favor of inclusion and fair treatment of others (Abrams & Killen, 2014; Rutland & Killen, 2015). Children are both the victims and the perpetrators of social exclusion. Yet they are also moral agents with developing abilities to reason about equity, justice, and inclusion, and developing capacities to act on their convictions.

From early childhood through adolescence, children must navigate a social world with conflicting messages about inclusion and exclusion. They hear disparate messages from peers, parents, teachers, and the media on a daily basis, while also forming their own conceptions of group identity, group membership, and friendship based on personal interactions (Killen, Elenbaas, & Rutland, 2015; Killen, Mulvey, & Hitti, 2015; Rutland, Killen, & Abrams, 2010). In fact, children's capacity to weigh positive messages about equality against negative messages about status and group-specific stereotypes is the focus of our ongoing research in this area.

In this chapter, we will outline our perspective on intergroup social exclusion as a form of prejudice, highlighting closely related work on the detrimental impact of discrimination on child development. Because our empirical research program examining intergroup social exclusion also spotlights children's capacity to *include*, we will introduce the integrative theoretical model that has guided our work in this area, bridging research on children's social development and moral development. Many aspects of social life revolve around determining who will be included or excluded in various personal, group, community, and institutional contexts. This model provides a framework for interpreting what is known in this area thus far, and for identifying the most robust constructs and necessary considerations for investigation regarding children's everyday decisions about inclusion and exclusion.

In particular, we will emphasize three areas of research that have made major contributions to understanding social inclusion and exclusion decisions in childhood and adolescence. We aim to present a broad and balanced perspective on the role of intergroup contact and friendships, the role of peer group norms, and the role of parents and teachers in contributing to inclusion and exclusion in childhood. While providing a background on the state of research to date, each of these three sections will also pinpoint very recent research in this area. These studies, emphasized later, shed new light on pressing issues of inclusion and exclusion, and complex interplay of moral reasoning and intergroup attitudes in children's decisions.

1.1 Recognizing Intergroup Social Exclusion in Childhood

As previously mentioned, many children regularly face exclusion from social and peer groups because of stereotypes, biases, and prejudice. Yet, most of the research on peer relations and exclusion in childhood has focused on instances where children are rejected because of individual personality traits like extreme shyness or aggressiveness. These two research foci, the former on *intergroup social exclusion* (the topic of this chapter) and the latter on *interpersonal peer rejection*, represent different views on exclusion in childhood.

Recently, Killen, Mulvey, and Hitti (2013) outlined the key differences between these two views. Developmental research on interpersonal rejection has documented how patterns of victimization and bullying behavior reflect individual differences in children's temperament, attachment, confidence, and social-cognitive skills like intention attribution (Dodge et al., 2003; Gunnar, Sebanc, Tout, Donzella, & van Dulmen, 2003; Ladd, 2006; Masten et al., 2009). For example, children who are extremely shy, fearful, and wary are more vulnerable to victimization, whereas children who are highly externalizing are at risk for becoming bullies (Hodges, Boivin, Vitaro, & Bukowski, 1999; Olweus, 1993; Rubin et al., 2006). Intergroup social exclusion, by contrast, refers to instances when children are excluded by peers based on their group membership. That is, social exclusion is a form of prejudice and discrimination whereby children face rejection because of their gender, ethnicity, sexual orientation, or another type of group membership (Horn & Sinno, 2014).

Accordingly, research on intergroup social exclusion has investigated social processes like group identity, ingroup bias, outgroup threat, and stereotypes, rather than individual differences in personality or traits that make certain children more vulnerable to exclusion. In fact, whereas developmental outcomes for interpersonally rejected children are improved by interventions targeting children's social skills, competence, and resilience (Bierman, 2004; Rubin et al., 2006), intervention programs addressing intergroup social exclusion aim to increase awareness for all children by reducing systemic prejudice and bias (Rutland & Killen, 2015).

Importantly, with age, children and adolescents make this differentiation between interpersonal rejection and intergroup social exclusion when judging the legitimacy of these distinct exclusion contexts. That is, children from multiple cultures and countries (for a review, see Helwig, Ruck, & Peterson-Badali, 2014) reason that intergroup exclusion (based on social groups like gender, nationality, and culture) is unfair, and interpret interpersonal rejection (on the basis of traits such as shyness) either as a conventional issue pertinent to the functioning of the group or in terms of individual choice and autonomy.

1.1.1 Prevalence of Social Exclusion in Development

In many cases, however, intergroup social exclusion is covert or subtle, and decisions regarding whom to include or exclude from a group invoke complex issues at the intersection of fairness, group identity and dynamics, and individual prerogatives. In intergroup contexts, biases can often influence one's decison-making, resulting in the exclusion of children who do not match the group on a dimension like religion, race, or gender.

Exclusive intergroup attitudes, including stereotypes and prejudice, have been examined extensively in adult populations for more than 50 years (Dovidio, Glick, & Rudman, 2005; Dovidio, Hewstone, Glick, & Estes, 2010). Yet biases, and exclusion resulting from biases, emerge in childhood and develop in adolescence. In fact, stereotypes and assumptions about groups are reflected in children's peer interactions from as early as the preschool years (Bigler & Liben, 2006; Rutland et al., 2010).

Intergroup social exclusion has been widely documented in countries around the world and is disproportionally experienced by children and adolescents from cultural minority groups as well as by girls and nonheterosexual youth (Møller & Tenenbaum, 2011; Nesdale, 2004; Verkuyten, 2008). Likewise experiences of social exclusion occur from early childhood through adolescence. For instance, even preschoolers have been found to use gender stereotypes about activity preferences to determine whether a boy or a girl should be allowed to join a play group (Killen, Pisacane, Lee-Kim, & Ardila-Rey, 2001; Theimer, Killen, & Stangor, 2001).

1.2 Consequences of Intergroup Social Exclusion in Childhood

Thus, intergroup biases that promote exclusion emerge early in development, in most societies around the world, and often persist across childhood and adolescence. As a result, many children—both excluded and excluders—miss opportunities for positive development through friendships and interaction with others from diverse backgrounds. Most research on the impact of intergroup social exclusion has focused on the detrimental outcomes of discrimination, including exclusion, for children who are members of stigmatized groups. This research highlights both the prevalence and impact of social exclusion as a form of prejudice.

Because participation in peer groups and friendships is an important part of social life, prolonged experiences of exclusion can be very harmful for children's well-being. Children who are the targets of persistent exclusion and prejudicial attitudes are at risk for elevated experiences of anxiety, depression, and substance abuse, as well as decreased academic motivation (Douglass et al., 2014; Neblett et al., 2008; Seaton et al., 2012). For example, in the United States, Asian-American and Latino adolescents report being the target of more instances of discrimination and exclusion than do European-American adolescents (Huynh & Fuligni, 2010). Likewise, higher rates of reported discrimination among these groups are associated with lower grade point averages and self-esteem, as well as higher depressive symptomology, distress, and physical complaints (Huynh & Fuligni, 2010). As another example, Latino and African-American adolescents attending majority European-American schools report more exclusion and social stress than peers from the same racial or ethnic background attending diverse schools, indicating that children from minority racial or ethnic groups are at increased risk for exclusion in more homogeneous social environments (Graham, Bellmore, Nishina, & Juvonen, 2009). Further, females are under-represented in academic, professional, and political positions (Horn & Sinno, 2014).

Thus, many of the detrimental impacts of social exclusion on development have been clearly identified; prolonged experiences of exclusion harm children psychologically and physically. Positive intergroup social experiences, by contrast, promote academic success and productive work experiences in adulthood (Buhs & Ladd, 2001; Coie, Terry, Lenox, & Lochman, 1995; DeRosier, Kupersmidt, & Patterson, 1994; Orfield & Lee, 2005; Prinstein & Aikins, 2004).

1.3 Combating Exclusion Through Consideration of Fairness

Because of the prevalence, early emergence, and persistence of intergroup biases throughout development, it is imperative for research to address children's perspectives on intergroup social exclusion in order to understand why, and under what circumstances, children and adolescents exclude peers on the basis of group membership. Until children are able to develop meaningful relationships with others from different backgrounds, detect and discourage exclusive attitudes in their peers, and understand what makes intergroup social exclusion wrong, progress toward true equity in development will be limited (Ruck & Tenenbaum, 2014; Tatum, 2003; Wilson & Rodkin, 2011).

Fortunately, as members of social groups, children often seek a balance between social and group concerns and moral concerns regarding the just treatment of others. That is, children do not always hold stereotypes, enforce exclusive norms, or reject peers on the basis of biases or prejudice. In fact, there are times when children strongly favor of inclusion and equality (Killen, Elenbaas, et al., 2015; Smetana, Jambon, & Ball, 2014). This is because, at the same time that biases and prejudice are emerging and developing, children are also developing their moral concerns for the well-being of others.

In fact, one of the significant developmental processes that enables children to be inclusive, rather than exclusive, is the emergence of conceptions of fairness, justice, and rights (Killen & Smetana, 2015). Alongside research on the early origins of exclusion and discrimination, our work has demonstrated how children balance moral concerns about fairness and others' welfare with social concerns about benefitting their social ingroup or adhering to stereotypic assumptions.

In the following section we will outline the integrative theoretical model that has guided our work in this area, bridging research on children's social development and moral development. Later in this chapter, we will use this theoretical model to review not only how children perpetuate exclusion and discrimination, but also how they reason about fairness and other's welfare, accenting research that reveals children's concerns for equity and justice, and identifying when and why children challenge exclusive attitudes and advocate for intergroup inclusion.

2. SOCIAL REASONING DEVELOPMENTAL MODEL FOR UNDERSTANDING INTERGROUP SOCIAL EXCLUSION IN CHILDHOOD

We have applied our theoretical model, called the social reasoning developmental (SRD) model, to investigate children's judgments, decisions, and reasoning regarding intergroup social exclusion. This research, to date, has demonstrated that, when children make decisions about inclusion and exclusion in intergroup social contexts, they reason about multiple moral and social group considerations, weighing their concerns for fairness with their developing knowledge about group identity and how groups function. The SRD model integrates the social domain theory perspective on moral development (Smetana et al., 2014; Turiel, 2006) with developmental social identity theories (Nesdale, 2004; Verkuyten, 2007) and theories of group dynamics in childhood (Abrams & Rutland, 2008). We will briefly review each of these theories later, in order to provide a background for interpreting the research findings that follow.

2.1 Developmental Social Identity Theories

Research in social psychology from the perspective of social identity theory (Tajfel & Turner, 1979) has long held that individuals are motivated to view their ingroup (i.e., members of the social groups that they belong to) favorably and that this can lead to biases against or dislike of members of relevant outgroups. Children also exhibit preference for ingroup members, seek to present a positive image of themselves to their ingroup (Rutland, Cameron, Milne, & McGeorge, 2005), and sometimes bolster their sense of group identity by excluding outgroup others (Nesdale, 2004; Verkuyten & Steenhuis, 2005).

Preference for one's ingroup, however, does not always lead to dislike for outgroups. Whether or not children exhibit biases against members of outgroups varies as a function of how strongly they identify with their ingroup, whether or not they feel that their ingroup is being threatened, and their perceptions of group norms and expectations around prejudicial treatment of outgroup members (Nesdale, Griffiths, Durkin, & Maass, 2007; Nesdale, Maass, Durkin, & Griffiths, 2005; Rutland, Cameron, Milne, et al., 2005).

2.2 Developmental Subjective Group Dynamics

Group norms have also been a focus of research in developmental subjective group dynamics (Abrams & Rutland, 2008). Research in this area has demonstrated that, with age, children begin to define group membership and identity in terms of a set of shared norms, traditions, and histories, in addition to external, observable characteristics (e.g., skin color for race, hair length for gender) (Abrams, Rutland, Cameron, & Marques, 2003; Abrams, Rutland, Pelletier, & Ferrell, 2009). With age, children expect individuals to endorse these shared norms in order to ensure the smooth functioning of the group, and in order to sustain their group membership (Abrams, Rutland, Ferrell, & Pelletier, 2008), as nonadherence to a group norm can be considered grounds for exclusion (Mulvey & Killen, 2015).

2.3 Social Domain Theory

Research in developmental psychology from the perspective of social domain theory (Nucci, 1981; Turiel, 1983) has provided evidence that, when reasoning about social contexts, events, and interactions, children consider three central domains of knowledge: moral, societal, and personal (Smetana et al., 2014). The moral domain pertains to issues of fairness, justice, and rights. The societal domain pertains to issues of norms, conventions, and expectations. The personal domain pertains to issues of individual prerogative, choice, or preference. These forms of knowledge are central to social life and are reflected in the reasoning of adults and children considering both straightforward and complex inclusion and exclusion decisions.

When determining how to judge an instance of intergroup social exclusion, or how to proceed when an inclusion decision is needed, children must weigh moral concerns about fairness with societal concerns about norms and expectations as well as personal prerogatives. Children care deeply about acceptance, respect, equality, and fairness, and there are many instances in which they advocate for these principles rather than adhering to stereotypic assumptions about group membership. In the following sections, we will return to these three theories, and their integrated application in the SRD model, in order to interpret recent research revealing the implications of social and moral concerns when children make decisions about inclusion and exclusion in intergroup contexts.

3. CONTRIBUTORS TO INCLUSION AND EXCLUSION DECISIONS: ROLE OF INTERGROUP CONTACT AND FRIENDSHIPS

As mentioned earlier, research in the area of developmental social identity has revealed that children hold ingroup biases (i.e., are motivated to view their ingroup in a positive light), and conversely, dislike of relevant outgroups can result in intergroup social exclusion (Nesdale, 2004; Verkuyten & Steenhuis, 2005). Considerable research in developmental science has focused on the social and contextual variables that support children of all ages in developing positive intergroup attitudes, including inclusive and tolerant attitudes toward outgroup members. One important social contextual variable is intergroup contact. In addition to reducing prejudice overall (Tropp & Prenovost, 2008), greater opportunities for contact with members of a relevant social outgroup can lead to more proactive attitudes about inclusion for both majority and minority status children and adolescents.

3.1 School Diversity

For instance, school racial and ethnic diversity is a strong predictor of positive learning outcomes, heightened civic engagement, and preparation of students for a diverse workforce (Orfield & Lee, 2005). This is because diversity provides opportunities for intergroup contact and the establishment of friendships across group boundaries (Bellmore, Nishina, Witkow, Graham, & Juvonen, 2007; Shelton, Douglass, Garcia, Yip, & Trail, 2014; Wilson & Rodkin, 2011). For example, racial and ethnic minority students feel safer, less harassed, and less lonely, and report higher self-worth the more racial and ethnic diversity they experience in their classrooms (Juvonen, Nishina, & Graham, 2006). Moreover, children and adolescents reporting intergroup contact in the form of cross-race friendships view interracial peer exclusion as more wrong than do children and adolescents with very low reported contact (Crystal, Killen, & Ruck, 2008). Thus, positive and cooperative interaction with members of other social groups improves not only immediate interpersonal relations but prepares children for diverse workplaces and adult social spaces.

Environmental diversity has an impact on children's inclusive attitudes from very early in development. For example, among 3–5-year-old Anglo-British children, greater intergroup contact with African Caribbean-British, East Asian-British, and Indian-British peers is associated with reduced rates of stereotypes about these outgroups (Rutland, Cameron, Bennett, & Ferrell, 2005). In fact, both racial minority and majority children report more inclusive attitudes in diverse schools. For example, two recent studies found that, whereas younger European-American children in racially homogeneous schools demonstrated implicit negative assumptions about the possibility of friendship between racial majority and minority peers, children at the same age, in the same school district, enrolled in racially diverse schools, held much more positive expectations for intergroup friendship

(McGlothlin & Killen, 2006). Likewise, racial minority adolescents who report greater contact with outgroup peers are more likely than their peers reporting little intergroup contact to rate intergroup exclusion as more wrong and to assert that they would intervene if they witnessed exclusion (Ruck, Park, Killen, & Crystal, 2011).

Thus, frequent positive contact with peers of different racial, religious, or socioeconomic backgrounds can improve intergroup relations for children from diverse backgrounds. Intergroup contact can set the stage for reducing stereotypes and biases, leading to more inclusive attitudes. One key mechanism whereby diversity improves intergroup attitudes is by providing opportunities for friendships across group boundaries, as outlined in the next section.

3.2 Intergroup Friendships

Forming friendships that cross-group boundaries (i.e., cross-group friendships) can be difficult for children, who often worry about being perceived negatively or being rejected by unfamiliar outgroup peers (Shelton, Richeson, & Bergsieker, 2009). For example, a recent study by Hitti and Killen (2015) revealed that non-Arab-American 12 and 16 year olds assumed that a group of Arab-American peers would prefer to befriend another Arab-American peer (choosing their friends on the basis of ethnic match) instead of a non-Arab American peer when making inclusion decisions. In contrast, they expected that their own group (non-Arab-Americans) to be inclusive, choosing new friends based on a match of hobbies and activity preferences and ignoring ethnicity. These findings demonstrate how negative assumptions about social groups perpetuate exclusive attitudes and behaviors.

Thus, one important reason why diversity promotes more inclusive attitudes is that it provides children with the chance to engage in close friendships with peers of other backgrounds. In fact, considerable evidence indicates that cross-group friendships are a significant predictor of children's intergroup attitudes, including attitudes about inclusion and exclusion (see chapter "Children's Intergroup Relationships and Attitudes" by Bigler et al., this volume; Davies, Tropp, Aron, Pettigrew, & Wright, 2011). As one example, among 7–11-year-old ethnically German children attending diverse schools, children who reported more cross-ethnic friendships with Turkish peers also held more positive attitudes about members of this ethnic group (Feddes, Noack, & Rutland, 2009). Beyond mere acquaintance, however, friendship quality also predicts attitudes about inclusion. For example, one study found that 6–12-year-old African-American and European-American children from racially diverse schools who reported closer cross-group friendships (friendships involving a high level of intimacy, emotional security, and loyalty) also reported more positive attitudes toward peers of other races than did children of the same age who reported more casual cross-race friendships or few cross-race friendships (Aboud, Mendelson, & Purdy, 2003).

Interestingly, under certain conditions, mere *awareness* of a positive friendship between an ingroup member and an outgroup member (i.e., "extended" intergroup contact) is also effective at improving intergroup attitudes among children who do not have the opportunity to engage in personal friendships with outgroup members (Cameron, Rutland, Hossain, & Petley, 2011). Research on extended contact (through peer networks or book reading) has examined inclusive and exclusive attitudes toward stigmatized groups including disabled individuals (Cameron & Rutland, 2006) and refugees (Cameron, Rutland, Brown, & Douch, 2006), and highlights how, when direct contact is difficult, just hearing about others who endorse positive norms of friendship can still help elementary-aged children reject stereotypes and biases in favor of inclusion.

3.3 Inclusive Policies

In addition to providing opportunities for friendship with peers of other social groups, school policies regarding diversity and tolerance play an important role in children's judgments about exclusion. Extensive research in the area of intergroup contact, as well as developmental social identity and subjective group dynamics, has revealed that certain conditions increase the likelihood that contact will yield positive results. Specifically, bringing groups together as equal in status, in noncompetitive situations endorsed by individuals in positions of authority, with the aim of attaining joint goals increases the likelihood that intergroup contact will result in a reduction in prejudice (Aboud et al., 2003; Allport, 1954; Dovidio et al., 2005; Pettigrew & Tropp, 2006).

Along these lines, policies at the school level can promote inclusion in development. For example, adolescents attending schools with safe school practices regarding sexual orientation (e.g., policies, professional development) evaluate exclusion on the basis of sexual orientation as more wrong, and use more moral reasoning in justifying their judgments, than adolescents attending schools without such practices (Horn & Szalach, 2009). Thus, policies of diversity and inclusion can have a positive impact on children's intergroup attitudes by establishing norms about inclusion on an institutional level (Russell, Kosciw, Horn, & Saewyc, 2010).

In short, adults and children alike can promote consideration of equity, justice, and inclusion by facilitating intergroup contact, cross-group friendships, and explicit support for diversity of perspectives. Beyond simply bringing groups together, opportunities for close friendships across group boundaries and broader policies of tolerance can have positive and wide-ranging effects for reducing stereotypes and promoting equality in development.

4. CONTRIBUTORS TO INCLUSION AND EXCLUSION DECISIONS: ROLE OF PEER GROUP NORMS

In addition to the norms and expectations set at the neighborhood, school, or local level by policies of diversity and inclusion, peer group norms have a significant impact on children's intergroup attitudes, including attitudes about inclusion and exclusion. As mentioned earlier, research in developmental subjective group dynamics has revealed that, with age, children expect individuals to endorse the norms shared by their group (Abrams & Rutland, 2008; Abrams et al., 2008). In regard to social exclusion in particular, children are more likely to demonstrate exclusive attitudes toward outgroup members if they believe that such actions are condoned by their peer ingroup (Nesdale et al., 2005; Rutland, Cameron, Milne, et al., 2005).

4.1 Adherence to Stereotypic Norms

Interestingly (and troublingly), shared norms and expectations can also reflect stereotypes about the preferences or traits of certain social groups. Nesdale and his colleagues have conducted a series of studies on the role of school and group norms on intergroup attitudes (Nesdale & Lawson, 2011; Nesdale, Zimmer-Gembeck, & Roxburgh, 2014). Their findings reveal how norms that condone or reject forms of intergroup bullying have an impact on children's attitudes. For example, older children often expect negative outcomes for those who deviate from gender norms about appropriate activities for males and females. One recent study by Mulvey and Killen (2015) revealed that older children and early adolescents personally supported individuals' decisions to challenge groups' gender stereotypic activity preferences by suggesting that the group try a nonstereotypic activity (e.g., a girl in an all-girls group that always does ballet suggests that the group play football instead). However, they expected that individuals who advocated for such changes, especially boys who expressed interest in gender nonstereotypic activities (e.g., ballet), would not be well received by their groups and would likely be excluded.

Likewise, older adolescents evaluate the exclusion of peers due to sexual orientation as more acceptable than other forms of discrimination such as teasing, harassing, or assaulting a gay or lesbian peer, and are more likely to refer to social norms and personal choice in regards to exclusion of a sexual minority peer (Heinze & Horn, 2009; Horn, 2006). Thus, exclusion of an individual because of nonconformity to group or social norms is often perceived as legitimate, particularly among older children and adolescents.

These findings reveal the detrimental impact of stereotypic and exclusive norms on children's decisions about inclusion and exclusion in intergroup contexts. Yet, closely related work, outlined in the following sections, also reveals many instances in which children attempt to subvert, or even take direct action against, restrictive and exclusive customs and assumptions. As outlined in the SRD perspective, children often seek a balance between adhering to group traditions and ensuring that others are treated fairly, emphasizing the frequent intersection of moral and social concerns in everyday life.

4.2 Distinguishing Group and Individual Perspectives

Children are aware of the relevance of peer group norms for inclusion and exclusion decisions from an early age. Yet, at the same time, they recognize that the way that groups work is not always supportive of justice and equality. For instance, a study by Cooley and Killen (2015) revealed that young children personally supported a deviant group member who stood up for equality, while at the same time recognizing that their group might not support this individual. This study was the first one to demonstrate "group nous" in early childhood, which is the ability to understand that what the individual believes is right may be different from the group's perspective.

This same pattern of differential evaluations has also been found in older children's expectations about an after-school club's opinion of an individual who advocated for equal allocation of money between clubs when the usual approach was to seek more for the ingroup (Killen, Rutland, Abrams, Mulvey, & Hitti, 2013; Mulvey, Hitti, Rutland, Abrams, & Killen, 2014). These findings highlight children's developing concerns for fairness, as well as their attempts to assert their own views on equal treatment in situations where bias is the norm. Concurrently, as mentioned earlier, children are increasingly aware that changing group customs is not easy to do, and deviating or dissenting from prevailing norms carries the risk of personal exclusion from the ingroup. Thus, in middle childhood and adolescence in particular, children begin to connect everyday experiences of exclusion from groups with larger, systemic inequalities in their social environment.

4.3 Impact of Group Status

Along these same lines, several studies have shown that children who are members of groups ranked lower on status hierarchies are more likely to view social exclusion as unacceptable relative to their higher status peers. For example, several studies have revealed that older racial minority children and adolescents are less likely than their racial majority counterparts to view socially excluding a peer as acceptable, particularly in situations like cross-race dating (Killen, Henning, Kelly, Crystal, & Ruck, 2007). Further, in later childhood, girls in many countries around the world have been found to be less accepting of exclusion of any kind than boys (Killen, Lee-Kim, McGlothlin, Stangor, & Helwig, 2002; Park & Killen, 2010). These findings suggest that membership in a traditionally excluded group (e.g., by race or gender) can lead children to more negatively evaluate exclusion experienced by others.

Likewise, when evaluating instances of interethnic exclusion, early adolescents from ethnic minority backgrounds (both in the United States and other countries) have been found to attribute more positive emotions (e.g., pride) to ethnic outgroup members who exclude an ethnic minority individual from a group than do early adolescents from ethnic majority backgrounds (Killen & Malti, 2015; Malti, Killen, & Gasser, 2012). Thus, children whose social groups are the targets of habitual exclusion not only evaluate such behavior more negatively than their same-aged peers from majority group backgrounds, but they also assume that the excluding group feels proud of their biased actions.

A recent study by Cooley and Killen (2016) suggests that these assumptions may not be entirely unfounded. As shown in Fig. 1, European-American 13–14 year olds in this study expected that peers of their racial group would be less likely to include an African-American peer than another European-American peer in everyday opportunities for inclusion (e.g., sitting together on the bus), unlike 8–9 year olds who did not differ in their expectations for inclusion by race of the target (see Fig. 1). Underscoring the points made earlier regarding misperceptions of exclusivity, these findings suggest that minority group children often perceive hostile attitudes toward inclusion from majority groups (i.e., believe that majority groups feel good about excluding outgroup members). These attitudes further underscore the cycle of intergroup misunderstanding and cynicism about inclusion that begins in childhood and adolescence.

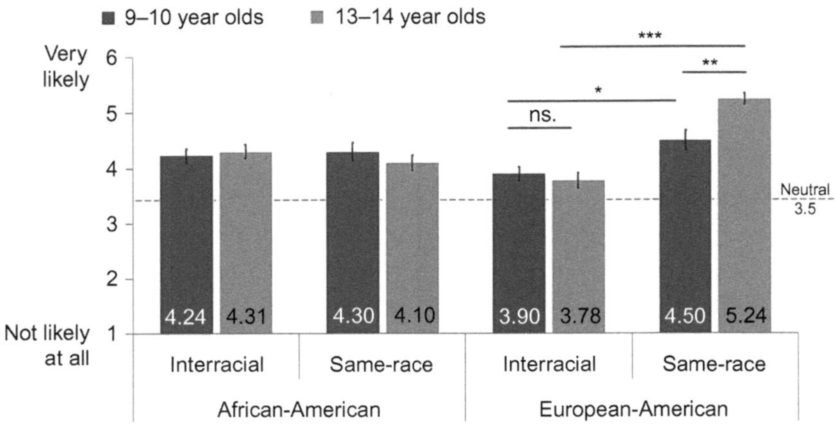

Fig. 1 Likelihood of peer inclusion in interracial and same-race situations by participant race and age (Cooley & Killen, 2016). Higher scores indicate greater likelihood of inclusion. Error bars represent standard errors of the mean. *Horizontal line* indicates scale midpoint (representing neither likely or unlikely).

4.4 Group Status and Social Inequalities

Further, recent research has examined whether children's awareness of group's status is related to their perspectives on resource allocation. The denial of resources based on group membership (such as race, gender, and culture) is a form of social exclusion. Elenbaas, Rizzo, Cooley, and Killen (2015) investigated whether children would rectify an inequality of resources between racial groups. Younger children (African-American and European-American) demonstrated a form of ingroup bias by selectively correcting an inequality that placed their own racial group at a disadvantage (that is, allocating more resources to their ingroup when their ingroup had been shown to have fewer resources than an outgroup). Conversely, younger children demonstrated more mixed responses toward correcting an inequality when their outgroup was disadvantaged (Elenbaas et al., 2015). With age, children were able to take into consideration immediate inequalities (correcting a disparity of resources between two groups) and also broader societal inequalities. Older children demonstrated awareness of which racial groups (in this case, African-American groups) were more often the targets of discrimination and differential access to resources on a broader societal level (Elenbaas & Killen, in press). Related work by Olson and colleagues has also revealed that older children are able to reject an unequal status quo in favor of rectifying resource inequalities between African-

American and European-American peers, particularly when inequality reflects recognizable societal disparities (Olson, Dweck, Spelke, & Banaji, 2011). These findings indicate that children are aware of social inequalities early, and in certain conditions take corrective action to promote equal access to resources.

The SRD model, then, emphasizes how, from early childhood through adolescence, children must navigate a social world with conflicting messages about inclusion and exclusion, weighing potentially conflicting messages from peers, parents, teachers, and the media, while forming their own conceptions of group identity and fairness based on personal interactions. In the next section, we outline relevant research on the unique roles that adults play in the development of inclusion and exclusion decisions in childhood and focus on recent work examining children's decisions in light of conflicting messages from adult and peer sources.

5. CONTRIBUTORS TO INCLUSION AND EXCLUSION DECISIONS: ROLE OF TEACHERS AND PARENTS

As introduced in Section 3, environmental diversity is more likely to result in positive attitudes about inclusion if increased contact is endorsed by individuals in positions of authority (Pettigrew & Tropp, 2006). On the other hand, research has also demonstrated that adults (including parents and teachers) play a role in the onset and development of prejudice, bias, and exclusive attitudes (Nesdale et al., 2005; Pahlke, Bigler, & Suizzo, 2012; Seaton et al., 2012). Teachers, for example, can unknowingly hold stereotypic beliefs about academic abilities based on race (Steele, 1997), and parents can show differential or preferential treatment based on gender, such as by granting more autonomy to sons than to daughters (Killen, Park, Lee-Kim, & Shin, 2005).

Equally as important as parents' and teachers' aims in discussing groups and intergroup relations with children are children's own interpretations of these messages, and the impact that this reciprocal process has on inclusion and exclusion decisions at the level of the peer group. Research from the SRD perspective, as well as related work drawing on social identity and socialization perspectives more broadly, has begun to address the roles that parents and teachers can play, both directly and indirectly, in the facilitation of inclusive intergroup attitudes in childhood and adolescence.

5.1 Teachers

Teachers occupy an important and unique position in children's lives. With regard to intergroup relations, they are often the adults charged with implementing any school diversity initiatives at the level of the classroom. More broadly, teachers make many vital decisions regarding how to structure a considerable number of children's daily activities. They also transmit both covert and explicit messages about the importance of inclusion.

For example, one study of Dutch, Turkish, Moroccan, and Surinamese 10–13 year olds living in The Netherlands found that ethnic minority children reported experiencing fewer instances of name-calling, teasing, and exclusion when they believed they could tell their teacher about unfair behavior toward them and their teacher would take action (Verkuyten & Thijs, 2002). Other studies have also shown that Dutch and Turkish children who report higher levels of multicultural education in the classroom (e.g., discussions regarding the need to be fair to others and recognize different cultures within the classroom) demonstrate more positive intergroup attitudes than their peers who report few discussions along these lines (Kinket & Verkuyten, 1999). Thus, teachers' commitment to addressing issues of intergroup exclusion, as well as engagement in explicit discussions about the importance of inclusion, has a direct positive impact on their students' intergroup attitudes and well-being.

Interestingly, some research shows that children are critical of teachers who do demonstrate intergroup biases or advocate for intergroup exclusion. For instance, one study investigated 8–12-year-old Danish children's reasoning about peer and teacher statements about excluding Muslim peers (e.g., Shahar wants to play Ludo, but the teacher says that she cannot play because there are already three Danish boys and girls playing. Instead, the teacher says that a Danish classmate can play). Children found it less acceptable for a teacher to endorse exclusion than for a peer to endorse exclusion and were critical of teachers who allowed exclusion of Muslim children from peer groups (Møller & Tenenbaum, 2011).

5.2 Parents

Parental discourse about intergroup relations can also contribute to the acquisition of prejudicial attitudes as well as concerns for fairness and inclusion between groups. Research on parental racial and ethnic socialization, for example, has revealed that parents of racial and ethnic minority children are faced with the challenge of discussing inclusion and equality while at the same time preparing their children for a social world where they may face biases, discrimination, and exclusion (Hughes, 2003; Neblett et al., 2008;

see chapter "A Transactional/Ecological Perspective on Ethnic–Racial Identity, Socialization, and Discrimination" by Hughes et al., this volume).

Considerable research has revealed that, by preparing their children for potential exclusion, parents can promote resilience and adaptive strategies than enable their children to thrive and combat the detrimental effects on discrimination psychological health and well-being (Harris-Britt, Valrie, Kurtz-Costes, & Rowley, 2007; Neblett, Terzian, & Harriott, 2010; Sellers, Caldwell, Schmeelk-Cone, & Zimmerman, 2003). Likewise positive messages about cultural pride and knowledge have been shown to be positively related to self-esteem and identity development among racial and ethnic minority adolescents (White-Johnson, Ford, & Sellers, 2010). As another example, African-American adolescents who report hearing more egalitarian messages from their parents (e.g., all people are equal regardless of their race) also report more positive group identity and more positive psychological adjustment on a range of measures (Neblett et al., 2008).

Racial and ethnic minority children are able to integrate these messages from parents with their own experiences in peer groups, drawing progressively stronger connections between their own daily experiences and overarching societal biases with age. When evaluating the exclusion of an African-American child from a group of European-American peers, for example, African-American children and adolescents have been found to reason about the wrongfulness of this action in the larger context of society by elaborating on the negative consequences of discrimination (Killen et al., 2002; Killen & Stangor, 2001).

By contrast, racial and ethnic majority (e.g., European-American) parents often adopt a colorblind approach to discussing intergroup relations with their children, perhaps because of worries that discussing discrimination, or even pointing out differences, may create biases where there were none before (Pahlke et al., 2012). This is not the case, however. Awareness of and alertness to the possibility of prejudice helps younger children overcome intergroup biases (Pahlke et al., 2012), helps older children detect instances of discrimination in everyday peer interactions (Apfelbaum, Pauker, Ambady, Sommers, & Norton, 2008), and helps adolescents recognize the importance of social policies promoting inclusion for underrepresented groups (Hughes & Bigler, 2011).

5.3 Weighing Adult and Peer Messages

Further, children may weigh peer and parental attitudes regarding inclusion and exclusion differently with age, as they focus increasingly on loyalty to peer groups in later childhood (Abrams & Rutland, 2008), and seek increased autonomy from parents in adolescence (Daddis, 2011; Smetana, 2011). With age, children often face challenges in weighing larger school- and neighborhood-wide norms against unique peer group norms. Peer group attitudes, for example, can come into conflict with overarching institutional policies, such as when a school is racially diverse and teachers promote equality, but cross-group friendships are not valued by certain segments of the student population.

For example, a recent study by McGuire, Rutland, and Nesdale (2015) assessed 5–11 year olds decisions about inclusion of outgroup peers in a context of conflicting norms put forth by their school and their peer group. In this study, children were participants in a drawing competition; the school-wide norm for the competition was presented as inclusive, in that teachers advocated for friendliness between the two teams, but the team-level norm was presented as either inclusive (i.e., You have to like and include all the members of the other team) or exclusive (i.e., You cannot like or be friendly to any members of the other team). Results revealed that the inclusive school-wide norm promoted more positive attitudes toward the outgroup relative to no stated norm, except when children were held accountable to their team which held an exclusive norm. That is, an inclusive school-level norm was found to be most successful when peer-level norms were also inclusive. When messages from adults and peers were mismatched, however, unfair or exclusive attitudes at the level of the peer group undermined the success of a large-scale adult-initiated attempt at acceptance and inclusion.

6. INTERGROUP SOCIAL EXCLUSION IN CONTEXT: CONCLUSIONS

Children who are excluded because of their religion, nationality, race, gender, sexual orientation, or (dis)ability (among other types of group membership) are at risk for a range of negative psychological and physical outcomes. Likewise children who reject friendships with others because of biases and stereotypes also face long-term negative consequences. In this chapter, we have outlined our perspective on intergroup social exclusion as a form of prejudice, using our integrative SRD model to highlight many of the factors that contribute to consideration of fairness, justice, and inclusion in development (Killen, Elenbaas, et al., 2015; Rutland et al., 2010).

Children's biases, adherence to group norms, and discriminatory actions contribute to the cycle of social exclusion that begins early in development.

Everyday choices about restricting access to peer groups reflect the social hierarchies of children's worlds, and these are no less damaging than the discriminatory behaviors that permeate adult social relations. Yet, as members of social groups, children often seek a balance between preserving group customs, equal and just treatment of others, adherence to societal norms, and expectations from both peers and parents. Children display genuine concern for justice and others' welfare in intergroup contexts, from early in development. In fact, these different orientations coexist within individuals throughout the life span. With age, children must weigh stereotypes and motives to ensure fairness, consider ingroup vs outgroup identity, balance adherence to social norms with promotion of inclusion and equality, and consider others' welfare as well as the consequences of deviating from exclusive norms.

While the detrimental impacts of social exclusion are evident in the psychological and physical harm of discrimination, the origins of thinking about intergroup interactions, status, and inclusion are often less apparent. In this way, developmental science makes a vital contribution to understanding why and how social exclusion exists and persists in society. Fortunately, as outlined in this chapter, recent research points to the ways in which diversity in children's social environments, including schools and peer groups, inclusive norms on several levels, and messages regarding the wrongfulness of prejudice from adults can promote positive and inclusive intergroup attitudes and behavior. The ongoing challenge for research in this area is to uncover the negative intergroup attitudes that motivate exclusive behaviors and encourage the development of children's capacity to resist biases in favor of inclusion and fair treatment of others.

REFERENCES

Aboud, F. E., Mendelson, M. J., & Purdy, K. T. (2003). Cross-race peer relations and friendship quality. *International Journal of Behavioral Development, 27*, 165–173. http://dx.doi.org/10.1080/01650250244000164.

Abrams, D., & Killen, M. (2014). Social exclusion of children: Developmental origins of prejudice. *Journal of Social Issues, 70*, 1–11. http://dx.doi.org/10.1111/josi.12043.

Abrams, D., & Rutland, A. (2008). The development of subjective group dynamics. In S. R. Levy & M. Killen (Eds.), *Intergroup attitudes and relations in childhood through adulthood* (pp. 47–65). New York, NY: Oxford University Press.

Abrams, D., Rutland, A., Cameron, L., & Marques, J. (2003). The development of subjective group dynamics: When in-group bias gets specific. *British Journal of Developmental Psychology, 21*, 155–176. http://dx.doi.org/10.1348/026151003765264020.

Abrams, D., Rutland, A., Ferrell, J. M., & Pelletier, J. (2008). Children's judgments of disloyal and immoral peer behavior: Subjective group dynamics in minimal intergroup contexts. *Child Development, 79*, 444–461. http://dx.doi.org/10.1111/j.1467-8624.2007.01135.x.

Abrams, D., Rutland, A., Pelletier, J., & Ferrell, J. M. (2009). Children's group nous: Understanding and applying peer exclusion within and between groups. *Child Development, 80*, 224–243. http://dx.doi.org/10.1111/j.1467-8624.2008.01256.x.

Allport, G. W. (1954). *The nature of prejudice*. Oxford, UK: Addison-Wesley.

Apfelbaum, E. P., Pauker, K., Ambady, N., Sommers, S. R., & Norton, M. I. (2008). Learning (not) to talk about race: When older children underperform in social categorization. *Developmental Psychology, 44*, 1513–1518. http://dx.doi.org/10.1037/a0012835.

Bellmore, A. D., Nishina, A., Witkow, M. R., Graham, S., & Juvonen, J. (2007). The influence of classroom ethnic composition on same- and other-ethnicity peer nominations in middle school. *Social Development, 16*, 720–740. http://dx.doi.org/10.1111/j.1467-9507.2007.00404.x.

Bierman, K. L. (2004). *Peer rejection: Developmental processes and intervention strategies*. New York, NY: Guilford Press.

Bigler, R. S., & Liben, L. S. (2006). A developmental intergroup theory of social stereotypes and prejudice. In R. V. Kail (Ed.), *Advances in child development and behavior: Vol. 34* (pp. 39–89). San Diego, CA: Elsevier Academic Press.

Buhs, E. S., & Ladd, G. W. (2001). Peer rejection as an antecedent of young children's school adjustment: An examination of mediating processes. *Developmental Psychology, 37*, 550–560. http://dx.doi.org/10.1037/0012-1649.37.4.550.

Cameron, L., & Rutland, A. (2006). Extended contact through story reading in school: Reducing children's prejudice toward the disabled. *Journal of Social Issues, 62*, 469–488. http://dx.doi.org/10.1111/j.1540-4560.2006.00469.x.

Cameron, L., Rutland, A., Brown, R., & Douch, R. (2006). Changing children's intergroup attitudes toward refugees: Testing different models of extended contact. *Child Development, 77*, 1208–1219. http://dx.doi.org/10.1111/j.1467-8624.2006.00929.x.

Cameron, L., Rutland, A., Hossain, R., & Petley, R. (2011). When and why does extended contact work? The role of high quality direct contact and group norms in the development of positive ethnic intergroup attitudes amongst children. *Group Processes & Intergroup Relations, 14*, 193–206. http://dx.doi.org/10.1177/1368430210390535.

Coie, J., Terry, R., Lenox, K., & Lochman, J. (1995). Childhood peer rejection and aggression as predictors of stable patterns of adolescent disorder. *Development and Psychopathology, 7*, 697–713. http://dx.doi.org/10.1017/S0954579400006799.

Cooley, S., & Killen, M. (2015). Children's evaluations of resource allocation in the context of group norms. *Developmental Psychology, 51*, 554–563. http://dx.doi.org/10.1037/a0038796.

Cooley, S., & Killen, M. (2016). Explicit and implicit forms of racial bias in childhood: Role of contact and identity in children's evaluations of peer inclusion. In *Paper presented at the society for personality and social psychology annual convention. San Diego, CA*.

Crystal, D., Killen, M., & Ruck, M. (2008). It is who you know that counts: Intergroup contact and judgments about race-based exclusion. *British Journal of Developmental Psychology, 26*, 51–70. http://dx.doi.org/10.1348/026151007X198910.

Daddis, C. (2011). Desire for increased autonomy and adolescents' perceptions of peer autonomy: "Everyone else can; why can't I?" *Child Development, 82*, 1310–1326. http://dx.doi.org/10.1111/j.1467-8624.2011.01587.x.

Davies, K., Tropp, L. R., Aron, A., Pettigrew, T. F., & Wright, S. C. (2011). Cross-group friendships and intergroup attitudes: A meta-analytic review. *Personality and Social Psychology Review, 15*, 332–351. http://dx.doi.org/10.1177/1088868311411103.

DeRosier, M., Kupersmidt, J. B., & Patterson, C. J. (1994). Children's academic and behavioral adjustment as a function of the chronicity and proximity of peer rejection. *Child Development, 65*, 1799–1813. http://dx.doi.org/10.2307/1131295.

Dodge, K. A., Lansford, J. E., Burks, V. S., Bates, J. E., Pettit, G. S., Fontaine, R., et al. (2003). Peer rejection and social information-processing factors in the development of aggressive behavior problems in children. *Child Development, 74*, 374–393. http://dx.doi.org/10.1111/1467-8624.7402004.

Douglass, S., Yip, T., & Shelton, J. N. (2014). Intragroup contact and anxiety among ethnic minority adolescents: Considering ethnic identity and school diversity transitions. *Journal of Youth and Adolescence, 43*, 1628–1641. http://dx.doi.org/10.1007/s10964-014-0144-5.

Dovidio, J. F., Glick, P., & Rudman, L. (2005). *Reflecting on the nature of prejudice: Fifty years after Allport.* Malden, MA: Blackwell.

Dovidio, J. F., Hewstone, M., Glick, P., & Estes, V. (2010). *Handbook of prejudice, stereotyping, and discrimination.* Thousand Oaks, CA: Sage Publications.

Elenbaas, L., & Killen, M. (in press). Children rectify inequalities for disadvantaged groups. *Developmental Psychology.*

Elenbaas, L., Rizzo, M. T., Cooley, S., & Killen, M. (2015). Children rectify social inequalities regarding access to educational resources. In *Paper presented at the society for research in child development biennial meeting. Philadelphia, PA.*

Feddes, A. R., Noack, P., & Rutland, A. (2009). Direct and extended friendship effects on minority and majority children's interethnic attitudes: A longitudinal study. *Child Development, 80*, 377–390. http://dx.doi.org/10.1111/j.1467-8624.2009.01266.x.

Graham, S., Bellmore, A., Nishina, A., & Juvonen, J. (2009). "It must be me": Ethnic diversity and attributions for peer victimization in middle school. *Journal of Youth and Adolescence, 38*, 487–499. http://dx.doi.org/10.1007/s10964-008-9386-4.

Gunnar, M. R., Sebanc, A. M., Tout, K., Donzella, B., & van Dulmen, M. M. (2003). Peer rejection, temperament, and cortisol activity in preschoolers. *Developmental Psychobiology, 43*, 346–358. http://dx.doi.org/10.1002/dev.10144.

Harris-Britt, A., Valrie, C. R., Kurtz-Costes, B., & Rowley, S. J. (2007). Perceived racial discrimination and self-esteem in African American youth: Racial socialization as a protective factor. *Journal of Research on Adolescence, 17*, 669–682. http://dx.doi.org/10.1111/j.1532-7795.2007.00540.x.

Heinze, J. E., & Horn, S. S. (2009). Intergroup contact and beliefs about homosexuality in adolescence. *Journal of Youth and Adolescence, 38*, 937–951. http://dx.doi.org/10.1007/s10964-009-9408-x.

Helwig, C. C., Ruck, M. D., & Peterson-Badali, M. (2014). Rights, civil liberties, and democracy. In M. Killen & J. G. Smetana (Eds.), *Handbook of moral development* (2nd ed., pp. 46–69). New York: Psychology Press.

Hitti, A., & Killen, M. (2015). Expectations about ethnic peer group inclusivity: The role of shared interests, group norms, and stereotypes. *Child Development, 86*, 1522–1537. http://dx.doi.org/10.11.11/cdev.12393.

Hodges, E. V., Boivin, M., Vitaro, F., & Bukowski, W. M. (1999). The power of friendship: Protection against an escalating cycle of peer victimization. *Developmental Psychology, 35*, 94–101. http://dx.doi.org/10.1037/0012-1649.35.1.94.

Horn, S. S. (2006). Heterosexual adolescents' and young adults' beliefs and attitudes about homosexuality and gay and lesbian peers. *Cognitive Development, 21*, 420–440. http://dx.doi.org/10.1016/j.cogdev.2006.06.007.

Horn, S. S., & Sinno, S. M. (2014). Gender, sexual orientation, and discrimination based on gender and sexual orientation. In M. Killen & J. G. Smetana (Eds.), *Handbook of moral development* (2nd ed., pp. 317–339). New York, NY: Psychology Press.

Horn, S. S., & Szalach, L. A. (2009). School differences in heterosexual students' attitudes about homosexuality and prejudice based on sexual orientation. *European Journal of Developmental Science, 3*, 64–79.

Hughes, D. (2003). Correlates of African American and Latino parents' messages to children about ethnicity and race: A comparative study of racial socialization. *American Journal of Community Psychology, 31*, 15–33. http://dx.doi.org/10.1023/a:1023066418688.

Hughes, J. M., & Bigler, R. S. (2011). Predictors of African American and European American adolescents' endorsement of race-conscious social policies. *Developmental Psychology*, *47*, 479–492. http://dx.doi.org/10.1037/a0021309.

Huynh, V. W., & Fuligni, A. J. (2010). Discrimination hurts: The academic, psychological, and physical well-being of adolescents. *Journal of Research on Adolescence*, *20*, 916–941. http://dx.doi.org/10.1111/j.1532-7795.2010.00670.x.

Juvonen, J., Nishina, A., & Graham, S. (2006). Ethnic diversity and perceptions of safety in urban middle schools. *Psychological Science*, *17*, 393–400. http://dx.doi.org/10.1111/j.1467-9280.2006.01718.x.

Killen, M., Elenbaas, L., & Rutland, A. (2015). Balancing the fair treatment of others while preserving group identity and autonomy. *Human Development*, *58*, 253–272. http://dx.doi.org/10.1159/000444151.

Killen, M., Henning, A., Kelly, M. C., Crystal, D., & Ruck, M. (2007). Evaluations of interracial peer encounters by majority and minority U.S. children and adolescents. *International Journal of Behavioral Development*, *31*, 491–500. http://dx.doi.org/10.1177/0165025407081478.

Killen, M., Lee-Kim, J., McGlothlin, H., Stangor, C., & Helwig, C. (2002). How children and adolescents evaluate gender and racial exclusion. *Monographs of the Society for Research in Child Development*, *67*(4) 1–129.

Killen, M., & Malti, T. (2015). Moral judgments and emotions in contexts of peer exclusion and victimization. *Advances in Child Development and Behavior*, *48*, 249–276. http://dx.doi.org/10.1016/bs.acdb.2014.11.007.

Killen, M., Mulvey, K. L., & Hitti, A. (2013). Social exclusion in childhood: A developmental intergroup perspective. *Child Development*, *84*, 772–790. http://dx.doi.org/10.1111/cdev.12012.

Killen, M., Mulvey, K. L., & Hitti, A. (2015). Social development and intergroup relations. In M. Mikulincer, P. R. Shaver, J. F. Dovidio, & J. A. Simpson (Eds.), *APA handbook of personality and social psychology*: *Vol. 2. Group processes* (pp. 177–201). Washington, DC: American Psychological Association. http://dx.doi.org/10.1037/14342-007.

Killen, M., Park, Y., Lee-Kim, J., & Shin, Y. (2005). Evaluations of children's gender stereotypic activities by Korean parents and nonparental adults residing in the United States. *Parenting, Science and Practice*, *5*, 57–89. http://dx.doi.org/10.1207/s15327922par0501_3.

Killen, M., Pisacane, K., Lee-Kim, J., & Ardila-Rey, A. (2001). Fairness or stereotypes? Young children's priorities when evaluating group exclusion and inclusion. *Developmental Psychology*, *37*, 587–596. http://dx.doi.org/10.1037/0012-1649.37.5.587.

Killen, M., & Rutland, A. (2011). *Children and social exclusion: Morality, prejudice, and group identity*. Malden, MA: Wiley-Blackwell. http://dx.doi.org/10.1002/9781444396317.

Killen, M., Rutland, A., Abrams, D., Mulvey, K. L., & Hitti, A. (2013). Development of intra- and intergroup judgments in the context of moral and social-conventional norms. *Child Development*, *84*, 1063–1080. http://dx.doi.org/10.1111/cdev.12011.

Killen, M., Rutland, A., & Ruck, M. (2011). Promoting equity, tolerance, and justice in childhood. *SRCD policy report: Sharing child and youth development knowledge: Vol. 25* (pp. 1–33).

Killen, M., & Smetana, J. G. (2015). Origins and development of morality. In M. E. Lamb (Ed.), *Handbook of child psychology and developmental science: Vol. 3* (7th ed., pp. 701–749). NY: Wiley-Blackwell.

Killen, M., & Stangor, C. (2001). Children's social reasoning about inclusion and exclusion in gender and race peer group contexts. *Child Development*, *72*, 174–186. http://dx.doi.org/10.1111/1467-8624.00272.

Kinket, B., & Verkuyten, M. (1999). Intergroup evaluations and social context: A multilevel approach. *European Journal of Social Psychology*, *29*, 219–237. http://dx.doi.org/10.1002/1099-0992/33.0.CO2-X.

Ladd, G. W. (2006). Peer rejection, aggressive or withdrawn behavior, and psychological maladjustment from ages 5 to 12: An examination of four predictive models. *Child Development*, 77, 822–846. http://dx.doi.org/10.1111/j.1467-8624.2006.00905.x.

Malti, T., Killen, M., & Gasser, L. (2012). Social judgments and emotion attributions about exclusion in Switzerland. *Child Development*, *83*, 697–711.

Masten, C. L., Eisenberger, N. I., Borofsky, L. A., Pfeifer, J. H., McNealy, K., Mazziotta, J. C., et al. (2009). Neural correlates of social exclusion during adolescence: Understanding the distress of peer rejection. *Social Cognitive and Affective Neuroscience*, *4*, 143–157. http://dx.doi.org/10.1093/scan/nsp007.

McGlothlin, H., & Killen, M. (2006). Intergroup attitudes of European American children attending ethnically homogeneous schools. *Child Development*, 77, 1375–1386. http://dx.doi.org/10.1111/j.1467-8624.2006.00941.x.

McGuire, L., Rutland, A., & Nesdale, D. (2015). Peer group norms and accountability moderate the effect of school norms on children's intergroup attitudes. *Child Development*, *86*, 1290–1297. http://dx.doi.org/10.1111/cdev.12388.

Møller, S. J., & Tenenbaum, H. R. (2011). Danish majority children's reasoning about exclusion based on gender and ethnicity. *Child Development*, *82*, 520–532. http://dx.doi.org/10.1111/j.1467-8624.2010.01568.x.

Mulvey, K. L., Hitti, A., Rutland, A., Abrams, D., & Killen, M. (2014). When do children dislike ingroup members? Resource allocation from individual and group perspectives. *Journal of Social Issues*, *70*, 29–46. http://dx.doi.org/10.1111/josi.12045.

Mulvey, K. L., & Killen, M. (2015). Challenging gender stereotypes: Resistance and exclusion. *Child Development*, *86*, 681–694. http://dx.doi.org/10.1111/cdev.12317.

Neblett, E. W., Terzian, M., & Harriott, V. (2010). From racial discrimination to substance use: The buffering effects of racial socialization. *Child Development Perspectives*, *4*, 131–137. http://dx.doi.org/10.1111/j.1750-8606.2010.00131.x.

Neblett, E. W., White, R. L., Philip, C. L., Nguyên, H. X., & Sellers, R. M. (2008). Patterns of racial socialization and psychological adjustment: Can parental communications about race reduce the impact of racial discrimination? *Journal of Research on Adolescence*, *18*, 477–515. http://dx.doi.org/10.1111/j.1532-7795.2008.00568.x.

Nesdale, D. (2004). Social identity processes and children's ethnic prejudice. In M. Bennett & F. Sani (Eds.), *The development of the social self* (pp. 219–245). New York, NY: Psychology Press. http://dx.doi.org/10.4324/9780203391099_chapter_8.

Nesdale, D., Griffiths, J. A., Durkin, K., & Maass, A. (2007). Effects of group membership, intergroup competition and out-group ethnicity on children's ratings of in-group and out-group similarity and positivity. *British Journal of Developmental Psychology*, *25*, 359–373. http://dx.doi.org/10.1348/026151006X150382.

Nesdale, D., & Lawson, M. J. (2011). Social groups and children's intergroup attitudes: Can school norms moderate the effects of social group norms? *Child Development*, *82*, 1594–1606. http://dx.doi.org/10.1111/j.1467-8624.2011.01637.x.

Nesdale, D., Maass, A., Durkin, K., & Griffiths, J. (2005). Group norms, threat, and children's racial prejudice. *Child Development*, *76*, 652–663. http://dx.doi.org/10.1111/j.1467-8624.2005.00869.x.

Nesdale, D., Zimmer-Gembeck, M. J., & Roxburgh, N. (2014). Peer group rejection in childhood: Effects of rejection ambiguity, rejection sensitivity, and social acumen. *Journal of Social Issues*, *70*, 12–28. http://dx.doi.org/10.1111/josi.12044.

Nucci, L. P. (1981). Conceptions of personal issues: A domain distinct from moral or societal concepts. *Child Development*, *52*, 114–121.

Olson, K. R., Dweck, C. S., Spelke, E. S., & Banaji, M. R. (2011). Children's responses to group-based inequalities: Perpetuation and rectification. *Social Cognition*, *29*, 270–287. http://dx.doi.org/10.1521/soco.2011.29.3.270.

Olweus, D. (1993). *Bullying at school: What we know and what we can do*. Malen, MA: Blackwell Publishing.

Orfield, G., & Lee, C. (2005). *Why segregation matters: Poverty and educational inequality*. Cambridge, MA: The Civil Rights Project, Harvard University.

Pahlke, E., Bigler, R. S., & Suizzo, M.-A. (2012). Relations between colorblind socialization and children's racial bias: Evidence from European American mothers and their preschool children. *Child Development, 83*, 1164–1179. http://dx.doi.org/10.1111/j.1467-8624.2012.01770.x.

Park, Y., & Killen, M. (2010). When is peer rejection justifiable?: Children's understanding across two cultures. *Cognitive Development, 25*, 290–301. http://dx.doi.org/10.1016/j.cogdev.2009.10.004.

Pettigrew, T. F., & Tropp, L. R. (2006). A meta-analytic test of intergroup contact theory. *Journal of Personality and Social Psychology, 90*, 751–783. http://dx.doi.org/10.1037/0022-3514.90.5.751.

Prinstein, M. J., & Aikins, J. W. (2004). Cognitive moderators of the longitudinal association between peer rejection and adolescent depressive symptoms. *Journal of Abnormal Child Psychology, 32*, 147–158. http://dx.doi.org/10.1023/B:JACP.0000019767.55592.63.

Rubin, K. H., Bukowski, W. M., & Parker, J. G. (2006). Peer interactions, relationships, and groups. In N. Eisenberg, W. Damon, & R. M. Lerner (Eds.), *Handbook of child psychology: Social, emotional, and personality development: Vol. 3* (6th ed., pp. 571–645). Hoboken, NJ: John Wiley & Sons Inc.

Ruck, M. D., Park, H., Killen, M., & Crystal, D. S. (2011). Intergroup contact and evaluations of race-based exclusion in urban minority children and adolescents. *Journal of Youth and Adolescence, 40*, 633–643. http://dx.doi.org/10.1007/s10964-010-9600-z.

Ruck, M. D., & Tenenbaum, H. R. (2014). Does moral and social conventional reasoning predict British young people's judgments about the rights of asylum-seeker youth? *Journal of Social Issues, 70*, 47–62. http://dx.doi.org/10.1111/josi.12046.

Russell, S. T., Kosciw, J., Horn, S., & Saewyc, E. (2010). Safe schools policy for LGBTQ students. In *SRCD Policy Report: Sharing Child and Youth Development Knowledge: Vol. 24* (pp. 1–25).

Rutland, A., Cameron, L., Bennett, L., & Ferrell, J. (2005a). Interracial contact and racial constancy: A multi-site study of racial intergroup bias in 3–5 year old Anglo-British children. *Journal of Applied Developmental Psychology, 26*, 699–713. http://dx.doi.org/10.1016/j.appdev.2005.08.005.

Rutland, A., Cameron, L., Milne, A., & McGeorge, P. (2005b). Social norms and self-presentation: Children's implicit and explicit intergroup attitudes. *Child Development, 76*, 451–466. http://dx.doi.org/10.1111/j.1467-8624.2005.00856.x.

Rutland, A., & Killen, M. (2015). A developmental science approach to reducing prejudice and social exclusion: Intergroup processes, social-cognitive development, and moral reasoning. *Social Issues and Policy Review, 9*, 121–154. http://dx.doi.org/10.1111/sipr.12012.

Rutland, A., Killen, M., & Abrams, D. (2010). A new social-cognitive developmental perspective on prejudice: The interplay between morality and group identity. *Perspectives on Psychological Science, 5*, 279–291. http://dx.doi.org/10.1177/1745691610369468.

Seaton, E. K., Yip, T., Morgan-Lopez, A., & Sellers, R. M. (2012). Racial discrimination and racial socialization as predictors of African American adolescents' racial identity development using latent transition analysis. *Developmental Psychology, 48*, 448–458. http://dx.doi.org/10.1037/a0025328.

Sellers, R. M., Caldwell, C. H., Schmeelk-Cone, K. H., & Zimmerman, M. A. (2003). Racial identity, racial discrimination, perceived stress, and psychological distress among African American young adults. *Journal of Health and Social Behavior, 44*, 302–317. http://dx.doi.org/10.2307/1519781.

Shelton, J. N., Douglass, S., Garcia, R. L., Yip, T., & Trail, T. E. (2014). Feeling (mis)understood and intergroup friendships in interracial interactions. *Personality and Social Psychology Bulletin*, *40*, 1193–1204. http://dx.doi.org/10.1177/0146167214538459.

Shelton, J. N., Richeson, J. A., & Bergsieker, H. B. (2009). Interracial friendship development and attributional biases. *Journal of Social and Personal Relationships*, *26*, 179–193. http://dx.doi.org/10.1177/0265407509106707.

Smetana, J. G. (2011). *Adolescents, families, and social development: How teens construct their worlds.* New York, NY: Wiley/Blackwell.

Smetana, J. G., Jambon, M., & Ball, C. (2014). The social domain approach to children's moral and social judgments. In M. Killen & J. G. Smetana (Eds.), *Handbook of moral development* (2nd ed., pp. 23–45). New York, NY: Taylor & Francis Publishers.

Steele, C. M. (1997). A threat in the air: How stereotypes shape intellectual identity and performance. *The American Psychologist*, *52*, 613–629. http://dx.doi.org/10.1037/0003-066X.52.6.613.

Tajfel, H., & Turner, J. C. (1979). An integrative theory of intergroup conflict. In W. G. Austin & S. Worchel (Eds.), *The social psychology of intergroup relations* (pp. 33–47). Monterey, CA: Brooks-Cole.

Tatum, B. D. (2003). *Why are all the black kids sitting together in the cafeteria?: And other conversations about race.* New York, NY: Basic Books.

Theimer, C. E., Killen, M., & Stangor, C. (2001). Young children's evaluations of exclusion in gender-stereotypic peer contexts. *Developmental Psychology*, *37*, 18–27. http://dx.doi.org/10.1037/0012-1649.37.1.18.

Tropp, L. R., & Prenovost, M. A. (2008). The role of intergroup contact in predicting children's interethnic attitudes: Evidence from meta-analytic and field studies. In S. R. Levy & M. Killen (Eds.), *Intergroup attitudes and relations in childhood through adulthood* (pp. 236–248). New York, NY: Oxford University Press.

Turiel, E. (1983). *The development of social knowledge: Morality and convention.* Cambridge, England: Cambridge University Press.

Turiel, E. (2006). The development of morality. In N. Eisenberg, W. Damon, & R. M. Lerner (Eds.), *Handbook of child psychology: Vol. 3. Social, emotional, and personality development* (6th ed., pp. 863–932). Hoboken, NJ: John Wiley & Sons Inc.

Verkuyten, M. (2007). Ethnic in-group favoritism among minority and majority groups: Testing the self-esteem hypothesis among preadolescents. *Journal of Applied Social Psychology*, *37*, 486–500. http://dx.doi.org/10.1111/j.1559-1816.2007.00170.x.

Verkuyten, M. (2008). Perceived discrimination, ethnic minority identity, and self-esteem. In S. M. Quintana & C. McKown (Eds.), *Handbook of race, racism, and the developing child* (pp. 339–365). Hoboken, NJ: John Wiley & Sons Inc.

Verkuyten, M. (2011). Assimilation ideology and outgroup attitudes among ethnic majority members. *Group Processes & Intergroup Relations*, *14*, 789–806. http://dx.doi.org/10.1177/1368430211398506.

Verkuyten, M., & Steenhuis, A. (2005). Preadolescents' understanding and reasoning about asylum seeker peers and friendships. *Journal of Applied Developmental Psychology*, *26*, 660–679. http://dx.doi.org/10.1016/j.appdev.2005.08.002.

Verkuyten, M., & Thijs, J. (2002). Racist victimization among children in The Netherlands: The effect of ethnic group and school. *Ethnic and Racial Studies*, *25*, 310–331. http://dx.doi.org/10.1080/01419870120109502.

White-Johnson, R. L., Ford, K. R., & Sellers, R. M. (2010). Parental racial socialization profiles: Association with demographic factors, racial discrimination, childhood socialization, and racial identity. *Cultural Diversity and Ethnic Minority Psychology*, *16*, 237–247. http://dx.doi.org/10.1037/a0016111.

Wilson, T., & Rodkin, P. C. (2011). African American and European American children in diverse elementary classrooms: Social integration, social status, and social behavior. *Child Development*, *82*, 1454–1469. http://dx.doi.org/10.1111/j.1467-8624.2011.01634.x.

CHAPTER FIVE

Children's Intergroup Relations and Attitudes

Rebecca S. Bigler*[,1], John M. Rohrbach*, Kiara L. Sanchez[†]
*University of Texas at Austin, Austin, TX, United States
[†]Rice University, Houston, TX, United States
[1]Corresponding author: e-mail address: rebeccabigler28@gmail.com

Contents

Abstract

The existence of warm, intimate, supportive, and egalitarian relationships between members of differing social outgroups is likely, at the societal level, to facilitate cooperation and cohesion, and at the individual level, to promote positive social, educational, and occupational outcomes. The developmental pathway from intergroup contact to intergroup attitudes as it operates among children is not, however, well understood. In our chapter, we review and integrate selected social and developmental science related

Equity and Justice in Developmental Science: Implications for Young People, Families, and Communities (S.S. Horn, M.D. Ruck & L.S. Liben, Eds.)
Advances in Child Development and Behavior (J.B. Benson, Series Ed.), Vol. 51
ISSN 0065-2407 http://dx.doi.org/10.1016/bs.acdb.2016.05.005

to intergroup relations and attitudes with the goal of proposing a conceptual model of the pathway from intergroup contact to positive intergroup attitudes among youth.

1. INTRODUCTION

Intergroup relations (a term we use to include *intergroup contact, interaction, and friendship*) and intergroup attitudes (a term we use to include *knowledge, beliefs*, and *evaluations* concerning social groups) are pressing concerns worldwide. Conflict among groups is a major source of war and other forms of violence and aggression. Maltreatment and other forms of injustice (e.g., inequitable distribution of resources) frequently are tied to group membership. Furthermore, global migration is increasing the diversity of the people within most geographic regions of the world, bringing people into closer proximity to individuals who differ from themselves with respect to group membership, including groups based on religious affiliation, race and ethnicity, economic status, gender, culture, and sexual orientation. Ensuring that intergroup relations and attitudes are positive is, and will continue to be, a significant challenge for humanity.

Intergroup relations and attitudes have been a concern of psychological scientists for nearly a century (Kruglanski & Stroebe, 2012). Much of the extant empirical work has been conducted within the United States (US) and the United Kingdom (UK). Our own expertise is grounded in the US and thus we focus primarily (albeit not exclusively) on the region. Furthermore, much of the focus of intergroup research has been on causes and amelioration of *negative* relations and attitudes, including social stereotyping and exclusion (Ruck, Park, Killen, & Crystal, 2011; Sherif, Harvey, White, Hood, & Sherif, 1961; Williams, 1947). Such a focus is understandable given the enormous human costs associated with negative intergroup relations and attitudes, including war and violence. Less attention has been directed at identifying the person and contextual variables associated with positive intergroup relations (i.e., affectionate, trusting, supportive, and close relationships with outgroup individuals) and attitudes. In addition to the less pressing nature of the topic, it is possible that a lack of consensus about the ideals associated with these positive constructs plays a role. With respect to the negative end of the intergroup relations and attitudes continuum, the complete absence of hostility and prejudice is a broadly held ideal. With respect to the positive end of the continuum, no single ideal is broadly endorsed. For example, individuals may exhibit no outgroup hostility or prejudice, but simultaneously exhibit ingroup favoritism (e.g., a Christian who exhibits positive attitudes toward and treatment of Muslims but prefers Christians to Muslins across settings). Such situations produce de facto social segregation, which is common in the US. Indeed, levels of explicit stereotyping and prejudice toward many stigmatized groups, including African Americans, women, sexual minorities, and physically disabled individuals have declined over time (see Rifkin, 2009). At the same time, warm, intimate relationships across groups are still relatively uncommon. That is, children and adults continue to form their most intimate bonds—including close friendships—with members of their own social groups (McPherson, Smith-Lovin, & Cook, 2001; Young, 2011). Whether the formation of close, intimate, trusting cross-group relationships represents an ideal goal (or not) may depend on its impact on social equity and justice.

How do intergroup relations and attitudes relate to social equity and justice? Negative intergroup relations and attitudes undoubtedly produce social inequity and injustice. But is the mere absence of intergroup hostility—something akin to tolerance and neutrality—sufficient to promote equity and justice? Is the adoption of a "separate but equal" ideal concerning intergroup relations and attitudes sufficient to produce social equity and justice? We believe that the ability to form affectionate, intimate, trusting, and supportive relationships with outgroup members is a vital component of positive intergroup attitudes (Davies, Tropp, Aron, Pettigrew, & Wright, 2011), with highly meaningful consequences for social equity and justice. Specifically, we argue that intergroup relations, especially cross-group friendships, significantly affect intergroup attitudes (and vice versa), and that cross-group friendship is vital to the creation of equitable and just societies.

1.1 Scope and Significance of the Problem

Intergroup relations have important implications at individual, societal, and global levels. At the individual level, children's intergroup relations shape their experiences within schools, neighborhoods, and communities (e.g., via interactions with teachers, police, and doctors), with important consequences for their developmental outcomes. We hypothesize, for example, that children with close, affectionate ties to cross-group peers are more likely to detect and challenge others' stereotyping, prejudice, and discrimination (e.g., exclusion) than children without such ties (e.g., Ruck et al., 2011). At the societal level, intergroup relations have important consequences for the effectiveness with which institutions function, including educational, military, and governmental institutions. It is easy to imagine, for example, that White teachers with affectionate, intimate, and trusting relationships with cross-race individuals reduce racial achievement gaps more effectively than their colleagues without such relationships, and similarly, that White police officers who have affectionate, intimate, and trusting relationships with cross-race individuals promote community safety more effectively than their colleagues who lack such relationships. At the global level, intergroup relations have important implications for the ability of international organizations to solve worldwide problems (e.g., global warming and human trafficking). Those leaders who have affectionate, intimate, and trusting relationships with outgroup individuals may negotiate collective solutions to world problems more effectively than those leaders who do not. At the same time, we recognize that positive intergroup relations are not without risks and drawbacks; positive intergroup contact can create unfulfilled expectations of equitable treatment (see Saguy, Tausch, Dovidio, & Pratto, 2009) and can be cognitively and emotionally taxing to achieve (Trawalter, Richeson, & Shelton, 2009). Nonetheless, the alternative (i.e., the creation of tolerant and civil, but emotionally distant relationships with outgroup members) seems to us to carry a greater number of disadvantages.

One major challenge for promoting positive intergroup relations is that interpersonal similarity promotes the formation of affectionate, intimate, and trusting relationships. The notion that individuals prefer others similar to themselves is widespread among laypeople. It is evident in Plato's observation that "similarity begets friendship" and in variations on the proverb "birds of a feather flock together," which are common in many languages (Schug, Yuki, Horikawa, & Takemura, 2009). Scientific work supports the notion that homophily (i.e., similarity) facilitates social connection (McPherson et al., 2001), even among children as young as three (Fawcett & Markson, 2010). Of course, individuals are members of multiple social groups simultaneously. Researchers have begun to examine intergroup attitudes using the lens of intersectionality (i.e., examining how differing social identities interact with one another to shape outcomes; Cole, 2009). It seems likely, however, that overall similarity provides an organizing principle, such that those individuals who share greater numbers of social group memberships show greater levels of ingroup favoritism toward one another. It is also true, however, that some individuals develop close friendships across group boundaries—and even across multiple group boundaries.

The psychological processes that shape how, when, and why children come to form close social bonds with outgroup members, and the consequences of such friendships for their lives, are increasingly recognized as important topics for psychological study (see Killen, Mulvey, & Hitti, 2013; Turner & Cameron, 2016).

1.2 Chapter Goals

The primary purpose of this chapter is to provide a selective review and integration of literatures within social and developmental psychology concerning intergroup relations with the goal of proposing a conceptual model of the pathway from intergroup contact to positive intergroup attitudes in children. This chapter is divided into five major sections. Following this introduction, a second section provides a brief review of historical approaches to understanding the pathway from intergroup contact to positive intergroup attitudes and overview of our own approach. The third section introduces our new model of the pathway from intergroup contact to intergroup attitudes and the four core processes of the pathway model are described. In the fourth section, the factors hypothesized to affect these processes are outlined. The fifth and final section provides a brief summary of our conclusions.

2. HISTORICAL APPROACHES AND OVERVIEW OF OUR MODEL

2.1 Historical Approaches to Intergroup Relations

In the aftermath of World War II, social scientists became interested in intergroup relations, particularly the formation and reduction of negative intergroup attitudes (Allport, 1954; Williams, 1947). The single most influential construct that appeared in the psychological literature on intergroup attitudes during the following decades was termed "contact." First proposed by Allport in 1954, the Contact Hypothesis outlined key environmental factors that facilitate positive intergroup contact and reduce prejudice. Allport claimed that intergroup contact, when it is characterized by five conditions, successfully reduces prejudice and intergroup conflict. The first of these conditions is that the groups involved have similar rank or prestige. The second and third conditions, respectively, require that group members share—and work jointly to achieve—common, superordinate goals. The fourth condition is that groups acknowledge and abide by social norms that encourage intergroup contact. The fifth condition is that members of respective groups interact within casual settings. Unfortunately, stereotyping and prejudice often block the creation of the conditions necessary to reduce them. For example, individuals with highly negative attitudes toward a particular outgroup typically are unwilling to interact in fair, cooperative, and communal ways with outgroup members.

In 1998, Pettigrew, a former student of Allport, proposed Intergroup Contact Theory, which expanded on Allport's hypothesis by identifying the processes by which intergroup contact reduces prejudice. Specifically, Pettigrew (1998) argued that (a) learning about outgroups, (b) changing behavioral patterns, (c) developing affective ties, and (d) reappraising beliefs about one's ingroup facilitate the positive effects of intergroup contact. Furthermore, Pettigrew (1998) described several processes and mediating factors hypothesized to affect the degree to which positive intergroup experiences with particular outgroup members are generalized to other intergroup situations, other outgroup members, and other social groups. We incorporate and expand on this work here. Although Allport (1954) and Pettigrew (1998) theorized about the formation and change of intergroup attitudes among children, neither focused on the social or cognitive constraints associated with childhood that may impact intergroup relations. Recent developmental work has sought to fill this gap (see Killen et al., 2013; Turner & Cameron, 2016), and also serves as a basis for our thinking.

2.2 Overview of Our Model

We draw upon contact theory and research (Allport, 1954; Pettigrew, 1998), as well as developmental theory and research (Bigler & Liben, 2006, 2007; Killen et al., 2013; Turner & Cameron, 2016), to posit an integrative model, General Intergroup Friendship Theory (GIFT), of successive processes of contact, interaction, friendship, and intergroup attitude formation and change. The model is named for the crucial role of friendship in producing positive intergroup attitudes. The contribution of the model lies in synthesizing the literature to produce an overarching framework for understanding the distinct roles of contact, interaction, and friendship—and unique sets of situational, social, cognitive, and affective factors that impact these processes—in shaping children's intergroup attitudes.

Our model is designed to be generalizable across social groups and thus informative about the pathway from intergroup contact to positive attitudes among individuals from differing genders, races, religions, etc. In the tradition of Allport and Pettigrew, we focus on race, religion, and nationality, but unlike most intergroup researchers (e.g., Davies et al., 2011; Pettigrew & Tropp, 2006), we also focus on gender. Of course, particular social groups (e.g., those based on gender, race, and sexual orientation) have unique historical backgrounds and contemporary sociological characteristics. We identify differences (as well as similarities) in cross-group contact, interaction, friendship, and attitudes with respect to particular groups (race, gender, nationality) and build them into our model as factors that shape these constructs (see Brown & Bigler, 2005).

The focal point for this work is intergroup *relations* (contact, interaction, friendship with outgroup members) and thus our model starts with the child's encounter with an outgroup member. Importantly, children may (or may not) have a well-developed attitude toward the group prior to their encounter. Bigler and Liben (2006) provide a theoretical account of the causes of children's intergroup attitudes that includes many factors and is beyond the scope of this chapter. It is important for our purposes here that readers know that intergroup relations (contact, interaction, friendship with outgroup members) is only one of many causal influences on children's intergroup attitudes. Bigler and Liben (2006) posited that encounters with outgroup members sometimes lead to the reification, and sometime lead to the modification, of intergroup attitudes. Their model does not, however, address factors that shape the likelihood of encountering outgroup individuals, or the interpersonal processes of interaction and friendship that sometimes follow from encountering a cross-group individual. These are the core processes to which we now turn.

3. CORE PROCESSES IN INTERGROUP RELATIONS AND ATTITUDES

Our model of the pathway from intergroup contact to intergroup attitudes, titled GIFT and depicted in Fig. 1, includes four core processes. These core processes are represented as rectangles in the center of the model (see Fig. 1), and include: (1) intergroup contact, (2) intergroup interaction, (3) intergroup friendship, and (4) intergroup attitudes. Each core process is shaped by exogenous and endogenous factors, depicted as ovals in the model, and described in the latter half of this chapter.

3.1 Intergroup Contact

The first core process in the pathway from intergroup contact to positive intergroup attitudes is encountering outgroup members. Pettigrew and Tropp's (2006) meta-analysis of hundreds of studies of intergroup relations provides strong evidence that contact with outgroup members promotes

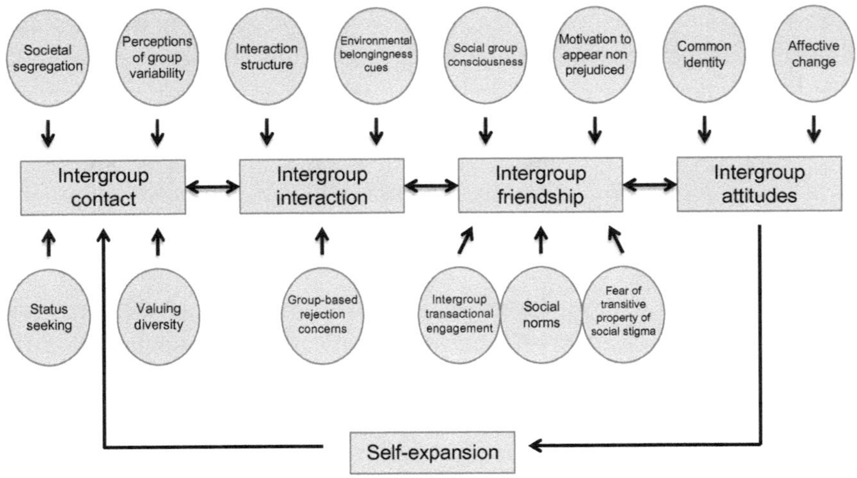

Fig. 1 Processes involved in the pathway from intergroup contact to intergroup attitudes rectangles depict core processes. Ovals depict contextual and individual difference variables hypothesized to impact core processes.

positive intergroup attitudes. However, the extant literature is limited in revealing why this is the case.

One limitation to the extant literature is that researchers often fail to disentangle the effects of contact on attitude *formation* vs attitude *change*. Most work implicitly assumes that individuals have negative intergroup attitudes prior to contact, and thus is framed as a test of whether contact improves such attitudes. For example, Allport (1954) and Pettigrew and Tropp (2006) argued that segregation facilitates negative intergroup attitudes because opportunities for stereotype disconfirmation are absent or rare under such conditions. That is, stereotypes are believed to be *undermined* by personal experiences with outgroup members.

Additional causal mechanisms appear to link segregation to negative intergroup attitude formation. For instance, developmental intergroup theory (Bigler & Liben, 2006) posits that when children are exposed to segregation, they construct hypotheses about the causes of the observed nonrandom distribution of persons across contexts. These hypotheses tend to be essentialist and supportive of the status quo. For example, children exposed to racial segregation are likely to assume that Whites and Blacks are different in meaningful, innate ways and these beliefs, in turn, cause children to interact preferentially with same-race peers (or self-segregate). This inferential process appears to operate even when children are observers (rather than members) of the target social groups and when the groups in questions are novel and hence unfamiliar to participants (Bigler & Liben, 2006, 2007). In sum, new work suggests that intergroup contact may function in more complex ways than previously described to affect children's intergroup attitudes.

A second limitation to the literature is that researchers rarely define or quantify contact at the psychological level. Most approaches compare the intergroup attitudes of individuals who spend time within segregated vs integrated contexts—or who are known to have interacted in some capacity (Pettigrew & Tropp, 2006)—but little is typically known about the extent or nature of such contact. For example, many researchers have found that European American children attending racially homogeneous schools were more likely to hold negative racial attitudes than European American children attending racially heterogeneous schools (Killen et al., 2013). What mechanism accounts for the effect? Is the number of African American children (a) encountered in the hallway, (b) included on the school's football team, or (c) enrolled in one's academic courses predictive of White children's attitudes? Is the absolute number of positive interactions or ratio of positive to negative Black–White interactions within such settings relevant? Or is the degree of segregation within schools a proxy for the formation of close, intimate cross-race friendship? Does the formation of these relationships, among the subset of children who develop them, drive the finding concerning intergroup contact?

Importantly, the relation between intergroup contact and intergroup attitudes is moderate in size and varies across studies (Pettigrew & Tropp, 2006). Such variation is not, however, attributable to variations in Allport's conditions for positive contact. Pettigrew and Tropp (2006) reported that Allport's optimal conditions for contact failed to predict individuals' intergroup attitude. As a consequence, they argued, in part, that mere exposure to outgroups causes liking to increase. However, many other researchers have noted that merely placing groups together often does little to produce positive intergroup outcomes (Dixon, Durrheim, & Tredoux, 2005; Pfeifer, Brown, & Juvonen, 2007). Gender represents one of the most powerful illustrations of the limits of mere contact for promoting positive intergroup attitudes. Nearly all children come into contact with both men and women countless times every day, often within their own families. As a result, no interventions of which we are aware seek to increase cross-gender contact per se. Nonetheless, levels of gender stereotyping and prejudice are quite high among children, suggesting that contact per se has limited power to explain children's intergroup attitudes. However, contact is important because it is a necessary precursor of two additional, sequential processes—intergroup interaction and friendship—that are likely to be more powerful predictors of the development of positive intergroup attitudes (Turner & Cameron, 2016).

3.2 Intergroup Interaction

The second core process in the pathway from intergroup contact to positive intergroup attitudes is *interpersonal interaction* with outgroup members. Importantly, contact with outgroup members may not progress to interaction at all. That is, youth may encounter outgroup members without engaging in interaction, as, for example, when children encounter cross-race others in movie theaters, stores, and restaurants. Such situations are likely to be common. For example, many US schools make use of tracking, or grouping students by academic skills and performance. Because academic performance is correlated with poverty and race in the US, such schools can appear racially integrated on paper but the students within such schools often fail to share classrooms or activities with cross-race others. As noted earlier, it is possible that contact alone without the subsequent processes of interaction and friendship (e.g., passing cross-group others in the hall without interacting) positively affects intergroup attitudes through mere exposure. But such effects are likely to be trivial, especially when individuals endorse negative intergroup attitudes prior to contact.

Some encounters with outgroup members will engender interactions and these interaction can be characterized along a continuum from negative (e.g., imbued with negative emotions such as anxiety, defensiveness, anger, and frustration) to positive (imbued with positive emotions such interest and warmth). In the middle of the continuum are interactions that are mundane and perfunctory, arousing neutral emotion. Nonverbal behavior exhibited during cross-group interactions is illustrative of this variation and appears to play a role in shaping interpersonal outcomes and intergroup attitudes (Weisbuch, Pauker, & Ambady, 2009). For example, a recent meta-analysis by Toosi, Babbitt, Ambady, and Sommers (2012) found that individuals express more friendly nonverbal behavior in same- than cross-race dyads, leading to more negative impressions within cross- than same-race dyads. Although rarely studied, it is likely that interactions between dyads comprised of cross-group children are also characterized by more negative—and fewer positive—nonverbal signals than interactions between dyads comprised of same-group children (see Hebl, Foster,

Mannix, & Dovidio, 2002). Individuals also consciously and unconsciously distance themselves, physically and psychologically, from outgroup members to avoid potential interaction. With regard to race, for example, White children and adults often geographically distance themselves from people of color (e.g., avoiding walking or sitting near them), thereby minimizing interpersonal interactions (Goff, Steele, & Davies, 2008; Lackey, 2013; Turner, West, & Christie, 2013). Similarly, children are much more likely to avoid interacting with cross-gender than same-gender peers (Martin, Fabes, & Hanish, 2014).

One reason for avoiding cross-group interactions is that they tend to be uncomfortable and stressful (Blascovich, Mendes, Hunter, Lickel, & Kowai-Bell, 2001). Indeed, such interactions have been shown to induce anxiety among high-status (Devine, Evett, & Vasquez-Suson, 1996; Ickes, 1984; Stephan & Stephan, 1985) and low-status (Richeson & Trawalter, 2008) group members. Prior experience with outgroup members influences the level of anxiety experienced in intergroup interactions; those individuals with the most contact are the least likely to feel anxious (Britt, Boniecki, Vescio, Biernat, & Brown, 1996; Brown, Maras, Masser, Vivian, & Hewstone, 2001; Dijker, 1987; Islam & Hewstone, 1993; Stephan, Diaz-Loving, & Duran, 2000; Stephan & Stephan, 1985; Stephan, Ybarra, & Bachman, 1999; Trawalter et al., 2009; West, Shelton, & Trail, 2009). Thus, those individuals who might benefit the most from cross-group contact (because they have few outgroup friends) are most likely to experience such interactions as stressful and, as a consequence, as negative.

Unfortunately, the sources of stress during cross-group interactions are not well understood. It is likely that behavioral patterns play a role, such that dyads from differing groups bring different styles and skills to interacting, and that these differences are a source of tension. For example, boys and girls, at the group level, differ in their tendency to engage in rough and tumble play (Maccoby, 2002). Some girls appear to find boys' attempts to engage them in such play aversive (Maccoby, 2002; Martin et al., 2014). Furthermore, behaviors that are construed as confirming negative social stereotypes (e.g., boys are aggressive, girls cry easily) are unlikely to lead to close intimate relationships and may instead reinforce negative intergroup attitudes. This notion is consistent with the evidence that children experience frequent cross-gender interaction but that these interactions rarely become the basis of close friendship and, in turn, fail to counteract children's high levels of gender stereotyping and prejudice (Martin et al., 2014). Friendships are likely to grow out of positive rather than negative intergroup interactions.

3.3 Intergroup Friendship

The third core process in the pathway from intergroup contact to positive intergroup attitudes is the development of warm, close, meaningful, supportive, and trusting relationships with cross-group individuals. Just as intergroup contact does not necessarily lead to intergroup interaction, intergroup interaction does not inevitably lead to intergroup friendship (Saguy & Chernyak-Hai, 2012; Saguy et al., 2009).

What is known about children's friendships with outgroup members? We know that they are relatively uncommon. Same-group friendships are more common than cross-group friendships for race (Aboud, Mendelson, & Purdy, 2003), gender (Martin et al., 2014), age (e.g., French, 1987), and immigrant status (Verkuyten & Martinovic, 2006). However, when children and adults form close friendships with outgroup members, evidence suggests that these relationships are particularly potent in promoting positive intergroup attitudes and behaviors (Hewstone, Cairns, Voci, Hamberger, & Niens, 2006; Levin, van Laar, & Sidanius, 2003; McLaughlin-Volpe, Aron, Wright, & Reis, 2002; Page-Gould, Mendoza-Denton, & Tropp, 2008; Paolini, Hewstone, Cairns, & Voci, 2004; Turner & Cameron, 2016; Turner, Hewstone, & Voci, 2007). However, friendships require that interactions persist over time and lead to affect and beliefs marked by trust, warmth, and closeness. It is vital, therefore, to identify factors that cause cross-group interactions to evolve into friendships.

3.4 Intergroup Attitudes

The final core process in our model concerns intergroup attitudes. We posit that the development of warm, intimate, and supportive relationships with members of a social outgroup produces positive intergroup attitude formation and change among youth. As argued earlier, children who merely encounter outgroup members on the street or within stores, or who interact with such individuals exclusively in formal, structured manners, are unlikely to develop positive intergroup attitudes as a result. Instead, the experience of having a close outgroup friend is hypothesized to causes one to develop positive views of that individual's social group (see Turner & Cameron, 2016, for a similar argument).

Consistent with the notion that friendship affects intergroup attitudes, experimental research with adults has shown that inducing cross-race friendships improves intergroup attitudes (Mendoza-Denton & Page-Gould, 2008, Page-Gould, Mendoza-Denton, Alegre, & Siy, 2010; Page-Gould et al.,

2008; West, Pearson, Dovidio, Shelton, & Trail, 2009). No work has yet employed experimental methodologies to test the consequences of cross-race friendship for children's racial attitudes. However, a quasi-experimental study of gender relations among preschoolers by Martin and colleagues is suggestive of a causal role of friendship in positive intergroup attitudes (Martin et al., 2014). In their study, preschool teachers in a "Buddy Up" intervention condition assigned children to mixed-sex dyads that participated in everyday collaborative activities several times over the course of the week (e.g., drawing, blowing bubbles together, tossing balls to one another). "Buddies" were rotated each week to allow students the opportunity to develop friendships with multiple cross-sex peers. Teachers in the control condition conducted classroom activities as usual. Controlling for children's initial levels of aggression, exclusion, and harassment, analyses of teachers' ratings of children's behaviors at the conclusion of the intervention revealed a significant decrease in aggression toward both male and female peers, less exclusion of both male and female peers, and less gender-related harassment for children who had interacted with a cross-sex buddy as compared to those in the control condition.

4. FACTORS THAT SHAPE CORE PROCESSES

4.1 Factors Affecting Intergroup Contact

4.1.1 Overview

Four factors are hypothesized to govern the frequency with which children encounter outgroup members (represented by ovals in Fig. 1). The first of these factors—societal segregation—is a characteristic of the environment (e.g., school, neighborhood) over which children typically have no control. For example, a child might live within a culture that is widely and routinely segregated by gender or not (e.g., Saudi Arabia and United States, respectively). The remaining factors—perceptions of between- and within-group variability, status seeking and valuing diversity—are factors at the individual level that are hypothesized to affect youth's tendency to self-segregate (i.e., avoid contact with outgroup members by, for example, electing to join clubs and organizations that are comprised of proportionally fewer outgroup members).

4.1.2 Societal Segregation

Societal-level segregation refers to the sorting of individuals by group membership into specific physical spaces (e.g., regions, cities, neighborhoods, schools, organizations, and work settings), and includes *de jure* or *de facto* grouping. Social groups vary in the degree to which they are characterized by societal segregation. Historical and contemporary patterns of segregation by race, religion, and sexual orientation are illustrative. Despite temporary declines in racial segregation following the *Brown v. Board of Education* ruling, racial and ethnic segregation of US schools has returned nearly to its high pre-Brown levels; most Black and Latino students today attend schools in which children of color comprise 90% or more of the student body (Frankenberg & Orfield, 2012). In contrast, religious segregation in schools has declined. Historically, many US children attended schools based on religious group membership (e.g., Catholic schools and Jewish schools), but that trend has waned. For example, approximately 6500 Catholic schools are operating today—down from nearly 13,000 in the 1960s (NCEA, 2013). Segregation based on sexual orientation shows yet another form of change of over time. Throughout most of US history, institutions did not segregate based on sexual orientation but instead instituted policies aimed at negating the existence of sexual minorities or rendering them invisible (e.g., declaring consensual same-sex sexual behavior illegal and treating homosexuality as a mental illness). Increasing public recognition of sexual minority individuals brought segregation and exclusion (President Eisenhower's Executive Order 10450; D'Emilio, 1998). Over time, some sexual minorities began to form separate communities (i.e., neighborhoods, churches, and schools). For instance, in 1985, the Harvey Milk High School, geared toward sexual minority youth, opened in New York City. Moreover, many large American cities now have what are termed "gayborhoods" (e.g., Castro in San Francisco, Boystown in Chicago, West Hollywood in Los Angeles), representing a form of de facto segregation.

Many societies are characterized by contentious battles over whether, and how, to regulate integration of social groups. The US Supreme Court, for example, has issued multiple rulings related to the legality of strategies for segregating (Plessey v. Ferguson, Brown v. Board of Education) and integrating (Regents of California v. Bakke, Fisher v. University of Texas) individuals along racial and ethnic lines (see Frankenberg & Orfield, 2012). Similar battles have occurred concerning sexual minority individuals' right to serve in the US military (i.e., the repeal of "Don't Ask, Don't Tell"). Additionally, a heated debate is currently being waged over policies related to the use of gender segregation within public schools (Pahlke, Bigler, & Patterson, 2014).

How does societal integration affect children's intergroup contact? It seems obvious that institutional segregation limits opportunities for intergroup contact (i.e., encounters) with outgroup members. This is likely to be especially true for members of proportionally large rather than small groups. For example, the large-scale creation of high schools designed specifically for sexual minority youth would produce modest reductions in such youth's interactions with straight peers, but would more drastically reduce the proportion of straight youth that have contact with sexual minority peers. The absence of contact is likely to decrease children's opportunities to modify established negative attitudes via exposure to counter-stereotypic outgroup members (Allport, 1954; Pettigrew & Tropp, 2006). More powerfully, however, the absence of contact negates the opportunity for interaction and friendship formation. Consistent with this notion, Knifsend and Juvonen (2014) and Wilson, Rodkin, and Ryan (2014) reported that when children had fewer cross-ethnicity classmates, they had disproportionately greater numbers of same-ethnicity friends.

In addition to restricting children's opportunities for intergroup contact, societal segregation is hypothesized to affect intergroup contact by shaping children's cognitions about outgroups. Children strive to make sense of the contexts in which they are embedded. As outlined by Bigler and Liben (2006, 2007), children who are exposed to societal segregation (e.g., encounter organizations, such as schools, whose members comprise a single social group) are likely to construct reasons for the nonrandom sorting of individuals across contexts, inferring that social groups are inherently, deeply, and meaningfully different. For example, children who witness racial segregation within or across schools are likely to view racial groups as characterized by high levels of within-group similarity and between-group difference, and to endorse stereotypic beliefs about race (Bigler & Liben, 2006).

4.1.3 Perceptions of Group Variability

Although children's ecologies are characterized by greater or lesser degrees of institutional segregation over which they have no control, children may also *elect* to embed themselves within more or less segregated contexts (e.g., groups, activities, and organizations). One individual difference hypothesized to drive the tendency for children to prefer more versus less segregated contexts is perceptions of group variability, a cognitive aspect of intergroup attitudes. Children differ in the extent to which they interpret social groups as marking meaningful dimensions of differences; some children perceive high levels of variability across, and low levels of variability within, social groups (Guinote, Mouro, Pereira, & Monteiro, 2007). Children often view the source of between-group variation as innate (e.g., essentialist; see Gelman, 2003). Regardless of the perceived source, we hypothesize that children who perceive high levels of between-group variability (i.e., "We are different from them") and low levels of within-group variability, especially concerning the outgroup (referred to as *outgroup homogeneity*, "they are all alike") will be less likely to seek outgroup contact than their peers.

Correlational studies indicate links between perceptions of group variability and contact with outgroups. In the case of race, high school students in South Africa who perceived higher levels of within-group variability had more cross-race friendships than their peers (Swart, Hewstone, Christ, & Voci, 2010). In the case of gender, children who endorse more gender-stereotypic beliefs (e.g., believe that girls and boy differ substantially from each other) spend more time in same-sex peer groups than their peers who endorse fewer gender-stereotypic beliefs (see Martin et al., 2014). Similarly, children and adults who endorse essentialist beliefs about gender (e.g., "Boys and girls' brains are different so they learn science differently") are more likely to be affiliated with sex-segregated than coeducational institutions (Pahlke et al., 2014). Although we posit that perceptions of group variability are causally related to intergroup contact, the association between the two constructs is also likely to reflect causal effects that run in the reverse direction; increased contact with outgroup members is likely to produce modest increases in the perceptions of outgroup heterogeneity (see Fig. 1).

4.1.4 Status Seeking

The second individual difference hypothesized to affect the frequency with which children come into contact with outgroup members is status seeking. As early as age 8, some children are motivated by a desire to appear high in social status (Rodkin, Ryan, Jamison, & Wilson, 2013). We hypothesize that status seeking affects children's willingness to enter spaces shared by cross-group others, albeit it does so differently among members of groups that are higher and lower in social status. Among members of higher status groups, concerns about status are hypothesized to drive avoidance of cross-group contact, whereas among members of lower status groups, concerns about status are hypothesized to facilitate cross-group contact. Support for this hypothesis comes from a study of social goal orientation and cross-race friendship by Wilson et al. (2014). They reported that within a school context in which African Americans were high in status (i.e., perceived as cool), students who were motivated by status concerns were especially interested in befriending African Americans. Thus, among African Americans, status seeking predicted increases in segregation from fall to spring; among European Americans, it predicted decreases in segregation from fall to spring. Future work should examine the role of status seeking within other domains. For example, our model predicts that elementary school-age boys who are high in status concerns will be more likely to avoid girls than will be those boys who are low in status concerns. The reverse may be true following puberty, when status is associated with heterosexual romantic success. In the case of sexual orientation, sexual majority youth who seek contact with sexual minorities peers (e.g., by joining gay-straight alliances) may be lower in status seeking than their peers.

4.1.5 Valuing Diversity

A third individual difference hypothesized to affect the frequency with which children come into contact with outgroup members is the degree to which they value diversity. Overall, the US is characterized by increasingly pro-diversity social norms (Chemers, Oskamp, & Constanzo, 1995; Dovidio & Gaertner, 2000; Gurin, Dey, Hurtado, & Gurin, 2002; McConahay, 1983). Individuals' support for diversity is diminished, however, when it competes with other values (e.g., status, money, and power; Rohrbach & Bigler, 2013). As a consequence, individuals' major decisions, such as where one elects to buy a house and enroll one's children in school, do not seem to be driven as strongly by diversity valuing as by other values (see Bishop, 2008). Nonetheless, those children who value interacting with others who differ from themselves are, we argue, more likely to seek out contact with outgroup members than their peers. Consistent with this view, Tropp and Bianchi (2006) reported that individuals who valued diversity more strongly showed greater interest in intergroup contact than individuals who valued diversity less strongly.

4.2 Developmental Changes in Intergroup Contact

We could locate no work that has examined whether overall levels of contact per se with outgroup members changes over the life course. Rather than expecting age to universally increase (or decrease) intergroup contact, we expect age to moderate the effects of each of the factors hypothesized to affect intergroup contact. For example, the power of societal-level segregation to predict levels of contact with outgroup members is likely to diminish as children age. As they move into adolescence (a period marked by increased autonomy and identity formation), youth have more power to choose with whom they interact and socialize (Eccles, 1999). For example, they may influence parental decisions about the schools that they attend and be able to transport themselves to new intergroup contexts. Additionally, as children age, they are likely to become more concerned with social status and more cognizant of diversity as a potential personal value. Thus, individual differences in status seeking and valuing diversity may be more predictive of intergroup contact among older than young children.

4.3 Factors Affecting Intergroup Interactions

4.3.1 Overview

Two aspects of the immediate environment are hypothesized to shape the quality of children's intergroup interaction: interaction structure and environmental belongingness cues. In addition, we argue that group-based rejection concerns, a relational process in which individuals develop, interpret, and act on perceived rejection on the basis of one's social group membership influence social and cognitive aspects of children's intergroup interactions (see Fig. 1).

4.3.2 Interaction Structure

Interactions occur within settings that vary along a continuum from highly *structured* (constrained by predetermined goals or expectations; e.g., ordering food in restaurant) to highly *unstructured* (unconstrained by a predetermined goals or expectation; hanging out at mall). Cross-group interactions that are unstructured are likely to be particularly challenging for youth. The lack of a goal can leave children (a) without a common basis for conversation and interaction, (b) self-conscious of their behavior, and (c) insecure about their social skills. For example, Whites who engage in unstructured (but not structured) interracial interactions tend to experience concerns about appearing prejudiced (Apfelbaum, Pauker, Ambady, Sommers, & Norton, 2008; Apfelbaum & Sommers, 2009; Apfelbaum, Sommers, & Norton, 2008), whereas African Americans tend to focus on ensuring the interaction goes smoothly (Shelton, Richeson, & Salvatore, 2005). In the case of gender, those children who feel less efficacious in their ability to understand, communicate with, and engage in activities with cross-gender peers tend to have fewer cross-gender friends than their peers (Martin et al., 2014).

Structured settings (e.g., basketball practice) seem to ameliorate some of the potential negative aspects of intergroup interactions (Babbitt & Sommers, 2011). However, structured interactions can be problematic as well, especially when they make social stereotypes salient. In the case of race, the requirement that cross-race dyads discuss the topic of race (rather than a neutral topic) appears to make Whites anxious, undermining the quality of the interaction (Richeson & Trawalter, 2008). In the case of gender, some structured interactions (e.g., group classroom assignments) may lead boys to adopt dominant, and girls to adopt subservient, roles. Thus, we propose that cross-group interactions that are structured to avoid social stereotypes provide the best initial basis for positive intergroup interaction. However, as will become clear later, experiences within structured interactions alone, even when they are positive, are insufficient to produce close, intimate cross-group friendships. The experience of attending school, working, or playing a sport alongside members of a differing social groups does not, we argue, produce friendship or positive intergroup attitudes among youth, unless accompanied by interactions within unstructured environments that promote friendship.

4.3.3 Environmental Belongingness Cues

A second factor hypothesized to affect the quality of children's cross-group interactions concerns the characteristics of the environment in which interactions are embedded. Individuals typically manipulate their environment to reflect their personality, beliefs, and values (Gosling, Ko, Mannarelli, & Morris, 2002). The manifestation of personality in physical environments can extend beyond the individual to larger entities or institutions (e.g., schools and workplace) and can influence one's sense of belonging in an environment and concerns about being judged based on one's identity (i.e., social identity contingencies; Purdie-Vaughns, Steele, Davies, Ditlmann, & Crosby, 2008). We propose that settings that promote a sense of belonging among ingroup and outgroup members lead children to experience more positive cross-group interactions than settings that promote the belongingness among only a single group (e.g., females, Christians).

Evidence concerning the power of environmental cues to affect social perceptions and motivations comes from work on gender and STEM. Murphy, Steele, and Gross (2007) showed men and women STEM college majors an advertisement for a college STEM conference that featured either a gender balance (1 male:1 female) or uneven balance (3 men: 1 woman) in conference attendees. Women who viewed the unbalanced video reported lower levels of belongingness and expressed less desire to participate in the conference (Murphy et al., 2007). Additional environmental cues, such as classroom decor, can impact women's interest in STEM fields. For instance, computer science classrooms with stereotypical items (e.g., Star Trek posters) compared to classrooms with nonstereotypical items (e.g., nature posters) negatively affected women's interest, anticipated success, and feelings of belonging in computer science (Cheryan, Meltzoff, & Kim, 2011; Cheryan, Plaut, Davies, & Steele, 2009). The language spoken within an environment also appears to serve as a belongingness cue. Aboud and Sankar (2007) found that elementary school-age children attending bilingual schools were equally likely to have same- and cross ethno-linguistic friends, perhaps because the presence of their native language led both groups to feel valued.

4.3.4 Group-Based Rejection Concerns

A third factor hypothesized to affect the quality of intergroup interactions is youth's concern about rejection on the basis of their social group membership. Within all social relationships, individuals risk rejection in some form. Awareness of rejection can influence one's perception of both current and potential interpersonal relationships (Buckley, Winkel, & Leary, 2004; Downey & Feldman, 1996; Williams, Cheung, & Choi, 2000). Based on prior experience, some individuals develop anxious expectations of rejections in interpersonal interactions (i.e., rejection sensitivity; Downey & Feldman, 1996; Feldman & Downey, 1994). Importantly, interpersonal rejection can occur on the basis of personal attributes such as one's sense of humor, or social group membership, such as one's sexual orientation (Pachankis, Goldfried, & Ramrattan, 2008), race (Mendoza-Denton, Downey, Purdie, Davis, & Pietrzak, 2002), or gender (London, Downey, Romero-Canyas, Rattan, & Tyson, 2012). We propose that children who enter into cross-group interactions with heightened concerns about group-based rejection are more likely than their peers to experience negative interactions.

Support for this notion comes from studies of cross-race interactions. Individuals show heightened concern about race-based rejection when they interact with others who appear racially prejudiced. One marker of racial prejudice is a racially homogeneous friendship network (e.g., White individuals with exclusively White friends). African Americans expect a more difficult interaction when presented with a White partner who has a racially homogeneous friendship network compared to a more diverse friendship network (Wout, Murphy, & Steele, 2010). Similarly, Whites are more likely to be concerned about being rejected by a Black partner who ostensibly has a Black rather than a White best friend (Shapiro, Baldwin, Williams, & Trawalter, 2011). Although there is little available evidence on the topic, we expect that children also attend to the diversity of their peers' social networks and such information, in turn, affects the degree to which they experience rejection concerns. If such speculation is correct, these processes may comprise one of the ways in which the "climate" within schools and classrooms affects children's intergroup relations.

4.4 Developmental Changes in Intergroup Interactions

To date, few studies have investigated age-related changes in the quality of children's in vivo interactions with outgroup members. This gap represents a serious limitation to understanding intergroup attitudes and relations, and we hope our model spurs research on the topic. As children age, their schemas for social groups (definitions, norms, and stereotypes) become more sophisticated (McKown & Weinstein, 2003; Rhodes, 2012), affecting, in turn, their interactions with outgroup members. It seems possible that young children, whose understanding of social groups is more limited, might enjoy more successful cross-group interactions than older children. For example, young children—at the group level—are likely to know fewer stereotypes and be less reflective and self-conscious about behaviors within cross-group interactions than older children. Thus, stereotype threat concerns within interactions should be less common among younger than older youth. At the same time, youths' limited experience with, and understanding of, outgroups' histories, customs, preferences, etc., may undermine cross-group (but not same-group) interactions (Turner & Cameron, 2016). For example, a mother who participated in one of our studies reported that upon coming across the movie *The Wizard of Oz*, an African American 5-year-old said to her White classmate, "Oh, you have the White one! I have the Black one!" Her classmate, being unfamiliar with *The Wiz* and the terminology for race, was befuddled, and as a result, the interaction faltered and ended.

4.5 Factors Affecting Intergroup Friendship

4.5.1 Overview

The likelihood that youth who interact with outgroup members will develop reciprocal friendships with these individuals is hypothesized to be regulated by five factors (depicted in Fig. 1): (1) social group consciousness,

(2) motivation to appear nonprejudice, (3) intergroup transactional engagement, (4) social norms, and (5) fear of the transitive property of social stigma.

4.5.1.1 Social Group Consciousness

Some youth, but not others, readily communicate about social groups (e.g., their meaning, between- and within-group variations, biases). We speculate that this individual difference carries consequences for cross-group friendship formation, with those individuals who are willing to discuss group differences being more likely to form friendships with outgroup members than their reticent peers.

There are several possible motivations for noting and discussing (versus ignoring and avoiding) the topic of social group membership. One such motivation concerns individuals' views of social justice and how it might be achieved. Some adults believe that social equity has already been achieved, or is best achieved by emphasizing common humanity and downplaying factors that are associated with difference, including social group membership. In the case of race, this belief is referred to as colorblindness (Neville, Lilly, Lee, Duran, & Browne, 2000; Wolsko, Park, Judd, & Wittenbrink, 2000). Individuals who subscribe to colorblind ideology are reluctant to address, or even acknowledge, race in common, everyday interactions—even when it is relevant (Apfelbaum, Sommers, et al., 2008; Norton, Sommers, Apfelbaum, Pura, & Ariely, 2006). For example, Apfelbaum, Pauker, et al. (2008) asked children to play a game in which they were presented with photographs of diverse individuals. The goal was to guess the picture their partner was holding while asking as few questions as possible. Despite the utility of inquiring about targets' race, White children, especially those over age 10, avoided using race to narrow down the possible choices. This effect is particularly strong when Whites interact with Black partners (Norton et al., 2006).

Ironically, individuals who adopt a colorblind ideology appear at a disadvantage in forming quality interracial relationships. African Americans perceive Whites who avoid mentioning race as more likely to be racially biased than Whites who discuss race (Apfelbaum, Sommers, et al., 2008). Moreover, those who adopt a colorblind mentality are more likely to develop and display explicit and implicit bias (Richeson & Nussbaum, 2004; Son & Shelton, 2011; Vorauer, Gagnon, & Sasaki, 2009; Wolsko et al., 2000) and tend to justify racial resentment (Norton et al., 2006). Adopting a colorblind mentality in burgeoning interracial friendships may lead to a less intimate friendship or worse, deteriorate the acquaintanceship before a friendship can develop. Although social group consciousness is more acceptable for many social categories than for race, we nonetheless argue that children who are (a) attentive to, (b) willing to acknowledge, and (c) open and enthusiastic about discussing and learning about the meaning the social groups are especially likely to develop friendships with outgroup members.

4.5.1.2 Motivation to Appear Nonprejudiced

The motivations that drive individuals to respond to outgroup members without stereotyping and prejudice differ across individuals, and can stem from internal (i.e., one's ideals for the self) or external (i.e., one's desire to avoid being labeled a racist by others) sources (Devine et al., 1996; Richeson & Shelton, 2007). Whether youth are driven primarily by internal or external motivation is likely to affect their behavior in cross-group interactions. With respect to race, individuals who are externally motivated to respond without prejudice are more threatened by outgroup members (Bean et al., 2012), which may lead them to avoid acknowledging or discussing race with newly formed cross-race acquaintanceships. Similarly, those who are externally motivated to avoid sexism may avoid discussing gender-related topics (e.g., unequal pay, and feminism) with cross-gender peers (Klonis, Plant, & Devine, 2005; Plant & Devine, 1998) and, as a consequence, their cross-gender friendships may lack intimacy relative to same-gender friendships. In contrast, youth who are internally motivated to avoid social stereotyping and prejudice may both seek out and respond nondefensively to feedback from outgroup peers about the quality of their interactions, including information about insensitive or offensive behaviors. No research to date has examined whether youth's motivation to appear nonprejudice affect the formation or maintenance of cross-group friendships.

4.5.1.3 Intergroup Transactional Engagement

The success of interactions in fostering close friendships depends on interpersonal behaviors that convey intimacy, including disclosing personal information and acting in a caring manner (Reis & Shaver, 1988). Self-disclosure, supportiveness, and openness, as well as the total number and frequency of interactions, are important predictors of friendship formation and maintenance (Fehr, 1996; Hays, 1984; Oswald, Clark, & Kelly, 2004).

Among elementary school-age children, same-race friendships yield higher levels of intimacy and are more stable across time than cross-race friendships (Aboud et al., 2003; Hallinan & Williams, 1987). One possible explanation for the discrepancy is that same- and cross-race friends differ in the quality of activities they participate in together. One study using a nationally representative sample of U.S. teenagers found that cross-race friends reported fewer shared activities than same-race friends (Kao & Joyner, 2004), which have been found to be key in promoting positive intergroup attitudes (e.g., Turner et al., 2007; Wagner, van Dick, Pettigrew, & Christ, 2003). Similar effects have been reported among adults (Davies et al., 2011). For instance, White college freshmen who were paired with a cross-race rather than same-race roommate were less likely to engage in intimacy-building behaviors and less likely to consider their roommate a friend (Trail, Shelton, & West, 2009).

The lack of intimacy-building behaviors may be a result of stereotypic perceptions of cross-group others, such as underestimating mutual interests (Shelton, Richeson, & Bergsieker, 2009; Vorauer, 2005). However, if they emerge, intimacy-building behaviors are likely to promote quality cross-race friendships (Davies et al., 2011). For instance, self-disclosure in cross-race friendship appears to improve intergroup attitudes by creating a sense of empathy for outgroup members (Turner et al., 2007) and reinforcing the idea that outgroup contact is valuable (Davies, Aron, Wright, Brody, & McLaughlin-Volpe, 2010; Page-Gould et al., 2008; van Dick et al., 2004). Additionally, shared activities may induce a common identity (e.g., basketball player, musician), which appears to foster cross-group friendship and positive intergroup attitudes (West, Pearson, et al., 2009), to (discussed later).

4.5.1.4 Social Norms

Humans look to others to infer how they should behave (Aronson, Wilson, & Akert, 2005). Indeed, individuals are informed of how to behave via social norms enforced by their group (Cialdini, Kallgren, & Reno, 1991). *Descriptive norms* provide a behavioral index for individuals (Schultz, Nolan, Cialdini, Goldstein, & Griskevicius, 2007), whereas *injunctive norms* indicate the extent to which a behavior is approved of within a group (Reno, Cialdini, & Kallgren, 1993). Both types of social norms influence intergroup behavior, affecting the degree to which individuals (a) like outgroup members (Nesdale & Dalton, 2011), (b) discriminate against outgroup members (Shapiro & Neuberg, 2008), and (c) recognize stereotyping and discrimination when it occurs (O'Brien, Kinias, & Major, 2008). For example, Rutland and colleagues have reported that children's desire to uphold ingroup norms can influence their decision to reject or accept others in intergroup contexts (Abrams, Palmer, Rutland, Cameron, & Van de Vyer, 2013; Rutland, Cameron, Milne, & McGeorge, 2005).

Social norms concerning cross-group friendships appear present across the lifespan. For example, it is generally expected that men and women will form more same-sex than cross-sex friendships (Adams, 1985; Lee & Troop-Gordon, 2011). It is common for children to claim that members of the other gender have "cooties" and are unlikable. Indeed, many adults view children's rejection of cross-sex peers as friends normative and acceptable (Bigler & Liben, 2006). Likewise, it appears that even young children are aware that individuals are expected to befriend members of their own social groups (Rhodes, 2012). For example, Killen and her colleagues have found that children are sensitive to social norms regarding intergroup relations (McGlothlin & Killen, 2006, 2010). Children's perceptions of their parents' normative beliefs regarding intergroup relationships significantly predict the degree to which children seek cross-race friendships and romantic relationships (Edmonds & Killen, 2009; Mwamwenda, 1998). Thus, we expect that cross-group friendships are more likely within environments in which social norms support their existence.

4.5.1.5 Fear of Transitive Property of Social Stigma

An additional factor that it is likely to affect cross-group friendship formation is the degree to which individuals view others' social networks as representative of their values. The adage "A man is known by the company he keeps" suggests that humans look to others' social network for information. For instance, with regard to race, individuals' use information about the racial diversity of others' social networks to make predictions about the ease with which interactions are likely to occur (Wout et al., 2010) and the likelihood of rejection (Shapiro et al., 2011).

Awareness that one's social network conveys information about the self may lead to concerns about the category membership of the individuals one befriends. The formation of friendships with outgroup members may constitute a threat of backlash from ingroup members (e.g., social rejection and limited access to social capital). Cross-group interactions, because they are typically neither affectionate nor intimate, are unlikely to carry the same level of threat associated with cross-group friendship. With respect to gender, for example, Maccoby (2002) speculated that young children avoid playing with cross-sex peers out of concern about being teased by ingroup members. Although backlash and black sheep effects are well documented (Abrams et al., 2013), children's awareness and fear of the phenomena, and consequent effects on their motivation to form and maintain cross-group friends, is understudied.

4.6 Developmental Changes in Intergroup Friendships

The predictors and qualities of friendships change across age. For example, many adolescents (but few children) report that friends are their most important source of support and influence (Collins & Steinberg, 2007). More so than childhood friendships, adolescent friendships are characterized by support, companionship, security, loyalty, intimacy, equality, and investment, as well as reciprocity in liking, affect, self-disclosure, cooperation, and responsiveness (Bukowski, Motzoi, & Meyer, 2009). Thus, it is likely that cross-group friendships established in childhood that do not develop these qualities will dissipate across adolescence. Furthermore, it is likely that the factors hypothesized to affect intergroup friendship operate to differing degrees across childhood and adolescence.

For example, as they age, children become more aware of, and concerned about, how others may perceive them (Malloy, Albright, & Scarpati, 2007). This developing awareness may be the cause of White children's reluctance to mention race, for example, after the age of 10 years. Similarly, although young children are aware of social norms dictating ingroup favoritism (Rhodes, 2012), children are likely to grow increasingly conscious of the negative perceptions that are likely to occur as a result of their own befriending of outgroup members, perhaps especially those from lower status or stigmatized groups, as they acquire more sophisticated perspective-taking skills. Indeed, such consciousness may not emerge until middle childhood (approximately age 8 year), which is when cross-race and cross-gender friendships begin to dwindle (Aboud et al., 2003; Maccoby, 2002). This awareness, paired with children's concerns about social rejection, may motivate them to avoid forming new intergroup friendships and to disengage from established outgroup friendships.

4.7 Factors Affecting Intergroup Attitudes

The cognitive and emotional mechanisms by which cross-group friendships produce attitude formation and change are not well understood. We argue that two factors, one cognitive and one emotional, contribute to children's intergroup attitude change as a function of friendships: common identity and affective change.

4.7.1 Common Identity

As early as 1954, Allport argued that the formation of a superordinate identity with outgroup members (e.g., an American identity among racially diverse individuals) elicits positive intergroup attitudes. Somewhat later, Sherif et al. (1961) argued that intergroup interaction aimed at achieving a common goal leads to decreased prejudice, in part because such interactions create a common identity. The common ingroup identity model (Gaertner & Dovidio, 2000) posits that the recategorization of outgroup members into a shared, superordinate category promotes more harmonious intergroup interactions. Consistent with this model, empirical studies indicate that inducing a common ingroup identity reduces intergroup bias and creates positive intergroup attitudes (Cameron, Rutland, Brown, & Douch, 2006; Gaertner & Dovidio, 2000; Riek, Mania, Gaertner, McDonald, & Lamoreaux, 2010).

It is clear that the formation of a common identity (and consequent decreases in intergroup antipathy) does not require friendship with particular outgroup individuals. Although friendship is not necessary for the formation of a common identity, it is certainly likely to promote it. When forming close relationships with others, people often feel a sense of interpersonal closeness. Closeness or intimacy in relationships can be described as "sharing that which is inmost with others" (McAdams, 1988, p. 18). People tend to represent close social partners (e.g., friends and family) as overlapping with their own sense of self (Aron, Aron, Tudor, & Nelson, 1991) or as forming a common identity (Agnew, Loving, Le, & Goodfriend, 2004). The extent to which individuals incorporate a social partner's traits into their own self-views varies across individuals (Aron et al., 1991 and predicts a host of relational outcomes, including relationship satisfaction (Lewandowski, Nardone, & Raines, 2010), closeness (Aron & Fraley, 1999), and relational understanding (Waugh & Fredrickson, 2006).

Children appear to incorporate the self into views of the ingroup beginning as early as 4 years of age (Patterson & Bigler, 2006; Sani & Bennett, 2009). Some youth also appear to incorporate aspects of outgroups into their self-identities, producing what is referred to as *social identity complexity* by Knifsend and Juvonen (2014). In their study of US seventh graders, social identity complexity mediated the link between cross-ethnic friendships and ethnic intergroup attitudes when youth attended a school with a high proportion of cross-ethnic peers. Thus, it seems likely that youth whose cross-group friendships lead them to incorporate aspects of outgroups (e.g., the activities, skills, and preferences associated with outgroups in their culture) into their self identity are especially likely to develop positive intergroup attitudes.

4.7.2 Affective Change

Although cognitive dimensions of intergroup interactions (e.g., common identity and recategorization) are important aspects of attitude change, affective dimensions of intergroup relations appear to be even more powerful agents of attitude change (see Tropp & Pettigrew, 2005). Affect (e.g., feelings of comfort vs anxiety, empathy vs dispassion, and liking vs disdain) is an important component of cross-group interaction and cross-group friendships (discussed earlier), and appears to be strongly related to intergroup attitude change associated with cross-group friendship (Herek & Capitanio, 1996; Levin et al., 2003; McLaughlin-Volpe et al., 2002; Paolini et al., 2004; Pettigrew, 1998; Wright, Aron, & Tropp, 2002).

Much of the evidence concerning the role of affect in intergroup attitude change concerns race. Past research on cross-race friendships has examined effects of the total number of intergroup interactions—and their level of intimacy—on general outgroup attitudes. Overall, results indicate that greater numbers of cross-group interactions predict more positive outgroup attitudes, but only among those individuals who have friendships with outgroup members (McLaughlin-Volpe et al., 2002). Additionally, Pettigrew (1998) found that cross-race friendships predicted reduced prejudice, especially on measures that assess affective responses toward outgroup (e.g., sympathy and admiration). Similarly, Swart et al.'s (2010) study of South African youth found that anxiety and empathy during interactions mediated the relation of cross-race friendships and positive intergroup attitudes.

Prejudice is often rooted in negative affect (e.g., contempt and disgust; Brown & Henriquez, 2008; Embrick, Walther, & Wickens, 2007; Olatunji, 2008). The experience of positive emotions within the context of cross-group friendships appears to undermine such negative affect. Based on previous work, we expect that the emotions that youth experience during close friendships with outgroup individuals (comfort, empathy, and liking) facilitate the generalization of positive attitudes to the entire outgroup.

4.8 Developmental Changes in Intergroup Attitudes

Children show evidence of stereotyping and prejudice towards many social groups by 4 years of age (Doosje et al., 2011; Raabe & Beelmann, 2011). Most contemporary theoretical models posit that intergroup attitudes are the result of interactions between the organismic characteristics (e.g., cognitive constraints and proclivities) that children bring to their social worlds and the contexts in which they are embedded. For instance, Bigler and Liben (2006) suggest that children look to adults for cues about which dimensions of human variation are important. According to developmental intergroup theory, the presence of social category labeling and the explicit and implicit sorting of individuals along particular dimensions (e.g., race and gender) renders some social categories psychologically salient and, in turn, leads children to categorize groups on those particular dimensions. These categorizations develop into stereotypes and prejudices as a result of internally driven (e.g., essentialist thought) and externally driven (detecting group-attribute links in the environment) processes. Importantly, age-related increases in the sophistication and flexibility of children's cognitive skills generally produce reductions in children's social stereotyping and prejudice (Bigler & Liben, 2006). However, relatively little is known about how the process of friendship formation intersections with children's cognitive abilities and intergroup attitudes.

It may be that younger children are less able than older children to construct a self-identity that includes outgroup members, even as they form outgroup friendships. Indeed, young children lack hierarchical and multiple classification abilities, which may prevent them from viewing themselves as sharing a superordinate identity with outgroup members (e.g., males and female are both humans) or as having traits or skills that are associated with both ingroups and outgroups (e.g., liking both dolls and trucks). Conversely, it is possible that young children's cognitive limitations are facilitative of some cross-group friendships. For example, preschool children tend to center on some particular dimension (e.g., color) of stimuli and have difficulty turning their attention to alternative dimensions (e.g., shape). It is possible that children center on one particular dimension of their peers (e.g., gender), undermining their attention to other categories. Thus, for example, two boys of differing ethnicities may be more likely to become friends in earlier than later childhood.

4.9 Pathway Between Intergroup Attitudes and Intergroup Contact

Intergroup attitudes are not an endpoint with respect to individuals' outcomes but instead shape one's future social behaviors. Thus, our model includes a directional arrow from intergroup attitudes to intergroup contact (see Fig. 1). Specifically, we propose that positive intergroup attitudes play a causal role in increasing intergroup contact. In addition, however, we propose an individual difference variable that may mediate this feedback loop: self-expansion.

4.9.1 Self-Expansion

Self-expansion provides an explanation for why individuals seek and maintain relationships (Aron, Aron, & Norman, 2001). According to self-expansion theorists, humans have a fundamental need to expand their sense of self by exploring and acquiring new identities, learning new perspectives, or participating in novel activities. The goal of self-expansion is to boost one's potential self-efficacy in achieving goals by increasing access to resources (Aron & McLaughlin-Volpe, 2002). One process by which individuals expand the self is the formation of close relationships with individuals who are perceived to provide access to resources. Including aspects of others into the self (discussed in the previous section) is the mechanism by which close relationships promote self-expansion and, in turn, self-efficacy. In other words, including another person's resources, identities, and perspectives into one's self-concept creates a more complex sense of self and, in turn, provides a larger pool of available resources.

With regard to intergroup relations, cross-group friendships provide individuals with unique opportunities for self-expansion. For instance, individuals who perceived a new friend as different from themselves (e.g., cross-sex, cross-religious, and cross-political orientation) were more likely to modify their self-concept (i.e., report new unique self-descriptions) over the course of a 6-week period (McLaughlin-Volpe, 2002). Specifically, befriending outgroup members may provide a diverse set of potential resources (beyond one's own ingroup) and motivate an individual to seek additional cross-group contact (Wright et al., 2002). Indeed, inducing cross-race friendships among individuals who are highly prejudiced reduces negative intergroup attitudes and increases motivation to seek novel friendships with outgroup members (Page-Gould et al., 2008). Unfortunately, very little research has investigated the potential role of self-expansion as a motivator of outgroup contact among youth.

5. CONCLUSIONS

The central goal of this chapter was to selectively review and synthesize research within social and developmental psychology concerning intergroup attitudes and behavior and propose a integrative model, GIFT, of the processes by which intergroup contact influences and shapes intergroup attitudes. GIFT contains four core processes: (1) intergroup contact, (2) intergroup interaction, (3) intergroup friendship, and (4) intergroup attitudes. Bidirectional causal pathways link each core process, and each process is shaped by a set of contextual, cognitive, social, and affective variables. The model is designed to be applicable to all potential intergroup contexts but is not meant to be exhaustive. Intergroup relations are complex and it is likely that additional factors have causal influence on the four core processes.

Like others (e.g., Killen et al., 2013; Turner & Cameron, 2016), we highlight the role of friendship in the processes of children's intergroup attitude formation and change. Most children and adults come into contact with others who are members of differing social groups (races, religions, gender) during the course of their daily lives, while engaging in work (job, school) and leisure activities (traveling, shopping). Most of these individuals—from both same- and other social groups—will not become close social partners and, we argue, such encounters have trivial effects on intergroup attitudes. Instead most individuals form their closest social bonds with same-group others, an occurrence that, perhaps because it is so common, is considered routine, normative, and acceptable. We argue, however, that the formation of close social bonds with cross-group others is a vital component of positive intergroup attitudes and crucial to creating and maintaining social equity and justice.

By providing a more comprehensive model than was previously available, we hope to spark systematic research that will provide a more accurate understanding of the pathway from intergroup contact to positive intergroup attitudes among youth. Longitudinal empirical work is especially needed on the individual and contextual factors that are predictive of children's attempts to establish and retain cross-group friendships, and the consequences of cross-group friendships for children's self-esteem, sense of belonging, knowledge of and commitment to ending social injustice, social-emotional well-being, and cognitive competence. It is possible, for example, that environmental or contextual factors are especially important in guiding the formation and maintenance of cross-group friendships in early childhood, and that individuals differences in children's qualities (e.g., social group consciousness, motivations to appear nonprejudice) play more powerful roles in later childhood and adolescences. It will also be important for researchers to adopt experimental methods to manipulate children's opportunities for, and experiences with, cross-group peers and adults, to clarify relations among children's qualities, their opportunities for and experiences with cross-group friendships, and the consequences of such friendships for developmental outcomes. Guided by new insights, researchers can design and test additional interventions aimed at promoting positive intergroup interactions and attitudes. Furthermore, researcher can assess whether positive intergroup interactions, especially cross-group friendship, are predictive of behaviors that produce social equity and justice.

REFERENCES

Aboud, F., Mendelson, M., & Purdy, K. (2003). Cross-race peer relations and friendship quality. *International Journal of Behavioral Development, 27*, 165–173.

Aboud, F., & Sankar, J. (2007). Friendship and identity in a language-integrated school. *International Journal of Behavioral Development, 31*, 445–453.

Abrams, D., Palmer, S. B., Rutland, A., Cameron, L., & Van de Vyer, J. (2013). Evaluations of and reasoning about normative and deviant ingroup and outgroup members: Development of the black sheep effect. *Developmental Psychology, 50*, 258–270.

Adams, R. G. (1985). People would talk: Normative barriers to cross-sex friendships for elderly women. *The Gerontologist, 25*, 605–611.

Agnew, C. R., Loving, T. J., Le, B., & Goodfriend, W. (2004). In D. Mashek & A. P. Aron (Eds.), *Handbook of closeness and intimacy* (pp. 103–115). Mahwah, NJ: Lawrence Erlbaum.

Allport, G. (1954). *The nature of prejudice*. Reading, MA: Addison-Wesley.

Apfelbaum, E. P., Pauker, K., Ambady, N., Sommers, S. R., & Norton, M. I. (2008). Learning (not) to talk about race: When older children underperform in social categorization. *Developmental Psychology, 44*, 1513–1518.

Apfelbaum, E., & Sommers, S. R. (2009). Liberating effects of losing executive control: When regulatory strategies turn maladaptive. *Psychological Science, 20*, 139–143.

Apfelbaum, E., Sommers, S. R., & Norton, M. I. (2008). Seeing race and seeming racist? Evaluating strategic colorblindness in social interaction. *Journal of Personality and Social Psychology, 95*, 918–932.

Aron, A., Aron, E. N., & Norman, C. (2001). Self-expansion model of motivation and cognition in close relationships and beyond. In M. Clark & G. Fletcher (Eds.), *Interpersonal processes: Vol. 2. Blackwell's handbook of social psychology*. Oxford: Blackwell Publishers.

Aron, A., Aron, E. N., Tudor, M., & Nelson, G. (1991). Close relationships as including other in the self. *Journal of Personality and Social Psychology, 60*, 241–253.

Aron, A., & Fraley, B. (1999). Relationship closeness as including other in the self: Cognitive underpinnings and measures. *Special Issue: Social Cognition and Relationships, 17*, 140–160.

Aron, A., & McLaughlin-Volpe, T. (2002). Including others in the self: Extensions to own and partner's group memberships. In M. Brewer & C. Sedikides (Eds.), *Individual self, relational self, and collective self: Partners, opponents, or strangers*. New York, NY: Psychology Press.

Aronson, E., Wilson, T. D., & Akert, A. M. (2005). *Social psychology* (5th ed.). Upper Saddle River, NJ: Prentice Hall.

Babbitt, L. G., & Sommers, S. R. (2011). Framing matters: Contextual influences on interracial interactions outcomes. *Personality and Social Psychology Bulletin, 37*, 1233–1244.

Bean, M. G., Slaten, D. G., Horton, W. S., Murphy, M. C., Todd, A. R., & Richeson, J. A. (2012). Prejudice concerns and race-based attentional bias: New evidence from eye-tracking. *Social Psychological and Personality Science, 3*, 722–729.

Bigler, R. S., & Liben, L. S. (2006). A developmental intergroup theory of social stereotypes and prejudice. In R. V. Kail (Ed.), *Advances in child development and behavior: Vol. 34* (pp. 39–89). San Diego, CA: Elsevier.

Bigler, R. S., & Liben, L. S. (2007). Developmental intergroup theory: Explaining and reducing children's social stereotyping and prejudice. *Current Directions in Psychological Science, 16*, 162–166.

Bishop, B. (2008). *The big sort.* New York, NY: Mariner Books.

Blascovich, J., Mendes, W. B., Hunter, S. B., Lickel, B., & Kowai-Bell, N. (2001). Perceiver threat in social interactions with stigmatized others. *Journal of Personality and Social Psychology, 80*, 253–267.

Britt, T. W., Boniecki, K. A., Vescio, T. K., Biernat, M., & Brown, L. M. (1996). Intergroup anxiety: A person x situation approach. *Personality and Social Psychology Bulletin, 22*, 1177–1188.

Brown, C. S., & Bigler, R. S. (2005). Children's perceptions of discrimination: A developmental model. *Child Development, 76*, 533–553.

Brown, M. J., & Henriquez, E. (2008). Socio-demographic predictors of attitudes towards gays and lesbians. *Individual Differences Research, 6*, 193–202.

Brown, R., Maras, P., Masser, B., Vivian, J., & Hewstone, M. (2001). Life on the ocean wave: Testing some intergroup hypotheses in a naturalistic setting. *Group Processes & Intergroup Relations, 4*, 81–97.

Buckley, K. E., Winkel, R. E., & Leary, M. R. (2004). Reactions to acceptance and rejection: Effects of level and sequence of relational evaluation. *Journal of Experimental Social Psychology, 40*, 14–28.

Bukowski, W. M., Motzoi, C., & Meyer, F. (2009). Friendship as process, function, and outcome. In K. H. Rubin, W. M. Bukowski, & B. Laursen (Eds.), *Handbook of peer interactions, friendships, and groups* (pp. 217–234). New York, NY: Guilford.

Cameron, L., Rutland, A., Brown, R., & Douch, R. (2006). Changing children's intergroup attitudes toward refugees: Testing different models of extended contact. *Child Development, 77*, 1208–1219.

Chemers, M., Oskamp, S., & Constanzo, M. (1995). *Diversity in organizations: New perspectives for a changing workplace.* Thousand Oaks: Sage.

Cheryan, S., Meltzoff, A. N., & Kim, S. (2011). Classrooms matter: The design of virtual classrooms influences gender disparities in computer science classes. *Computers & Education, 57*, 1825–1835.

Cheryan, S., Plaut, V. C., Davies, P. G., & Steele, C. M. (2009). Ambient belonging: How stereotypical cues impact gender participation in computer science. *Journal of Personality and Social Pscyhology, 97*, 1045–1060.

Cialdini, R. B., Kallgren, C. A., & Reno, R. R. (1991). A focus theory of normative conduct: A theoretical refinement and reevaluation of the role of norms in human behavior. *Advances in Experimental Social Psychology, 21*, 201–234.

Cole, E. R. (2009). Intersectionality and research in psychology. *American Psychologist, 64*, 170–180.

Collins, W. A., & Steinberg, L. (2007). Adolescent development in interpersonal context. *Handbook of child psychology: Vol. 3* (p. 16).

Davies, K., Aron, A., Wright, S. C., Brody, S., & McLaughlin-Volpe, T. (2010). *The fast-friends project: Some initial results of an intergroup contact intervention.* (Unpublished raw data).

Davies, K., Tropp, L. R., Aron, A., Pettigrew, T. F., & Wright, S. C. (2011). Cross-group friendships and intergroup attitudes: A meta-analytic review. *Personality and Social Psychology Review, 15*, 332–351.

D'Emilio, J. (1998). *Sexual politics, sexual communities: The making of a homosexual minority.* Chicago, IL: University of Chicago Press.

Devine, P. G., Evett, S. R., & Vasquez-Suson, K. A. (1996). Exploring the interpersonal dynamics of intergroup contact. In R. M. Sorrentino & T. E. Higgins (Eds.), *Handbook of motivations and cognition* (pp. 423–464). New York, NY: Guilford Press.

Dijker, A. J. (1987). Emotional reactions to ethnic minorities. *European Journal of Social Psychology, 17*, 305–325.

Dixon, J., Durrheim, K., & Tredoux, C. (2005). Beyond the optimal contact strategy: A reality check for the contact hypothesis. *American Psychologist, 60*, 697–711.

Doosje, B., Mateus Figueiredo, A. C., Van Hemert, D. A., Dotsch, T., Wirtz, C., Kroos, M., et al. (2011). *A meta-analysis on in-group bias among children: The role of age, relative group status and group threat.* (Manuscript submitted for publication).

Dovidio, J. F., & Gaertner, S. L. (2000). Aversive racism and selection decisions: 1989 and 1999. *Psychological Science, 11*, 315–319.

Downey, G., & Feldman, S. I. (1996). Implications of rejection sensitivity for intimate relationships. *Journal of Personality and Social Psychology, 70*, 1327–1343.

Eccles, J. (1999). The development of children ages 6 to 14. *The Future of Children, 9*, 30–44.

Edmonds, C., & Killen, M. (2009). Do adolescents' perceptions of parental racial attitudes relate to their intergroup contact and cross-race relationships? *Group Processes and Intergroup Relations, 12*, 5–21.

Embrick, D. G., Walther, C. S., & Wickens, C. M. (2007). Working class masculinity: Keeping gay men and lesbians out of the workplace. *Sex Roles, 56*, 757–766.

Fawcett, C. A., & Markson, L. (2010). Similarity predicts liking in 3-year-old children. *Journal of Experimental Child Psychology, 105*, 345–358.

Fehr, B. (1996). *Friendship processes.* Thousand Oaks, CA: Sage.

Feldman, S., & Downey, G. (1994). Rejection sensitivity as a mediator of the impact of childhood exposure to family violence on adult attachment behavior. *Development and Psychopathology, 6*, 231–247.

Frankenberg, E., & Orfield, G. (Eds.), (2012). *The resegregation of suburban schools: A hidden crisis in American education.* Boston, MA: Harvard Education Press.

French, D. C. (1987). Children's social interaction with older, younger, and same-age peers. *Journal of Social and Personal Relationships, 4*, 63–86.

Gaertner, S. L., & Dovidio, J. F. (2000). *Reducing intergroup bias: The common ingroup identity model.* New York, NY: Psychology Press.

Gelman, S. (2003). *The essential child: Origins of essentialism in everyday thought.* New York, NY: Oxford University Press.

Goff, P. A., Steele, C. M., & Davies, P. G. (2008). The space between us: Stereotype threat and distance in interracial contexts. *Journal of Personality and Social Psychology, 94*, 91–107.

Gosling, S. D., Ko, S. J., Mannarelli, T., & Morris, M. E. (2002). A room with a cue: Personality judgments on offices and bedrooms. *Journal of Personality and Social Psychology, 82*, 379–398.

Guinote, A., Mouro, C., Pereira, M. H., & Monteiro, M. B. (2007). Children's perceptions of group variability as a function of status. *International Journal of Behavioral Development, 31*, 97–104.

Gurin, P., Dey, E. L., Hurtado, S., & Gurin, G. (2002). Diversity and higher educations: Theory and impact on educational outcomes. *Harvard Educational Review, 72*, 330–366.

Hallinan, M. T., & Williams, R. A. (1987). The stability of students' interracial friendships. *American Sociological Review, 52*, 653–664.

Hays, R. B. (1984). The development and maintenance of friendship. *Journal of Social and Personal Relationships, 1*, 75–98.

Hebl, M. R., Foster, J. B., Mannix, L. M., & Dovidio, J. F. (2002). Formal and interpersonal discrimination: A field study of bias toward homosexual applicants. *Personality and Social Psychology Bulletin, 28*, 815–825.

Herek, G. M., & Capitanio, J. P. (1996). "Some of my best friends": Intergroup contact, concealable stigma, and heterosexuals' attitudes toward gay men and lesbians. *Personality and Social Psychology Bulletin, 22*, 412–424.

Hewstone, M., Cairns, E., Voci, A., Hamberger, J., & Niens, U. (2006). Intergroup contact, forgiveness, and experience of "The Troubles" in Northern Ireland. *Journal of Social Issues, 62*, 99–120.

Ickes, W. (1984). Compositions in Black and White: Determinants of interaction in interracial dyads. *Journal of Personality and Social Psychology, 47*, 330–341.

Islam, M. R., & Hewstone, M. (1993). Dimensions of contact as predictors of intergroup anxiety, perceived out-group variability, and out-group attitude: An integrative model. *Personality and Social Psychology Bulletin, 19*, 700–710.

Kao, G., & Joyner, K. (2004). Do race and ethnicity matter among friends? Activities among interracial, interethnic, and intraethnic adolescent friends. *The Sociological Quarterly, 45*, 557–573.

Killen, M., Mulvey, K. L., & Hitti, A. (2013). Social exclusions in childhood. *Child Development, 84*, 772–790.

Klonis, S. C., Plant, A. E., & Devine, P. G. (2005). Internal and external motivation to respond without sexism. *Personality and Social Psychology Bulletin, 31*, 1237–1249.

Knifsend, C., & Juvonen, J. (2014). Social identity complexity, cross-ethnic friendships, and intergroup attitudes in urban middle schools. *Child Development, 85*, 709–721.

Kruglanski, A. W., & Stroebe, W. (2012). *Handbook of the history of social psychology*. New York, NY: Taylor & Francis.

Lackey, S. (2013). It takes two to tango: Stigma consciousness, intergroup anxiety, and avoidance of interactions between Blacks and Whites. *Dissertation Abstracts International, 73*, 1–72.

Lee, E., & Troop-Gordon, W. (2011). Peer processes and gender role development: Changes in gender atypicality related to negative peer treatment and children's friendships. *Sex Roles, 64*, 90–102.

Levin, S., van Laar, C., & Sidanius, J. (2003). The effects of ingroup and outgroup friendship on ethnic attitudes in college: A longitudinal study. *Group Processes and Intergroup Relations, 6*, 76–92.

Lewandowski, G. W., Jr., Nardone, N., & Raines, A. J. (2010). The role of self-concept clarity in relationship quality. *Self and Identity, 9*, 416–433.

London, B., Downey, G., Romero-Canyas, R., Rattan, A., & Tyson, D. (2012). Gender-based rejection sensitivity and academic self-silencing in women. *Journal of Personality and Social Psychology, 102*, 961–979.

Maccoby, E. E. (2002). Gender and group process: A developmental perspective. *Current Directions in Psychological Science, 11*, 54–58.

Malloy, T., Albright, L., & Scarpati, S. (2007). Awareness of peers' judgments of oneself: Accuracy and process of metaperception. *International Journal of Behavioral Development, 31*, 603–610.

Martin, C. L., Fabes, R. A., & Hanish, L. (2014). Gendered-peer relationships in educational contexts. In J. Benson (Series Ed.) & L. S. Liben & R. S. Bigler (Vol. Eds.), *Advances in child development and behavior: Vol. 47. The role of gender in educational contexts and outcomes* (pp. 151–187). San Diego, CA: Elsevier.

McAdams, D. P. (1988). *Power, intimacy, and the life story: Personological inquiries into identity*. New York, NY: Guilford.

McConahay, J. B. (1983). Modern racism and modern discrimination: The effects of race, racial attitudes, and context on simulated hiring decisions. *Personality and Social Psychology Bulletin, 9*, 551–558.

McGlothlin, H., & Killen, M. (2006). Intergroup attitudes of European American children attending ethnically homogeneous schools. *Child Development, 77*, 1375–1386.

McGlothlin, H., & Killen, M. (2010). How social experience is related to children's intergroup attitudes. *European Journal of Social Psychology, 40*, 625–634.

McKown, C., & Weinstein, R. (2003). The development and consequences of stereotype consciousness in middle childhood. *Child Development, 74*, 498–515.

McLaughlin-Volpe, T. (2002). *The intergroup contact effect as including an outgroup other in the self.* State University of New York at Stony Brook (Unpublished doctoral dissertation).
McLaughlin-Volpe, T., Aron, A., Wright, S. C., & Reis, H. T. (2002). *Intergroup social interactions and intergroup prejudice: Quantity versus quality.* (Unpublished manuscript).
McPherson, M., Smith-Lovin, L., & Cook, J. M. (2001). Birds of a feather: Homophily in social networks. *Annual Review of Sociology, 27*, 415–444.
Mendoza-Denton, R., Downey, G., Purdie, V. J., Davis, A., & Pietrzak, J. (2002). Sensitivity to status-based rejection: Implications for African American students' college experience. *Journal of Personality and Social Psychology, 83*, 896–918.
Mendoza-Denton, R., & Page-Gould, E. (2008). Can cross-group friendships influence minority students' well-being at historically white universities? *Psychological Science, 19*, 933–939.
Murphy, M. C., Steele, C. M., & Gross, J. J. (2007). Signaling threat: How situational cues affect women in math, science, and engineering settings. *Psychological Science, 18*, 879–885.
Mwamwenda, T. S. (1998). African university students' responses to questions on interracial marriage. *Psychological Reports, 83*, 658.
National Catholic Educational Association. (2013). *U.S. catholic elementary and secondary schools: The annual statistical report on schools, enrollment, and staffing.* Arlington, VA: National Catholic Educational Association.
Nesdale, D., & Dalton, D. (2011). Children's social groups and intergroup prejudice: Assessing the influence and inhibition of social group norms. *British Journal of Developmental Psychology, 29*, 895–909.
Neville, H. A., Lilly, R. L., Lee, R. M., Duran, G., & Browne, L. (2000). Construction and initial validation of the color-blind racial attitudes scale. *Journal of Counseling Psychology, 47*, 59–70.
Norton, M. I., Sommers, S. R., Apfelbaum, E. P., Pura, N., & Ariely, D. (2006). Color blindness and interracial interaction: Playing the political correctness game. *Psychological Science, 17*, 949–953.
O'Brien, L. T., Kinias, Z., & Major, B. (2008). How status and stereotypes impact attributions to discrimination: The stereotype-asymmetry hypothesis. *Journal of Experimental Social Psychology, 44*, 405–412.
Olatunji, B. O. (2008). Disgust, scrupulosity and conservative attitudes about sex: Evidence for a mediational model of homophobia. *Journal of Research in Personality, 42*, 1364–1369.
Oswald, D. L., Clark, E. M., & Kelly, C. M. (2004). Friendship maintenance: An analysis of individual and dyad behaviors. *Journal of Social and Clinical Psychology, 23*, 413–441.
Pachankis, J. E., Goldfried, M. R., & Ramrattan, M. E. (2008). Extension of the rejection sensitivity construct to the interpersonal functioning of gay men. *Journal of Consulting and Clinical Psychology, 76*, 306–317.
Page-Gould, E., Mendoza-Denton, R. Alegre, Alegre, J. M., & Siy, J. O. (2010). Understanding the impact of cross-group friendship on interactions with novel outgroup members. *Journal of Personality and Social Psychology, 98*, 775–793.
Page-Gould, E., Mendoza-Denton, R., & Tropp, L. R. (2008). With a little help from my cross-group friend: Reducing anxiety in intergroup contexts through cross-group friendship. *Journal of Personality and Social Psychology, 95*, 1080–1094.
Pahlke, E., Bigler, R. S., & Patterson, M. M. (2014). Reasoning about single-sex schooling for girls among students, parents, and teachers. *Sex Roles, 14*, 261–271.
Paolini, S., Hewstone, M., Cairns, E., & Voci, A. (2004). Effects of direct and indirect cross group friendships on judgments of catholics and protestants in Northern Ireland: The mediating role of an anxiety-reduction mechanism. *Personality and Social Psychology Bulletin, 30*, 770–786.

Patterson, M. M., & Bigler, R. S. (2006). Preschool children's attention to environmental messages about groups: Social categorization and the origins of intergroup bias. *Child Development, 77*, 847–860.

Pettigrew, T. F. (1998). Intergroup contact theory. *Annual Review of Psychology, 49*, 65–85.

Pettigrew, T. F., & Tropp, L. R. (2006). A meta-analytic test of intergroup contact theory. *Journal of Personality and Social Psychology, 90*, 751–783.

Pfeifer, J. H., Brown, C. S., & Juvonen, J. (2007). Prejudice reduction in schools. *Social Policy Report, 11*, 3–23.

Plant, A. E., & Devine, P. G. (1998). Internal and external motivation to respond without prejudice. *Journal of Personality and Social Psychology, 75*, 811–832.

Purdie-Vaughns, V., Steele, C. M., Davies, P. G., Ditlmann, R., & Crosby, J. R. (2008). Social identity contingencies: How diversity cues signal threat or safety for African Americans in mainstream institutions. *Journal of Personality and Social Psychology, 94*, 615–630.

Raabe, T., & Beelmann, A. (2011). Development of ethnic, racial, and national prejudice in childhood and adolescence: A multinational meta-analysis of age differences. *Child Development, 82*, 1715–1737.

Reis, H. T., & Shaver, P. (1988). Intimacy as an interpersonal process. In S. Duck, D. F. Hay, S. E. Hobfoll, W. Ickes, & B. M. Montgomery (Eds.), *Handbook of personal relationships: Theory, research and interventions*. Oxford, England: Wiley & Sons.

Reno, R. R., Cialdini, R. B., & Kallgren, C. A. (1993). The transsituational influence of social norms. *Journal of Personality and Social Psychology, 64*, 104–112.

Rhodes, M. (2012). Naïve theories of social groups. *Child Development, 83*, 1900–1916.

Richeson, J. A., & Nussbaum, R. J. (2004). The impact of multiculturalism versus colorblindness on racial bias. *Journal of Experimental Social Psychology, 40*, 417–423.

Richeson, J. A., & Shelton, J. N. (2007). Negotiating interracial interactions: Costs, consequences, and possibilities. *Current Directions in Psychological Science, 16*, 316–320.

Richeson, J. A., & Trawalter, S. (2008). The threat of appearing prejudiced and race-based attentional biases. *Psychological Science, 19*, 98–102.

Riek, B. M., Mania, E. W., Gaertner, S. L., McDonald, S. A., & Lamoreaux, M. J. (2010). Does a common ingroup identity reduce intergroup threat? *Group Processes & Intergroup Relations, 13*, 403–423.

Rifkin, J. (2009). *The empathetic civilization: The race to global consciousness in a world in crisis*. New York, NY: Penguin.

Rodkin, P. C., Ryan, A. M., Jamison, R., & Wilson, T. (2013). Social goals, social behavior, and social status in middle childhood. *Developmental Psychology, 49*, 1139–1150.

Rohrbach, J. M., & Bigler, R. S. (2013). Whites' cross-race friendships (but not behavior) predict racial attitudes. In *Poster presented at the annual meeting of the Society for Personality and Social Psychology. New Orleans, Louisiana.*

Ruck, M. D., Park, H., Killen, M., & Crystal, D. S. (2011). Intergroup contact and evaluations of race-based exclusion in urban minority children and adolescents. *Journal of Youth and Adolescences, 20*, 622–643.

Rutland, A., Cameron, L., Milne, A., & McGeorge, P. (2005). Social norms and self-presentation: Children's implicit and explicit intergroup attitudes. *Child Development, 76*, 451–466.

Saguy, T., & Chernyak-Hai, L. (2012). Intergroup contact can undermine disadvantaged group members' attributions to discrimination. *Journal of Experimental Social Psychology, 48*, 714–720.

Saguy, T., Tausch, N., Dovidio, J. F., & Pratto, F. (2009). The irony of harmony: Intergroup contact can produce false expectations for equality. *Psychological Science, 20*, 114–121.

Sani, F., & Bennett, M. (2009). Children's inclusion of the group in the self: Evidence from a self-ingroup confusion paradigm. *Developmental Psychology, 45*, 503–510.

Schug, J., Yuki, M., Horikawa, H., & Takemura, K. (2009). Similarity attraction and actually selecting similar others: How cross-societal differences in relational mobility affect interpersonal similarity in Japan and the USA. *Asian Journal of Social Psychology, 12*, 95–103.
Schultz, W. P., Nolan, J. M., Cialdini, R. B., Goldstein, N. J., & Griskevicius, V. (2007). The constructive, destructive, and reconstructive power of social norms. *Psychological Science, 18*, 429–434.
Shapiro, J. R., Baldwin, M., Williams, A. M., & Trawalter, S. (2011). The company you keep: Fear of rejection in intergroup interaction. *Journal of Experimental Social Psychology, 47*, 221–227.
Shapiro, J. R., & Neuberg, S. L. (2008). When do the stigmatized stigmatize? The ironic effects of being accountable to (perceived) majority group prejudice-expression norms. *Journal of Personality and Social Psychology, 95*, 877–898.
Shelton, J. N., Richeson, J. A., & Bergsieker, H. B. (2009). Interracial friendship development and attributional biases. *Journal of Social and Personal Relationships, 26*, 179–193.
Shelton, J. N., Richeson, J. A., & Salvatore, J. (2005). Expecting to be the target of prejudice: Implications for interethnic interactions. *Personality and Social Psychology Bulletin, 31*, 1189–1202.
Sherif, M., Harvey, O. J., White, B. J., Hood, W. R., & Sherif, C. W. (1961). *Intergroup conflict and cooperation: The robbers cave experiment*. Norman: University of Oklahoma Book Exchange.
Son, D., & Shelton, N. J. (2011). Stigma consciousness among Asian Americans: Impact of positive stereotypes in interracial roommate relationships. *Asian American Journal of Psychology, 2*, 51–60.
Stephan, W. G., Diaz-Loving, R., & Duran, A. (2000). Integrated threat theory and intercultural attitudes: Mexico and the United States. *Journal of Cross-Cultural Psychology, 31*, 240–249.
Stephan, W. G., & Stephan, C. W. (1985). Intergroup anxiety. *Journal of Social Issues, 41*, 157–175.
Stephan, W. G., Ybarra, O., & Bachman, G. (1999). Prejudice toward immigrants. *Journal of Applied Social Psychology, 29*, 2221–2237.
Swart, H., Hewstone, M., Christ, O., & Voci, A. (2010). The impact of crossgroup friendship in South Africa: Affective mediators and multigroup comparisons. *Journal of Social Issues, 66*, 309–333.
Toosi, N. R., Babbitt, L. G., Ambady, N., & Sommers, S. R. (2012). Dyadic interracial interactions: A meta-analysis. *Psychological Bulletin, 138*, 1–27.
Trail, T. E., Shelton, N. J., & West, T. V. (2009). Interracial roommate relationships: Negotiating daily interactions. *Personality and Social Psychology Bulletin, 35*, 671–684.
Trawalter, S., Richeson, J. A., & Shelton, J. N. (2009). Predicting behavior during interracial interactions: A stress and coping approach. *Personality and Social Psychology Review, 13*, 243–268.
Tropp, L. R., & Bianchi, R. A. (2006). Valuing diversity and interest in intergroup contact. *Journal of Social Issues, 62*, 533–551.
Tropp, L. R., & Pettigrew, T. F. (2005). Differential relationships between intergroup contact and affective and cognitive dimensions of prejudice. *Personality and Social Psychology Bulletin, 31*, 1145–1158.
Turner, R. N., & Cameron, L. (2016). Confidence in contact: A new perspective on promoting cross-group friendship among children and adolescents. *Social Issues and Public Policy, 10*, 212–246.
Turner, R. N., Hewstone, M., & Voci, A. (2007). Reducing explicit and implicit outgroup prejudice via direct and extended contact: The mediating role of self-disclosure and intergroup anxiety. *Journal of Personality and Social Psychology, 93*, 369–388.

Turner, R. N., West, K., & Christie, Z. (2013). Out-group trust, intergroup anxiety, and out-group attitude as mediators of the effect of imagined intergroup contact on intergroup behavioral tendencies. *Journal of Applied Social Psychology*, *43*, E196–E205.

van Dick, R., Wagner, U., Pettigrew, T. F., Chris, O., Wolf, C., Petzel, T., et al. (2004). Role of perceived importance in intergroup contact. *Interpersonal Relations and Group Processes*, *87*, 211–227.

Verkuyten, M., & Martinovic, V. (2006). Understanding multicultural attitudes: The role of group status, identification, friendships, and justifying ideologies. *International Journal of Intercultural Relations*, *30*, 1–18.

Vorauer, J. D. (2005). Miscommunications surrounding efforts to reach out across group boundaries. *Personality and Social Psychology Bulletin*, *31*, 1653–1664.

Vorauer, J. D., Gagnon, A., & Sasaki, S. J. (2009). Salient intergroup ideology and intergroup interaction. *Psychological Science*, *20*, 838–845.

Wagner, U., van Dick, R., Pettigrew, T. F., & Christ, O. (2003). Ethnic prejudice in East and West Germany: The explanatory power of intergroup contact. *Group Processes & Intergroup Relations*, *6*, 22–36.

Waugh, C. E., & Fredrickson, B. L. (2006). Nice to know you: Positive emotions, self-other overlap, and complex understanding in the formation of a new relationship. *The Journal of Positive Psychology*, *1*, 93–106.

Weisbuch, M., Pauker, K., & Ambady, N. (2009). The subtle transmission of race bias via televised nonverbal behavior. *Science*, *326*, 1711–1714.

West, T. V., Pearson, A. R., Dovidio, J. F., Shelton, N. J., & Trail, T. E. (2009). Superordinate identity and intergroup roommate friendship development. *Journal of Experimental Social Psychology*, *45*, 1266–1272.

West, T. V., Shelton, J. N., & Trail, T. E. (2009). Relational anxiety in interracial interactions. *Psychological Science*, *20*, 289–292.

Williams, R. M. (1947). *The reduction of intergroup tensions*. New York, NY: Social Science Research Council.

Williams, K. D., Cheung, C. K. T., & Choi, W. (2000). Cyberostracism: Effects of being ignored over the internet. *Journal of Personality and Social Psychology*, *79*, 748–762.

Wilson, T. M., Rodkin, P. C., & Ryan, A. M. (2014). The company they keep and avoid: Social goal orientation as a predictor of children's ethnic segregation. *Developmental Psychology*, *50*, 1116–1124.

Wolsko, C., Park, B., Judd, C. M., & Wittenbrink, B. (2000). Framing interethnic ideology: Effects of multicultural and color-blind perspectives on judgments of groups and individuals. *Journal of Personality and Social Psychology*, *78*, 635–654.

Wout, D. A., Murphy, M. C., & Steele, C. M. (2010). When your friends matter: The effect of white students' racial friendship networks on meta-perceptions and perceived identity contingencies. *Journal of Experimental Social Psychology*, *46*, 1035–1041.

Wright, S. C., Aron, A., & Tropp, L. R. (2002). Including others (and groups) in the self: Self-expansion and intergroup relations. In J. P. Forgas & K. D. Williams (Eds.), *The social self: Cognitive, interpersonal, and intergroup perspectives*. New York, NY: Psychology Press.

Young, J. T. N. (2011). How do they 'end up together'? A social network analysis of self-control, homophily, and adolescent relationships. *Journal of Quantitative Criminology*, *27*, 251–273.

CHAPTER SIX

Power, Process, and Protection: Juveniles as Defendants in the Justice System

Jennifer L. Woolard*,[1], Kristin Henning[†], Erika Fountain*
*Georgetown University, Washington, DC, United States
[†]Georgetown University School of Law, Washington, DC, United States
[1]Corresponding author: e-mail address: jlw47@georgetown.edu

Contents

Abstract

The juvenile court was created in 1899 in part to remedy the unfairness of trying youth in the adult criminal justice system, but its success at rectifying those problems is unclear. One concern is that the vast majority of youth who are adjudicated delinquent are adjudicated after waiving their right to trial and entering a guilty plea. Fairness and equity in the plea bargaining process are premised on the assumption that youth have the capacity to understand and elect between available options and will be given a

Equity and Justice in Developmental Science: Implications for Young People, Families, and Communities (S.S. Horn, M.D. Ruck & L.S. Liben, Eds.)
Advances in Child Development and Behavior (J.B. Benson, Series Ed.), Vol. 51
ISSN 0065-2407 http://dx.doi.org/10.1016/bs.acdb.2016.04.002

meaningful opportunity to choose without coercion and deception. In legal terms, the Constitution will only sanction a plea when the defendant makes a knowing, voluntary, and intelligent waiver of her right to trial. In this chapter, we briefly describe the juvenile court process and explain the circumstances of a plea bargain, which constitutes both a waiver of Constitutional rights and an agreement to certain conditions. Then we evaluate the research and practice knowledge regarding the legal components of a valid waiver—that it must be knowing and voluntary. We consider how information, capacity, and circumstance contribute to a knowing waiver. Then we examine how procedural justice, paternalism, and coercion may affect a voluntary waiver. Throughout, we consider whether the people, policies, and practices meant to assess and safeguard that waiver decision fulfill their intended purpose.

Most adolescents engage in some type of behavior that could meet the legal definition of a delinquent act, and most governments have specific systems to respond to such behavior. Cross-cultural data indicate the onset of offending occurs between ages 8 and 14, the frequency of offending peaks between ages 15 and 19, and the peak of desistance occurs between ages 20 and 29 (Farrington, 2005; Monahan & Piquero, 2009). A variety of international standards address the processing of children in a nation's justice system, including the United Nations Standard Minimum Rules for the Administration of Juvenile Justice (United Nations, 1985), the Convention on the Rights of the Child (United Nations, 1989), the United Nations Guidelines for the Prevention of Juvenile Delinquency (United Nations, 1990), and the United Nations Rules for the Protection of Juveniles Deprived of their Liberty (United Nations Office on Drugs & Crime, 2006).

Nations vary in their philosophies of intervention but most have created a completely separate system to intervene with youths differently than adults. Remarkably, the creation of a separate justice system for youth in the US state of Illinois in 1899 quickly spread throughout the United States and globally to the vast majority of nations (Zimring & Langer, 2015). As Weithorn (2005) notes, governments have multiple systems with which to respond to "troubled and troublesome" youth, including mental health, health, and child welfare systems. The entry point chosen can set in motion a chain of events that is difficult to interrupt and may have long-lasting consequences.

In the United States, sanctity of the family is paramount but not impermeable; through its parens patriae power the state may step in and "act as a parent" when a youth's parents are unwilling or unable to do so. Most American support and intervention systems for children and families, including the juvenile justice system, are primarily reactive, only engaging youth once behavior labeled as offending occurs. The system then deemphasizes preventive intervention and expends most of its resources on youth who are already at risk or identified as delinquent. The efficacy and biases of the system's surveillance and detention action determine which youth are drawn into the system at all. As we shall see, the juvenile justice system disproportionately affects poor minority youth.

The American juvenile court in 1899 was justified in part by the belief that the adult criminal justice system was inadequate for youth and that the state's paternalistic intervention would return wayward children to the path of law-abiding behavior (Tannenhaus, 2002). This new more equitable approach would use different language, and emphasize individualized rehabilitation over punishment. Two youth with the same offense could receive vastly different responses from the court; fairness was to be found in the appropriate use of the court's discretion, not the consistency of responses across youth or offense type. Over time, Constitutional protections afforded adult defendants were extended to youth to rein in that unbridled discretion and promote consistency. Some power was returned to youth, or at least their attorneys, to hold the state accountable and protect youths' Constitutional rights.

Today, the American juvenile court simultaneously attempts to protect public safety, rehabilitate youth, and exercise or restrain the power to incarcerate youth. Each state maintains its own separate juvenile justice system that follows three basic phases: a preadjudication phase in which a youth enters the system, an adjudication phase that determines guilt, and a post-adjudication phase that specifies the disposition or sentence.

The vast majority of American juveniles choose to plead guilty and give up their rights to an adjudicatory hearing and to an appeal on the merits of the allegation. Fairness and equity are premised on the assumption that youth have the capacity to understand the plea bargaining process and that they will be given a meaningful opportunity to choose without coercion and deception. Pleading guilty engages defendants and their lawyers in sophisticated cognitive analysis and complex decision making. Evaluating a plea offer requires an abstract analysis of what might or might not happen in the future—a skill that is challenging for the most astute adult and almost impossible for a youth without the assistance of counsel. Many developmental features of adolescence—including limited life experience, deference to adult authority figures, poor risk perception, and susceptibility to peer influence—can lead youth to make poor and unsatisfying decisions in the plea bargaining process. The choices they make as immature teenagers are likely not the same choices they would make as fully mature adults.

Can any juvenile justice system assume that developmentally immature youth make informed and voluntary decisions about pleading guilty? In this chapter, we interrogate that assumption using the American juvenile justice system. First, we briefly describe the history of US juvenile courts and explain how the typical case process results in a plea bargain. Then we examine what a youth needs to understand and appreciate to make an informed decision about a plea. Finally, we examine how procedural justice, paternalism, and coercion may undermine the voluntariness of a youth's decision to plead guilty. Throughout, we consider whether the people, policies, and practices meant to assess and safeguard that waiver decision fulfill their intended purpose.

1. THE US JUVENILE JUSTICE SYSTEM IN CONTEXT

The US juvenile court was created in 1899 in part to remedy the unfairness of trying youth in the adult criminal justice system (Tannenhaus, 2002). The juvenile justice system began with an explicitly paternalistic approach that characterized the presenting offense as merely symptomatic of larger problems that needed to be "solved" (Woolard & Scott, 2009). The early court assumed that court involvement was universally positive; no iatrogenic effects would result. The court's invention was not simply a benign intervention to "save children" and produce model citizens, however. Ward's (2012) investigation of juvenile justice history argues that the system must be understood as "components of a contested and dynamically racialized social system in which racial, class, and gender identities and power relations constantly shape group opportunity, influence, benefits, and burdens" (p. 7). Not only were black youth treated differently than white youth, but black advocates were excluded from leadership and administration of juvenile justice.

The fairness of that approach was called into question during the "due process" wave of juvenile justice reform. In a series of cases brought before the US Supreme Court in the 1960s, attorneys questioned the assumption that intervention incurred no costs to youth. The Court in Kent v. U.S. (1966) concluded youth received the "worst of both worlds," meaning that the juvenile justice system was not providing the promised rehabilitative intervention. Instead, youth faced significant deprivations of liberty without the constitutional rights guaranteed to adults in the criminal system. The most significant case, In re Gault (1967) involved a youth who was committed to a juvenile correction facility until his 21st birthday for an alleged offense (making an obscene phone call) that would have resulted in a fine or minimal jail time for an adult. The majority ruled that youth must be afforded some due process and constitutional rights, including the right to an attorney, the right to timely notification of charges, the right against self-incrimination, and the right to confront witnesses at trial. While some saw the reforms as the only way to protect children's rights from biased and unbridled judicial discretion, others were concerned that due process reforms undermined the court's original individualized approach to rehabilitative intervention and render a separate juvenile justice system unnecessary (Zimring, 1978, 1982).

Challenges to fairness and equity reemerged in the 1980s as public safety officially trumped rehabilitation in most states and some predicted a generation of juvenile "super-predators" that would wreak havoc on society (Dilulio, 1996, February 28). Stoked by these fears, states increased the harshness of punishment in juvenile court and expanded the avenues for prosecution in adult court (Woolard & Scott, 2009). Forty-five states allow some juveniles to be tried in adult criminal court through a judicial hearing (judicial waiver), a prosecutor's charging decision (prosecutorial discretion), or as required by statute (statutory exclusion) (Griffin, Addie, Adams, & Firestine, 2011). As a result, more youth were exposed to sentencing practices reserved for the worst offenders including life without parole (LWOP) and the death penalty (until it was banned in 2005). These sentences, which are banned by the UN Convention on the Rights of the Child (United Nations, 1989), are not commonly applied to juvenile offenders around the world. Although a handful of countries have laws allowing LWOP for juveniles, the only country with known cases of juveniles sentenced to LWOP is the United States (De la Vega & Leighton, 2008).

Reform has since shifted to an era in which developmental differences between juveniles and adults are recognized and leveraged in attempts to create a more nuanced approach to juvenile offending (Scott, 2013). Citing research on the immature decisional capacities that may compromise youths' effectiveness as defendants and culpability for crimes (e.g., Scott & Steinberg, 2008), the US Supreme Court eliminated the death penalty for youths (Roper v. Simmons, 2005), LWOP for nonhomicide offenses by youth (Graham v. Florida, 2010), and mandatory LWOP for adolescent homicide offenders (Miller v. Alabama, 2011). Some youth still may be transferred to the criminal justice system and processed as an adult.

2. REALITIES OF THE JUVENILE JUSTICE SYSTEM

Although a majority of the more than 74 million American youth self-report behaviors that could be labeled delinquent, only a subset of allegedly delinquent youth come to the attention of authorities. About 1.7 million cases were brought through juvenile courts in 2010 (Hockenberry & Puzzanchera, 2013). Of those, approximately 80% originate through law enforcement officials who also have the discretion to do nothing or divert the youth to alternative programs. The remaining 20% of cases come from other sources—community members, school officials, or parents (Sickmund & Puzzanchera, 2014).

2.1 "System" Is a Collection of Independent Organizations

The juvenile justice system is actually a collection of separate organizations with different roles, including law enforcement, the prosecuting attorney, the defense attorney, the judiciary, and departments of youth services/probation (Bishop, Leiber, & Johnson, 2010). Each of the organizational entities operates in a separate bureaucracy and is linked to the other organizations through the flow of cases. A variety of decisions by these organizations determine whether a case proceeds or is removed from further processing. The first decision point begins with an intake officer who recommends that a prosecutor dismiss, divert/process informally, or advance the case. Intake officers are usually part of a court services or probation unit that has a treatment and rehabilitation orientation and prioritizes the needs of youth. The prosecuting attorney represents the agency that focuses on community safety and accountability and prioritizes those concerns over the best interests of the youth.

The decision to advance a case is made solely by the prosecutor, whose goals of accountability and justice drive the process forward. If the case is advanced, a delinquency petition is filed with the court (or, under certain conditions, the juvenile may be moved to the adult court process). In the adjudication phase, the child is found delinquent or not through a hearing (somewhat like a trial) or enters a plea of guilty. Here the judge is the final arbiter of whether a youth is found delinquent or not. As with adult criminal cases (Durose & Langan, 2007), the vast majority of delinquency adjudications are resolved by pleas. Although national data are lacking, several state reports confirm that guilty pleas are the norm and trials are rare (e.g., Puritz & Sterling, 2010). For example, Scali and Song (2010) found that 95% of juvenile cases in South Carolina resulted in guilty pleas, the vast majority of which took place at the initial hearings.

Emmelman (1996) describes a typical sequence of interactions that comprise the plea process. In practice, prosecutors will typically extend a plea offer through defense counsel. Attorneys evaluate the offer in light of how serious the charge is (both in absolute terms and relative to crime in their community), how strong the evidence is against their clients, and "who" their client is (e.g., demographics, offending history). Ideally, defense counsel will investigate the facts, review the state's evidence, evaluate the credibility of witnesses, and identify legal challenges that might lead to the exclusion of the state's evidence. Then attorneys may negotiate the terms of the offer with the prosecutor by providing positive information about the client, comparing this case to other cases, and sometimes suggesting that further litigation might be their client's best option. Lawyers then present the youth with the state's offer, inform the client of the likely consequences of any plea, and advise the youth about whether to accept or decline. Finally, at the plea hearing, the judge will determine whether the facts support the plea and whether the youth's decision meets the legal definition of "knowing and voluntary."

If found delinquent by trial or plea, the juvenile is then scheduled for a disposition hearing for which officials (usually probation officers) prepare a detailed report about the youth and provide recommendations for disposition (i.e., sentence). The final disposition is rendered by the judge but involves input from defense attorneys, prosecuting attorneys, and probation officers, each of whom has different perspectives. Probation officers tend to emphasize a rehabilitation and treatment perspective. Prosecutors emphasize accountability and public safety and defense attorneys emphasize rights and rehabilitation. More than half of youth receive a disposition of probation (OJJDP, 2015) and some are sent to correctional facilities.

2.2 Youth of Color and Girls Receive Disproportionate Contact and Confinement

Decades of research document the system's disproportionate confinement of minority youth (e.g., Kempf-Leonard, 2007), and gender disparities in processing and outcome (e.g., National Research Council and Institute of Medicine, 2001). These disparities are not unique to the United States; globally, youth from various disadvantaged groups are disproportionately represented in judicial systems (Ruck, Keating, Saewyc, Earls, & Ben-Arieh, 2016). Youth of color are less likely to receive lenient or treatment-oriented approaches and more likely to receive more punitive sentences than white youth. For example, Bridges and Steen (1998) identified differences by youth race in probation reports' explanations of offending and attributions for those classified as moderate risk. Reports on black youth emphasized stable, internal risk factors whereas reports on whites emphasized external factors. In another study, youth of color were more likely to be sentenced to facilities emphasizing physical activity programing whereas white youth were more likely to be sent to smaller more therapeutic facilities (Fader, Kurlychek, & Morgan, 2014). Race and ethnicity also interact with gender in complicated ways. Moore and Padavic (2010) found that for lower levels of severity and prior record, black females received harsher sentences than whites. With greater offense severity, though, the race effect was reversed. Some reductions in disproportionate processing and outcomes have occurred. A number of initiatives focused on structured and evidence-based decision making have successfully reduced some of these disparities, particularly in the use of pretrial detention (e.g., Annie E. Casey Foundation, Models for Change). Although black–white disparities in incarceration have declined in the past decade (Davis & Sorenson, 2012), they still remain.

Bishop et al. (2010) argue that both differences in offending and differences in processing contribute to racial and ethnic disparities. That literature is too extensive to be reviewed here. Of particular interest to our chapter's focus on justice system processing, though, is Bishop and colleagues proposal that decision points that are "loosely coupled," meaning that multiple agencies are involved in the decision to advance a case further into the system (e.g., intake, sentence), do not often produce a decision based on consensus. Instead, that decision point must accommodate multiple organizational goals. It is precisely this combination of competing goals that allow the opportunity for nonlegal factors such as stereotype and bias to influence outcomes.

2.3 Many Youth Are Not Represented by Attorneys

Youth have a constitutional right to be represented by an attorney and, if they cannot afford to hire a private attorney (i.e., are indigent) the court appoints an attorney to represent them. States use three mechanisms to provide indigent defense representation—public defender offices (usually government employees), contract attorneys (nonprofit corporations or private attorneys who contract annually with governments to represent indigent defendants), and assigned/appointed counsel systems (a list of private attorneys from which the court appoints case-specific representation) (Mann, 2010; Owens, Accetta, Charles, & Shoemaker, 2015). Programs providing representation to youth who cannot afford to hire a private attorney are significantly overworked and underresourced (Bright, 2010). States also vary widely in their funding for public defense. In 2004, 24 states covered up to 100% of indigent defense funds while others (14 states) paid under 25% for indigent defense costs, requiring county governments to fill in the gap. Per capita spending on public defense ranges from $4.00 to approximately $40.00 (Worden, Davies, & Brown, 2011). This underfunding particularly undermines access for indigent youth (Levick & Desai, 2007). Feld and Schaefer's (2010) Minnesota study of access to counsel identified rates of representation that varied from 20% to 95% by county, what Feld (1991) calls "justice by geography." Similarly, the National Juvenile Defender Center has documented a wide range of representation across states (Puritz, Burrell, Schwartz, Soler, & Warboys, 2002). Lack of access to counsel may deprive youth of necessary advocacy and advice, which in turn may exacerbate the racial and ethnic disparities in processing highlighted earlier.

2.4 Attorneys Play a Critical Role in the Protection of Youth Rights

The importance of access to counsel came into stark relief in 2008 with the "Kids for Cash" scandal in Pennsylvania (Ecenbarger, 2012). Elected on a "tough on juvenile crime" platform, Juvenile Court Judge Mark Ciavarella wanted a new juvenile detention facility built in his county but public funds were unavailable. Instead, he talked with private contractors who put together a proposal and paid Judge Ciavarella what they called a "finder's fee" for his contribution to the project. Simultaneously, the Luzerne County President Judge Michael Conahan guaranteed annual payments of over 1 million dollars from the county for use of the facility and ordered all juvenile probation officers to commit their clients to the new facility. That guarantee allowed the contractors to finance the facility's construction. From 2003 to 2008, Judge Ciaveralla implemented policies that increased the use of automatic detention for minor offenses (e.g., skipping school) resulting in approximately 2500 children who were hastily adjudicated without legal counsel and incarcerated in that same private facility that generated a "fee" of more than half a million dollars. In 2011, Mark Ciavarella was found guilty in federal court and sentenced to 28 years.

Admittedly an extreme example, the Pennsylvania scandal highlights two key elements of the juvenile justice system upon which our chapter focuses—the role of attorneys and the youth's decision to waive the right to a trial in order to accept a plea agreement. Although the accused has the right to make any final decision about whether or not to accept a plea (American Bar Association, 2015a), defense counsel plays a critical role in the plea process. Defendants have a Sixth Amendment right to the effective assistance of counsel in the plea bargaining process (Lafler v. Cooper, 2012; Missouri v. Frye, 2012) and defenders have an ethical obligation to advise and guide clients through the plea decision (e.g., Mann, 2010). As we review in later sections, scant empirical research systematically examines how this process plays out in court.

3. WAIVING THE CONSTITUTIONAL RIGHT TO TRIAL

Accused youth have a Constitutionally protected right to trial and to confront witnesses against them at trial (Amendment VI of the US Constitution). The plea decision involves both entering a plea of guilty and waiving the right to a trial. A defendant may relinquish this right only if she makes a knowing and voluntary waiver (McCarty v. United States, 1969). In Godinez v. Moran (1993), the United States Supreme Court held that competence to stand trial and competence to plead guilty are equivalent competencies. In the plea context, an accused must be competent to understand the rights she is giving up as well as the short- and long-term consequences of a plea.

3.1 Developmental Differences in the Capacities to Understand the Waiver Process

A number of studies have demonstrated that capacities relevant to competence to stand trial, which according to the Court are equivalent to those of competency to plead, increase with age. Grisso et al. (2003) assessed competence-related capacities among a sample of 1300 youth and young adults ages 10–25, half of whom were under pretrial incarceration, using the MacArthur Competence Assessment Tool–Criminal Adjudication (MacCAT-CA; Poythress et al., 1999). Almost 60% of 11–13-year-olds and 50% of the 14–15-year-olds demonstrated mild to significant impairment on the Understanding subscale. Those two age groups significantly differed from each other and the older adolescent and young adult group, each of which had less than 40% of participants with similar impairments.

To further investigate youths' understanding, Woolard and Fountain (in preparation) reexamined the data from Grisso and colleagues (2003) to focus on questions within the MacCAT-CA Understanding subscale that specifically evaluated understanding of the role of the defense lawyer. We tested whether youth were less likely than young adults to understand the very basis of the defense attorney's role—to be on the side of the defendant herself. The likelihood of correctly understanding the defense attorney's role increased with age and IQ. About three quarters of 11–13-year-olds understood the role compared to more than 90% of older adolescents and young adults. No effects of race, ethnicity, gender, socioeconomic status, or justice system status were found. It appears that the impairment associated with age occurs for the youngest adolescents, particularly when they have a lower IQ.

Moreover, younger adolescents were also less likely to understand some of the rights that are given up when pleading guilty. About 75% of all participants, regardless of age, understood that a guilty plea prevents one from convincing the judge of innocence. Only about 6% of the 11–13-year-olds, 20% of the 14–15-year-olds, and about 30% of the 16–17-year-olds were able to identify any rights that are given up by pleading guilty. Forty percent of the young adults were able to identify at least one right that is waived in those circumstances.

Beyond lacking basic legal knowledge of their rights, the cognitive and psychosocial capacities that youth need to make knowing and informed decisions are precisely those that are undergoing developmental changes during adolescence, changes that will not be complete in some cases until well into young adulthood. Brain development during adolescence consists of structural and functional changes that affect executive functioning such as decision making and planning. During adolescence, two major structural changes occur in the prefrontal cortex: (1) myelination, or white matter increases, which speeds up neural processing and (2) pruning or gray matter volume decreases (Blakemore & Choudhury, 2006; Gogtay et al., 2004). These structural developmental changes provide preliminary evidence that the prefrontal cortex functioning is becoming more efficient perhaps by the strengthening of primary synaptic connections (myelination) and the elimination of rarely used ones (pruning). Findings also suggest that phylogenetically (i.e., evolutionarily) older brain areas tend to develop before newer ones (Gogtay et al., 2004), suggesting that areas associated with executive function (i.e., prefrontal cortex), develop after areas implicated in motivation and emotional processing (i.e., limbic system) (Casey, Jones, & Hare, 2008). As we discuss, the different rates of maturation help explain developmental differences in legally relevant decisional capacities.

One way to understand the structural and functional brain changes during adolescence is through a dual systems model that highlights the importance of two networks—the socioemotional network and the cognitive control system (e.g., Steinberg, 2010). Converging research confirms that different parts of the brain are active during different aspects of decision making, that different brain systems mature on different time tables, and that, compared to adults, adolescents recruit different parts of the brain during decision-making tasks (Steinberg, 2010).

The socioemotional network, or brain systems responsible for emotion, rewards, and social processing, undergoes major changes in early adolescence, which is also a time of increased sensation seeking, increased/easier emotional arousal, and increased attentiveness to social information from peers. Early adolescents in particular are more likely to engage in sensation seeking—activities that are novel, exciting, and rewarding. Studies suggest that adolescents do so in part because they are more sensitive to rewards, particularly those that are immediately available (e.g., Cauffman et al., 2010; Steinberg et al., 2009). For example, in a study that used an increasing risk dynamic paradigm (i.e., the probability of a negative outcome increases with each additional decision) to measure risky decision making, researchers found that in affective (emotionally laden) settings adolescents were more likely to make risky decisions compared to children and adults (Figner, Mackinlay, Wilkening, & Weber, 2009).

Moreover, it is not just a myth that teens are more sensitive than adults to perceived and actual influences of their peers. For example, adolescents took more risks in a driving game when their peers were in the room than children and adults in the same situation (Gardner & Steinberg, 2005). Interestingly, all three groups engaged in the same amount of risky behavior when they completed the task alone. Peer influence can be direct (e.g., friends encouraging one to do something risky) or indirect (e.g., doing something risky to avoid the potential for peer rejection even in the absence of direct pressure). The capacity to resist peer influence appears to grow during middle adolescence (ages 14–18) but not before (Steinberg & Monahan, 2007). Given the fact that most adolescents who commit crime do so in groups, the susceptibility to peer influence during the teen years cannot be underestimated.

So, adolescence is characterized by a socioemotional system that is easily aroused and highly sensitive to social feedback in ways that are different from both children and adults. This arousal and sensitivity can have an adaptive value by helping teens meet the novel social challenges they face as adolescents and prepare them for adulthood. But, they can also lead teens to make decisions that might threaten their own well-being and the well-being of others (Casey & Caudle, 2013).

At the same time, the entire developmental period of adolescence is characterized by a still-immature cognitive control system. The capacity for planning, future orientation, and the ability to regulate oneself involves prefrontal and anterior cingulate portions of the brain that continue to develop well into young adulthood. Sometimes called the "CEO" of the brain, these areas activate during what we might consider mature or deliberate thinking—the abilities to identify and consider future consequences, understand possible sequences of events, and control impulses. Throughout the entirety of adolescence, these portions of the brain involved in executive function do not demonstrate adult-like patterns of performance during laboratory tasks that require the young person to think ahead, control impulses, and balance short-term rewards with long-term consequences (e.g., Casey, Jones, & Somerville, 2011).

For example, teens are more likely to focus on the short-term immediate consequences of a decision rather than the possible long-term consequences (e.g., Steinberg et al., 2009), even when discussing decisions such as police interrogation, attorney consultation, and plea agreement considerations (e.g., Grisso et al., 2003). Steinberg and colleagues (2009) examined self-reported ability to plan ahead, ability to anticipate consequences, and time perspective among 930 individuals aged 10–30 in a normative community sample. Adolescents aged 12–15 scored significantly lower on planning than individuals younger than 12 and older than 15 years old. Additionally, time perspective and the ability to anticipate consequences increased linearly with age. This is not surprising given that younger adolescents are known to consider fewer long-range consequences of their decisions. As part of the competence to stand trial study described earlier, Grisso and colleagues (2003) also provided the adolescents and young adults with three separate legal decision-making scenarios and had participants list the consequences associated with each decision. Their consequences were then coded as being either short-term or long-term, and the long-term consequences were averaged across all scenarios for a total "future orientation" score. Similarly, Grisso and colleagues (2003) found that compared to older adolescents (aged 16–17), young adolescents (11–13) provided the fewest amount of long-term consequences.

Research provides evidence that adolescents as a group, particularly mid-adolescents (ages 14–17), are less able to control impulses, less able to resist pressure from peers, less likely to think ahead, more likely to take risks, less likely to give weight to potential costs and losses of risky behavior, and more driven by the thrill of rewards. These effects hold true across the entire span of adolescence, decreasing with age into young adulthood. Moreover, the effects of immaturity are probably even greater outside the control of a laboratory. Compared to adults, juveniles' cognitive capacity is undermined by that socioemotional system in circumstances that are not controlled, deliberate, and calm—circumstances that may encompass much of adolescent delinquency risk (e.g., Casey & Caudle, 2013). In other words, the adolescent brain reaches heightened emotional reactivity in mid-adolescence before it develops the capacity to regulate those emotions in late adolescence and early adulthood (Steinberg, 2010). Theory suggests the integration of the two systems develops with maturation, thus bringing the influence of each system into greater balance and perhaps contributing to the reduction in risky behavior we see in adulthood.

Now, adolescents do have some capacity for self-control but, while still developing, it is more easily overwhelmed by circumstances than adults. Because much youth crime is committed in groups (Zimring, 1982) and peer influence peaks in mid-adolescence (e.g., Gardner & Steinberg, 2005), youths' decisions may also be a function of their desires to do what they believe their peers want them to do, to protect the peers who were involved in the offense, and to impress their friends. Recent laboratory studies suggest that adolescents are uniquely sensitive to motivational cues such as immediate rewards (compared to delayed rewards) and happy faces (compared to neutral or fearful faces) (e.g., Casey & Caudle, 2013). When these are present, their cognitive control system, which is still immature, cannot meet the challenge of inhibiting their attention or potential action. The systems that regulate or control the self are there but do not perform as effectively in the face of strong motivation or incentive. One analogy might be a muscle that is still being strengthened. When challenged with too much weight, it simply cannot perform as well yet. So adolescents are less able to marshal their developing self-regulatory capacities in emotional, reward-driven situations such as the peer interactions that are increasingly common during this age. As teens mature into young adults they become better able to control impulses, regulate their emotions, have greater foresight, and plan ahead in similar circumstances.

Even with these developmental differences, attorneys can scaffold youths' decision making and mitigate some impairments. Attorney–youth interaction is the primary way youths receive and process information about a plea offer. Once a plea offer has been extended by the prosecutor, the lawyer's first and most basic responsibility is to advise the child of the plea offer (Missouri v. Frye, 2012). Professional Rules and Standards require defense counsel to keep their clients advised of any significant developments in the case and promptly communicate and explain all plea proposals (American Bar Association, 2015a, 2015b; National Juvenile Defender Center, 2012). The lawyer (and the court) must also ensure that the child enters the plea with a complete understanding of the consequences (American Bar Association, 2015b; National Juvenile Defender Center, 2012). As such, to ensure a child's complete understanding, the attorney must obtain all the necessary and relevant information, convey that information to the youth in a way that he/she can receive it, and process the information adequately and effectively with the youth.

Although adolescents' cognitive and psychosocial limitations might undermine their effective participation in the attorney–client relationship, defense counsel have heightened responsibilities when representing children. The lawyer's responsibility is not just to passively or neutrally list alternatives, but to offer a realistic appraisal of all of the legal and nonlegal advantages and disadvantages of a contemplated course of action and to structure the counseling process in a way that ensures the youth will identify and evaluate all of the available options and choose the best alternative. The attorney's typical explanation of concepts like "plea" and "trial" will likely have little meaning to a youth. An attorney may undermine the youth's right to choose between trial and plea not only by failing to communicate the plea offer and its consequences, but also by failing to counsel the youth in a way that is appropriate for her age and developmental capacity.

However, effective counseling by an attorney can maximize the youth's limited cognitive capacities and improve the youth's judgment and insight (Henning, 2005). Attorneys could help scaffold an adolescent defendant's understanding if they spend adequate time together and communicate in a way that is appropriate for the youth's age and developmental capacity. For example, Viljoen, Klaver, and Roesch (2005) interviewed 150 defendants between the ages of 11–17 about their understanding of the Miranda warnings (Miranda v. Arizona, 1966) as well as their factual understanding and appreciation of the trial process. Their results suggested that the amount of time spent with a defense attorney indeed increased capacities relevant to Miranda and adjudicative competence. Time is a luxury for most youth, however. Even when youth are provided with an opportunity to consult with counsel before a plea, the consultation may occur in a holding cell moments before the plea hearing. Regardless of what and how knowledge is communicated and discussed, youth in courts across the country are often forced to make plea decisions under extreme time pressure.

Of course, the potential for attorneys to improve a youth's understanding will not be realized unless the youth actually has access to a lawyer. As noted earlier, a significant percentage of youth remain unrepresented (National Juvenile Defender Center, 2015). In many jurisdictions, children are asked whether they wish to plea at the very first court appearance—often without the advice of any counsel. In other jurisdictions, children are given a written plea form when they enter the courthouse. These forms are meant to inquire as to whether the defendant comprehends the plea decision but no attorney is assigned to help them read and understand it. The lack of assistance is highly problematic because preliminary research evaluating the comprehensibility of tender of plea forms found that fewer than 5% of forms would be comprehensible to the average juvenile or adult defendant. Redlich and Bonventre (2015) examined approximately 200 different tender of plea forms used for juvenile and adult defendants in various jurisdictions. The authors found that only 4.3% of the forms were comprehensible at a sixth grade reading level (i.e., the average reading level of juvenile defendants).

In summary, developments in psychology and brain science demonstrate that youth may be inadequately equipped to make decisions characterized by incomplete or inadequate information, significant short- and long-term consequences, time pressure, and emotional stress. On average, adolescents' underdeveloped decisional abilities may be taxed beyond capacity in ambiguous, fast paced, emotional situations, although some adolescents can be scaffolded by extended, thoughtful, methodical counsel to produce informed decisions in the juvenile justice system. Realistically, the plea process more often resembles the former than the latter.

4. DEVELOPMENTAL DIFFERENCES IN THE CAPACITIES TO VOLUNTARILY WAIVE THE RIGHT TO TRIAL

Youth plead guilty for a myriad of reasons in the juvenile justice system. Key stakeholders have a tremendous influence on a child's decision to plead guilty and a significant impact on a child's perception of justice and fairness within the system. In this section, we use procedural justice as a theoretical frame for examining the mechanisms that promote, protect, or undermine youth voluntariness and justice.

4.1 Youth May Enter the Process Anticipating Unfairness

As the Supreme Court recognized in the case In re Gault (1967), the appearance and actuality of fairness, impartiality, and orderliness in the juvenile court may be just as, if not more, therapeutic for the youth than programing. That is, the youth's perception about whether she is being treated fairly in the system is "integral to the child's behavioral and psychological development" (In re Amendment to Rules of Juvenile Procedure, 2001). Studies of both American (Piquero, Fagan, Mulvey, Steinberg, & Odgers, 2005) and Canadian youth (Sprott & Greene, 2010) suggest that adolescents' perceptions of judges and attorneys affect their overall attitudes about the legitimacy of the legal system itself. The effects of youths' perceptions on perceived legitimacy occur above and beyond youths' initial views of system legitimacy and their case-specific outcomes. For example, Canadian youths' views of the prosecutor, defense attorney, judge, and overall assessment of the legal system became more negative between their first court appearance and their sentencing hearing, indicating they experienced less procedural justice and viewed the legal system as less legitimate (Sprott & Greene, 2010).

Fair decision-making procedures included being treated with respect and impartiality by authorities litigants can trust and being given an opportunity to participate in proceedings (Fagan & Tyler, 2005; Penner, Viljoen, Douglas, & Roesch, 2014; Tyler, 2000). In a juvenile case, the youth has voice when she is given an opportunity to tell her story and express her own views and opinions before important decisions are made (Lind, Kanfer, & Earley, 1990). Because meaningful choice is virtually impossible without information, youth in court are also likely to measure fairness and impartiality by access to information (Winick, 1999). Information relieves stress, increases the respondent's understanding and acceptance of procedures, and may increase the respondent's expectations for a positive result. Individuals who obtain information about the law and the legal process also perceive that they have greater control within the system. Lawyers who encourage a child to take a plea without fully investigating the allegations or understanding the facts or helping the child understand the link between the facts and the elements may leave the child with a perception that the system is unfair.

Adolescent expectations about unfairness within the legal system cannot only influence their legal attitudes but their legal decisions as well. For example, Woolard, Harvell, and Graham (2008) examined how feelings of anticipatory injustice influenced legal decision making across various legal scenarios, including considering a plea offer. Interviews with almost 1400 youth (ages 10–17) and adults (ages 18–25), in pretrial confinement and in the community demonstrated that adolescents with higher levels of anticipatory injustice were less likely to recommend accepting a plea offer. Future analyses of these data will examine the explanations that adolescents gave for their choices. It is possible that those expecting injustice may not believe the plea offer is legitimate or fair and instead would recommend relying on an adversarial trial and facing uncertain sentencing outcomes. Overall, adolescents' expectations for and experience of the court process itself may interact with ongoing cognitive and psychosocial development to undermine their views of the justice system's legitimacy and lead them to make decisions that may not serve their best interests.

4.2 Youth May Misinterpret Interaction Among System Officials

Buss (2015) argues that not only do the court system and individual stakeholders fail to meaningfully engage youth, it "ostentatiously treats them as outsiders" (p. 315). Perhaps more concerning, she writes

> *[I]s the message that the entire court-full of professionals, including the young person's own lawyer, and even more significantly the judge, are on a single team that excludes the young person. (p. 317)*

Different court systems, and even individual courts, operate in a culture that is both formal and informal (Dixon, 1995; Ulmer & Kramer, 1998). The social regularities (Seidman, 1990) of a court manifest in explicit procedures (e.g., process for bringing a plea before the court) and implicit guidelines (e.g., "the going rate" for a particular crime, specific negotiating strategies for individual stakeholders) that create the context in which attorneys and youths engage in the plea process. Ulmer and Kramer (1998) describe "courts as communities of action and communication based on court actors' shared workplace, interdependent working relationships between key sponsoring agencies (prosecutor's office, bench, defense bar), and local legal culture" (p. 251). In other words, relationships among justice professionals existed before an individual youth's case and will extend well beyond her time in court. Without that context and a fully developed capacity to take other people's perspective (e.g., Scott, Reppucci, & Woolard, 1995), a youth may not know how to interpret her limited experience with these ongoing relationships. In a jurisdiction where the prosecution and defense bar are collegial, for example, the youth may believe Buss's (2015) claim above that everyone is on the same team, a team that does not include the youth. And there may actually be some truth to that claim, particularly in systems in which benevolent paternalism loses sight of the need for fair process and loyal defense advocacy.

4.3 Youth May Be Particularly Susceptible to Pressure from Prosecutors

Prosecution's focal concerns prioritize public safety and accountability over youth needs and treatment amenability (Bishop et al., 2010). These interests focus on the offense itself, and likely on punishment/accountability. Despite Constitutional safeguards designed to preclude the state from coercing a plea from a defendant (U.S. v. Jackson, 1968), prosecutors also manipulate the plea process by extending unconscionably coercive offers, such as those that require the child to plead guilty to avoid transfer to adult court, extended incarceration in juvenile or adult facilities, or multiple serious charges that overstate the child's true conduct. Because prosecutors have virtually unfettered discretion and immense power to convince a defendant to plea, a child presented with such a Hobson choice might even plead guilty to a crime she did not commit just to avoid the alternatives. It does not help that, unlike trials which take place in the child's presence, plea bargains are negotiated between the prosecutor and defense counsel outside of the child's presence.

4.4 Youths May Have Difficulty Resisting Paternalistic Pressure from Defense Attorneys

The child's attorney is an advisor (American Bar Association, 2015a). As such, the lawyer is ethically bound to advise the client of the advantages and disadvantages of any plea offer after investigation and meaningful evaluation of the evidence and likely witnesses. The lawyer's insight, guidance, and advice at this stage are critical. The lawyer's conversation with her client is so important at the plea bargaining stage that the Supreme Court has attempted to regulate it (Lafler v. Cooper, 2012) by finding that defendants who reject a lenient plea offer and go to trial due to counsel's bad advice, with the result of a harsher sentence, have a potential remedy. Unfortunately, the juvenile court's long history of paternalism has had a significant impact on the plea process. Lawyers who are coopted by the paternalism of the juvenile court and believe the child needs services may manipulate the child to take a plea. Lawyers with less benign motives may even encourage youth to plead to save time and reduce overwhelming caseloads.

The plea evaluation is a particularly abstract process. Children decide whether to plea after hypothesizing about various outcomes based on the lawyer's best guess about the strength and weaknesses of the state's case, the likelihood that essential witnesses will attend the trial, how credible the state's witnesses will appear in court, how the judge will perceive the evidence, and how the judge will sentence the child if the judge finds the child guilty. Lawyers may consciously and subconsciously control the child's choices by manipulating the information they provide about available options and anticipated outcomes. Lawyers may intentionally omit critical information or frame the discussion to highlight the options the lawyer thinks are best and diminish those options the lawyer rejects.

Attorneys' recommendations might be more influential for youth compared to adults because of youth's deference to adults. For example, Grisso and colleagues (2003) evaluated adolescents' abilities to make adult-like decisions by interviewing adolescents and young adults regarding how they would respond in each one of these scenarios (i.e., speaking to police, considering a prosecutor's plea offer, and consulting with a defense attorney) and found adolescents 15 and younger were more likely than older adolescents to make compliant decisions. Specifically, adolescents were more likely to make decisions that complied with authority figures' requests (e.g., confessing to police, accepting plea offered by the prosecutor, fully disclosing to the defense attorney).

Adolescents may also struggle to bring up disagreements they have with their attorneys in part as a result of this deference. In another example, Viljoen et al. (2005) examined the legal decisions of approximately 150 adolescent defendants (<18 years). They asked young defendants what they would do if they disagreed with their attorney. Younger adolescents were the least likely to consider appealing their cases or to discuss disagreements with their attorneys. These characteristics of young adolescents leave them at a disadvantage.

Lawyers for children have a special duty to engage youth in developmentally appropriate language, repeat information as many times as the youth needs to hear it, and provide youth with ample time to ask questions and understand the issues (Henning, 2005). The lawyer should also ensure there is a comfortable physical and emotional environment for the counseling. The National Juvenile Defense Standards require defenders to "explain to the client in developmentally appropriate language, the strengths, and weaknesses of the prosecution's case, the benefits and consequences of accepting a plea, and any rights the client may be forfeiting by pleading guilty" (National

Juvenile Defender Center, 2012, Standard 4.9). The Standards emphasize the importance of ensuring that youth understand plea colloquies by requesting a recess or continuance to assist the client if necessary (Standard 4.10). In the early stage of the interview, it is especially important for the lawyer to be nonjudgmental and provide genuine, noncontingent acceptance, and empathy. Given research suggests that psychosocial aspects of decision making—such as trust for adults—are likely to improve as the attorney–client relationship improves (Schmidt, Reppucci, & Woolard, 2003), the lawyer should build rapport with the youth over time and allocate sufficient time for thorough one-on-one counseling. When provided with all of the relevant information and given all of the appropriate cognitive and emotional supports, a youth may make well-reasoned decisions about the plea.

Attorneys play a significant role in securing procedural justice and therapeutic outcomes in a juvenile case. An accused child is powerless to make critical decisions in her case without information about the elements of an offense, the defenses available, and the advantages and disadvantages of a plea. The attorney not only arms the client with information and makes the proceedings seem less coercive, but the child's relationship with her lawyer is also the primary means by which an accused child may exercise or waive important constitutional rights. It is also the lens through which the child views, understands, and evaluates the juvenile court system, and it is the relationship through which the child comes to understand broader notions of law, liberty, justice, and fairness. Ultimately, when the lawyer is not overbearing in counseling and delays advice until he has established an appropriate rapport with the client, the child retains individual autonomy and is free to reject the lawyer's opinion (Henning, 2005).

4.5 Judges' Assessments of Voluntariness Are Not Developmentally Sensitive

To protect the accused against a coercive plea, court rules typically require the judge (a) determine whether there is a factual basis for accepting the plea and (b) to address the defendant personally on the record to determine whether any promises, force, or threats were used to obtain the plea (known as the judicial colloquy). The courts depend on lawyers to investigate the allegations and advise defendants of any defenses that might apply. The court will also ask the defendant to state on the record whether he or she agrees with the factual basis of the offense as proffered (American Bar Association, 2015b, Sections 14-1.5 and 14-1-6). While the judicial colloquy in particular is an essential safeguard against coercive and uncounseled pleas, the reality is that these colloquies are very poorly executed in most juvenile courts across the country. Judges often address youth in sophisticated legal language, ask leading questions that call for "yes" and "no" answers, speak in a tone that clearly conveys to the child that assent is expected, and rarely give children an opportunity to ask questions. If judges do not address youth in developmentally appropriate language, the youth may not fully understand what a promise of leniency or a coerced plea decision actually mean. Likewise, defense counsel rarely prepare children for the plea colloquy, effectively leaving the child to navigate this confusing and unfamiliar process by herself in the courtroom.

4.6 Parents May Not Always Act in Their Youth's Best Interests

Parents may have a multitude of goals for their child's plea decisions. Some parents may force their child to plead guilty to avoid the time and costs associated with accompanying the youth to court. Other parents may see the juvenile justice system as a resource. It is important to note that some parents without access to adequate social capital may rely on the juvenile court as an important source of social control of their children and social support for them as parents. Moreover, Richardson's (2014) longitudinal study of underresourced African American families in Harlem documented the view that confinement is one way to protect children's health and life, providing a safe haven that is otherwise unavailable. The rich ethnographic portrait of those families highlights the complicated context in which youth and families operate a context that is not unique to those families. Several studies document that a significant number of parents report using the juvenile justice system as a last resort to access mental health treatment for their children that is otherwise unavailable (e.g., Cocozza, Skowyra, & Shufelt, 2010; Osher & Hunt, 2002; Skowyra & Cocozza, 2007; U.S. General Accounting Office, 2003; Vitanza et al., 1999).

It is highly likely that, irrespective of parents' goals, they lack adequate and accurate knowledge about how the justice system works. Woolard and colleagues' (2008) interviews with 170 parent–child pairs documented significant deficits in knowledge among parents about the process of interrogation. For example, although about 70% of parents correctly understand the components of the Miranda warnings, only one-half of parents correctly believed that police were legally allowed to lie during interrogation. If similar misconceptions abound regarding the plea process, even well-intentioned parents may provide advice that ultimately does a disservice to their children.

5. IMPLICATIONS FOR YOUTHS' WELL-BEING

First, adolescents' limited ability to conceive of and appreciate the long-term risks and consequences of a choice leave them vulnerable to manipulation from prosecutors, defense attorneys, and/or parents. These age-based aspects of fairness and susceptibility to influence increase the likelihood that youth choose to waive the right to a trial and accept a plea bargain because of their ongoing cognitive and psychosocial development. If faced with a similar situation as an adult, these same youth might make different choices about their plea agreement.

Second, experiences of unfairness may negatively affect legal socialization. Legal socialization is the process by which individuals develop an understanding of the laws or rules within society, the institutions that create those laws, and the people within the institutions that enforce the laws or rules (Trinkner & Cohn, 2014). Once engaged with the system, children who feel coerced into pleading guilty or who plead guilty without fully understanding the evidence against them may have a lasting impression of unfairness. When children perceive legal rules, procedures, and actors as unfair, they have less respect for the law and legal authorities and are less likely to comply with the law in the future (Penner et al., 2014). By contrast, when children believe the legal system has treated them with fairness, respect, and dignity, they are more inclined to accept the legitimacy of authority figures and be less cynical about laws (Trinkner & Cohn, 2014). Because adolescence is a time when attitudes are being formed about the legal system (Fagan & Tyler, 2005), youths' experiences and perceptions of fairness and justice during adolescence may have a substantial impact on their risk of offending in the long term. Socialization that is primarily driven by fair, procedurally just, social interactions with legal authorities may ultimately affect individuals' decisions whether to violate or obey laws (Trinkner & Cohn, 2014).

Third, collateral consequences can influence a youth's future opportunities. Pleading guilty in juvenile court can have important ramifications beyond the particular sentence that may be imposed. Collateral consequences are the consequences that indirectly result from a conviction. For example, juvenile convictions may prevent a youth from obtaining public housing, affect eligibility to serve in the military, require her to register as a sex offender, and lead to school expulsion (Henning, 2004; Pinard, 2006). Some states may include juvenile convictions in calculations that impose enhanced sentences on adults (e.g., a "strike" in a three strikes law) (Pinard, 2006). Because of their ongoing development, youth are not well situated to truly comprehend the implications of these future consequences and are likely to discount their importance when deciding whether to accept a plea. Moreover, the collateral consequences of a plea agreement may have important implications for the family. For example, some public housing authorities may check whether any family member, including a juvenile, has been convicted of an offense. In some circumstances, a youth's delinquency adjudication could render the entire family ineligible for public housing (Henning, 2004). In sum, an adolescent's choice to take a plea agreement may result in collateral consequences that can harm their developmental pathway, reduce the chance for desistance, and increase their chance of reoffending.

6. RECOMMENDATIONS

Zimring and Langer (2015) argue that a maturational approach to juvenile justice, rather than a rehabilitative approach, now predominates globally in juvenile justice systems. A maturational approach assumes that most youth will naturally mature out of offending behaviors as they enter young adulthood and reserves intervention for those youth that need additional resources to follow that course. The rehabilitation approach assumes that offending youth will not necessarily naturally desist from patterns of offending and require active rehabilitative intervention to change their developmental path.

In January 2015, the World Congress on Juvenile Justice convened 900 participants from 80 countries to produce a Final Declaration that reaffirmed and promoted numerous philosophical, political, and policy approaches to children (under age 18) in conflict with the law. Among other things, the declaration noted "Institutions, laws, and procedures applicable to juvenile justice should be specifically adapted to children, to the greatest extent feasible" (item 13) and that specialized training for all justice stakeholders on international standards and children's rights should occur. In light of our review of the United States' approach to juvenile justice generally and the process of plea agreements specifically, we offer several recommendations consistent with the declaration.

First, defense attorneys should provide more effective representation through better training. Attorneys must have the capacity and then take the time to engage their client in developmentally sensitive ways. Organizations like the National Juvenile Defender Center and the MacArthur Foundation Models for Change offer training and resource materials to assist defense attorneys (as well as judges and prosecutors) understand adolescent development and incorporate that knowledge into their practice.

Second, the structure of defense representation must be more effectively resourced. While most attorneys will notify clients of plea offers that have been extended by the state, the adequacy of the attorney's advice can be severely compromised in most jurisdictions by the attorney's lack of discovery of the state's evidence (the process by which the defense receives relevant information from the prosecutor before trial) and by the lack of time to investigate. Attorneys who cannot investigate are ill-equipped to assess the likely advantages and disadvantages of the plea.

Third, prosecutors should offer a developmentally appropriate and procedurally just approach to plea agreements. In doing so, they may still advance their goals of protecting public safety and holding youth accountable. In fact, developmentally appropriate procedures may actually increase the likelihood that youth will understand and comply with sanctions and experience positive legal socialization. Applying Tyler's four aspects of procedural justice to the plea context, O'Hear (2008) suggests that before starting plea negotiations, prosecutors should make sure defendants have had a meaningful opportunity to tell their side of the story (e.g., through counsel) (voice), develop objective criteria to guide plea negotiations, and explain positions taken in negotiations (neutrality); expressly acknowledge arguments for more lenient treatment (trustworthiness); and refrain from pressure tactics like exploding offers and charging threats (respect).

Fourth, case processing must provide more time and attention to youth, particularly during the judicial colloquy about pleas. Youths' decision-making capacities are more effective when they are activated under conditions with less time pressure and less emotional salience. This holds true in the judicial colloquy. Not only should judges have a more developmentally appropriate and effective colloquy, they need to take the time to engage the youth in this process. All stakeholders should be educated on adolescent development (brain and behavior) and the implications for the plea and adjudication/disposition process. Understanding functional and structural brain development is important when considering adolescent culpability within the context of the juvenile justice system. The lengthy maturation of brain regions implicated in executive functioning combined with evidence of poorer performance on behavioral tasks bolsters what most already suspect to be true regarding adolescents, strengthening the argument that adolescents are indeed different from adults. Adolescents' poor planning, increased impulsivity, and susceptibility to peer influence argue for reduced culpability and highly greater risk of impaired performance as defendants compared to adults. Neuroscience allows for a better understanding of the underlying mechanisms related to these functions. Poor executive functioning coincides with difficulty in these processes, which inevitably can hinder decision making (Johnson, Blum, & Giedd, 2009).

7. CONCLUSION

Can a young person be empowered to exercise her constitutional rights and, if he so chooses, make a knowing and voluntary waiver? Our review suggests that it is possible but not probable given developmental, relational, resource, and system challenges. Youth must marshal capacities not yet fully developed to make a potentially life-altering decision with incomplete (or incorrect) information under difficult circumstances. Attorneys who represent children in juvenile cases have a unique and difficult task of honoring the child's autonomy while simultaneous recognizing and accommodating those developmental features that undermine sound decision making. The attorney's success in establishing and maintaining this delicate balance will determine whether the child experiences the system as one that is fair and just. As such, the attorney–client relationship is a significant vehicle through which many children come to understand the concepts of law and justice and experience fairness or unfairness in the juvenile justice system. Buss (2015) calls for attorneys to work *with* their clients, not for or on their clients. Systemic changes must produce the time, resources, and attention needed to do so.

REFERENCES

American Bar Association. (2015a). *Model rules of professional conduct.* Washington, DC: American Bar Association.

American Bar Association. (2015b). *ABA standards for criminal justice: Prosecution and defense function* (4th ed.). Washington, DC: American Bar Association.

Bishop, D., Leiber, M., & Johnson, J. (2010). Contexts of decision making in the juvenile justice system: An organizational approach to understanding minority overrepresentation. *Youth Violence and Juvenile Justice*, *8*, 213–233.

Blakemore, S. J., & Choudhury, S. (2006). Development of the adolescent brain: Implications for executive function and social cognition. *Journal of Child Psychology and Psychiatry, 47*, 296–312.

Bridges, G. S., & Steen, S. (1998). Racial disparities in official assessments of juvenile offenders: Attributional stereotypes as mediating mechanisms. *American Sociological Review, 63*, 554–570.

Bright, S. B. (2010). Legal representation for the poor: Can society afford this much injustice? *Missouri Law Review, 75*, 1–33.

Buss, E. (2015). The developmental stakes of youth participation in American juvenile court. In T. Gal & B. Duramy (Eds.), *International perspectives and empirical findings on child participation: From social exclusion to child-inclusive policies* (pp. 303–331). New York: Oxford University Press.

Casey, B. J., & Caudle, K. (2013). The teenage brain: Self control. *Current Directions in Psychological Science, 22*, 82–87.

Casey, B. J., Jones, R. M., & Hare, T. A. (2008). The adolescent brain. *Annals of the New York Academy of Sciences, 1124*, 111–126.

Casey, B. J., Jones, R. M., & Somerville, L. H. (2011). Braking and accelerating of the adolescent brain. *Journal of Research on Adolescence, 21*, 21–33.

Cauffman, E., Shulman, E. P., Steinberg, L., Claus, E., Banich, M. T., Graham, S., et al. (2010). Age differences in affective decision making as indexed by performance on the Iowa gambling task. *Developmental Psychology, 46*, 193–207.

Cocozza, J. J., Skowyra, K. R., & Shufelt, J. L. (2010). *Addressing the mental health needs of youth in contact with the juvenile justice system in system of care communities: An overview and summary of key issues.* Washington, DC: Technical Assistance Partnership for Child and Family Mental Health.

Davis, J., & Sorenson, J. R. (2012). Disproportionate minority confinement of juveniles: A national examination of black–white disparity in placements, 1997–2006. *Crime and Delinquency, 59*, 115–139.

De la Vega, C., & Leighton, M. (2008). Sentencing our children to die in prison: Global law and practice. *University of San Francisco Law Review, 42*(4), 983–1044.

DiIulio, J. J. (1996). *Fill churches, not jails: Youth crime and "superpredators." Testimony before the Senate Committee on the Judiciary, Subcommittee on Youth Violence.* Retrieved from, http://www.brookings.edu/research/testimony/1996/02/28crime-diiulio.

Dixon, J. (1995). The organizational context of criminal sentencing. *American Journal of Sociology, 100*, 1157–1198.

Durose, M. R., & Langan, P. A. (2007). *Felony sentences in state courts, 2004.* Washington, DC: Bureau of Justice Statistics, Office of Justice Programs, U.S. Department of Justice.

Ecenbarger, W. (2012). *Kids for cash: Two judges, thousands of children, and a $2.8 million kickback scheme.* New York, NY: The New Press.

Emmelman, D. S. (1996). Trial by plea bargain: Case settlement as a product of recursive decision making. *Law and Society Review, 30*, 335–360.

Fader, J. J., Kurlychek, M. C., & Morgan, K. A. (2014). The color of juvenile justice: Racial disparities in dispositional decisions. *Social Science Research, 44*, 126–140.

Fagan, J., & Tyler, T. R. (2005). Legal socialization of children and adolescents. *Social Justice Research, 18*, 217–241.

Farrington, D. P. (2005). Introduction to integrated developmental and life-course theories of offending. In D. P. Farrington (Ed.), *Integrated developmental and life course theories of offending: Advances in criminological theory: Vol. 14* (pp. 1–14). Brunswick, NJ: Transaction Publishers.

Feld, B. (1991). Justice by geography: Urban, suburban, and rural variations in juvenile justice administration. *Journal of Criminal Law and Criminology, 82*, 156–210.

Feld, B., & Schaefer, S. (2010). The right to counsel in juvenile court: The conundrum of attorneys as an aggravating factor at disposition. *Justice Quarterly*, *27*, 713–741.
Figner, B., Mackinlay, R. J., Wilkening, F., & Weber, E. (2009). Affective and deliberative processes in risky choice: Age differences in risk taking in the Columbia card task. *Journal of Experimental Psychology: Learning, Memory, and Cognition*, *35*, 709–730.
Gardner, M., & Steinberg, L. (2005). Peer influence on risk taking, risk preference, and risky decision making in adolescence and adulthood: An experimental study. *Developmental Psychology*, *41*, 625–635.
Godinez v. Moran, 509 U.S. 389 (1993).
Gogtay, N., Giedd, J. N., Lusk, L., Hayashi, K. M., Greenstein, D., Vaituzis, A. C., et al. (2004). Dynamic mapping of human cortical development during childhood through early adulthood. *Proceedings of the National Academy of Sciences*, *21*, 8174–8179.
Graham v. Florida, 560 U.S. 48 (2010).
Griffin, P., Addie, S., Adams, B., & Firestine, K. (2011). *Trying juveniles as adults: An analysis of state transfer laws and reporting: Juvenile Offenders and Victims: National Report Series Bulletin*. Washington, DC: Office of Juvenile Justice and Delinquency Prevention.
Grisso, T., Steinberg, L., Woolard, J., Cauffman, E., Scott, E., Graham, S., et al. (2003). Juveniles' competence to stand trial: A comparison of adolescents' and adults' capacities as trial defendants. *Law and Human Behavior*, *27*, 333–363.
Henning, K. (2004). Eroding confidentiality in delinquency proceeding: Should schools and public housing authorities be notified? *New York University Law Review*, *79*, 520–611.
Henning, K. (2005). Loyalty, paternalism, and rights: Client counseling theory and the role of child's counsel in delinquency cases. *Notre Dame Law Review*, *81*, 245–324.
Hockenberry, S., & Puzzanchera, C. (2013). *Juvenile court statistics 2013*. Pittsburgh, PA: National Center for Juvenile Justice.
In re Amendment to Rules of Juvenile Procedure, 804 So.2d 1206 (Fla. 2001).
In re Gault. 387 U.S. 1 (1967).
Johnson, S. B., Blum, R. W., & Giedd, J. N. (2009). Adolescent maturity and the brain: the promise and pitfalls of neuroscience research in adolescent health policy. *Journal of Adolescent Health*, *45*, 216–221.
Kempf-Leonard, K. (2007). Minority youths and juvenile justice: Disproportionate minority contact after nearly 20 years of reform efforts. *Youth Violence and Juvenile Justice*, *5*, 71–87.
Kent v. U.S., 383 U.S. 541 (1966).
Lafler v Cooper, 132 S.Ct. 1376 (2012).
Levick, M., & Desai, N. (2007). Still waiting: The elusive quest to ensure juveniles a constitutional right to counsel at all stages of the juvenile court process. *Rutgers University Law Review*, *60*, 175–205.
Lind, E. A., Kanfer, R., & Earley, P. C. (1990). Voice, control, and procedural justice: Instrumental and noninstrumental concerns in fairness judgments. *Journal of Personality and Social Psychology*, *59*, 952–959.
Mann, P. E. (2010). Ethical obligations of defense attorneys to their clients. *Missouri Law Review*, *75*, 715–750.
McCarty v. United States, 394 U.S. 459 (1969).
Miller v. Alabama, 132 S. Ct. 2455 (2011).
Miranda v. Arizona, 384 U.S. 436 (1966).
Missouri v. Frye, 132 S.Ct. 1399 (2012).
Monahan, K. C., & Piquero, A. R. (2009). Investigating the longitudinal relation between offending frequency and offending variety. *Criminal Justice and Behavior*, *36*, 653–673.
Moore, L. D., & Padavic, I. (2010). Racial and ethnic disparities in girls' sentencing in the juvenile justice system. *Feminist Criminology*, *5*, 263–285.

National Juvenile Defender Center. (2012). *National juvenile defense standards.* Washington, DC: National Juvenile Defender Center.
National Juvenile Defender Center. (2015). *State assessments.* Retrieved from, http://njdc.info/our-work/juvenile-indigent-defense-assessments/.
National Research Council and Institute of Medicine (2001). *Juvenile crime, juvenile justice.* Panel on juvenile crime: Prevention, treatment, and control. In J. McCord, C. S. Widom, & N. A. Crowell (Eds.), *Committee on law and justice and board on children, youth, and families.* Washington, DC: National Academy Press.
O'Hear, M. M. (2008). Plea bargaining and procedural justice. *Georgia Law Review, 42,* 407–431.
Office of Juvenile Justice and Delinquency Prevention (OJJDP). Statistical briefing book. (2015). At http://www.ojjdp.gov/ojstatbb/ (accessed 01.07.15).
Osher, T., & Hunt, P. (2002). *Involving families of youth who are in contact with the juvenile justice system.* Delmar, NY: National Center for Mental Health and Juvenile Justice.
Owens, S. D., Accetta, E., Charles, J. J., & Shoemaker, S. E. (2015). *Indigent defense services in the United States, FY 2008-2012—Updated.* Washington, DC: Bureau of Justice Statistics, Office of Justice Programs, U.S. Department of Justice.
Penner, E. K., Viljoen, J. L., Douglas, K. S., & Roesch, R. (2014). Procedural justice versus risk factors for offending: Predicting recidivism in youth. *Law and Human Behavior, 38,* 225–237.
Pinard, M. (2006). The logistical and ethical difficulties of informing juveniles about the collateral consequences of adjudications. *Nevada Law Journal, 6,* 1111–1126.
Piquero, A. R., Fagan, J., Mulvey, E. P., Steinberg, L., & Odgers, C. (2005). Developmental trajectories of legal socialization among serious adolescent offenders. *The Journal of Criminal Law & Criminology, 96,* 267–298.
Poythress, N., Nicholson, R., Otto, R., Edens, J., Bonnie, R., Monahan, J., et al. (1999). *The MacArthur competence assessment tool–criminal adjudication: Professional manual.* Odessa, FL: Psychological Assessment Resources.
Puritz, P., Burrell, S., Schwartz, R., Soler, M., & Warboys, L. (2002). *A call for justice: An assessment of access to counsel and quality of representation in delinquency proceedings.* Washington, DC: National Juvenile Defender Center.
Puritz, P., & Sterling, R. W. (2010). *West Virginia: An assessment of access to counsel and quality of representation in juvenile delinquency court.* Washington, DC: National Juvenile Defender Center.
Redlich, A. D., & Bonventre, C. L. (2015). Content and comprehensibility of juvenile and adult tender-of-plea forms: Implications for knowing, intelligent, and voluntary guilty pleas. *Law and Human Behavior, 39,* 162–176.
Richardson, J. B. (2014). I want him locked up: Social capital, African American parenting strategies, and the juvenile court. *Journal of Contemporary Ethnography, 43,* 488–522.
Roper v. Simmons, 543 U.S. 551 (2005).
Ruck, M. D., Keating, D. P., Saewyc, E. M., Earls, F., & Ben-Arieh, A. (2016). The United Nations convention on the rights of the child: Its relevance for adolescents. *Journal of Research on Adolescence, 26,* 16–29.
Scali, M. A., & Song, J. S. (2010). *South Carolina indigent defense: A report on access to counsel and quality of representation in delinquency proceedings.* Washington, DC: National Juvenile Defender Center.
Schmidt, M. G., Reppucci, N. D., & Woolard, J. L. (2003). Effectiveness of participation as a defendant: The attorney–juvenile client relationship. *Behavioral Sciences and the Law, 21,* 175–198.
Scott, E. S. (2013). Children are different: Constitutional values and justice policy. *Ohio State Journal of Criminal Law, 11,* 71–105.

Scott, E. S., Reppucci, N. D., & Woolard, J. L. (1995). Evaluating adolescent decision making in legal contexts. *Law and Human Behavior, 19*, 221–244.

Scott, E. S., & Steinberg, L. (2008). *Rethinking juvenile justice.* Boston, MA: Harvard University Press.

Seidman, E. (1990). Pursuing the meaning and utility of social regularities for community psychology. In P. Tolan, C. Keys, F. Chertok, & L. Jason (Eds.), *Researching community psychology: Issues of theory and methods* (pp. 91–100). Washington, DC: American Psychological Association.

Sickmund, M., & Puzzanchera, C. (2014). *Juvenile offenders and victims: 2014 national report.* Pittsburgh, PA: National Center for Juvenile Justice.

Skowyra, K., & Cocozza, J. (2007). *Blueprint for change: A comprehensive model for the identification and treatment of youth with mental health needs in contact with the juvenile justice system.* Delmar, NY: National Center for Mental Health and Juvenile Justice.

Sprott, J. B., & Greene, C. (2010). Trust and confidence in the courts: Does the quality of treatment young offenders receive affect their views of the courts? *Crime and Delinquency, 56*, 269–289.

Steinberg, L. (2010). A behavioral scientist looks at the science of adolescent brain development. *Brain and Cognition, 72*, 160–164.

Steinberg, L., Graham, S., O'Brien, L., Woolard, J., Cauffman, E., & Banich, M. (2009). Age differences in future orientation and delay discounting. *Child Development, 80*, 28–44.

Steinberg, L., & Monahan, K. C. (2007). Age differences in resistance to peer influence. *Developmental Psychology, 43*, 1531–1543.

Tannenhaus, D. S. (2002). The evolution ofjuvenile courts in the twentieth century: Beyond the myth of immaculate construction. In M. K. Rosenheim, F. E. Zimring, D. S. Tanenhaus, & B. Dorn (Eds.), *A century of juvenile justice* (pp. 42–73). Chicago: University of Chicago Press.

Trinkner, R., & Cohn, E. S. (2014). Putting the social back in legal socialization: Procedural justice, legitimacy, and cynicism in legal and nonlegal authorities. *Law and Human Behavior, 38*, 602–617.

Tyler, T. (2000). Social justice: Outcome and procedure. *International Journal of Psychology, 35*, 117–125.

U.S. General Accounting Office. (2003). *Child welfare and juvenile justice: Federal agencies could play a stronger role in helping states reduce the number of children placed solely to obtain mental health services.* Washington, DC: U.S. General Accounting Office.

Ulmer, J. T., & Kramer, J. H. (1998). The use and transformation of formal decision-making criteria: Sentencing guidelines, organizational contexts, and case processing strategies. *Social Problems, 45*, 248–267.

United Nations. (1985). *United Nations standard minimum rules for the administration of juvenile justice ("The Beijing Rules").* A/RES/40/33, New York, NY: United Nations. Retrieved from, http://www2.ohchr.org/english/law/pdf/beijingrules.pdf.

United Nations. (1989). *Convention on the rights of the child.* A/RES/44/25, New York, NY: United Nations.

United Nations. (1990). *United nations guidelines for the prevention of juvenile delinquency ("The Riyadh guidelines").* A/RES/45/112, New York, NY: United Nations. http://www2.ohchr.org/english/law/juvenile.htm.

United Nations Office on Drugs and Crime. (2006). *Manual for the measurement of juvenile justice indicators.* New York: United Nations.

United States v. Jackson, 390 U.S. 570 (1968).

Viljoen, J. L., Klaver, J., & Roesch, R. (2005). Legal decisions of preadolescent and adolescent defendants: Predictors of confessions, pleas, communication with attorneys, and appeals. *Law and Human Behavior, 29*, 253–277.

Vitanza, S., Cohen, R., Hall, L. L., Wechsler, H., Cohen, J., Rothrock, A., et al. (1999). *Families on the brink: The impact of ignoring children with serious mental illness. Results of a national survey of parents and other caregivers.* Washington, DC: National Alliance for the Mentally Ill.
Ward, G. (2012). *The black child-savers: Racial democracy and juvenile justice.* Chicago: University of Chicago Press.
Weithorn, L. (2005). Envisioning second-order change in America's response to troubled and troublesome youth. *Hofstra Law Review, 33*, 1305–1506.
Winick, B. J. (1999). Therapeutic jurisprudence and the civil commitment hearing. *Journal of Contemporary Legal Issues, 10*, 37–60.
Woolard, J.L., & Fountain, E. (in preparation). Comparing juvenile and adult understanding of the right to waive trial and plead guilty.
Woolard, J. L., Harvell, S. A., & Graham, S. (2008). Anticipatory in justice among adolescents: Age and racial/ethnic differences in perceived unfairness of the justice system. *Behavioral Sciences and the Law, 26*, 207–226.
Woolard, J. L., & Scott, E. S. (2009). The legal regulation of adolescence. In R. M. Lerner & L. Steinberg (Eds.), *Contextual influences on adolescent development: Vol. 2. Handbook of adolescent psychology* (3rd ed., pp. 345–371). New York: Wiley.
Worden, A. P., Davies, A. L. B., & Brown, E. K. (2011). A patchwork of policies: Justice, due process, and public defense across American states. *Albany Law Review, 74*, 1423–1463.
Zimring, F. E. (1978). *Confronting youth crime: Report of the twentieth century fund task force on sentencing policy toward young offenders.* New York: Holmes and Meier Publishers.
Zimring, F. E. (1982). *The changing legal world of adolescence.* New York, NY: Free Press.
Zimring, F. E., & Langer, M. (2015). One theme or many? The search for deep structure in global juvenile justice. In F. E. Zimring, M. Langer, & D. S. Tannenhaus (Eds.), *Juvenile justice in global perspective* (pp. 383–411). New York: New York University Press.

CHAPTER SEVEN

Social Justice and the Environmental Commons

Constance A. Flanagan[1], Rachel Byington, Erin Gallay, Allison Sambo
School of Human Ecology, University of Wisconsin-Madison, Madison, WI, United States
[1]Corresponding author: e-mail address: caflanagan@wisc.edu

Contents

Abstract

In this chapter, we build on the scholarship on youth civic engagement by turning attention to the environmental commons as a space for political action. We begin with a definition of the term and arguments about ways that social justice is implied in it. Following that, we raise several psychological challenges to motivating action on behalf of the environmental commons and discuss the critical experiences and actions that can defy those challenges. Finally, drawing from Ostrom's empirical evidence opposing

Equity and Justice in Developmental Science: Implications for Young People, Families, and Communities (S.S. Horn, M.D. Ruck & L.S. Liben, Eds.)
Advances in Child Development and Behavior (J.B. Benson, Series Ed.), Vol. 51
ISSN 0065-2407 http://dx.doi.org/10.1016/bs.acdb.2016.04.005

a *tragedy of the commons*, we discuss practices consistent with a social justice approach that nurture in younger generations an identification with and commitment to the environmental commons and discuss how this orientation would benefit human beings, democracies, and the earth.

1. INTRODUCTION

Over the past few decades there has been an exponential increase in scholarship on civic/political action as a domain of youth development. Whereas the political socialization models from earlier eras emphasized intergenerational transmission of political attitudes and behaviors, the new scholarship has drawn attention to the agency of youth as contributing members of their communities. Convergent evidence from this body of work points to several key findings. First, youth's civic interest and engagement is motivated and sustained when they feel that they have a voice, are respected, and matter to fellow residents of their communities (Eccles & Gootman, 2001). Second, young people's sense of incorporation (solidarity with fellow community members and identification with community institutions) is positively associated with assuming social responsibility for individuals and groups in the broader community (Flanagan, Kim, Collura, & Kopish, 2015). Third, attention to political issues is generated by controversy, by discussion and exchange of different perspectives, and by beliefs that it matters to take a stand (Flanagan, 2013). Fourth, civic engagement and volunteering are correlated with happiness, self-esteem, life satisfaction, and well-being (Piliavin & Siegl, 2007). Fifth, engaging in community affairs in one's youth is a precursor to voting, volunteering, and assuming community leadership roles in adulthood (McFarland & Thomas, 2006). Finally, in the course of constructing their personal identities and aspirations for the future, young people also are imagining the kind of society they want to inhabit and are constructing political theories that guide their behaviors (Flanagan, 2013).

A good deal of the new scholarship has emphasized the benefits of civic engagement for the social incorporation of younger generations. Less attention has been paid to the potential of youth's civic action to challenge the status quo. The exception is the expanding field of youth organizing and activism that has drawn attention to myriad forms of social injustice experienced primarily by those who reside in ethnic minority and low-income communities (see edited volume by Conner & Rosen, 2016).

Youth organizing/activism reframes issues that, all too often, are dismissed as "personal" problems into social justice issues that require political solutions. In activist projects, young people identify issues that concern them and advocate to redress the injustice. Prominent themes in youth activist projects include reform of public education and the poor quality of urban schools, the school to prison pipeline and the prison industrial complex, racial profiling, police brutality, and state injunctions against the right to assemble in public spaces.

Actions typically focus on change at the local level, but local struggles raise broader political questions of resource distribution and racial, social, and economic justice. Adults are involved as partners and allies who work with young people to build skills in community organizing, power analysis, and strategies for institutional and societal change. But the young people are the agents of change. Through the actions that they take and the relationships that they form in organizing campaigns, youth develop a sense of empowerment and earn identities as community leaders (Christens & Kirshner, 2011; Conner & Rosen, 2016; Kirshner, 2015).

In this chapter, we build on this body of work and turn attention to the environmental commons as a space for political action. Elsewhere we have argued that young people's theories about the environmental commons are political theories because they concern membership in the polity and the prerogatives and responsibilities associated with that membership (Flanagan & Gallay, 2014). Here we extend that work first by defining the environmental commons and discussing its relevance to civic life and to children's and adolescents' rights. Following that we lay out a set of claims about how social justice is implied in an environmental commons framework. Next, we review Bandura's assertions about selective moral disengagement from environmental responsibility. To address these impediments to moral action, we summarize the three elements that Prilleltensky (2012) contends are essential to challenge injustice and illustrate how each element can be enacted in eco-justice practice, using examples from our work on *Youth and the Environmental Commons*. Finally, we discuss the design principles that Ostrom identified as those that enable communities to conserve the environmental commons and discuss ways that these principles can be realized in eco-justice stewardship practice.

2. CONCEPTUAL DEFINITIONS AND FRAMEWORK

The "environmental commons" is an expansive term that refers to the natural resources on which life depends (air, water, land, food) and the public spaces (public schools, public parks, town halls, and the Internet) where people gather and negotiate how and why they will care for those resources, for one another, and for the communities they inhabit (Bowers, 2006; Flanagan & Gallay, 2014; Martusewicz, Edmundson, & Lupinacci, 2015). The term implies that: (a) the resources that sustain healthy lives belong to all people and (b) the public spaces where people assemble are rights of all people (Gallay, Lupinacci, Sarmiento, Flanagan, & Lowenstein, 2016).

By invoking natural resources, we do not signify nature as an entity apart from people but instead emphasize the interdependence of humans with one another and with other living things. This treatment of nature contrasts with the view that was historically promulgated by the environmental movement, i.e., a pristine entity apart from the everyday lives of urban dwellers. Historically, the environmental movement, led largely by White men, treated nature and the environment as synonymous. Even today predominant representations of humans in the natural environment (in advertising, consumption, and outdoor recreation) are people who are White, middle-class, and young. As Finney (2014) suggests in her book, *Black Faces, White Spaces*, such images constrain our imagination and our beliefs about who has knowledge and who cares about the environment. In fact, contrary to these stereotypical images, scores of contemporary environmental justice organizations are led by youth of color who apply an intersectional analysis linking race, class, and the environment to address the root causes of environmental injustice and offer hopeful solutions (Quiroz-Martinez, Wu, & Zimmerman, 2005). But this was not always the case.

Although we owe a debt to the 19th century conservationists who preserved wilderness areas from rampant exploitation, most paid little attention to the negative impacts of urban pollution on the health of residents. In addition, the claiming of wilderness areas by "civilized men" was accomplished by removing Indigenous people from those lands and denigrating their cultural and spiritual relationships with nature. Not only did colonizers remove Native people from their lands; they also uprooted them from their tribal communities and traditional practices.

As late as the 1970s, official U.S. policies criminalized the transmission of cultural knowledge across generations. For example, according to Harnon (2001), federal and state laws in Alaska were developed with Euro-American fishing interests in mind. Prioritizing the interests of the dominant group created problems for Indigenous people by criminalizing many aspects of cultural practices related to subsistence and ultimately suppressing some that had been part of the traditional way of life. In other cases, state policies ignored federal policy (Nesperer, 2002). For example, in Wisconsin, the Ojibwe peoples retained their rights to hunt, fish, and gather in treaties signed with the federal government in 1837, 1842, and 1854. However, for generations, these rights were ignored by state officials. Into the 1980s that ignorance resulted in the arrest of tribal members and the confiscation of their equipment. Not surprisingly, suppression of Indigenous practices over many generations led to a loss in Traditional Ecological Knowledge (TEK)—a holistic understanding of the interdependence and fragile balance between people, plants, and animals in a local ecology (Turner, Ignace, & Ignace, 2000).

Over time, the focus on pristine nature that had predominated in the environmental movement was complemented by an environmental justice orientation that mobilized people from blue-collar and ethnic minority backgrounds to demand more attention to connections between environmental and human health (Mohai, Pellow, & Roberts, 2009; Sandler & Pezzullo, 2007). Some of these changes occurred on the world stage as the eradication of poverty through development was coupled with rescuing the earth from environmental destruction. Poverty was barely mentioned at the 1970 World Conference on the Environment in Stockholm. By the time of the 1992 Earth Summit in Rio, however, the global south had made it clear that the benefits of development had been reaped by the global north and the costs would no longer be borne by keeping people in the global south in poverty (Hart, 1997).

Today, when ethnic minority youth engage in environmental action, they are motivated by an awareness of the intersections of social justice issues such as social class and racial/ethnic inequities in environmental and human health (Quiroz-Martinez et al., 2005). Eco-Justice is an emerging field that demonstrates various ways that environmental destruction is rooted in a hierarchical value system that places greater value on certain races, genders, and social classes of humans and privileges humans over other species (Martusewicz et al., 2015). The Eco-Justice emphasis on the interdependence of humans with other living things values the TEK of Native American tribal groups which stresses that the identity and culture of a tribal group are rooted in a particular place. As Scott Momaday (1974) reflected, "To [the Indian] the sense of place is paramount. Only in reference to the earth can he persist in his true identity." Forty years later, environmental activist, Winona LaDuke, offered a similar sentiment saying, "The land calls us. It calls us home. And it makes us the people our ancestors wish us to be" (Loew, 2014).

3. ENVIRONMENTAL COMMONS AND CIVIC LIFE

Our definition of the environmental commons also invokes the rights of all people to public spaces for assembly and decision making (Gallay, Lupinacci, et al., 2016). The principle that all people have a right to assemble in public spaces and a right to monitor and make decisions about the environmental commons reveals our position on the debate about the "Tragedy of the Commons" (Hardin, 1968). On one side of this debate, scholars contend that human beings, driven by self-interest, will maximize their own goals at the expense, and ultimately the destruction, of the commons (Hardin, 1968). The logic of this position is that, since everyday people are incapable of managing their commons, states and markets should have control. To be clear, we are not arguing against the role of government policies to preserve the commons but are emphasizing the other side of the debate as articulated by the Nobel Prize winner, Elinor Ostrom. As she has argued, relying *only* on governments and markets reduces the voices of everyday people to their roles as consumers and voters. Assuming that people will destroy the commons also ignores the evidence: throughout the world people regularly engage in collective decision making to manage their environmental commons (Ostrom, 2010).

Engaging in *collective* rather than individual decision making is key for effectively managing and preserving the commons. For example, with respect to climate change, research has shown that individuals have a low sense of personal efficacy, given the magnitude and global nature of the problem (Kerr & Kaufman-Gilliland, 1997). Leveraging the social context in which people make decisions and emphasizing the power of the group to effect change (i.e., collective efficacy) is a more effective strategy (Roser-Renouf, Maibach, Leiserowitz, & Zhao, 2014).

The emphasis on collective action in environmental commons work reveals our civic republican interpretation of liberty and democracy which holds that citizens can only guarantee their liberty by participating in communities where they deliberate with fellow residents. This interpretation diverges from a "liberal" or thin version of democracy that stresses the rights of citizens to live independent lives, to determine *on their own* how they want to live without discussing with fellow members of their communities how "We" should live together (Sandel, 1996).

A civic republican interpretation of liberty implies a sense of belonging to a larger public, a concern for the whole, a moral bond with the community and appreciation of the interdependence of one's own with the community's fate (Flanagan, 2013). Engaging in such work can communicate a basic lesson about democracy. As legal scholar, Post (2006), has pointed out, democracy concerns the *authorship* of decisions, that is, who gets to decide. If young people are going to identify with and have a stake in the environmental commons, they have to have opportunities to author decisions about the commons with others who are affected by those decisions.

4. ENVIRONMENTAL COMMONS AND CHILD RIGHTS

Activism for the environmental commons is political work for which there are no age prerequisites. Such work expands the discussion of civic engagement beyond narrow frameworks of electoral politics where, typically, those under 18 do not have a voice. Everyone, regardless of age or background, has a stake and thus, environmental commons work can engender an intergenerational awareness that "we" are in this together.

Nor is the civic action of young people merely preparatory for a time when their voice will matter. In fact, youths' actions matter in the here and now, in part because of the cumulative impact of environmental choices. By virtue of the fact that their bodies and brains are still forming, younger people are especially vulnerable to environmental risks and will have to live longer with the consequences (United Nations, 2003). If anything, younger generations should have a greater voice than their elders on issues that concern the future of life on earth as it is their futures that are at stake.

The framework of an environmental commons as a basis for youth social justice action draws attention to the major categories of rights outlined in the United Nations Convention on the Rights of the Child (CRC; United Nations General Assembly, 1989). The focus on natural resources that sustain life (e.g., right to clean water) alludes to children's rights to survival, development, and basic health. The fact that civil wars are now being waged over control of such resources evokes articles in the CRC calling for children's right to protection from all forms of violence. Besides rights to protection, many articles refer to children's and adolescents' capacities to participate in decision making. To do so they should have rights to access information, to have education for responsible citizenship, rights to think freely and to assemble with others, and to express opinions on matters that affect the commons (Ruck, Keating, Saewyc, Earls, & Ben-Arieh, 2016).

5. SOCIAL JUSTICE IMPLICATIONS OF THE ENVIRONMENTAL COMMONS FRAMEWORK

There are many social justice implications of adopting an environmental commons framework. First, because the commons provide the resources essential to sustaining life, it is unjust when powerful actors extract and privatize those resources. Second, because natural resources are finite, consumption by more privileged groups exacts unjust costs on less powerful groups. Third, there are inequities in power to affect decisions about the commons. Fourth, as an interdependent system, human actions have impacts on other parts of the system—on other species, places, or generations. Finally, insofar as time spent in nature promotes well-being, the fact that all people do not have equal access to green spaces is a social justice issue.

5.1 Privatization of the Commons

The environmental commons denotes access to resources (water, air, land, food) that sustain human life and proposes that those resources are not private commodities but rather belong to everyone. Historically, a pattern of social injustice has been repeated—when resources that were owned in common were enclosed or extracted, privatized in the interests of a few at the expense of the rest (Swineheart, 2013)—from the enclosure acts of the mid-18th century to the appropriation of tribal lands and fishing rights to the policies of resource extraction from the colonies for the empire (Shiva, 1997). Enclosure of these commons today includes the privatization and bottling of water, the commercialization of indigenous groups' hunting and fishing areas, the patenting and commodification of seeds, and the sale of mineral and energy rights in combination with extraction practices that release toxic pollution into the atmospheric and hydrologic systems.

5.2 Inequities in Benefits and Burdens of Natural Resource Use

A second reference to social justice implied in the term is the fact that natural resources are finite. Overconsumption of resources by privileged groups exacts unjust costs on less powerful groups. For example, across the globe, the cumulative impact of the carbon footprint of White privileged groups and their extraction of natural resources has exacted costs on Indigenous groups whose traditional ways of living in concert with nature are compromised (Klein, 2014; Le Guen, Iliev, Lois, Atran, & Medin, 2016). Likewise, those populations who have contributed the least in greenhouse gases will likely experience the worst impacts of climate change (Samson, Berteaux, McGill, & Humphries, 2011). Globally, women and girls are a vulnerable group in light of the large role they play in providing for the basic needs of families such as growing food, fishing, and gathering water and firewood. In the majority world, deforestation, droughts, and polluted water sources mean that females are spending more time and walking longer distances in search of clean, safe water and of firewood for cooking.

Within the United States, ethnic minority and low-income communities bear the environmental costs of the "American" way of life. Waste disposal, toxic manufacturing, and other land uses that compromise health are disproportionately located in low-income communities. The lower a person's income, the more likely it is that s/he will be exposed to toxins and suffer from diseases caused by environmental factors and the less likely s/he is to have easy access to healthy food or to live in a community with safe outdoor spaces (Grist, 2006).

Youth organizing around environmental justice reveals a deep awareness of how race and class inequities intersect with environmental issues. For example, in Detroit, youth and adults have been organizing against the political decisions that locate trash incinerators in their backyards and the health consequences associated with those decisions such as high levels of asthma in their neighborhoods (Gallay, Lupinacci, et al., 2016). Awareness of the intersections of oppressive systems develops as young people work alongside their elders to lay claim to the commons. Cross-generational partnerships and the intersections of justice issues also are common in Indigenous communities where youth learn traditional farming and fishing practices and ecological knowledge from elders that are often combined with struggles for self-determination and sovereignty and the protection of sacred burial, cultural, and spiritual sites (Byington, 2015; Loew, 2014; Quiroz-Martinez et al., 2005).

5.3 Inequities in Power to Affect Decisions About the Commons

Third, since the health and well-being of children and families depend on their access to healthy air, water, and land, they should have a say in how decisions about their local environmental commons are made. However, there are questions of justice in the management and distribution of environmental resources that reflect differences in the power (social class, racial/ethnic, gender, majority/minority world) to make or affect decisions (Adger, Paavola, Huq, & Mace, 2006). For example, gender gaps in education and sociopolitical power mean that females in the majority world, whose everyday lives are impacted by worsening environmental conditions, have little voice in affecting community decisions (Agarwal, 2001). In contrast, when large numbers of women are involved in policy making, pro-environmental policies are more common: according to cross-national studies, countries with higher proportions of women in Parliament are more likely to ratify environmental treaties (Norgaard & York, 2005).

Social class differences in political power also have been well documented. In the United States, Bartels (2008) has shown that economically advantaged families have more political clout and elected officials are far more likely to attend to their concerns than to matters that affect the disadvantaged. Such class differences in political clout have been traced to the early and cumulative effects in childhood of being born into poverty (Verba, Burns, & Schlozman, 2003) including fewer opportunities for civic practice in schools (Kahne & Middaugh, 2009), greater stress experienced and lower social capital accrued in disadvantaged families, and events such as getting arrested or leaving high-school before graduating (Flanagan & Levine, 2010). Due to the social class composition of schools, the advantages to political knowledge that middle-class adolescents gain from discussing current events in their families are further enhanced by attending school with classmates who also discuss current events at home (Flanagan et al., 2014).

5.4 Interdependence—Spaces, Species, and Generations

A fourth social justice issue is raised by the ecological principle of interdependence—the impacts of actions on a system—whether that impact is felt in other geographical areas, by other living things, or by other generations. The principle of interdependence may refer to the fact that watersheds or atmospheres cross geographical or political boundaries. The very nature of rivers and the flow of air in the atmosphere mean that the actions that take place in one community affect the fates of other communities one may never know. What takes place "upstream" has a great effect on communities "downstream." Likewise, as the science on climate change has made clear, as an interdependent system, the use of resources in the form of burning fossil fuels exacts a cost on other parts of the system, increasing water and air temperatures, melting of the ice cap, rising sea levels, flooding of low-lying areas, and salinization of the ground for growing crops.

The principle of interdependence also reminds us that issues of equity and justice apply to other nonhuman species. The community, as Aldo Leopold described it, is "the land": soil, water, plants, and animals collectively. The implications for our moral obligations were captured by his statement, "All ethics evolved so far rest upon a single premise: that the individual is a member of a community of interdependent parts" (Leopold, 1948, p. 204). The global implications of this interdependence are captured by scholar-activist, Shiva (2005) who writes about the equality, rights, and worth of all life on earth. In the kind of society that she has dubbed an *Earth Democracy*, citizens of the planet would be aware of their connections with the "community of all beings supported by the earth" (p. 1).

Finally, the principle of interdependence refers to intergenerational obligations, such as the depletion of a finite resource by older generations having unjust implications for the well-being of future generations. This is why Native people have followed the practice of being mindful of the next seven generations when they make decisions about the use of natural resources (Loew, 2014). The seven generations principle and the concept of interdependence also figure in the socialization of youth: tribal leaders emphasize the need to make younger generations aware of their responsibility to take care of the land so that the land takes care of the people (Yazzie Ashley cited in Doan-Crider, Simms Hipp, Lone Fight, Small, & Yazzie Ashley, 2013).

5.5 Equity in Access to Green Spaces

Finally, equal access to green outdoor spaces is a social justice issue raised by a focus on the environmental commons. In light of the health promoting properties of time spent in nature, easy access to natural areas should be a right that everyone enjoys, not a privilege for those who can afford it. Psychological health (increased levels of awe, vitality, and attention) seem to be improved by time spent in the natural environment. Natural environments also contain health promoting chemical and biological agents such that even breathing in the air may boost immune systems and reduce stress and depression (Kuo, 2015). Besides the benefits to individuals, green outdoor common spaces can build social ties and feelings of belonging to the larger community. Research in large housing projects has demonstrated that, other things being equal, residents who live adjacent to greener common spaces have stronger feelings of belonging to their community: they report more social activities and visitors, know more of their neighbors, and have more positive views of neighbors' inclinations to help others (Kuo, Sullivan, Coley, & Brunson, 1998).

6. MORAL DISENGAGEMENT FROM ENVIRONMENTAL RESPONSIBILITY

The social justice challenges that environmental degradation pose for the future of life on earth make it arguably the greatest civic challenge facing younger generations. At the same time, moral disengagement from environmental responsibility is common. Bandura (2007) points to three loci where people may absolve themselves of a sense of personal accountability: by displacing responsibility onto others, by minimizing the harmful effects, and by ignoring or marginalizing recipients of those harmful effects. Concerning displacement and diffusion of responsibility, rather than be accountable or think of themselves as agents of change, individuals may decide that science, technology, or government will fix the problem. Analyses of the environmental attitudes and behaviors of U.S. high-school seniors between 1976 and 2005 bear this out: in every year, youth were more likely to absolve themselves of personal accountability and assign responsibility for the environment to the government and consumers (Wray-Lake, Flanagan, & Osgood, 2010). But youth were not only or always free riders. There were years when they were more likely to take personal action to preserve the environment (e.g., using public transportation or bike riding). Notably, these were the same years when they believed that resources were scarce and that technology would not provide an easy fix to the problem of finite resources. And in those years when they realized that something had to be done, not only did they reduce their own environmental footprint, but they also wanted the government to be proactive in protecting the environment. Taken together, these results suggest that education about finite resources could be effective in combatting a "free rider" mentality and in marshalling youths' commitments to having all hands on deck.

Bandura (2007) points to two other loci where moral disengagement from environmental responsibility occurs. At the outcome locus, people may disregard or minimize the harmful effects and at the recipient locus, they may ignore or marginalize the victims. Disregarding or minimizing harmful environmental effects may be due to what Nixon (2011) has referred to as the slow violence of environmental decline, that is, the plodding, cumulative, and intergenerational impacts that exacerbate vulnerabilities—of ecosystems and of people with little power—and that fuel conflicts and wars over life-sustaining resources. The slow violence that characterizes climate change makes it difficult for human impact on the environment to penetrate people's consciousness as a problem to be reckoned with. By the time the impact is obvious, it may be too late for action (Giddens, 2009). According to a sizable body of research, most people underestimate the risks of climate change, believing that the threats are distant—temporally, socially, and spatially (Van der Linden, Maibach, & Leiserowitz, 2015).

Disregarding the negative impact of humans on the environment also occurs due to what Kahn (2002) has called "environmental generational amnesia." In interviews with children in a Texas bayou, he observed that, although children understood in the abstract that pollution and garbage harm a clean environment, only one-third of those interviewed felt that pollution affected them directly. Kahn explained this seeming contradiction by noting that, if a polluted environment is the only one a child has known, then that level of environmental harm seems normal. He coined the term, "environmental generational amnesia" to reflect the psychological phenomenon of each generation experiencing more environmental degradation than was experienced by their parents' generation and of that more degraded environment becoming the new normal. If this is the case, nurturing the commitments of younger generations to the environmental commons will require two things: first, an awareness that human impact can be both positive and negative and second, that alternative, less polluted communities and worlds are possible.

As in any movement for social change, challenging assumptions that the status quo is okay is no small task: according to system justification theory, defending the status quo is the default for most people. As Jost and his colleagues argue (Jost, Frederico, & Napier, 2009), people typically accept the way things are rather than try to challenge the system. Justifying the system requires relatively little cognitive effort, whereas challenging the status quo requires a capacity to see alternative perspectives to the way things are and to critique the system in light of those other possibilities. Challenging widely accepted practices is both cognitively and emotionally demanding and requires more cognitive complexity and tolerance of uncertainty and ambiguity than most people typically muster.

Bandura contends that moral disengagement from environmental responsibility also occurs at the recipient locus; i.e., people will ignore the consequences of human impact because they depersonalize, demote, or disregard those humans or other living things that are impacted. To combat this ignorance, it is important that people understand the interdependence of their fates with those of other living things. In fact, according to a meta-analysis of research on pro-environmental behavior, awareness of one's interdependence with other people and species motivates actions to protect that larger community (Bamberg & Moser, 2007).

Working with others to preserve the environmental commons seems to promote awareness of interdependence. As Ostrom and her colleagues demonstrated, whereas *isolated individuals* may focus only on their own interests and consequently overharvest common-pool resources (forests, water systems, fisheries), when people come together in local organizations, communicate and build trust, they appreciate the implications of their actions, reduce overharvesting, and manage resources in the interests of their common good.

An awareness of the ecology of human interdependence with other living things and an identification of one's own interests with the larger commons have been referred to as an environmental identity (Clayton, 2003). The psychological role of an environmental identity is similar to that of other collective identities—providing a sense of connection, identification, and commitment to a larger whole. Comparisons of environmental activists with their nonactivist peers show how deeply an identification with the natural environment is to the activist's sense of self (Alisat, Norris, Pratt, Matsuba, & McAdams, 2014). Activists attribute their love of and dedication to the environmental commons to an early education about and affinity for nature fostered through relationships with parents, grandparents, school, and community programs (Chawla, 1999). Like other collective identities, the connection that one feels to the larger whole (in this case, living things) motivates responsible actions on their behalf (Arnocky, Stroink, & De Cicco, 2007; Schultz, 2001). Not surprisingly, an environmental identity is positively related to time spent in nature (Dutcher, Finley, Luloff, & Johnson, 2007). According to integrative syntheses of the research, positive feelings about nature (enjoyment, connection, fulfillment) in one's childhood, also referred to as environmental sensitivity, predict a lifetime of responsible environmental behavior (Ernst & Theimer, 2011; Hungerford & Volk, 1990).

Moral disengagement may also occur if one ignores the implications of actions today on future generations. Psychologists have referred to attention paid to the impact of current actions on future generations as generative concern (Jia, Alisat, Soucie, & Pratt, 2015) and have defined it as a conscious preoccupation with the well-being of future generations and an awareness and sense of unrest about the impacts of one's actions on them (McAdams & de St. Aubin, 1992). Generative concern is positively correlated with pro-environmental behavior (Horwitz, 1996; Matsuba et al., 2012). But the longitudinal evidence is even more compelling: generative concerns expressed at age 23 predict environmental identity, behavior, and involvement at age 32, net of one's education, political orientation, and benevolent attitudes (Jia et al., 2015).

Thematic analyses of Jia et al.'s interview data revealed the processes through which generative concerns may motivate environmental behavior. Some of the young adults interviewed discussed their regrets about an instance of moral disengagement—when they felt the need to stand up and take action but lacked the courage—as a transformative moment. They had not expressed the generative concerns that they felt and regret about their inaction motivated them to take a stand in the future. For others, becoming parents crystallized their generative concerns into environmental action. Parenthood made some more aware of the impact of actions in the present on the future their children would inherit. Becoming parents also rekindled values about the natural world that their own parents had nurtured in them (Jia et al., 2015). The latter (multigenerational) theme is supported in other research which found that parents' generative concerns have a positive impact on their own and on their children's environmental values and behaviors (Pratt, Norris, Alisat, & Bisson, 2013). In summary, developmental research points to the importance of connecting with and respecting nature during one's childhood for the formation of environmental identities and of concerns about the quality of the environment for future generations.

7. CHALLENGING INJUSTICE: EVIDENCE FROM YOUTH AND THE ENVIRONMENTAL COMMONS

According to Prilleltensky (2012), three psychosocial mechanisms are necessary if people are going to challenge injustice: critical experiences, critical consciousness, and critical action. We discuss each and draw examples from our program of work on *Youth and the Environmental Commons* to illustrate that these mechanisms are at work in eco-justice education. We draw from interviews with 5th–12th graders who participated in stewardship education in three different projects. The first involved Native American youth living in an urban area who were involved in an intense summer learning experience on tribal lands that emphasized the indigenous knowledge and relationship of Native people with the land. The second concerned youth from ethnic minority and low-income urban communities who participated in a school-community partnership in which the youth gathered data and took action on an environmental problem affecting the quality of life in their community. The third used the same pedagogical model (of learning/action and school-community partnership) but took place in a depressed rural community that is rich in environmental resources such as lakes, forests, and wildlife.

The first mechanism for challenging injustice that Prilleltensky (2012) outlines is having one or more critical experiences that leave a strong impression, cause one to question assumptions about the status quo, and reveal that something is profoundly wrong. Interviews with young people in our program of work on *Youth and the Environmental Commons* have revealed how engaging in stewardship projects was a critical experience that caused them to question the status quo. For example, Native American adolescents from an urban area discussed the personal transformations that some experienced by connecting with the Indigenous environmental practices that are part of their heritage. As one young person reflected, "you get out of your comfort zone and not a lot of people like how that sounds but you just get out and be more part of, be more part of nature and that really helps; it just really gets you out of your own little world and just broadens your horizon" (Byington, 2015).

Likewise, when adolescents from a mid-western rural community reflected on what they learned from their stewardship projects, many referred to their increased awareness of human impact. The transformation in consciousness to which Prilleltensky alludes were invoked in responses such as, "I learned how careless some people can be, how litter affects animals and water" or "I learned littering can be extremely dangerous which changed my mind about everything" (Gallay, Marckini-Polk, Schroeder, & Flanagan, 2016). By having such experiences, young people would conclude that yesterday's normal is unacceptable today. But what should they do with that newfound awareness?

According to Prilleltensky, if things are going to change, critical experiences must be complemented by critical consciousness (combining awareness of the conditions causing the problem with what people can do to change those conditions) and critical action (practice that defies the status quo and refuses to accept that injustice is something that cannot be changed). Empirical work bears this out: among high-school seniors, positive attitudes toward protecting the environment are more likely to impact behavior when students feel that they can do something about the problem (Meinhold & Malkus, 2005). Likewise, research with adults indicates that people are more likely to act in environmentally responsible ways when they are knowledgeable about the environment, have an affective reaction to negative changes, and feel capable of taking actions to address the problem (Patchen, 2010; Van der Linden, 2014).

In our interviews with 5th–12th graders, we gained several insights into the elements of experiences that may lead to critical consciousness and action. First, by combining learning about human impact with actions to address the problem, young people learned that human impact can be positive as well as negative and that they could apply what they were learning to environmental problems: "Because we helped the creek get cleaner, we try to get the information out to the world. We try to protect the living things..." and "From the data we found we can help the problem and let other people see the results and maybe get them interested in helping" (Gallay, Marckini-Polk, et al., 2016). Second, as these quotes suggest, youth realized that environmental commons work was a collective action problem, one that cannot be accomplished either by individuals or by elected officials acting alone. When asked if they could accomplish the stewardship work alone, most were adamant that they could not, asserting not only that students need to work together but that they planned to recruit family, friends, and other community members into future projects. As one African-American in an urban community noted, "Don't just go to people with power, go to the citizens. The more citizens, the people are together, the more power we have." Another reflected on how he developed new communication skills, in fact, became a different person, through the collective practice of environmental action, "It had an impact on me. I'm not a people person, extroverted. This work will make me improve on myself in this way. Now I know how to talk, work with people, get people to work together. It changed how I acted" (Gallay, 2016). These students' reflections echo adults' perceptions about tackling a problem as overwhelming as climate change with political action more likely if one focuses on the context and believes in the collective efficacy of the group (Roser-Renouf et al., 2014).

Third, for some students, the work made them aware that citizens cannot displace their responsibilities and assume that government will take care of things. As one student from an urban area put it, "The stewardship project changed how I see community. It's not just council and the mayor. We have to take charge of our community. Take care of and help little ones grow up in our community. You don't have to sit around and wait for the big man to come around. We can do it. They need to know that big changes don't just start big. You can start small. That's what we did. We came together as a community to make change" (Gallay, 2016).

8. PRESERVING OUR ENVIRONMENTAL COMMONS

Environmental issues pose enduring challenges to the way we live our lives and should cause us to rethink the values and aspirations that guide our choices. Despite the fact that material consumption has become so integral to expressions of identity and status, lives measured in consumption and success indexed by income are aspirations that the planet cannot sustain (Giddens, 2009). The good news is that material goods, ego-enhancing values, and hedonism are not the pursuits that make people happy. Rather, human happiness is associated with eudaimonia, a virtue-driven sense of well-being that emphasizes the potential of humans to see "the good" in and to act in the best interests of one another (Ryan, Curren, & Deci, 2013).

Eudaimonic sources of happiness and self-transcending values also are good for the environment. Ecologically responsible behavior is positively correlated with well-being (Brown & Kasser, 2005), and people are more likely to engage in pro-environmental behaviors when they espouse self-transcending values such as social responsibility, societal welfare, and generativity (Grob, 1995; Pratt et al., 2013). Pro-environmental attitudes and behaviors also are positively correlated with endorsing egalitarian rather than hierarchical social arrangements (Patchen, 2010) and are inversely related to endorsing group stereotypes (Flanagan & Tucker, 1999). Adolescents' very images of democracy are harmonious with their environmental behaviors: youth who conceive of democracy in social inclusion rather than only in individual rights terms are more likely to engage in pro-environmental behaviors (Flanagan, 2013; Flanagan, Gallay, Gill, Gallay, & Nti, 2005).

Taken together, these studies point to the benefits of pro-environmental behavior for individual well-being and happiness and for the health of the planet. So how can we nurture in younger generations the self-transcending values that underlie pro-environmental behavior? Insights are provided in the work of Elinor Ostrom, who won the Nobel Prize in Economics for challenging conventional wisdom that a tragedy of the commons would be an inevitable outcome of people managing the commons.

8.1 Applying Ostrom's Design Principles to Stewardship Education

Based on studies of community-based organizations (CBOs) that successfully managed their environmental commons, Ostrom and her colleagues (Cardenas & Ostrom, 2006) determined that certain essential design principles were the foundation for their success. These included proximity to and knowledge about the local environmental context; identification with the group and its task; mutual respect and responsibility; and communication, collaboration, and collective interactions over time that enabled people to know one another and to build trust. In this final section, we illustrate how these elements can be realized in place-based eco-justice education.

8.2 Place-Based Stewardship Education

Ostrom's first principle, proximity to and knowledge about the local environmental context, echoes the emphasis on local place urged by proponents of children's participation in environmental action (Hart, 1997) and emphasized in place-based stewardship education. Consistent with a social justice framing of environmental issues, both point to the intimate links between health, well-being, and relationships in a local area and stewardship of the commons that people in that area share. The more proximal the experience of an environmental issue, the likelier it is that young people can both learn about and work with others to address it (Gallay, Marckini-Polk, et al., 2016). This emphasis on direct experience is consistent with social science research indicating that people are more likely to pay attention to and support policy on climate change if the risks are translated into relatable and concrete personal experiences (Van der Linden et al., 2015).

The value of a focus on local place for students' motivation and learning has long been a core theme in rural education research (Gallay, Marckini-Polk, et al., 2016; Gruenewald & Smith, 2008; Theobald, 2006). Scholars have pointed out that learning from and contributing to one's local community is a model of education that is in tension with the model that focuses on preparing them for jobs outside of their community. They have criticized the latter for responding narrowly to market forces, for a lack of civic accountability, and for creating a society "marked by few allegiances and almost no propensity to shoulder mutual obligations" (Theobald, 1997, p. 120). In contrast, and consistent with an environmental commons model of education, scholars of place argue that the dignity of a human life inheres in the positive impact one can have on the lives of others (Theobald, 2006). Education, according to Gruenewald and Smith (2008), should teach young people how to reinhabit communities—that is, to restore their relationships to other people and to the land. The focus on local place enables young people to identify with and feel that they belong to the local community.

In turn, that sense of belonging motivates feelings of responsibility for that place and civic action on its behalf (Flanagan & Gallay, 2014).

8.3 Identification with the Group and Its Task

This brings us to Ostrom's second principle, an identification with the group and its task. Research with youth and adults indicates that cooperation, commitment, and a sense of responsibility for the whole are higher when people identify with an organization or institution (Pearce & Larson, 2006; Ryan & Deci, 2000). When people identify with a group, they are more likely to make personal sacrifices on its behalf (Baumeister & Leary, 1995). Erikson (1968) alluded to this process as part of identity formation when he observed that adolescents will seek out groups where they find that their values and ideals and those of the group are concordant. Youniss (2009) extends this argument by noting that, when people identify and work with an organization or group, they are contributing to history. As he observes, when youth engage in civic work that work typically takes place in CBOs that have their own history, ideology, and professed sets of values that inform the work that they do. Thus, in choosing to work with a particular community organization, young people deepen and extend the reach of the values for which that organization stands.

Community action projects afford somewhat unique opportunities for extending the boundaries of the groups with which youth identify and for nurturing their civic identities. Longitudinal analyses following a U.S. sample of adolescents into young adulthood showed that, compared to other forms of extracurricular activities, involvement in community service, political action, and public performance in adolescence predicted voting, volunteering, and joining community organizations in adulthood (McFarland & Thomas, 2006). The authors point to the *public* quality of these activities, echoing Arendt's discussion of the public realm—where one's activities gain meaning because they are seen and heard by everyone.

In her book, *The Human Condition*, Arendt (1958) provides several mechanisms whereby activity in the public realm may nurture a commitment to the environmental commons: first, insofar as the public realm is the common world that gathers people together, activity in that realm helps them to realize their personal stake in the common good and motivates them to act in the interests of the whole. Second, the inclusive nature of the public realm should expand our civic and moral community and our perspectives on solutions to public problems. In the public realm people come from diverse backgrounds and experiences. By bringing their unique standpoints to discussions and actions in that realm, they enlarge the range of perspectives for solving public problems. Although people will choose different ways to live their own private lives, it is in the public realm that a wide range of beliefs on how best to live together in a civil society can be aired.

8.4 Mutual Respect, Responsibility, and Trust

When work in the public realm yields feelings of solidarity with the group and its goals, Ostrom's third principle—mutual respect and responsibility—underlies the process. The diverse membership in the public realm means that participation in that realm exposes youth to a wider range of "others" than would be typical in their family, school, and even in many extracurricular activities. In contrast to the more homogeneous interest-based groups that characterize most extracurricular clubs, community engagement via service or organizing offers adolescents opportunities to explore (individual and collective) identity with a more heterogeneous group of people in their community—people who may differ from them in age, race/ethnicity, religion, language, sexual orientation, or social class. Consequently, it should expand the groups with whom they interact and the boundaries of the communities for which they feel responsible. Compared to the more homogeneous range of "others" with whom they engage in extracurricular activities, community-based actions provide venues through which young people can meet individuals who are members of stereotyped groups (e.g., the elderly, the homeless). Such face-to-face encounters provide fodder for questioning group stereotypes, for expanding concepts of "our community" and the ties that bind members of that community together (Flanagan et al., 2015).

In the process of engaging with a heterogeneous mix of fellow residents of their community, young people may learn to respect and feel respected by people who are not "like them." Empirical work bears this out: adolescents who engage with the broader community through community service (regardless of whether it is mandated or voluntary) are more likely than peers who engage in other forms of extracurricular activities to respect fellow community members. Specifically, they are more likely to report that people in their community: work together to solve problems, try to make the community a good place to live, can count on others to help them out, trust each other, and are welcoming to newcomers (Flanagan et al., 2015). These positive feelings appear to be mutual insofar as youth who engage in community service also report the highest levels of intergenerational harmony, i.e., that adults in their community are nice to young people and that the generations get along well.

8.5 Relationships That Build Trust

Youths' interactions with diverse groups of others are relevant to Ostrom's final principle that focuses on processes that build trust, such as communication, collaboration, and collective interactions over time that enable people to know one another. The assumption underlying this principle is that trust is the result of collective work with diverse others—of relationships that are not founded on familiarity but on the willingness to wrangle with, to get to know one another, and to find common ground (Flanagan, 2013). Our trust in others is not augmented merely by joining groups. However, it is boosted by joining groups with a diverse membership and groups that engage in charitable work (Uslaner, 2002).

Undoubtedly, communicating with one another and listening to the diverse standpoints that people bring to decisions are part of the group dynamics that build trust. When the membership of a group is diverse, discussions increase the likelihood of finding common ground (Thomas & Louis, 2013). This may be due to the fact that discussions enable strangers to get to know one another and that, through this process, feelings of camaraderie and an appreciation of who *We* are together transcends individual differences.

According to experimental studies, when prisoner's dilemma games are preceded by a period of discussion, group identities form, competition and rivalry decrease, and cooperation increases (Orbell, van de Kragt, & Dawes, 1988). Likewise, longitudinal work following middle- and high-school students provides evidence that discussing different views expands group identities and increases feelings of solidarity and social trust. Over a period of 2 years, when students reported that their teachers encouraged them to share diverse perspectives on issues with one another, the youths' sense of student solidarity increased. In turn, those feelings of solidarity boosted the students' beliefs that fellow human beings (people they did not even know) were trustworthy and fair rather than out for their own gain (Flanagan & Stout, 2010). These dynamics illustrate the role of communication in building what Dewey (1927, p. 142) referred to as the *Great Community*: "Without such communication the Public will remain in eclipse." In short, the identity of a community or a people will remain in the dark unless those people assemble as a public, get to know one another, and together, work out how they will govern the commons that they share. The role of communication and civic friendship for sustaining a polity was first noted by Aristotle who wrote in the *Nicomachean Ethics* that laws and institutions cannot support governance in the absence of the comity and trust of citizens who appreciate that they share a common fate (Aristotle, 1947).

9. CONCLUSIONS

In this chapter, we have explored the environmental commons as a civic space where young people can have an impact well before they are old enough to vote. Because it refers to the natural resources essential for life and the decision-making processes for managing those resources, a focus on the environmental commons draws attention both to protection and participation rights outlined in the CRC. Despite the social justice issues raised by this framework, moral disengagement from environmental action is common. However, practices emphasized in eco-justice stewardship programs can provide the critical experiences necessary for overcoming moral disengagement if they focus on: human impact and the application of learning to public problem solving in the local community; the intersection of environmental with other social justice issues; collective actions that bring people from different backgrounds and generations together; processes that build trust; and an awareness of the interdependence of individual fates with those of other humans, living things, and future generations.

ACKNOWLEDGMENTS

We are grateful to the Spencer Foundation for supporting our program of work on Youth and the Environmental Commons.

REFERENCES

Adger, W. N., Paavola, J., Huq, S., & Mace, M. J. (2006). Toward justice in adaptation to climate change. In W. N. Adger, J. Paavola, S. Huq, & M. J. Mace (Eds.), *Fairness in adaptation to climate change* (pp. 1–19). Cambridge, MA: MIT Press.

Agarwal, B. (2001). Participatory exclusions, community forestry, and gender: An analysis for South Asia and a conceptual framework. *World Development, 29*(10), 1623–1648.

Alisat, S., Norris, J. E., Pratt, M. W., Matsuba, M. K., & McAdams, D. P. (2014). Caring for the earth: Generativity as a mediator for the prediction of environmental narratives from identity among activists and non-activists. *Identity: An International Journal of Theory and Research, 14*, 177–194.

Arendt, H. (1958). *The human condition*. Chicago, IL: University of Chicago Press.

Aristotle. (1947). Nicomachean ethics. In R. M. McKeon (Ed.), *Introduction to Aristotle*. New York: Random House. S. D. Ross, Trans.

Arnocky, S., Stroink, M., & De Cicco, T. (2007). Self-construal predicts environmental concern, cooperation, and conservation. *Journal of Environmental Psychology, 27*(4), 255–264.

Bamberg, S., & Moser, G. (2007). Twenty years after Hines, Hungerford, and Tomera: A new meta-analysis of psycho-social determinants of pro-environmental behavior. *Journal of Environmental Psychology, 27*, 14–25.

Bandura, A. (2007). Impeding ecological sustainability through selective moral disengagement. *International Journal of Innovation and Sustainable Development, 2*(1), 8–35.

Bartels, L. M. (2008). *Unequal democracy: The political economy of the new gilded age*. Princeton, NJ: Princeton University Press.

Baumeister, R., & Leary, M. R. (1995). The need to belong: Desire for interpersonal attachments as a fundamental human motivation. *Psychological Bulletin, 117*, 497–529.

Bowers, C. A. (2006). *Revitalizing the commons: Cultural and educational sites of resistance and affirmation*. Lanham, MA: Lexington Books.

Brown, K. W., & Kasser, T. (2005). Are psychological and ecological well-being compatible? The role of values, mindfulnesss, and lifestyle. *Social Indicators Research, 74*, 349–368. http://dx.doi.org/10.1007/s11205-004-8207-8.

Byington, R. (2015). *Urban American Indians: Understanding the role of cultural programs that teach elements of traditional practices*. Masters thesis, School of Human Ecology, University of Wisconsin-Madison.

Cardenas, J., & Ostrom, E. (2006). How norms help reduce the tragedy of the commons: A multi-layer framework for analyzing field experiments. In J. N. Drobak (Ed.), *Norms and the law* (pp. 105–136). New York: Cambridge University Press.

Chawla, L. (1999). Life paths into effective environmental action. *The Journal of Environmental Education, 31*, 15–26.

Christens, B. D., & Kirshner, B. (2011). Taking stock of youth organizing: An interdisciplinary perspective. *New Directions for Child and Adolescent Development, 134*, 27–42.

Clayton, S. (2003). Environmental identity: A conceptual and an operational definition. In S. Clayton & S. Opotow (Eds.), *Identity and the natural environment* (pp. 45–65). Cambridge, MA: MIT Press.

Conner, J., & Rosen, S. M. (Eds.), (2016). *Contemporary youth activism: Advancing social justice in the United States*. ABC-CLIO Greenwood.

Dewey, J. (1927). *The public and its problems*. New York: Holt.

Doan-Crider, D., Simms Hipp, J., Lone Fight, L., Small, V., & Yazzie Ashley, V. (2013). Keeping Native American communities connected to the land: Women as change agents. *Society for Range Management, 35*(6), 5. http://dx.doi.org/10.2111/RANGELANDS-D-13-00040.1.

Dutcher, D., Finley, J., Luloff, A., & Johnson, J. (2007). Connectivity with nature as a measure of environmental values. *Environment and Behavior, 39*, 474–493.

Eccles, J. S., & Gootman, J. A. (2001). *Community programs to promote youth development*. National Research Council and Institute of Medicine Committee on Community-Level Programs for Youth. Board on Children, Youth, and Families, Division of Behavioral and Social Sciences and Education. Washington, DC: National Academy Press.

Erikson, E. H. (1968). *Identity: Youth and crisis*. New York: W.W. Norton.

Ernst, J., & Theimer, S. (2011). Evaluating the effects of environmental education programming on connectedness to nature. *Environmental Education Research, 17*(5), 577–598. http://dx.doi.org/10.1080/13504622.2011.565119.

Finney, C. (2014). *Black faces, white spaces: Reimagining the relationships of African-Americans to the great outdoors*. Chapel Hill, NC: University of North Carolina Press.

Flanagan, C. (2013). *Teenage citizens: The political theories of the young*. Cambridge, MA: Harvard University Press.

Flanagan, C., & Gallay, E. (2014). Adolescents' theories of the "commons" In J. Benson (Ed.), *Advances in Child Development and Behavior: Vol. 46.* (pp. 33–55). Oxfordshire, UK: Elsevier. http://dx.doi.org/10.1016/B978-0-12-800285-8.00002-9.
Flanagan, C. A., Gallay, L. S., Gill, S., Gallay, E., & Nti, N. (2005). What does democracy mean? Correlates of adolescents' views. *Journal of Adolescent Research, 20*(2), 193–218. http://dx.doi.org/10.1177/0743558404273377.
Flanagan, C., Kim, T., Collura, J., & Kopish, M. A. (2015). Community service and adolescents' social capital. *Journal of Research on Adolescence, 25*(2), 295–309. http://dx.doi.org/10.1111/jora.12137.
Flanagan, C., Kim, T., Pykett, A., Finlay, A., Gallay, E., & Pancer, M. (2014). Adolescents' theories about economic inequality: Why are some people poor while others are rich? *Developmental Psychology, 50*(11), 2512–2525. http://dx.doi.org/10.1037/a0037934.
Flanagan, C., & Levine, P. (2010). Civic engagement and the transition to adulthood. *The Future of Children, 20*(1), 159–180. spring, www.futureofchildren.org.
Flanagan, C. A., & Stout, M. (2010). Developmental patterns of social trust between early and late adolescence: Age and school climate effects. *Journal of Research on Adolescence, 20*(3), 748–773. http://dx.doi.org/10.1111/j.1532-7795.2010.00658.x.
Flanagan, C. A., & Tucker, C. J. (1999). Adolescents' explanations for political issues: Concordance with their views of self and society. *Developmental Psychology, 35*(5), 1198–1209. http://dx.doi.org/10.1037/0012-1649.35.5.1198.
Gallay, E. (2016). *Students' commitments to the commons: Civic learning in EcoJustice place-based stewardship education.* Masters thesis, Eastern Michigan University.
Gallay, E., Lupinacci, J., Sarmiento, C., Flanagan, C., & Lowenstein, E. (2016). Race, class, and environmental stewardship. In J. Conner & S. M. Rosen (Eds.), *Contemporary youth activism: Advancing social justice in the United States.* ABC-CLIO Greenwood.
Gallay, E., Marckini-Polk, L., Schroeder, B., & Flanagan, C. (2016). Place-based rural stewardship education: Engendering an identification with the local commons. *Peabody Journal of Education, 91*, 155–175. http://dx.doi.org/10.1080/0161956X.2016.1151736.
Giddens, A. (2009). *The politics of climate change.* Cambridge, UK: Polity Press.
Grist. (2006). Introducing a seven-week series on the intersection of economic and ecological survival. *Grist Staff.* Retrieved on May 1, 2016 from, http://grist.org/article/pate/.
Grob, A. (1995). A structural model of environmental actions and behavior. *Journal of Environmental Psychology, 15*, 209–220.
Gruenewald, D. A., & Smith, G. A. (2008). *Place-based education in the global age: Local diversity.* New York: Psychology Press.
Hardin, G. (1968). The tragedy of the commons. *Science, 162*(3859), 1243–1248. http://dx.doi.org/10.1126/science.162.3859.1243.
Harnon, D. (Ed.), (2001). *Crossing Boundaries in Park Management. Proceedings of the 11th conference on research and resource management in parks and on public lands.* Hancock, MI: The George Right Society.
Hart, R. A. (1997). *Children's participation: The theory and practice of involving young citizens in community development and environmental care.* London, UK: Earthscan Publications.
Horwitz, W. A. (1996). Developmental origins of environmental ethics: The life experiences of activists. *Ethics and Behavior, 6*, 29–54.
Hungerford, H., & Volk, T. (1990). Changing learner behavior through environmental education. *The Journal of Environmental Education, 21*(3), 8–21. Retrieved from, http://www.tandfonline.com/doi/pdf/10.1080/00958964.1990.10753743.
Jia, F., Alisat, S., Soucie, K., & Pratt, M. (2015). Generative concern and environmentalism: A mixed methods longitudinal study of emerging and young adults. *Emerging Adulthood. 3*(5). http://dx.doi.org/10.1177/2167696815578338.

Jost, J. T., Frederico, C. M., & Napier, J. L. (2009). Political ideology: Its structure, functions, and elective affinities. *Annual Review of Psychology, 60*, 307–333. http://dx.doi.org/10.1146/annurev.psych.1160.110707.163600.

Kahn, P. H. (2002). Children's affiliations with nature: Structure, development, and the problem of environmental generational amnesia. In P. H. Kahn, Jr. & S. R. Kellert (Eds.), *Children and nature: Psychological, sociocultural, and evolutionary investigations* (pp. 93–116). Cambridge, MA: MIT Press.

Kahne, J. E., & Middaugh, E. (2009). Democracy for some: The civic opportunity gap in high school. In J. Youniss & P. Levine (Eds.), *Engaging young people in civic life* (pp. 29–58). Nashville: Vanderbilt University Press.

Kerr, N. L., & Kaufman-Gilliland, C. M. (1997). "...and besides, I probably couldn't have made a difference anyway": Justification of social dilemma defection via perceived self-inefficacy. *Journal of Experimental Social Psychology, 33*, 211–230.

Kirshner, B. (2015). *Youth activism: Defending the right to learn in an era of education inequality.* New York: NYU Press.

Klein, N. (2014). *This changes everything: Capitalism vs. the climate.* New York: Simon & Schuster.

Kuo, M. (2015). How might contact with nature promote human health? Promising mechanisms and a possible central pathway. *Frontiers in Psychology, 6*, 1093. http://dx.doi.org/10.3389/fpsyg.2015.01093.

Kuo, F. E., Sullivan, W. C., Coley, R. K., & Brunson, L. (1998). Fertile ground for community: Inner-city neighborhood common spaces. *American Journal of Community Psychology, 26*(6), 823–851.

Le Guen, O., Iliev, R., Lois, X., Atran, S., & Medin, D. L. (2016). A garden experiment revisited: Inter-generational change in environmental perception and management of the Maya Lowlands, Guatemala. *Journal of the Royal Anthropological Institute (N.S.), 19*, 771–794.

Leopold, A. (1948). *A sand county Almanac, and sketches here and there.* New York: Oxford University Press.

Loew, P. (2014). *Seventh generation earth ethics: Native voices of Wisconsin.* Wisconsin Historical Society Press.

Martusewicz, R. A., Edmundson, J., & Lupinacci, J. (2015). *EcoJustice education: Toward diverse, democratic, and sustainable communities* (2nd ed.). New York, NY: Routledge.

Matsuba, M. K., Pratt, M. W., Norris, J. E., Mohle, E., Alisat, S., & McAdams, D. P. (2012). Environmentalism as a context for expressing generativity and identity: Patterns among activists and uninvolved youth and midlife adults. *Journal of Personality, 80*, 1091–1115.

McAdams, D. P., & de St. Aubin, E. (1992). A theory of generativity and its assessment through self-report, behavioral acts, and narrative themes in autobiography. *Journal of Personality and Social Psychology, 62*, 1003–1015.

McFarland, D. A., & Thomas, R. J. (2006). Bowling young: How youth voluntary associations influence adult political participation. *American Sociological Review, 71*, 401–425. http://dx.doi.org/10.1177/000312240607100303.

Meinhold, J., & Malkus, A. (2005). Adolescent environmental behaviors. *Environment and Behavior, 17*, 511–532.

Mohai, P., Pellow, D., & Roberts, J. T. (2009). Environmental justice. *Annual Review of Environment and Resources, 34*, 405–430.

Nesperer, L. (2002). *The walleye wars: The struggle for Ojibwe spearfishing and treaty rights.* Lincoln, Nebraska: University of Nebraska Press.

Nixon, R. (2011). *Slow violence and the environmentalism of the poor.* Cambridge, MA: Harvard University Press.

Norgaard, K., & York, R. (2005). Gender equality and state environmentalism. *Gender & Society, 19*(4), 506–522. http://dx.doi.org/10.1177/0891243204273612.

Orbell, J. M., van de Kragt, A., & Dawes, R. M. (1988). Explaining discussion-induced cooperation. *Journal of Personality and Social Psychology, 54*, 811–819.

Ostrom, E. (2010). Beyond markets and states: Polycentric governance of complex economic systems. *American Economic Review, 100*(3), 641–672. http://dx.doi.org/10.1257/aer.100.3.641.

Patchen, M. (2010). What shapes public reactions to climate change? Overview of research and policy implications. *Analyses of Social Issues and Public Policy, 10*(1), 47–68.

Pearce, N. J., & Larson, R. W. (2006). How teens become engaged in youth development programs: The process of motivational change in a civic activism organization. *Applied Developmental Science, 10*, 121–131.

Piliavin, J. A., & Siegl, E. (2007). Health benefits of volunteering in the Wisconsin longitudinal study. *Journal of Health and Social Behavior, 48*(4), 450–464.

Post, R. (2006). Democracy and equality. *The Annals of the American Academy of Political and Social Science, 603*(1), 24–36. http://dx.doi.org/10.1177/0002716205282954. Faculty Scholarship Series, Paper 177, http://digitalcommons.law.yale.edu/fss_papers/177.

Pratt, M. W., Norris, J. E., Alisat, S., & Bisson, E. (2013). Earth mothers (and fathers): Examining generativity and environmental concerns in adolescents and their parents. *Journal of Moral Education, 42*(1), 12–27. http://dx.doi.org/10.1080/03057240.2012.714751.

Prilleltensky, I. (2012). Wellness as fairness. *American Journal of Community Psychology, 49*, 1–21. http://dx.doi.org/10.1007/s10464-011-9448-8.

Quiroz-Martinez, J., Wu, D. P., & Zimmerman, K. (2005). *ReGeneration: Young people shaping environmental justice.* Oakland, CA: Movement Strategy Center.

Roser-Renouf, C., Maibach, E. W., Leiserowitz, A., & Zhao, X. (2014). The genesis of climate change activism: From key beliefs to political action. *Climate Change.* http://dx.doi.org/10.1007/s10584-014-1173-5.

Ruck, M. D., Keating, D. P., Saewyc, E. M., Earls, F., & Ben-Arieh, A. (2016). The United Nations convention on the rights of the child: Its relevance for adolescents. *Journal of Research on Adolescence, 26*(1), 16–29. http://dx.doi.org/10.1111/jora.12172.

Ryan, R. M., Curren, R. R., & Deci, E. L. (2013). What humans need: Flourishing in Aristotelian philosophy and self-determination theory. In A. S. Waterman (Ed.), *The best within us: Positive psychology perspectives on eudaimonic functioning* (pp. 57–75). Washington DC: APA Books.

Ryan, R. M., & Deci, E. L. (2000). The darker and brighter sides of human existence: Basic psychological needs as a unifying concept. *Psychological Inquiry, 11*, 319–338.

Samson, J., Berteaux, D., McGill, B., & Humphries, M. (2011). Geographic disparities and moral hazards in the predicted impacts of climate change on human populations. *Global Ecology and Biogeography, 20*(4), 532–544. http://dx.doi.org/10.1111/j.1466-8238.2010.00632.x.

Sandel, M. J. (1996). *Democracy's discontent: American in search of a public philosophy.* Cambridge, MA: Belknap Press.

Sandler, R., & Pezzullo, P. (Eds.), (2007). *Environmental justice and environmentalism: The social justice challenge to the environmental movement.* Cambridge, MA: MIT Press.

Schultz, P. W. (2001). The structure of environmental concern: Concern for self, other people, and the biosphere. *Journal of Environmental Psychology, 21*, 327–339.

Scott Momaday, N. (1974). *Angle of geese and other poems.* D.R. Godine.

Shiva, V. (1997). *The enclosure and recovery of the commons: Biodiversity, indigenous knowledge, and intellectual property rights.* New Delhi: Research Foundation for Science, Technology, and Ecology.

Shiva, V. (2005). *Earth democracy: Justice, sustainability and peace.* Cambridge, MA: South End Press.

Swineheart, T. (2013). *The real history of the commons and today's environmental crisis*. Utne Reader May/June 2013. Retrieved from, http://www.utne.com/environment/history-of-the-commons-zm0z13mjzbla.aspx?PageId=3#ArticleContent.

Theobald, P. (1997). *Teaching the commons: Place, pride, and the renewal of community*. Boulder, CO: Westview Press.

Theobald, P. (2006). A case for inserting community into public school curriculum. *American Journal of Education*, *112*(3), 315–334.

Thomas, E. F., & Louis, W. R. (2013). Doing democracy: The social psychological mobilization and consequences of collective action. *Journal of Social Issues*, 7(1), 173–200.

Turner, N. J., Ignace, M. B., & Ignace, R. (2000). Traditional ecological knowledge and wisdom of aboriginal peoples in British Columbia. *Ecological Applications*, *10*(5), 1275–1287. http://dx.doi.org/10.1890/1051-0761(2000)010[1275:TEKAWO]2.0.CO;2.

United Nations. (2003). *World Youth Report: The global situation of young people*. United Nations Department of Economic and Social Affairs.

United Nations General Assembly. (1989). *Adoption of a convention on the rights of the child*. New York, NY: United Nations. November 17.

Uslaner, E. M. (2002). *The moral foundations of trust*. Cambridge, U.K.: Cambridge University Press.

Van der Linden, S. L. (2014). On the relationship between personal experience, affect and risk perception: The case of climate change. *European Journal of Social Psychology*, *44*, 430–440.

Van der Linden, S. L., Maibach, E., & Leiserowitz, A. (2015). Improving public engagement with climate change: Five "best practice" insights from psychological science. *Perspectives on Psychological Science*, *10*(6), 758–763. http://dx.doi.org/10.1177/1745691615598516.

Verba, S., Burns, N., & Schlozman, K. L. (2003). Unequal at the starting line: Creating participatory inequalities across generations and among groups. *The American Sociologist*, *34*(1–2), 45–69.

Wray-Lake, L., Flanagan, C. A., & Osgood, D. W. (2010). Examining trends in adolescent environmental attitudes, beliefs, and behaviors across three decades. *Environment and Behavior*, *42*(1), 61–85.

Youniss, J. (2009). When morality meets politics in development. *Journal of Moral Education*, *38*(2), 129–144.

CHAPTER EIGHT

Mixed-Status Immigrant Families in the United States: The Role of Social Justice in Intervention Research

Mackenzie D.M. Whipps[1], Hirokazu Yoshikawa
New York University, New York, NY, United States
[1]Corresponding author: e-mail address: mdw317@nyu.edu

Contents

Abstract

More than 4 million unauthorized parents of legal status children currently reside in the United States (Capps, Fix, & Zong, 2016). Developmental scientists and intervention researchers hoping to work with these mixed-status families face a myriad of challenges, largely generated from the population's policy-driven social exclusion. Despite the challenges, there is a moral imperative to work with and support parents and children currently living in mixed-status households. This chapter applies a social justice perspective, largely stemming from Prilleltensky's critical community psychological framework, to improve the relevance and usefulness of research on mixed-status families (Prilleltensky & Nelson, 1997). We discuss the utility of this social justice perspective

Equity and Justice in Developmental Science: Implications for Young People, Families, and Communities (S.S. Horn, M.D. Ruck & L.S. Liben, Eds.)
Advances in Child Development and Behavior (J.B. Benson, Series Ed.), Vol. 51
ISSN 0065-2407 http://dx.doi.org/10.1016/bs.acdb.2016.04.003

in theory building, study design and implementation, and dissemination of findings regarding mixed-status families, with exemplars from recent research.

Over 4 million US citizen children have at least one unauthorized immigrant parent (Capps, Fix, & Zong, 2016), representing over a quarter of all children with immigrant parents in the United States. Families like these—termed mixed-status families—often have family members living at the margins of society. Those "without papers" and their family members live with heightened anxiety and uncertainty (Brabeck & Xu, 2010). Since 1996, federal and state policies have essentially shut down any pathway to citizenship for individuals with unauthorized status in the United States (Dreby, 2012; Menjívar, 2006; Yoshikawa, Suarez-Orozco, & Gonzales, in press).

A wide diversity of mixed-status families currently resides in the United States. Mexican immigrants comprise the largest single nationality among those with unauthorized status, representing over half of this population (Capps, Koball, et al., 2016). Significant numbers of unauthorized immigrants also come from other Latin American countries, East Asia, Africa, and Europe (Passel & Cohn, 2011). Immigrant families with unauthorized members are far from a homogeneous community. Wide diversity exists across many domains, including country of origin, income and poverty, education levels, religious ideology, and dominant language spoken (American Psychological Association, 2012; Rosenblum & Ruiz Soto, 2015; Yoshikawa, Kholoptseva, & Suárez-Orozco, 2013).

The goal of this chapter is to provide a social justice perspective on theory, methods, and use of research regarding mixed-status families in the United States. We discuss implications for the work of both intervention researchers and developmental scientists. Intervention researchers, or action scientists more generally, are those researchers who seek to work with the populations that they study to improve outcomes. These can include policy researchers, program developers and evaluators, and researchers working within advocacy organizations, to name a few. This chapter will hopefully serve as a practical resource for intervention researchers who wish to work directly with this diverse community. Basic developmental scientists may also benefit from including a social justice perspective in their work with this population.

In this chapter, we discuss three areas in which a social justice perspective may enrich work with mixed-status families in the United States: theory building, research design and methodology, and the dissemination and use of research. With respect to theory, we contend that Prilleltensky's model of social justice, originating in critical community psychology, is applicable across many research contexts, including that of developmental science and intervention (Prilleltensky & Nelson, 1997). This particular social justice framework is highly compatible with most modern developmental theories. Design and methodology, too, can be improved and made more ethical with the addition of this social justice perspective. We discuss five specific methodological issues, including the role of quantitative vs qualitative data, recruiting participants from mixed-status families, protecting those participants, measuring the construct of authorization status itself, and approaches to ending a collaborative research program with attention to sustainability. Additionally in this section, we will discuss community-based participatory action research (PAR) as a viable alternative to traditional research paradigms when studying this population. Finally, we discuss the dissemination and use of data gained from these research activities and the role that a social justice perspective can play in this process.

1. CURRENT POLICY CONTEXTS

The recent history of US policy regarding unauthorized migration is one of increasing restrictions on a pathway to citizenship since the provisions of the Immigration Reform and Control Act of 1986 were ended in 1988. Through that act, roughly 70% of individuals then living with unauthorized status became legal permanent residents (Ngai, 2004). In 1996, the Illegal Immigration Reform and Immigrant Responsibility Act (IIRIRA) greatly expanded the circumstances in which unauthorized immigrants could be deported from the United States. Specifically, local law enforcement and other officials could for the first time rule individuals as inadmissible to the United States, thus initiating deportation without judicial oversight or review. This created the context for considerable state- and local-level variations in initiation of removal proceedings. IIRIRA also greatly expanded the definition of prior "aggravated felonies" that make a legal resident subject to deportation, to include crimes more minor than under previous laws (e.g., perjury, failing to appear in court for a crime where the potential sentence is 2 years or more, drunken driving, and shoplifting). In the absence of Congressional action on a pathway to citizenship, state- and local-level enforcement practices have become part of the everyday lives of the unauthorized. In addition, the Obama administration in the years

2010–2014 deported an unprecedented number of those with unauthorized status from the country (Preston, 2013; these numbers have since declined).

The political and legal context regarding immigration in the United States makes living and working in the United States an extremely stressful situation for individuals in mixed-status families. In addition, increasing anti-immigration sentiment in public and political debates has created an environment of hostility and discrimination, not only for immigrants without authorization, but also for their family members with legal status (Menjívar, 2011). The threat of permanent family separation and deportation can cause intense and lasting stress, as well as a feeling of harassment within immigrant communities (McEwen, Boyle, & Messias, 2015). As a result, many with unauthorized family members are suspicious of interacting with any government-connected group at all (Dreby, 2012; Gonzales & Chavez, 2012; Wong & Valdivia, 2014).

In an effort to increase social inclusion for many law-abiding immigrants lacking authorization, the Obama administration enacted executive orders in 2012 and 2014. The Deferred Action for Childhood Arrivals (DACA) order provides temporary legal status to immigrants who arrived in the United States as minors and have met certain residency and education requirements. In 2014, Obama proposed both an expansion of DACA as well as the Deferred Action for Parents of Americans and Lawful Permanent Residents (DAPA) executive order, which aims to provide temporary legal status to unauthorized parents of lawful residents or citizen children. Both policies specifically targeted unauthorized immigrants and mixed-status families. Estimates of impact range from about 4 to 5 million immigrants who may be eligible for deferred action under these new reforms (Capps, Fix, et al., 2016; White House, 2014). A recent report has indicated the potential impacts of DAPA on children of the unauthorized in terms of reduced poverty and increased access to resources (Capps, Koball, et al., 2016). However, DAPA and extended DACA have been enjoined in the courts, with the Supreme Court set to hear the case (the United States vs Texas) in the spring of 2016.

2. DEVELOPMENTAL CONTEXT

Historically, there has been little empirical study of the effect of having an unauthorized parent on child or youth development. However, in the last half-dozen years or so, there has been increasing attention to this issue. The research to date provides evidence that parent unauthorized status predicts lower levels of cognitive development, achievement, and educational progress across early and middle childhood, even after adjusting for confounding dimensions of socioeconomic status and for ethnicity (Brabeck, Sibley, Taubin, & Murcia, 2015; Brabeck & Xu, 2010; Ortega et al., 2009; Yoshikawa, 2011). Landale and colleagues found higher internalizing (depression, anxiety, withdrawal) and externalizing (aggressive and acting out) behavioral problems in a sample of Mexican-origin, primary-school-age children with unauthorized parents, relative to their counterparts with authorized or citizen parents (Landale, Hardie, Oropesa, & Hillemeier, 2015). By adolescence, parent unauthorized status was associated with higher levels of self-reported anxiety and depressive symptoms in a North Carolina sample (Potochnick & Perreira, 2010). Finally, a large-scale survey of Mexican-origin young adults showed that having an unauthorized mother, relative to an authorized one, was associated with between 1.25 and 1.5 fewer years of schooling (Bean, Leach, Brown, Bachmeier, & Hipp, 2011), a large and substantively meaningful effect. Thus, parental legal status appears to have developmental consequences above and beyond the associated characteristics of low levels of parental education and relatively high rates of income poverty.

3. BUILDING THEORY

3.1 Developmental Theories

In parallel with the rapid development of literature showing effects of parent unauthorized status on child development, theories and conceptual frameworks have been put forward describing the specific *contextual mechanisms* through which parental status may exert its effects. The two social ecological theories put forward vary in their developmental emphasis, with one concentrating on effects in early childhood (Yoshikawa & Kalil, 2011), and the other adding a broader lifespan developmental perspective (Suárez-Orozco, Yoshikawa, Teranishi, & Suárez-Orozco, 2011). These two frameworks acknowledge that policy, economic, and household network contexts in sending countries drive rates of emigration without papers. Both frameworks also contend that a variety of developmental contexts in the host country—interactions with legal and illegal authorities; social ties; experiences of detention or removal proceedings; and family socialization and stress processes—may explain the effects of this status on child and youth cognitive, socio-emotional and educational outcomes. In addition, following García Coll et al.'s (1996) and García Coll and Magnuson's (1997) model of the development of ethnic minority children in the United States, these theories have also incorporated the influence of stigma, discrimination, and marginalization, as well as countervailing positive effects of critical consciousness and involvement in activism on this population (Suárez-Orozco et al., 2011). Recently these theories have been extended to apply to unauthorized populations in other countries, such as the experience of Syrian refugees in the Middle East and Europe (a large majority of these population flows lack authorization, with increasing policy blocks to pathways to legal status or citizenship; Yoshikawa, 2015).

A recent consensus report of the National Academy of Sciences Committee on Integrating Immigrants into American Society placed the phenomenon of unauthorized status within assimilation and integration theory in sociology (Waters & Pineau, 2015). That Committee's report, while generally finding that second-generation and third-generation youth were integrating quite well into US society, as measured by such indicators as educational progress, cited mixed-status families and children in them facing unique structural barriers that blocked educational progress and employment (e.g., lack of access to federal tuition assistance and in many states, in-state tuition rates). Each of these developmental frameworks—the social ecological approach, Garcia Coll's theory of ethnic minority development, and assimilation and integration theory—carefully considers the role that authorization status of one's self or one's family might play in the positive development of an individual over time.

3.2 Social Justice Perspective

Just as psychological intervention researchers aim to act in a way to enhance wellbeing and positive development, community psychologists aim to improve lives by understanding and improving the relational and collective contexts in which individual development occurs (Prilleltensky & Nelson, 2009). Many in the field of community psychology see developmental outcomes, as well as familial and community outcomes, as partly determined by the relative power of those within the context of interest. The powerful frame the discourse and reap the benefits of globalization processes, while the vulnerable are often left to shoulder the burdens (Prilleltensky, 2012). In the context of global migration, lasting and real change for the most marginalized members of a society must come from a critical view of the structures in place that promote the status quo. For many community psychologists, viewing the developmental processes and outcomes for children in mixed-status families through the lens of a social justice perspective is therefore a moral imperative.

Prilleltensky (2012) recommends tackling issues of power and access directly by investigating three "prongs" of research, each with a different emphasis on the process and outcomes of power imbalance. Though Prilleltensky does not apply his critical community psychology framework directly to topics surrounding immigration, we argue that his theories are highly relevant. The three prongs that he urges psychologists to research are: (1) the impact of immigration (both authorized and unauthorized) on the lives of the actors involved; (2) the impact of interventions that aim to mitigate the negative and capitalize on the positive effects of migration; and (3) the barriers to justice and equity at the individual, organizational, and community levels.

Prilleltensky also suggests *emancipatory impact studies* as a promising avenue for reaching decision makers at the policy level. Intervention researchers, in particular, should strive to promote policies that emancipate, or increase the self-determination of, populations made vulnerable by globalization processes. The first step of this emancipation agenda is a phase of investigation to determine the likely impact of an immigration policy change. This investigation process is analogous to an environmental impact assessment (EIA), which would customarily be conducted prior to breaking ground on a large industrial or construction project (Carroll & Turpin, 2002). Just as an EIA would provide information about the likely impact of a project to regulatory bodies and the local community, so too could an emancipatory impact study assess the likely effects of an immigration policy or program change on the self-determination and wellbeing of the immigrant communities the policy targets. Such forecasting has been integrated into amicus briefs for the Supreme Court arguments in the DAPA/extended DACA case (and see Capps, Koball, et al., 2016).

Utilizing a social justice perspective, as conceptualized by Prilleltensky's (2012) three prongs, may help researchers study this population effectively and ethically. Later we examine three examples of strong programs of research that, while not explicitly taking a social justice approach, map well onto Prilleltensky's (2012) suggestion for justice in research.

The first program is the Mexican Migration Project, which for nearly three decades has annually investigated transnational migration patterns of Mexican migrants to and from the United States. The project began in 1987 as a partnership between American and Mexican researchers, Massey and Durand. Over 10,000 unauthorized immigrants and their families have since taken part in the study. Unique sampling and surveying methods have added important information to the more basic demographic sources of information, such as the Census Bureau or Immigration and Naturalization Services, on the topic of mixed-status families (Durand & Massey, 2004). The research coming out of the Mexican Migration Project clearly demonstrates a deep understanding of ecologically descriptive and social justice-leaning theory. Specifically, it closely aligns with prongs one and three described by Prilleltensky (2012). Mexican Migration Project studies have examined the impact of immigration, both authorized and unauthorized, on the lived experiences of the subjects and their families (prong one), including the role that it plays in marital strategy, home ownership, and social capital accrual (Curiel, 2004; Flores, Hernández-León, & Massey, 2004; Parrado, 2004). Studies using these data have also examined the role of specific barriers to equity at the community, national, and international level (prong three), including the ways local Mexican labor market forces and US border patrol enforcement alter migration and settlement behaviors (Aysa & Massey, 2004; Orrenius, 2004; Riosmena, 2004).

Brabeck, Sibley, et al. (2015) recent work investigating the moderating effect of social service usage on the impact of parental authorized status and academic learning outcomes is an excellent example of Prilleltensky's (2012) second prong. The authors used a social ecological framework to guide their studies, and found evidence that in middle childhood, the use of programs and policies like Medicaid, state-funded preschool, or childcare subsidies lessened the negative impact of unauthorized parental status on several academic outcomes. The findings highlight the need for greater outreach to low-income immigrant parents, including those with unauthorized status, to help them enroll their eligible citizen children in programs that may advance their learning.

The work of Dreby (2006, 2012, 2015) provides a third example of utilizing a social justice perspective in the study of mixed-status families. In much of her work, Dreby utilized ethnographic observation and inquiry within a social ecological theoretical framework to gain a deep understanding of the burdens of deportation and the experience of transnational parenting for Mexican mixed-status families. Specifically, she has studied the differential regional enforcement of federal deportation policy—as well as the threat of that enforcement—that continue to impact the lived experiences, fears, and agency of mixed-status families; and specific policy- and community-level barriers to justice for immigrants from mixed-status families (Dreby, 2006, 2012, 2015). Notably, she was also instrumental in creating a visualization tool, the Deportation Pyramid, for community advocates, policy researchers, and service providers to assess injury severity across several domains as a result of family or community experiences of deportation as a way to give back to the immigrant community with which she worked (Dreby, 2012). Ultimately, undertaking a research program like this is in line with *emancipatory impact studies* expressly suggested by Prilleltensky (2012). Due to this work, the immigration research community, at large, now has a deeper understanding of how policy enforcement impacts the lived experiences of Mexican immigrants within mixed-status and transnational families. Ideally, Prilleltensky (2012) writes, impact studies would assess effects of policy implementation *prior* to policy development and enactment. Recently, this has been done extensively by the leading policy research institute on migration in the United States, the Migration Policy Institute, with input from a variety of sociologists, psychologists, and other social scientists (e.g., Capps, Koball, et al., 2016; Yoshikawa & Kholoptseva, 2013).

4. ETHICAL DESIGN AND METHODS IN RESEARCH ON UNAUTHORIZED STATUS

Scientific research can be ethical when the benefits and the risks or burdens experienced by participants and their communities are reasonably balanced and judiciously dispersed among the participants (National Commission for the Protection of Human Subjects of Biomedical and Behavioral Research, 1979). Developmental and intervention research seeks to gain knowledge about a phenomenon, with the ultimate goal to utilize this knowledge to improve the lives of those under study (Wallerstein, Miller, & Buchanan, 2007). A poorly designed or executed study is likely a waste of participants' limited time and energy, with little hope for future knowledge, and therefore benefits, to materialize. For unauthorized immigrants, this is especially problematic as time is an extremely precious resource. Wages for unauthorized working parents, for example, are very often below the legal minimum, necessitating extremely long work hours (Yoshikawa, 2011). They may, as a result, simply have no "extra" time or energy to give to research endeavors.

Participants without authorization also risk much more than those who have authorization to live in the United States. Immigrant families with members who lack authorization are more likely to be economically marginalized and therefore at risk of exploitation in research. Parents without legal authorization are also more likely to lack English proficiency and higher education, both characteristics that can increase the risk of misunderstanding roles in research activities (APA, 2012; Mather, 2009; Mertens, 2012). Finally, the risk that a breach of confidentiality poses for immigrants without authorization is potentially much higher. Citizen children with unauthorized parents are less likely to be enrolled in public programs due to parents' lack of knowledge as well as fear of detection (Brabeck, Sibley, et al., 2015; Capps, Koball, et al., 2016; Yoshikawa, 2011). Therefore, if the benefit of research to the community is merely program development without attention to information and outreach, mixed-status families are less likely or able to reap those benefits.

Researchers in developmental science and intervention are expected to deliver on promises of benefit to participants. However, those researchers should devote additional time and energy evaluating the equity of the burdens and benefits of research when marginalized populations, like mixed-status families, are the communities of interest (National Commission for the Protection of Human Subjects of Biomedical and Behavioral Research, 1979). Evaluations and experiments should be meticulously designed to make efficient use of participants' limited resources, with the risks of participation well understood. In this section, we will consider implications of these ethical considerations for research methods used in studying mixed-status families. We will explore methods across five domains: the role of qualitative and quantitative methods; sampling participants; measurement of unauthorized status; community participation in research activities; and ending a program of research with attention to sustainability.

4.1 Qualitative and Quantitative Methods

Qualitative and quantitative methods both have their place in the study of mixed-status families. When researching populations that are hidden and relatively unstudied, it often makes practical sense to begin in a holistic, qualitative fashion (Creswell, 2012; Dreby, 2015; Yoshikawa, 2011). Immigrant populations in the United States, especially those that are unauthorized, are likely to be misrepresented if forced into a research heuristic used to study a less marginalized population. For instance, assumptions made about the reasons for emigration or the role of acculturation may be applicable to authorized immigrants, but not to those without authorization. Research in the qualitative tradition is often more sensitive to complex interactions and tend to preserves specificity of the communities under investigation (Ragin,

2014, pp. ix–x). Thus, in our view, qualitative methodology may do a better job of correcting for misinterpretations stemming from closed-ended measurement tools common in quantitative methodologies. Furthermore, qualitative data collection methods seek to give an authentic voice to vulnerable and hidden populations—a goal that is expressly prioritized in a social justice framework (Prilleltensky, 2012).

Quantitative data on mixed-status families are useful in their own right. These types of data can provide critical information such as size and distribution of the population, as well as estimates of the impact of unauthorized status on developmental outcomes of interest. Most fundamentally, quantitative methods have recently been developed to estimate the unauthorized population in the United States and at the state and county levels (e.g., using merging of multiple national datasets with multiple imputation to "crosswalk" across them; Van Hook, Bachmeier, Coffman, & Harel, 2015). Descriptive data on those enrolled in the DACA program provide another example of how quantitative data have suggested patterns of policy impacts. Wong and Valdivia (2014) found that 70% of DACA enrollees in their sample got their first job or started a new one after receiving deferred action, and over half said that DACA helped them to improve their family's financial situation. However, other studies show heightened anxiety and worry about unauthorized family members among DACA enrollees, compared to DACA nonenrollees (Teranishi, Suárez-Orozco, & Suárez-Orozco, 2015). Without surveys, such policy-relevant data would be difficult to uncover.

Mixed methods, or qualitative and quantitative methods in concert, provide a unique and helpful strategy when studying children in mixed-status households (Huston, Duncan, & Yoshikawa, 2016). Qualitative methods can provide context surrounding quantitative data, and may serve to generate hypotheses about how the dimension of legality moderates the impact of immigration, poverty, or racial minority status on developmental outcomes (Cahill, 2013). Once again, the Mexican Migration Project provides a good example of how to blend qualitative and quantitative data sources (Massey, 1987). The "ethnosurvey" methodology was developed by Durand and Massey (2004). It begins with an in-depth ethnographic observation, in this case of sending communities in Mexico. Researchers used those observations to create survey instruments designed to elicit individual and interpersonal information (both quantitative and qualitative). Ideally, consistent information is collected for each interviewee, but the order, timing, and phrasing of the inquiries are left to the discretion of the interviewer.

In addition to individual and interpersonal information, the interviewer/observer also gathers additional quantitative information on the family and community context. This methodology lends itself to scientifically rigorous, multilevel analysis, and also provides rich contextual information within which to interpret the findings of those analyses (Durand & Massey, 2004; Massey, 1987). The researchers have found it particularly useful for studying those without legal status, as the ethnosurvey format can feel less threatening to participants, and allows the interviewers to use their own discretion about when and how to ask sensitive questions (Massey & Capoferro, 2004).

4.2 Sampling Participants

To obtain adequate numbers of participants from a hidden population—especially one that may harbor fears of detection and distrust of authorities as is commonly the case in families with mixed authorization status—normally requires purposive sampling methods. This is because nationally representative sampling frames do not exist for this population. Different strategies under the umbrella of purposive sampling, however, have different strengths and weaknesses. When purposive sampling is conducted, the results are by their very nature not generalizable to the population at large (Shadish, Cook, & Campbell, 2002).

Snowball sampling techniques, in which participants are each asked to identify several others in their community within the intended sampling frame, is one serviceable strategy. Montealegre, Risser, Selwyn, McCurdy, and Sabin (2013) utilized this method for identifying immigrants with unauthorized status who were also HIV positive (a population at the intersection of multiple vulnerabilities) with great success. Núñez and Heyman (2007) also identified potential participants in this fashion, recruiting families with unauthorized members in their study of entrapment processes in US-Mexican border regions. These strategies are not always successful, however. In her study of transnational parenting practices for parents with unauthorized status, for instance, Dreby (2006) immersed herself in a Mexican immigrant community in New Jersey for several years prior to proposing her study. Even with credibility and personal ties to the community, the families that she interviewed were reluctant to refer her to others in similar circumstances. The families felt that transnational parenting was too sensitive of an issue to discuss openly within their community, and so the researcher essentially made contact with each family one at a time (Dreby, 2006).

Researchers can also use targeted sampling strategies, in which they seek out a site (or many sites) with a high density of immigrant parents with unauthorized status and randomly sample within that small target area (Massey & Capoferro, 2004; Watters & Biernacki, 1989). Durand and Massey found that sampling in this way was successful at generating reliable and accurate information about migratory patterns and life histories of US-Mexican migrants, despite the group's movement being largely "transient, circular, and clandestine" (Durand & Massey, 2004, p. 4). By studying a few communities at a time, each in great detail, the researchers have gained extensive knowledge about mixed-status families in the United States and Mexico.

Leveraging community-based organizations (CBOs) and advocacy groups that work directly with the unauthorized population to recruit participants can be a productive partnership for both researcher and community service providers. Immigrant-serving CBOs generally seek to serve special populations in culturally sensitive ways, and to increase community involvement and empowerment; they are unique in their credibility and visibility within the immigrant community, as well as their ability to form partnerships with other critical service providers (Hardina, 2006; Hong, 2011; Rusch, Frazier, & Atkins, 2015; Yoshikawa et al., 2014). In their 2014 study, Wong and Valdivia found that unauthorized Millennials trusted an advocacy organization (in this case, *United We Dream*) to keep their authorization status, and that of their family members, out of the hands of immigration enforcement officials.

4.3 Protecting Participants

The protection of participants who are unauthorized in research studies raises some of the same issues that come forward with the study of those whose behaviors are technically outside the law (e.g., use of controlled substances among parents not authorized to use them). For the unauthorized, protections include several processes that researchers have used. Protecting participant identities, for example, can include approaches that are not usually used in the research of legal immigration. For instance, extensive masking of data or composite cases in qualitative analysis can provide a certain level of anonymity to subjects. Certificates of confidentiality can be obtained, which protect participants in cases where their identities may otherwise be revealed. Data collection can be limited to strategies that do not obtain names or identifying information, such as in anonymous, online surveys. Data that do include identifying information must be kept password protected, databases encrypted, and transcriptions can include pseudonyms not just for the participant, but for all people mentioned. Finally, interpretive communities with understanding of this population, from both "insider" and "outsider" status, as well as checks on methods from those across a range of disciplinary perspectives, can be useful in assessing the ethics and acceptability of different research methods (Suárez-Orozco & Carhill, 2008).

4.4 Measuring Unauthorized Status

There is a growing consensus among immigration researchers that measuring authorization status is of critical importance, given the differences in outcomes and developmental mechanisms between authorized and unauthorized individuals and their families (Waters & Pineau, 2015). Measuring the legal status of a citizen child's parents, however, presents several challenges to researchers. Depending on their ages, children or youth may not be aware of their parents' authorization status. Some immigration researchers have contended that asking children directly about relatives' or parents' authorization status is not recommended, as children may not recognize the ramifications of the information they are providing (Yoshikawa & Suárez-Orozco, 2012).

Motivation to answer questions about "illegal" activity varies widely across populations of interest, data collection methods, and topic of research (Tourangeau & Yan, 2007). Asking directly on a survey "Are you authorized to be living in the United States at this time?" is a tactic used by some researchers (such as Brabeck & Xu, 2010). However, this may be threatening to some participants and may bias the population estimate (Brabeck, Lykes, Sibley, & Kene, 2015).

Other researchers have used a wide range of questions about citizenship, visa status, asylum status, and public program usage to infer whether an immigrant lacks authorization; this approach has been used in national studies of the size and characteristics of the unauthorized population (e.g., Passel, Cohn, Krogstad, & Gonzalez-Barrera, 2014), including studies that rely on the Survey of Income and Program Participation, the Immigration and Intergenerational Mobility in Metropolitan Los Angeles, and the American Community Survey (Bean, Brown, Bachmeier, Fokkema, & Lessard-Phillips, 2012; Capps, Koball, et al., 2016; Hall, Greenman, & Farkas, 2010). All of these approaches use multiple demographic indicators to first establish residents without citizenship and then estimate those with characteristics of the many alternative visa statuses in the noncitizen category (such as temporary protected status). This multistep process then results in a final estimate of those with unauthorized status.

More fundamentally, researchers must consider the risk to the participant when answering questions (both direct and indirect) about legal status. As of this writing, the Obama administration has made clear its intention to focus on only detaining or deporting immigrants with unauthorized status who commit violent crimes (Rosenblum, 2015). However, the relative "friendliness" of this change in administration practice does not ensure that policies or enforcement strategies of the next administration will retain the practice. Law enforcement has subpoenaed data collected for scientific investigation in the past. For instance, in 2010, a federal court subpoenaed data collected in Arizona schools on Mexican immigrant children and the quality of the education that they received as part of the legal challenge to overturn certain statewide education policies. The University of Arizona complied with the subpoena, providing confidential information to the state superintendent amidst strong protest from the researchers at UCLA who conducted the studies (Gándara & Orfield, 2010; Jaschik, 2010; The Civil Rights Project (Proyecto Derechos Cilives), 2010). Despite good faith efforts like Certificates of Confidentiality and various anonymity measures on the part of any research team, there is no guarantee that confidential data, including data on legal status, will not get subpoenaed in the future.

4.5 Community-Based Participatory Research

A social justice approach to studying mixed-status families requires prioritizing the needs of those families (Prilleltensky, 1990, 2012). One of the most straightforward and effective ways to do this is to involve participants and members of the unauthorized immigrant community in the process of research at each step. In other words, interventionists can engage in research with—instead of research on—mixed-status families (Hernández, Nguyen, Casanova, Suárez-Orozco, & Saetermoe, 2013; Rivas-Drake, Camacho, & Guillaume, 2016).

Community-based participatory research (CBPR), sometimes also referred to as PAR, grew out of a blending of two research traditions: participatory research in the global South and action research in the global North (Ferreira & Gendron, 2011). Originally used by researchers in the social sciences and adult education field, CBPR as a research orientation has grown in popularity and has become a preferred methodology for many psychologists who study marginalized populations (Burhansstipanov, Christopher, & Schumacher, 2005; Ferreira & Gendron, 2011). It is characterized by equal footing of all members of the research team: scientists, community organizers, and participants. CBPR replaces the traditional balance of power favoring researchers with a collaborative approach. Investigators are both learners and teachers, as are the community members under investigation (Ferreira & Gendron, 2011). There are many excellent resources for researchers interested in the rich history and modern uses of this method of action/intervention science (e.g., Khanlou & Peter, 2005; Wallerstein, Duran, Minkler, & Foley, 2005). In short, the primary goals of this method are the inclusion of the community under study in all research-related tasks, including problem identification; theory development; data collection, analysis, and dissemination; and use of research products (Ferreira & Gendron, 2011). Any involved party initiate a research or intervention relationship/collaboration; lines between community members and researchers often blur as relationships develop. This approach allows research and context experts to share information and resources with each other under a joint goal of servicing and understanding the community under investigation.

This approach to scientific inquiry has produced fruitful programs of research and fertile grounds for activism and community empowerment. For instance, in her study of unauthorized Latino youth in Utah, Caitlin Cahill and the Mestizo Arts and Activism Collective collaborated on a project, *Dreaming of No Judgment*, which sought to explore the lived experiences of immigrant youth in Salt Lake City, and to expand their role in the production of theory and knowledge on the topic of immigration (Cahill, 2010). The result was an impactful narrative of many young participants' embodied experiences "negotiating a toxic terrain of discrimination" (Cahill, 2010, p. 156). The project also allowed the youth collective to develop their own stories, and to express those narratives, in various forms, to policy makers and the larger research community on their terms.

CBPR also has its challenges and limitations. These challenges mostly stem from the relative newness of community-centered research methodologies in the United States. The provisions set out for the protection of human subjects in psychological research—including the Belmont report and the American Psychological Association guidelines—have largely ignored the moral obligation that a researcher has to society at large, instead focusing on the obligation that a researcher has to individual participants or clients (Prilleltensky, 1990). Brabeck, Lykes, et al. (2015) do an exemplary job of discussing how psychologists, including developmental and intervention researchers, might go about satisfying both sets of ethical obligations. The authors explore the challenges to using the individualistic, biomedical ethical framework on which the Belmont report is based, to evaluate methodologies that seek active participant and community engagement with research activities, like CBPR. The authors conclude that researchers should directly confront the tension between participant ownership of their own narrative and the need to protect anonymity, and to solicit feedback from the participating community members themselves on how these issues should be handled. These are reasonable goals, and should be considered "best practices" for those conducting research with unauthorized immigrants and their mixed-status families.

4.6 Ending a Program of Research with Attention to Sustainability

The final task for researchers who work closely with unauthorized immigrant communities is leaving a study site or research community. This is of particular concern for researchers working with the CBPR paradigm, but extends to developmental and intervention researchers who work closely with any community organization or cohesive group of participants. Community-academic partnerships are often long-term and mutually beneficial; despite this, however, programs of research often end without any sustained plan for ongoing partnership or exchange (Suarez-Balcazar, Harper, & Lewis, 2005). "Helicopter research"—the act of an outside investigator dropping in, conducting a study, and flying right back out—is antithetical to the social justice perspective (Ferreira & Gendron, 2011). Participatory research affords community members an opportunity to learn about the process of research and gives the investigator a chance to work with community organizations and policy makers in a process of mutual learning (Donovan, Wigdor, & Snow, 2003; Ferreira & Gendron, 2011). For instance, CBOs may be interested in training staff members in database management, program evaluation, or analytic skills (Suarez-Balcazar et al., 2005). It is the responsibility of the researcher to "leave something behind" that will be useful to the community under investigation, and to those that directly serve that community (Suarez-Balcazar et al., 2005, p. 94). Researchers should share usable knowledge, such as impact or fidelity evaluations, with the community at multiple points along the research path. Finally, projects should conclude with honest conversations about the shared successes and challenges of the partnership, as well as the next steps for each member of the partnership (Suarez-Balcazar et al., 2005). Such steps are more likely to result in sustained partnerships rather than, as often occur, an end to involvement with the communities that gave to the research process.

5. DISSEMINATION AND USE OF RESEARCH RESULTS

Shifting from objective observer of injustice to action scientist requires active engagement with policy level questions and the honing of dissemination skills. Researchers can solicit topics for study from the marginalized communities of interest, or they may choose to engage directly with policy makers (Tseng, 2012). Often those tasked with creating and evaluating policy are frustrated by the state of research (Moodie, 2009; Tseng, 2012). This has been true of policy research on mixed-status families. Much of the research on these communities has emerged in the last 5 years, and policy makers continue to seek empirical evidence that may not yet exist on the consequences of unauthorized status for child, youth, and family development (United States of America et al. v. State of Texas et al., 2016). Furthermore, many studies with policy applications are not framed as such, but rather are published in journals aimed at researchers in developmental science. Prilleltensky (2012) suggests that researchers frame their questions from the start in a way that will answer the very basic questions that plague practitioners: has a particular immigration policy aimed at unauthorized individuals impacted citizen children in important ways? Tseng (2012) likewise suggests strengthening the influence of policy makers and practitioners on research activities, encouraging nonacademic research consumers to actively seek out methodologically strong empirical evidence, and for empowering academic researchers to use their skills to bridge information gaps that exist.

Research education programs within the US context often do not prepare researchers to disseminate findings effectively (Tseng, 2012). A basic premise put forth by many community and critical psychologists concerned with social justice in research is that a clear plan of dissemination and use be agreed upon during study design and proposal writing. As Hernández et al. (2013) so eloquently summarize: "Unless the precise modes of benefit or tangible outcomes can be delineated, the indirect benefits we claim may be perceived as exaggerated at the least and as a form of benevolent racism at the worst" (p. 48). Before a single survey has been administered or a single family has been asked to risk their livelihood and future, researchers have an obligation to understand policy and practice questions that those communities may find useful, rather than solely building their questions from the research literature. In addition, engaging stakeholders from the beginning of the process on how to use the research findings can further inform early phases of a research project. Finally, briefs and executive summaries that are short and jargon-free are good starting points for dissemination efforts and websites and easy to navigate databases present another option for disseminating "what works" to policy makers and practitioners (Tseng, 2012).

Researchers should also pay careful attention to sensitively framing research findings during the dissemination phase. As Brabeck, Lykes, et al. (2015) noted, studies involving mixed-status families, especially within the CBPR framework, have the ability to be further marginalizing if they confirm stereotypes of the populations (for example, label those with unauthorized status as "illegal"). The authors also caution that it is incumbent on the researcher to dissect how their research may be used or interpreted, and how it may impact the lives of the community members they study.

6. CONCLUSIONS

In this chapter, we have endeavored to understand the role that developmental scientists and intervention researchers can play in advancing a social justice agenda in support of a critically marginalized population. As researchers, having access to dependable qualitative and quantitative data is necessary to effectively support mixed-status families, but there are challenges to the ethical creation of that knowledge. Prilleltensky's (1990, 2012) and Prilleltensky and Nelson (1997) critical community psychology framework can help guide researchers to appropriate topics and methods for study. Intervention researchers and developmental scientists must contend with balancing the need for useful research with the burdens of participation for this population (Mahalingam & Rabelo, 2013). At a minimum, appropriate contextual and cultural experts with strong ties to the specific unauthorized community under study should be consulted as theories are built, measures are created, participants are recruited, and results are interpreted (Suárez-Orozco & Carhill, 2008). The most effective way to do this is to involve the communities under study in the research from the very beginning and to engage in participatory research strategies (Ferreira & Gendron, 2011). Intervention researchers can gain knowledge about the lives of mixed-status families, and use that knowledge to improve the lives of those families, by using the guiding principles of the social justice perspective.

We have also highlighted some examples of current research programs seeking to change the status quo with high-quality scholarship in which the community has an authentic voice and genuine ownership. For the 4 million citizen children living in the United States with an unauthorized parent, this is not a trivial matter. Ethical research must be committed to deeply considering the unique strengths, needs, and vulnerabilities of this community, and to honor that commitment throughout all stages of research: theory development; design and implementation of measures; participant recruitment and data collection; analyzing and contextualizing the results; and disseminating the findings. The growing role of research evidence in policy and community advocacy magnifies the challenges and the opportunities for change, and those studying mixed-status families must be ready to embrace these challenges and opportunities head on.

ACKNOWLEDGMENT

H.Y.'s work on this chapter was partially supported by a grant to the Global TIES for Children Center from the New York University Abu Dhabi Research Institute.

REFERENCES

American Psychological Association (2012). *Crossroads: The psychology of immigration in the new century*. Washington, DC: American Psychological Association. Retrieved from, http://www.apa.org/topics/immigration/report.aspx.

Aysa, M., & Massey, D. S. (2004). Wives left behind: The labor market behavior of women in migrant communities. In J. Durand & D. S. Massey (Eds.), *Crossing the border: Research from the Mexican Migration Project* (pp. 131–144). New York, NY: Russell Sage.

Bean, F. D., Brown, S. K., Bachmeier, J. D., Fokkema, T., & Lessard-Phillips, L. (2012). The dimensions and degree of second-generation incorporation in US and European cities: A comparative study of inclusion and exclusion. *International Journal of Comparative Sociology*, *53*(3), 181–209.

Bean, F. D., Leach, M. A., Brown, S. K., Bachmeier, J. D., & Hipp, J. R. (2011). The educational legacy of unauthorized migration: Comparisons across U.S. immigrant groups in how parents' status affects their offspring. *International Migration Review*, *45*(2), 348–385.

Brabeck, K., Lykes, M. B., Sibley, E., & Kene, P. (2015). Ethical ambiguities in participatory action research with unauthorized migrants. *Ethics & Behavior*, *25*(1), 21–36.

Brabeck, K. M., Sibley, E., Taubin, P., & Murcia, A. (2015). The influence of immigrant parent legal status on U.S.-born children's academic abilities: The moderating effects of social service use. *Applied Developmental Science*. http://dx.doi.org/10.1080/10888691.2015.1114420.

Brabeck, K., & Xu, Q. (2010). The impact of detention and deportation on Latino immigrant children and families: A quantitative exploration. *Hispanic Journal of Behavioral Sciences*, *32*(3), 341–361.

Brief of Educator and Children's Advocates as Amici Curiae in Support of Petitioners, United States of America, et al. v. State of Texas, et al. (2016). No. 15-674.

Burhansstipanov, L., Christopher, S., & Schumacher, S. A. (2005). Lessons learned from community-based participatory research in Indian country. *Cancer Control, 12*(Suppl. 2), 70–76.

Cahill, C. (2010). 'Why do they hate us?' Reframing immigration through participatory action research. *Area, 42*(2), 152–161.

Cahill, C. (2013). Transcultural community building. In J. Hu (Ed.), *Transcultural cities: Border crossing and placemaking* (pp. 193–206). New York, NY: Routledge.

Capps, R., Fix, M., & Zong, J. (2016). *A profile of U.S. children with unauthorized parents.* Washington, DC: Migration Policy Institute.

Capps, R., Koball, H., Bachmeier, J. D., Ruiz Soto, A. G., Zong, J., & Gelatt, J. (2016). *Deferred action for unauthorized parents: Analysis of DAPA's potential effects on families and children.* Washington, DC: Migration Policy Institute.

Carroll, B., & Turpin, T. (2002). *Environmental impact assessment handbook: A practical guide for planners, developers and communities.* London, UK: Thomas Telford Publishing.

Creswell, J. W. (2012). *Qualitative inquiry and research design: Choosing among five approaches.* New York, NY: Sage.

Curiel, E. M. (2004). The Green Card as a matrimonial strategy: Self-interest in the choice of marital partners. In J. Durand & D. S. Massey (Eds.), *Crossing the border: Research from the Mexican Migration Project* (pp. 6–108). New York, NY: Russell Sage.

Donovan, M. S., Wigdor, M. K. L., & Snow, C. E. (Eds.), (2003). *Strategic education research partnership.* Washington, DC: National Academy Press.

Dreby, J. (2006). Honor and virtue: Mexican parenting in the transnational context. *Gender & Society, 20*(1), 32–59.

Dreby, J. (2012). The burden of deportation on children in Mexican immigrant families. *Journal of Marriage and the Family, 74*(4), 829–845.

Dreby, J. (2015). *Everyday illegal: When policies undermine immigrant families.* Berkeley, CA: University of California Press.

Durand, J., & Massey, D. S. (2004). What we learned from the Mexican Migration Project. In J. Durand & D. S. Massey (Eds.), *Crossing the border: Research from the Mexican Migration Project* (pp. 1–16). New York, NY: Russell Sage.

Ferreira, M. P., & Gendron, F. (2011). Community-based participatory research with traditional and indigenous communities of the Americas: Historical context and future directions. *The International Journal of Critical Pedagogy, 3*(3), 153–168.

Flores, N. Y., Hernández-León, R., & Massey, D. (2004). A comparison of urban and rural origin migration from Mexico to the United States. In J. Durand & D. S. Massey (Eds.), *Crossing the border: Research from the Mexican Migration Project* (pp. 184–200). New York, NY: Russell Sage.

Gándara, P., & Orfield, G. (2010). *AZ Horne v. Flores: Letter from Drs. Patricia Gandara and Gary Orfield, Aug. 11, 2010.* ESOLFlorida Online. Retrieved from, http://esolfl.blog.com/az-horne-v-flores-letter-from-drs-patricia-gandara-and-gary-orfield-aug-11-2010/.

García Coll, C., Crnic, K., Lamberty, G., Wasik, B. H., Jenkins, R., Garcia, H. V., et al. (1996). An integrative model for the study of developmental competencies in minority children. *Child Development, 67*(5), 1891–1914.

García Coll, C., & Magnuson, K. (1997). The psychological experience of immigration: A developmental perspective. In N. Landale (Ed.), *Immigration and the family: Research and policy on U.S. immigrants* (pp. 91–131). Hillsdale, NJ: Erlbaum.

Gonzales, R. G., & Chavez, L. R. (2012). "Awakening to a nightmare": Abjectivity and illegality in the lives of undocumented 1.5 generation Latino immigrants in the United States. *Current Anthropology, 53*(3), 255–281.

Hall, M., Greenman, E., & Farkas, G. (2010). Legal status and wage disparities for Mexican immigrants. *Social Forces, 89*(2), 491–514.

Hardina, D. (2006). Strategies for citizen participation and empowerment in non-profit, community-based organizations. *Community Development, 37*(4), 4–17.

Hernández, M. G., Nguyen, J., Casanova, S., Suárez-Orozco, C., & Saetermoe, C. L. (2013). Doing no harm and getting it right: Guidelines for ethical research with immigrant communities. *New Directions for Child and Adolescent Development*, *2013*, 43–60. http://dx.doi.org/10.1002/cad.20042.

Hong, S. (2011). Acts of leadership: Building powerful forms of parent participation in Chicago. In M. R. Warren & K. L. Mapp (Eds.), *A match on dry grass: Community organizing as a catalyst for school reform* (pp. 168–196). New York, NY: Oxford University Press.

Huston, A. C., Duncan, G. J., & Yoshikawa, H. (2016). Mixed methods contributions to understanding anti-poverty policies: Four case studies. In C. M. Hay (Ed.), *Methods that matter: Integrating mixed methods for more effective social science research*. Chicago, IL: University of Chicago Press.

Jaschik, S. (2010). Another subpoena for research. *Inside higher ed*. Retrieved from, https://www.insidehighered.com/news/2010/08/13/arizona.

Khanlou, N., & Peter, E. (2005). Participatory action research: Considerations for ethical review. *Social Science and Medicine*, *60*(10), 2333–2340.

Landale, N. S., Hardie, J. H., Oropesa, R. S., & Hillemeier, M. M. (2015). Behavioral functioning among Mexican-origin children: Does parental legal status matter? *Journal of Health and Social Behavior*, *56*(1), 2–18.

Mahalingam, R., & Rabelo, V. C. (2013). Theoretical, methodological, and ethical challenges to the study of immigrants: Perils and possibilities. *New Directions for Child and Adolescent Development*, *141*, 25–41.

Massey, D. S. (1987). Understanding Mexican migration to the United States. *American Journal of Sociology*, *92*(6), 1372–1403.

Massey, D. S., & Capoferro, C. (2004). Conceptual and methodological developments in the study of international migration. *International Migration Review*, *38*(3), 1075–1102.

Mather, M. (2009). *Children in immigrant families chart new path*. Washington, DC: Population Reference Bureau. Retrieved from, http://www.prb.org/pdf09/immigrantchildren.pdf.

McEwen, M. M., Boyle, J. S., & Messias, D. K. H. (2015). Undocumentedness and public policy: The impact on communities, individuals, and families along the Arizona/Sonora border. *Nursing Outlook*, *63*(1), 77–85.

Menjívar, C. (2006). Liminal legality: Salvadoran and Guatemalan immigrants' lives in the United States. *American Journal of Sociology*, *111*, 999–1037.

Menjívar, C. (2011). The power of the law: Central Americans' legality and everyday life in Phoenix, Arizona. *Latino Studies*, *9*(4), 377–395.

Mertens, D. M. (2012). Ethics and social justice in ethnocultural qualitative research. In D. K. Nagata, L. Kohn-Wood, & L. A. Suzuki (Eds.), *Qualitative strategies for ethnocultural research*. Washington, DC: American Psychological Association.

Montealegre, J. R., Risser, J. M., Selwyn, B. J., McCurdy, S. A., & Sabin, K. (2013). Effectiveness of respondent driven sampling to recruit undocumented Central American immigrant women in Houston, Texas for an HIV behavioral survey. *AIDS and Behavior*, *17*(2), 719–727.

Moodie, R. (2009). Where different worlds collide: Expanding the influence of research and researchers on policy. *Journal of Public Health Policy*, *30*, S33–S37.

National Commission for the Protection of Human Subjects of Biomedical and Behavioral Research (1979). *The Belmont report: Ethical principles and guidelines for the protection of human subjects of research*. Retrieved from, http://www.hhs.gov/ohrp/humansubjects/guidance/belmont.html.

Ngai, M. (2004). *Impossible subjects: Illegal aliens and the making of modern America*. Princeton, NJ: Princeton University Press.

Núñez, G., & Heyman, J. (2007). Entrapment processes and immigrant communities in a time of heightened border vigilance. *Human Organization*, *66*(4), 354–365.

Orrenius, P. M. (2004). The effect of U.S. border enforcement on the crossing behavior of Mexican migrants. In J. Durand & D. S. Massey (Eds.), *Crossing the border: Research from the Mexican Migration Project* (pp. 265–280). New York, NY: Russell Sage.

Ortega, A. N., Horwitz, S. M., Fang, H., Kuo, A. A., Wallace, S. P., & Inkelas, M. (2009). Documentation status and parental concerns about development in young US children of Mexican origin. *Academic Pediatrics*, *9*(4), 278–282.

Parrado, E. (2004). US migration, home ownership, and housing quality. In J. Durand & D. S. Massey (Eds.), *Crossing the border: Research from the Mexican Migration Project* (pp. 63–85). New York, NY: Russell Sage.

Passel, J. S., & Cohn, D. (2011). *Unauthorized immigrant population: National and state trends.* Washington, DC: Pew Research Center.

Passel, J. S., Cohn, D., Krogstad, J. M., & Gonzalez-Barrera, A. (2014). *As growth stalls, unauthorized immigrant population becomes more settled.* Washington, DC: Pew Research Center.

Potochnick, S. R., & Perreira, K. M. (2010). Depression and anxiety among first-generation immigrant Latino youth: Key correlates and implications for future research. *The Journal of Nervous and Mental Disease*, *198*(7), 470–477.

Preston, J. (2013). U.S. Deportations decline: Felons made up big share. *New York Times*, A20. Retrieved from, http://www.nytimes.com/2013/12/20/us/us-deportations-decline-felons-made-up-big-share.html.

Prilleltensky, I. (1990). Enhancing the social ethics of psychology: Toward a psychology at the service of social change. *Canadian Psychology, Psychologie Canadienne* *31*(4), 310.

Prilleltensky, I. (2012). The what, why, who, and how of globalization: What is psychology to do? *Journal of Social Issues*, *68*(3), 612–629.

Prilleltensky, I., & Nelson, G. (1997). Community psychology: Reclaiming social justice. In I. Prilleltensky & D. Fox (Eds.), *Critical psychology: An introduction* (pp. 166–184). Thousand Oaks, CA: Sage Publishing.

Prilleltensky, I., & Nelson, G. (2009). Community psychology: Advancing social justice. In D. Fox, I. Prilleltensky, & S. Austin (Eds.), *Critical psychology: An introduction (2nd ed.*, pp. 126–143). Thousand Oaks, CA: Sage Publishing.

Ragin, C. C. (2014). *The comparative method: Moving beyond qualitative and quantitative strategies.* Berkeley, CA: University of California Press.

Riosmena, F. (2004). Return versus settlement among undocumented Mexican migrants, 1980 to 1996. In J. Durand & D. S. Massey (Eds.), *Crossing the border: Research from the Mexican Migration Project* (pp. 265–280). New York, NY: Russell Sage.

Rivas-Drake, D., Camacho, T. C., & Guillaume, C. (2016). Just good developmental science: Trust, identity, and responsibility in ethnic minority recruitment and retention. *Advances in Child Development and Behavior*, *50*, 161–188.

Rosenblum, M. R. (2015). *Understanding the potential impact of executive action on immigration enforcement.* Washington, DC: Migration Policy Institute. Retrieved from, https://www.fairus.org/DocServer/GR/Understanding_the_Potential_Impact_of_Executive_Action_on_Immigration_Enforcement_July2015.

Rosenblum, M. R., & Ruiz Soto, A. G. (2015). *An analysis of unauthorized immigrants in the United States by country and region of birth.* Washington, DC: Migration Policy Institute. Retrieved from, http://www.migrationpolicy.org/research.

Rusch, D., Frazier, S. L., & Atkins, M. (2015). Building capacity within community-based organizations: New directions for mental health promotion for Latino immigrant families in urban poverty. *Administration and Policy in Mental Health and Mental Health Services Research*, *42*(1), 1–5.

Shadish, W. R., Cook, T. D., & Campbell, D. T. (2002). *Experimental and quasi-experimental designs for generalized causal inference.* Boston, MA: Houghton Mifflin Company.

Suarez-Balcazar, Y., Harper, G. W., & Lewis, R. (2005). An interactive and contextual model of community–university collaborations for research and action. *Health Education & Behavior, 32*(1), 84–101.
Suárez-Orozco, C., & Carhill, A. (2008). Afterword: New directions in research with immigrant families and their children. *New Directions for Child and Adolescent Development, 121*, 87–104.
Suárez-Orozco, C., Yoshikawa, H., Teranishi, R., & Suárez-Orozco, M. (2011). Growing up in the shadows: The developmental implications of unauthorized status. *Harvard Educational Review, 81*(3), 438–473.
Teranishi, R., Suárez-Orozco, C., & Suárez-Orozco, M. (2015). *In the shadows of the ivory tower: Undocumented undergraduates and the liminal state of immigration reform*. Los Angeles, CA: The Institute for Immigration, Globalization, and Education.
The Civil Rights Project (Proyecto Derechos Cilives) (2010). *9 Studies document the educational condition of Arizona's English learners*. Retrieved from, http://civilrightsproject.ucla.edu/news/press-releases/2010/9-new-studies-document-the-educational-condition-of-arizonas-english-learners.
Tourangeau, R., & Yan, T. (2007). Sensitive questions in surveys. *Psychological Bulletin, 133*(5), 859.
Tseng, V. (2012). The uses of research in policy and practice. *Social Policy Reports of the Society for Research in Child Development, 26*(2), 1–24.
Van Hook, J., Bachmeier, J. D., Coffman, D. L., & Harel, O. (2015). Can we spin straw into gold? An evaluation of immigrant legal status imputation approaches. *Demography, 52*(1), 329–354.
Wallerstein, N., Duran, B., Minkler, M., & Foley, K. (2005). Developing and maintaining partnerships with communities. In B. Israel, E. Eng, A. Schulz, & E. Parker (Eds.), *Methods in community based participatory research methods* (pp. 31–51). San Francisco, CA: Jossey-Bass.
Wallerstein, N., Miller, F. G., & Buchanan, D. R. (2007). Ethical issues in community-based participatory research: Balancing rigorous research with community participation in community intervention studies. *Progress in Community Health Partnerships: Research, Education, and Action, 1*(2), 153–160.
Waters, M. C., & Pineau, M. G. (Eds.), (2015). *The integration of immigrants into American society*.Washington, DC: National Academy Press. Report of the National Academy of Sciences Consensus Committee on integrating immigrants into American Society.
Watters, J. K., & Biernacki, P. (1989). Targeted sampling: Options for the study of hidden populations. *Social Problems, 36*(4), 416–430.
White House (2014). *Fact sheet: Immigrant accountability executive action*. Washington, DC: White House. Retrieved from, http://www.whitehouse.gov/the-press-office/2014/11/20/fact-sheet-immigration-accountability-executive-action.
Wong, T. K., & Valdivia, C. (2014). *In their own words: A nationwide survey of undocumented Millennials*. Washington, DC/New York, NY: United We Dream Network and Unbound Philanthropy. Retrieved from, http://unitedwedream.org/wp-content/uploads/2014/05/Undocumented-Millennials-Survey-Summary.pdf.
Yoshikawa, H. (2011). *Immigrants raising citizens: Undocumented parents and their young children*. New York, NY: Russell Sage Foundation.
Yoshikawa, H. (2015). *Being undocumented in the U.S. and the world: Implications for child and youth development (University lecture)*. New York, NY: New York University.
Yoshikawa, H., & Kalil, A. (2011). The effects of parental undocumented status on the developmental contexts of young children in immigrant families. *Child Development Perspectives, 5*(4), 291–297.
Yoshikawa, H., & Kholoptseva, J. (2013). *Unauthorized parents and their children's development: A synthesis of the evidence*. Washington, DC: Migration Policy Institute.

Yoshikawa, H., Kholoptseva, J., & Suárez-Orozco, C. (2013). The role of public policies and community-based organizations in the developmental consequences of parent undocumented status. *Social Policy Reports of the Society for Research in Child Development, 27*(3), 1–17.

Yoshikawa, H., & Suárez-Orozco, C. (2012). Deporting parents hurts kids. *The New York Times (Op-Ed)*. Retrieved from, http://www.nytimes.com/2012/04/21/opinion/deporting-parents-ruins-kids.html?_r=0.

Yoshikawa, H., Suarez-Orozco, C.S., & Gonzales, R.G. (in press). Unauthorized status and youth development in the United States: Society for Research on Adolescence consensus statement, *Journal of Research in Adolescence*.

Yoshikawa, H., Weiland, C., Ulvestad, K., Perreira, K., Crosnoe, R., Chaudry, A., et al. (2014). *Improving access of low-income immigrant families to health and human services: The role of community-based organizations*. Washington, DC: The Urban Institute.

CHAPTER NINE

And I Shot Her: On War, and the Creation of Inequities in the Development of Youths' Moral Capacities

Cecilia Wainryb[1], Stacia Bourne
University of Utah, Salt Lake City, UT, United States
[1]Corresponding author: e-mail address: wainryb@psych.utah.edu

Contents

Abstract

War creates a multifaceted web of inequities that encompass most levels of the ecology of youth development. These include psychosocial inequities bearing on war-exposed youth's limited access to medical and educational services and job-training and employment opportunities, as well as some of the unique psychological sequelae of trauma exposure. In this chapter we put forth a twofold argument. First, we argue that the protracted hardships of war also create enduring psychological inequities that go beyond the well-documented psychosocial needs and psychological trauma, and encompass other aspects of youths' healthy development; these are inequities inasmuch as they represent profound alterations of the developmental pathways available to war-affected youth. Second, we maintain that the psychological sciences must strive to understand such longstanding developmental inequities even if we do not, at this time, have the tools to fully address them.

Equity and Justice in Developmental Science: Implications for Young People, Families, and Communities (S.S. Horn, M.D. Ruck & L.S. Liben, Eds.)
Advances in Child Development and Behavior (J.B. Benson, Series Ed.), Vol. 51
ISSN 0065-2407 http://dx.doi.org/10.1016/bs.acdb.2016.05.003

The need for an equity agenda—an approach geared to addressing unfair disparities by prioritizing the most disadvantaged groups of children—is most stark in relation to war-affected youths. War creates a multifaceted web of inequities that encompass most levels of the ecology of youth development. Understandably, researchers have devoted most efforts to identifying inequities that can be addressed by intervention and policy. These include psychosocial inequities bearing on war-exposed youth's limited access to medical and educational services and job-training and employment opportunities, as well as some of the unique psychological sequelae of trauma exposure. In this chapter we put forth a twofold argument. First, we argue that the protracted hardships of war also create enduring psychological inequities that go beyond the well-documented psychosocial needs and psychological trauma, and encompass other aspects of youths' healthy development; these are inequities inasmuch as they represent profound alterations of the developmental pathways available to war-affected youth. Second, we maintain that the psychological sciences must strive to understand such longstanding developmental inequities even if we do not, at this time, have the tools to fully address them.

1. ON THE NEED FOR AN EQUITY AGENDA TARGETING WAR-AFFECTED POPULATIONS

During the 1990s, a consensus emerged within the international community that the principal goal of economic development policy was the reduction and eventual eradication of poverty. Poverty was understood as a multidimensional phenomenon comprising both material (income, assets) and nonmaterial (education, health, rights, security) deprivation (UNDP, 1990). The United Nations' Millennium Development Goals, or MDGs, a set of voluntary global goals designed to accelerate progress over a 15-year span in areas such as health and education, provided the international community with fairly clear targets toward the achievement of this objective.

And, indeed, the MDGs-based strategy helped make significant advances in the conditions around the world, with the number of people living in extreme poverty being reduced by 700 million people in a relatively short time-span. Nevertheless, toward the end of 2005, several economic development reports redirected policy makers' attention away from the extent of absolute deprivation, toward the large inequalities in people's life chances and outcomes. These reports, including the Human Development Report (UNDP, 2005) and the World Development Report (World Bank, 2006), articulated *principled* reasons for why policy makers should care about inequality, inasmuch as equality and justice are valued goals in and of themselves. In addition, and importantly, in demonstrating that poverty could not be reduced through growth alone and that inequity was hampering poverty-reduction efforts, these reports also articulated compelling *instrumental* justifications for an equity agenda—an agenda designed to narrow disparities among the most marginalized populations.

The shortcomings of the MDGs approach, with its focus on economic growth and the reduction of poverty, were further underscored by the release of the 2011 World Development Report, which focused on the intersection between economic development and political conflict. As it reported (World Bank, 2011, pp. 5–6),

> *No low-income fragile or conflict-affected country has yet achieved a single MDG. People in fragile and conflict-affected states are more than twice as likely to be undernourished as those in other developing countries, more than three times as likely to be unable to send their children to school, twice as likely to see their children die before age five, and more than twice as likely to lack clean water. On average, a country that experienced major violence over the period from 1981 to 2005 has a poverty rate 21 percentage points higher than a country that saw no violence ... The average cost of civil war is equivalent to more than 30 years of GDP growth for a medium-size developing country. Trade levels after major episodes of violence take 20 years to recover. In other words, a major episode of violence, unlike natural disasters or economic cycles, can wipe out an entire generation of economic progress.*

As illustrated by this excerpt, the World Bank underscored the alarming finding that the nearly 2 billion people living in conflict-affected states were left behind in the global efforts to end extreme poverty. Strikingly, whereas in the 1970s the largest concentration of individuals in extreme poverty, defined as those living on less than $1.25 a day, was found in stable low-income countries, by 2011 roughly one-third of the world's extreme poor lived in conflict-affected states. The World Bank also highlighted the cyclic nature of political instability by noting that 90% of the prior decade's civil wars had taken place in countries that had already experienced a civil war in the previous 30 years. Understandably, the report concluded with a forceful call for the urgent need for targeted action to redress the extraordinary inequities affecting populations living in the midst of armed conflict.

2. ON WAR-EXPOSURE, AND THE ALTERATION OF THE ECOLOGY OF YOUTH DEVELOPMENT

War profoundly alters the ecology of child development. The multidimensional, pervading, and continued adversities associated with war constitute the "normal" developmental context for a considerable proportion of the world's children. As estimated by the Organization for Economic Cooperation and Development (2014), close to 40% of people living in fragile states are below the age of 15 (by comparison, youth make up around 25% of the population in stable states). UN reports are equally disquieting. According to recent estimates, in 2009 nearly 1 billion children were living in regions affected by armed conflict; of these, approximately 300 million were younger than 5 years. This report also noted with concern the changing nature and tactics of armed conflict, such that wars are increasingly fought within states, involve nonstate actors such as rebel or terrorist groups, and lack clear battlefields, thus multiplying the risks for civilian populations. In the last two decades wars have killed an estimated 2 million children and left 6 million children disabled (UNICEF, 2009).

In what has become a pervasive and acutely toxic feature of today's armed conflicts, various forms of sexual violence against children are habitually used as a means for intimidation and reprisal. The distinctive sequelae of girls' sexual victimization during war are beginning to be understood (McKay, Robinson, Gonsalves, & Worthen, 2006). Whereas the plight of girls who become pregnant and give birth under such circumstances is receiving increasing attention, the fate of their children remains largely understudied. According to recent estimates, to date there are 500,000 children born from wartime rape, and evidence suggests that these children are at heightened risk for infanticide, abandonment, and discrimination in both conflict and postconflict settings, solely due to their biological origins (Carpenter, 2010). Boys also become victims of sexual violence in times of war. For example, in Afghanistan the practice of Bacha Bazi, a form of sexual slavery in which boys are sold to powerful men, including military and political leaders, for entertainment and sexual activities, remains widespread (Qobil, 2010). Furthermore, boys often endure additional trauma when forced to witness or perpetrate sexual violence against others (Betancourt, Borisova, Williams, Brennan, et al., 2010).

But modern wars not only augment physical dangers for children; wars increasingly target the infrastructure that supports healthy youth development.

The proliferation of attacks against schools and teachers have become a particularly destructive, but often overlooked, tactic of modern wars. In some contexts, schools are a prime recruiting ground for children, and school buildings are increasingly used as military bases. In 2013 alone there were 3643 documented attacks on education that included the bombing of schools as well as torture and intimidation against children and teachers; unsurprisingly, nearly 50 million children between the ages of 6 and 15 in conflict areas are out of school (Save the Children, 2013).

The tactics used in modern wars also often include deliberate attacks against hospitals and threats against doctors and nurses. The blockage of timely delivery of humanitarian assistance is also common, with an estimated 80 million children being denied humanitarian assistance. Although the complex effects of war on children's health are still poorly documented, estimates indicate that health and nutritional insecurity and decreased immunization among children are a common consequence of wars, with significant deleterious effects that are independent of the effects of poverty prior to war (Agadjanian & Prata, 2003).

Significantly compounding children's vulnerability, wars shatter family ties and extended social networks. In the last decade alone wars have displaced around 20 million children (UNICEF, 2009). In the course of displacement, large numbers of children are separated from their parents, often becoming lost when they flee from attacks or when their parents are imprisoned or recruited. In many cases, parents send their children off alone to seek safety or avoid recruitment; sometimes, they send their sons ahead of the family to find work or a place to live. As they flee, children are often compelled to walk for days with limited quantities of food and water, becoming undernourished and prone to illness or death; they often become victims of assault and exploitation. Millions of children end up lingering in refugee camps or displaced camps, likely longing, and perhaps also dreading, the possibility of repatriation to their violence-torn communities (UNICEF, 2009). Whether permanent or temporary, separation from parents, families, and communities leaves children unprotected, pervasively threatening their sense of safety and belonging. Arguably, this constitutes a most profound and life-altering disruption of the ecology of child development.

In some war contexts this disruption goes further and children's sense of identity is directly threatened, as when children are forcibly removed from their parents. Such was the infamous case of the Vietnam Babylift in the 1970s, when thousands of children were airlifted and given up for adoption in the United States and other countries, and more recently the 2007 kidnapping operation in Chad, that would forcibly remove hundreds of allegedly orphaned children in Darfur to be adopted in France and other European countries. In some contexts, such as during recent civil wars in many Latin American countries, repressive regimes resorted to separating children from their parents as a deliberate means for annihilating the future of those considered "subversive." For example, between 1976 and 1983, the Argentine government abducted and "disappeared" tens of thousands of civilians, many of them women of childbearing age. Hundreds of children born to these "disappeared" women in detention camps were given to military families and others associated with the regime. Those children became the "living disappeared" (Avery, 2004), and still today local and international human rights organizations continue searching for the (now adult) children, so they can be reunited with their surviving biological families (Rotabi, 2012).

Noteworthy also for its pernicious effects on child development is the practice, increasingly common in modern warfare, known as "child soldiering." According to recent estimates, 300,000 children, some as young as 7 or 8 year olds, are used as soldiers in armed conflicts around the world (UNICEF, 2009). Some of these youths are forcibly conscripted through abduction or threats of violence to themselves or their families, others are more subtly compelled by circumstances and join armed groups to escape poverty, to defend their communities, out of a feeling of revenge, or for some other reasons that makes the "choice" to enlist the lesser of the evils life presents them. Many start out in support functions such as porters, carrying heavy loads including ammunition or injured soldiers. Some act as lookouts, messengers, or cooks, and girls are often forced to serve as sexual slaves; many others take direct part in combat. Regardless of how children are recruited and of their roles, they are commonly exposed to, subjected to, and often forced to participate in abuse, killings, sexual violence, and other horrors (Wessells, 2006).

This grim cataloging makes it plain that war irrevocably alters the ecology of youth development, by posing severe physical dangers to children and their families, disrupting basic services and institutions, unsettling children's sense of predictability and security, and shattering the workings of interpersonal and social support systems. That such extreme and continued adversity would create profound and enduring distress in children (and adults) is not surprising. Thus, it is also unsurprising that psychological research has focused much of its efforts on identifying the nature of this distress.

3. ON WAR-EXPOSURE, AND THE PRIMACY OF PTSD AND EMOTIONAL DISTRESS

Apart from the approximately two million children who have been killed or died in wars in the last decades, the remaining close to one billion war-affected children evidently find ways to continue living. In truth, even harrowing experiences of violence, deprivation, displacement, abuse, and abandonment provide youth, on any single day, with some opportunities to make choices, solve problems, assume responsible roles, learn and use skills, deploy their adaptive and perhaps even creative capacities, make connections with others, and enjoy some measure of control over their lives. Another way to put this is to say that most war-affected children find ways to cope and adapt, even to learn, grow, and "get over it." What choice do they have?

But this enduring, this "getting over it," carries significant psychological costs. Understandably, given the fears and dangers implicated in war and violence, much of the psychological research has examined these costs in terms of trauma and psychopathology. Indeed, the lion's share of psychological research has been devoted to documenting the negative effects of war-exposure on children's psychological functioning, in particular, the many ways in which war contributes to subsequent emotional distress and, in some cases, longer-term psychopathology. It is now well established that children exposed to war are vulnerable to increased rates of PTSD, depression, anxiety, and externalizing behavior (Betancourt & Khan, 2008). More recently, considerable efforts have been devoted to understanding the unique mental health outcomes for youth conscripted into armed combat (Betancourt et al., 2010; Kerig & Wainryb, 2014), who are traumatized in ways that are complex and pervasive and that cast a shadow not only over their own adult lives but over those of their children.

This research also suggests, however, that emotional distress and PTSD symptoms are not distributed homogeneously among youth exposed to war, though conclusions regarding the magnitude of traumatization vary. In some estimates (Barenbaum, Ruchkin, & Schwab-Stone, 2004) the prevalence of symptoms ranges from 20% to 30% (among Israeli children after scud missile attacks and Lebanese children exposed to shelling), to 50% (among Cambodian refugee children and Central American refugee children), to up to 70–95% (among Kuwaiti children and children displaced during the Bosnian war). Among former child soldiers, too, there is significant variation in the prevalence of PTSD (Derluyn, Broekaert, Schuyten, & De Temmerman, 2004), with some studies reporting rates below 30% and others reporting rates of over 90%. Similarly, reports on the duration of symptoms also vary, with some studies indicating that symptoms are fleeting and others enduring, including some documenting significant levels of psychological dysfunction over 10 years (Barenbaum et al., 2004). This variability in the emotional effects of war-exposure has been explained in terms of the particularity of young people's circumstances, including demographic moderators such as social class or ethnicity, differences in the type and degree of exposure, the continuity of disruption, and the broad psychosocial milieu both during and after the conflict. The child's age at the time of war-exposure is also thought to explain diversity in symptoms; although most place the greatest vulnerability among children between 5 and 9 years (Kuterovac-Jagodic, 2003), ongoing work suggests that infancy (Feldman & Vengrober, 2011) and adolescence (Hammack, 2011; Wainryb & Recchia, 2015) also present distinct and significant challenges for coping with war-exposure.

Starting in World War II, psychologists (Freud & Burlingham, 1943) speculated that the presence of supportive parents could moderate the psychological impact of war trauma. Contemporary and more systematic research (Betancourt & Khan, 2008) has supported these early conclusions and provided abundant evidence of the integral role of parents, as well as peers and communities, for long-term mental health outcomes in war-exposed youths. Nevertheless, this support is too often compromised in wartime, not only because parents die and communities become shattered or displaced, but because even when parents and other adults are physically present, their capacities to provide nurturing and protection are often imperiled and, also, because youths' capacities to benefit from available support are diminished.

In fact, research has shown that whereas parents and other family members can moderate war-related hardship, they can also hinder children's adjustment when the adults themselves manage stress poorly. For example, studies have shown that the mother's level of PTSD symptoms was a significant predictor of PTSD symptoms in her children (Betancourt & Khan, 2008; Feldman & Vengrober, 2011). Research has furthermore shown that in contexts of war, family conflict and difficulties in partner relationships become exacerbated, contributing to dysfunctional interactions in the family ecology and harsh and punitive parenting practices, all of which in turn decrease the level of parental support and increase the rate of maltreatment

(Palosaari, Punamäki, Qouta, & Diab, 2013). At the conclusion of a two-generation study involving several hundreds of children and their parents from 7 war-affected communities in Northern Uganda, researchers (Saile, Ertl, Neuner, & Catani, 2014) remarked that whereas war-orphaned children were at an increased risk to experience deprivation and neglect, children whose parents were alive were at a higher risk for family violence. Importantly, family violence emerged as a significant predictor of poor child mental health even for children exposed to severe war violence.

A different challenge to the extent to which youth derive benefits from parents and other close relationships comes from the youth themselves; sadly, exposure to chronic violence can have devastating effects on youths' capacity to benefit from available support systems. For example, recent research (Borisova, Betancourt, & Willett, 2013) emphasized the family's critical role in the reintegration of former child soldiers and underscored specifically the positive impact that parental awareness about the most extreme forms of violence experienced and perpetrated by their children had for supporting these youths' recovery from trauma. Disturbingly, however, the majority of parents significantly underestimated the atrocities their children had been forced to perpetrate—an experience uniquely associated with debilitating traumatic impact (Betancourt et al., 2010; Wainryb, 2011). Although the relative paucity of parental knowledge may reflect parents' lack of interest or resistance to asking, this phenomenon is better understood as a function of youths' lack of disclosure. This would be unsurprising given that ongoing work (MacNair, 2002; Wainryb, 2011) suggests that the perpetration of harm against others might contribute to a specific set of posttraumatic reactions that interfere with seeking and accepting support from others, such as shame, self-condemnation, and alienation.

Similarly, the relationships and experiences afforded by more distal settings, such as educational and work-training programs, are also thought to be implicated in the mental health and adjustment of war-affected youth by creating a context of safety and normalcy and providing children with a sense of purpose and self-sufficiency (Betancourt & Khan, 2008). Therefore, the provision of emergency education programming is typically given priority in postconflict and displacement contexts. And yet, NGO providers often lament the low attendance of war-exposed youth in education and employment programs. This seeming squandering of opportunities may reflect the mental health and emotional consequences of war-exposure, including concentration problems, flashbacks, and a disruption of the self-regulatory and executive function capacities necessary for healthy functioning, as well as a foreshortened sense of future (Betancourt & Khan, 2008).

In sum, the lingering traumatic effects of war are well documented and should not be underestimated or minimized. Even if some children do not experience emotional distress, and despite what appears to be a continuous decrease in symptom severity over time, the proportion of children who do develop psychopathology is significant (Barenbaum et al., 2004; Betancourt & Khan, 2008). Furthermore, it has been well established that the psychological effects of trauma can emerge as "sleeper effects" years after exposure and that exposure to trauma increases the risks for vulnerability in the future. Untreated problems are likely to negatively affect the quality of youths' interpersonal relationships concurrently and in the future and also how these youths, years later, will fare as parents (Betancourt, 2015).

Psychologists' preoccupation with youths' traumatic responses is understandable given the overwhelming research evidence. Nevertheless, this focus has remained relatively narrow and has overlooked other important aspects of healthy personhood, thereby restricting our grasp of wars' effects on youths' development. Traumatic disorder is only one negative consequence of war-exposure; other consequences entail developmental disruptions that do not manifest themselves in an overt clinical fashion. One potentially serious problem involves disruptions in the development of moral capacities (Wainryb, 2011; Wainryb & Pasupathi, 2010). These effects are much less well understood; to these issues we turn in the next section.

4. ON WAR-EXPOSURE, AND THE DISRUPTION OF THE DEVELOPMENT OF MORAL CAPACITIES

Our analyses of the implications of war-exposure for the development of moral capacities are consistent with a relatively new trend in research—one that acknowledges that children are not just victims or passive recipients of war-related experiences, but active and engaged participants, predisposed to make sense of their experiences and to adapt to the circumstances that befall them (Hammack, 2011; Wainryb & Kerig, 2013; Wessells, 2006). Because of this, researchers now recognize the importance of examining not only how youth are affected by violence but also the meanings they construct about their war-related experiences. And yet, there has been a tendency in the research literature toward viewing meaning-making capacities as promoting coping and resilience. We argue that moving away from viewing youth as merely victims of war and acknowledging their sense of agency does not suggest inherently positive developmental pathways. Indeed, while the capacity for meaning-making might create resilience, it might also give rise to risks—risks that go beyond emotional distress and encompass youth's sense of their own and others' moral capacities (Wainryb, 2011; Wainryb & Pasupathi, 2010; Wainryb & Recchia, 2015).

But why would youth's capacity for meaning-making give rise to long-term risks? In what follows, we aim to show that the process of grappling with the meanings of their own and others' actions in the context of war is fraught for reasons that have been foreshadowed in this chapter. The sorts of extreme harms and atrocities that war-exposed children experience as victims and as perpetrators—killings, murder, torture, displacement, abductions—can challenge their basic faith in themselves and others as moral agents. War teaches youth that the body can easily be maimed, that relationships are as vulnerable as the body, and that adults, in spite of their authority and love, cannot protect children from harm. War also proves that anything is possible when it comes to violence; almost any form of violence that can be imagined, can be committed (Garbarino, 2008). Furthermore, parents and other adults are often absent or overwhelmed and unavailable for listening to children and scaffolding the process of meaning-making and, at the more collective level, polarized war rhetoric offers very little in the form of societal containment. And finally, exposure to violence tends to provoke the sort of hyperarousal that encourages numbing or avoidance rather than meaning-making and agency construction.

Unsurprisingly, therefore, the process of coping with and making sense of their own and others' actions during war may have pathogenic side effects; children may be forced into ways of making sense of morally laden events, and ways of thinking about themselves and others as moral agents and about justice in general, that are less than optimal—for the child, and for society. In what follows we rely on children's own accounts of war-events, drawn from our own research and from research conducted by others. We examine their stories for how they make sense of their experiences, and also for what they may not be saying about these experiences, as a means for illustrating four uniquely problematic forms of adaptation.

4.1 Constructing Polarized and Imbalanced Views of Right and Wrong

One of the most common ways in which war and political violence shape, and distort, youth's meaning-making about themselves and others and about justice, revolves around the construction of polarized "us-them" understandings.

People often view themselves and others as being at least in part meaningfully connected to, and defined by, their membership in groups, and rely on collective identities to make sense of some of their experiences. But in the context of war, and especially in the context of intractable historically grounded conflicts, collective identities that distinguish between groups in conflict (e.g., Palestinians and Israelis; Catholics and Protestants) become increasingly salient and self-defining (Bar-Tal, 2007). They also tend to become polarized, featuring idealized beliefs about the fairness of the in-group's goals and the goodness of its people along with delegitimizing beliefs about the unfairness of the out-group's goals and the callous or dishonest nature of its people. In turn, these polarized ways of thinking support a sense of cohesiveness and patriotism and offer a coherent framework for making sense of, and coping with, the challenges posed by continued violent conflict. To illustrate, consider the following two excerpts from interviews of Jewish-Israeli and Palestinian youth (Hammack, 2011, pp. 135–136 and 176–177, respectively):

> *I think the first thing, they should stop the terrorist attacks against us. The whole thing started because of the terrorist acts against us ... They actually started it. They fired first. They were the first to use suicide bombers. ... Of course, I think that I'm right—that my country's right. Everybody thinks that his country's right. Let's start from the first thing [Palestinian youth participating in the program] say, when they say, "I am from Palestine." I mean, there is no such country named Palestine. You can check the UN. There is no country written in the UN notebook called Palestine! There is such country called Israel. So he can say, "I'm a Palestinian from Israel." But when you say, "Hi, I'm from Palestine", "Jerusalem, Palestine" or something, it hurts the people that are from Israel and are from Jerusalem ... This is the problem: they don't have a country, and they feel like they have it. And they're speaking like there is no Israel!*
>
> *It's like we're supposed to fight for every inch of the country. It's ours, and they took it by force. We're gonna take it back by force, if we can. But we, we can't take it back by force! We don't have money. We're not allowed to have an army, weapons, nothing! This is why we use the freedom fighters ... I believe, if we're not gonna get our land back, we don't have to make peace. Everyone should fight until they die. ... And how come do they call the suicide bombers "terrorists" and not the Israeli government? They started all the violence! They invaded Palestine! It's like, we're just defending ourselves. What else can you do?! If your wife was raped and killed, your mother and father, your whole family was killed in front of you, and you were humiliated, your wife being raped in front of you, and your home destroyed, and you have no reason to live, and all the hate, and you have all the hate inside you, and all you could think of is revenge, right?!*

Both accounts illustrate how youth appropriate collective discourses to make sense of their own experiences and to articulate their own understandings about who "we" and "they" are as moral agents. The utter incompatibility of these viewpoints is palpable when both accounts are considered side by side; each highlights the validity and fairness of the in-group's positions, while contesting and delegitimizing the beliefs and actions of the out-group. To do so, each adolescent makes sense of the aggressive actions of his own group and those of the other group in relation to goals and beliefs that are consistent with the polarized ideologies reinforced by their respective communities. The Jewish-Israeli adolescent blames the conflict on the other group (*They actually started it. They fired first. They were the first to use suicide bombers*) and labels their actions as terrorist attacks; the Palestinian youth uses the same rhetoric to describe the Israelis' actions (*They started all the violence! They invaded Palestine!*) and turns the "terrorist" labels on them.

Previous research (Punamäki, 2009) has focused on the finding that when youth can rely on well-established ideological frameworks to make sense of war-events, they tend to experience less distress than do youth for whom such collective meanings are unavailable. This is precisely because, as evidenced in the two above accounts, polarized collective beliefs help youth make sense of the suffering they experience and provide a justification for the violence that they and their people perpetrate. Nevertheless, even while conferring a measure of psychological protection against war-related distress, the construction of a sense of moral agency and justice around polarized ideologically grounded beliefs may also constitute various forms of risk—both for individual development and for societies. Ideally, the construction of mature understandings of right and wrong and of people as moral agents involves the freedom and flexibility to explore a multiplicity of goals and self-views. But collective meaning-making frameworks, especially if entrenched, may make it difficult for war-exposed youth to realize that they and others are complex moral beings, with multiple and varying goals, including some that may differ from, or even be in conflict with, those of the collective. Therefore, grounding the construction of one's sense of agency and one's sense of justice solely on collective and polarized understandings may be too constraining and may interfere with the development of more flexible notions of self that are not so fundamentally bound up with the negatively interdependent collective identities (Wainryb & Recchia, 2015). In addition to these risks for individual development, the construction of polarized understandings of themselves and others and of justice also poses a societal risk inasmuch as such understandings tend to foster the continuation, and even exacerbation, of conflict and violence (Hammack, 2011; Punamäki, 2009).

It is also worth noting that the delegitimization of the out-group, or the "other," may at times be achieved in more subtle ways, not via an explicit representation of members of the out-group as unjustifiably aggressive, but via the erasure of their psychological presence or experience. Consider an example by an Enga adolescent from Papua New Guinea. The Enga are a horticultural population of some 300,000 people divided into 108 tribes. This tribal society has had a 350-year-long history of continuous and culturally sanctioned warfare, and view war as an acceptable solution to gain reparation or quell anger (Wiessner & Tumu, 1998). In this narrative excerpt (Wainryb & Pasupathi, 2010, p. 51), a 14-year-old boy describes engaging, together with his tribesmen, in harming another group after learning that a girl from their tribe had been raped by members of that group (the excerpt below was preceded by a detailed account of the rape, which is omitted here because it does not directly include any actions by the narrator):

> *[Male name] saw the girl bleeding and shouted to all of us clansmen. Me and some of my clansmen heard that and we took our bushknives and ran to the Akupa. We entered the dancing ground and checked to see if any of the rapists' clansmen where there. There were lots and lots of people there but none of the rapists' clansmen were there. We were very frustrated and we burned all their mess houses, like tea-houses and flour-houses. ... Then we went to another place in search of men to kill, but we couldn't find any. So we left their village and we went back to our village. Early the next morning my clansmen called out from every corner; the clansmen and women gathered in the village. The clansmen talked about the rape and said that we would go and attack the rapists' clan. After the discussion, we went to [village-name] and fought. We didn't bring any guns, we brought spears and arrows. We destroyed their gardens and we chopped down their big trees. ... While we were destroying their places, they shot one of our clansmen with a spear. The war went on for about one week and we realized that we weren't winning so the elders stopped the war.*

Elsewhere, we have called attention to the stark imbalance in the extent to which some youth exposed to violence represent the psychological experiences of in-group and out-group members (Wainryb & Pasupathi, 2010). In the above account, this youth's actions and those of his tribesmen—their engaging in violence and their ending of the violence—were made comprehensible via references to their goals, understandings, and emotions; their actions were related to what they knew or believed; their decisions and feelings were also represented. In contrast, the "others" in this conflict—the many members of the other tribe—were not represented, individually or collectively, in ways that included any discernible psychological agency. It may be that this kind of imbalanced construction of a restricted moral universe, wherein only they and members of their own group are represented as moral agents whose actions are guided by goals, intentions, beliefs, and emotions functions in ways similar to the polarized construction illustrated earlier, that delegitimizes the "other." Each of these ways may serve to facilitate, encourage, and justify engaging in acts of collective violence and warfare. As underscored by all three accounts in this section, themes of revenge and retaliation often accompany collective constructions of moral agency, whether polarized or imbalanced. And the endorsement and legitimization of revenge and retaliation have emerged as a disruptive and disturbing developmental pathway in violence-torn countries (Posada & Wainryb, 2008)—a developmental pathway that poses unique challenges for intervention that are not yet fully understood (Recchia, Wainryb, & Posada, in preparation).

4.2 Essentializing Moral Agency

The construction of a sense of themselves and the world around collective categories, though pervasive, is by no means the only way in which war-exposed youth make sense of their experiences. In particular, youth who become directly involved in political conflict as combatants and, in this role, engage in brutal behaviors, such as killings, abductions, or torture, face unique challenges in their efforts to make sense of their own actions and in reconciling them with their understandings of themselves as moral people. As a result, many of these youth construct their own sense of moral agency as essentialized—a rigidified or frozen understanding of themselves, one for which change or redemption appear impossible or unlikely. Consider the following account by a 16-year-old former youth combatant in Colombia shortly after he left the armed group (Wainryb, 2011, p. 289):

> *So the day that I hurt a person was the day that they killed my cousins. We were fighting the Autodefensas Campesinas, and in the battle three of my cousins died. That day we captured—we killed 25 paracos [members of the paramilitary], we captured 10, and the comandante's order was to dismember them and to send the pieces to each of their families. And that day was when—from the rage of having seen my cousins killed by those same people we had caught—I was so enraged that I started out by removing the fingers off a person with a power-saw, I cut the fingers off both hands, then an arm, I cut off the arm all around until I got to the shoulders, then I started out with the feet, I removed everything until I cut off his head, I took off his tongue, and I cut off the eyes, and I sent it all to his mom. That day I will never forget and I always carry this burden. Being here I remember it and sometimes I feel like crying for having done this to a person. And a few days later I thought about it and said to myself—how will be my death, will it be like that or how?*

As is the case with many accounts of youth combatants' experiences, this account implies a sense of coercion. This boy recounts an event when he was ordered to engage in devastating harm against others; he could have plausibly organized the events in terms of "I was ordered to...," "I had no choice...." And yet, he depicts his own actions not in terms of the orders he was given, but in ways that underscore his own sense of agency. This boy is trying to grapple with what *he* did; his explanation of his behavior hinges on his overwhelming rage and his powerful desire for revenge at the death of his cousins.

Unlike the collective type of explanations discussed in the previous section, essentialized constructions of one's moral agency provide little self-protection: this boy is facing his own anger and his capacity for wrongdoing. Moreover, he seems unable to bracket his wrongdoing within a given time or context, so that its negative effects are contained and the potential for a future, more positive, sense of self is ushered in. On the contrary, he appears to be haunted by his actions, in such a way that the consequences and implications of his actions for the sense of who he is and who he can be are inescapable. In his way of making sense of things, his experience of wrongdoing has a pervasive and enduring negative causal meaning in relation to his future self. Indeed, he projects himself into an unbearable and inescapable future (Wainryb, 2011; see also Lilgendahl, McLean, & Mansfield, 2013).

Research has shown that accounts that construct a sense of agency that is rigidified or frozen, or shackled to past events, may be maladaptive in the long term because such accounts, if sustained unchanged over a long time, tend to perpetuate the grip of unresolved events, meanings, and emotions, and limit growth and well-being (Pals, 2006). The profound shame and self-condemnation likely to surround this type of essentialized construction of moral agency may also become deeply problematic because they may lead to withdrawal, thereby decreasing the chances for corrective and reparative experiences (Litz et al., 2009). This in turn may put youth at risk of hopelessness, depression, or suicide. As a girl who had fought with Sierra Leone's Revolutionary United Front (RUF) confides (Denov, 2010, p. 187):

> *I feel depressed most of the time. I sometimes feel there is no hope for me because of the horrible things I have done. I just think of ending my life.*

This type of feeling is not uncommon. Understandably, too, youth making sense of their experiences in this way may not be capable of benefitting from the reintegration activities offered by most DDR programs, which center on fostering education and work-related skills. Feeling worthless, hopeless, and irredeemably bad is unlikely to be conducive to taking advantage of such future-oriented opportunities. For some youth, these enduring negative views of themselves may be linked to the continuation of violence and delinquent behavior in the postwar period, inasmuch as these self-views may not promote a motivation and commitment to make better, more moral, choices in the future (Wainryb, 2011). For others, these essentialized views of themselves usher in a powerful drive for redemption. Such is the story of Aki Ra, who as a young child was first forced to participate in the Khmer Rouge regime, where he was taught to shoot a gun and plant landmines, and later captured by the Cambodian army and the Vietnamese, who forced him to plant explosives on their behalf against the Khmer Rouge. Years later, when peace was restored to Cambodia, Aki Ra, by then a young man, set off as a lone deminer, clearing some 50,000 mines and unexploded ordnance over 20 years with a knife and a stick, without any protective gear or specialized equipment. As he explains in the award-winning documentary "A Perfect Soldier" made about his life (Lacocque, Bergreen, Fitoussi, & Severson, 2010,

> *When I was 10 years old, I detonated bombs to kill people. … From the age of 4 or 5 and all through my childhood I saw people stepping on mines and dying all the time. […] I was around 10 years old when I got to shoot people. We destroyed houses, older people were injured or killed. None of those who died were soldiers. … We were ordered to kill. If we didn't follow our orders, we could be killed. War is like that. During war we carried away the injured, and in the morning we found out if they were alive or not. It was normal. But I still remember their faces, I remember them a lot. […] I planted landmines that injured or killed many things, now I try to remove the landmines that I and others planted. … Today I clear mines to make up for what I did in the past.*

Aki Ra has since been featured on *National Geographic* and honored with the CNN Heroes award (Ruffins, 2010). Future research might help us understand what drives some of these youth into an antisocial pathway while others go on to seek redemption by putting their lives in mortal danger on a daily basis. We may never be able to tell, however, to what extent Aki Ra, and others like him, are driven to risk their lives in an effort to atone for the evils they committed or to subdue—or perhaps surrender to—the obdurate sense of their own evil. Nevertheless, and despite the fact that in his redemptive quest Aki Ra has surely saved thousands of limbs and lives, we are quite confident that his pathway reflects a vast distortion and narrowing of a young person's developmental pathway. Indeed, this way of making sense of war-experiences constricts some young people's choices and pleasures, cementing their lives firmly in their past experiences, perpetually shadowed by what came before.

It is worth noting that youth do not always link their actions as combatants to profoundly negative views of themselves. In many cases, in grappling with their war-experiences youth appear to derive from their actions a sense of competence and prestige. And yet, inasmuch as their sense of who they are becomes wholly organized around their war-related roles, in the post-conflict period, these self-views, even when positive, may interfere with the development of alternative, more future-oriented, self-conceptions. Consider, as examples, the following two accounts. The first was given by a 19-year-old girl who had been abducted at age 12 by the Lord's Resistance Army (LRA) in northern Uganda and spent more than 3 years in the bush; in a country that is traditionally patriarchal, many abducted girls attained an elevated social status within the LRA by becoming a commander's "wife," but many earned respect through skill and bravery on the battlefield (Ellison, 2012). The second account was produced by a 15-year-old boy in Uganda (Wessells, 2006, p. 174).

> *Chapu was the name of a great group of fighters in the LRA which the government's army feared very much. Because I was a great fighter, I was made to join Chapu. ... Now I am slowly getting used to this new life [in the reintegration center], but whenever I encounter difficulties here I get depressed. I sometimes feel that it would be good if I was in the bush still because at least there I had power and access to whatever I wanted. ... In the bush, you can get what you want from people because you have a gun, but here I do not have a gun. In the bush, we were free to do anything we want without much control. You could ambush vehicles, you could loot.*
>
> *They [the rebels] took me from my village and made me carry heavy loads like the other children. I was big and a good fighter ... I was promoted to commander and had my own unit. The enemy came, and we fought ... fought hard. There were lots of deaths and wounded people. In one battle, the UPDF [government army] ... captured me and three other boys and ... took us to a rehabilitation center in Gulu. I learned to make some things [carpentry] but wanted to go to school ... I went to school for some days but do not go there now. The children, they call me "rebel" ... My teacher could not understand and wanted me to obey him. How could I obey him? He has not been in combat and does not know what it is like to be a commander and decide for life and death ... Now I have no job and I'm on the street.*

As these accounts illustrate, the positive self-views these youths were able to construct based on their war-experiences did not serve them well once the war ended. These problems are also compounded by the fact that many war-exposed youth and the majority of youth combatants have not had the chance to develop the skills needed for adapting in the post-war period; for some of them, as seems to be the case with the boy in the preceding account, even when given access to educational and work-training resources that could allow them to construct alternative lives, their war-shackled self-understandings prevent them from taking advantage of the opportunities afforded them.

As mentioned earlier, research examining meaning-making of war-exposed youth has focused largely on youth who rely on collective ideologies to make sense of war-events and compared them to youth who cannot avail themselves of such collective frameworks for making sense of their experiences. In this section we have shown that youth also construct meanings about their war-experiences in ways that elude collective categories while nevertheless shackling them to their actions and roles in the armed conflict. Often, these rigid understandings are very negative; whether they usher in antisocial pathways or pathways of redemption-seeking and tortured heroism, they are typically linked to overwhelming distress and stunted or disrupted growth. But even when these essentialized self-views are positive, they bind youth to their war-experiences, thwarting their capacity to develop alternative self-conceptions, adapt to civil society, and pursue rich and more varied moral lives.

In the following sections, we describe two distinct ways in which youth may neglect to draw meaning from their war-experiences: while some engage in numbing strategies that disrupt their ability to draw self-relevant meanings from their experiences, others actively search for meaning in their experiences but fail to find it. Although the first strategy buffers distress symptoms in the short term, each of these patterns is linked to problematic developmental outcomes in the longer term.

4.3 Numbing Moral Agency

Numbing and avoidance are common psychological responses in the immediate aftermath of trauma and prevalent among youth exposed to high levels of political violence (Jones, 2002), perhaps especially youth combatants who have themselves perpetrated violence against others (Wainryb, 2011), permeating the ways in which youth account for their war-experiences. Consider, as examples, the following two accounts, one told by a 14-year-old Somali boy who describes having participated in various war-related activities (Human Rights Watch, 2012, p. 29), and the second by a 14-year-old Colombian girl, a recently demobilized youth combatant, who was asked to describe an incident when her actions harmed another person (Wainryb, 2011, p. 284).

> *I was given two jobs, to whip women and to punish boys who had music on their mobile phones. I would make them swallow the memory card. I made 20 youth swallow the cards and I must have whipped 50 women. I would go with older men backing me up. They were about 30 years old and there were five of them.*
>
> *Well, that time, we were in—well, there were some young guerrilleros, maybe they were running away, and they got caught near Bolivar. And so my comandante got a hold of one of these guerrilleros and he took him, and he did—he extracted lots of information out of him, and then he tied him up like this, tied his feet up with a rope, a polyester rope, and then he tortured him. He cut off his fingers really really fast, and he destroyed his hands, and he—he did hundreds of things to him. AND YOU …? I was there, I was the one who gave the comandante the knives, I sharpened the knives and handed them over to him. IS THERE ANYTHING ELSE THAT YOU REMEMBER ABOUT THAT TIME? That's what we did over there, that's how we participated.*

In contrast to narrators who construct their war-experiences in polarized, imbalanced, or essentialized terms, the two narrators above fail to articulate any sense in which their actions arise from their own psychological experience. Indeed, the most striking characteristic of these accounts is what they do *not* include: these accounts are devoid of references to goals, thoughts, or emotions. The Somali boy depicts a harrowing experience by referencing solely who did what, where, and when; he does not describe why he thought he was ordered to whip women or to punish boys for having music; he does not describe why he obeyed, or how he felt about doing so. He also does not tell us what he felt or thought about it in the aftermath, or whether he would have liked to have done anything differently. Similarly, the Colombian girl conveys a fairly detailed sense of what happened, down to the type of rope they used, but references to her thoughts or feelings during the events or in their aftermath are wholly absent. In fact, although the above account represents this girl's recollection of an event when she had hurt another person, she did not include herself in the story until the interviewer directly asked her, "*And you …?*"

These narrators' conspicuous numbing of their agency is reminiscent of findings from research indicating that the capacities to think, organize, and integrate experience often collapse in the face of threat or trauma and, in their stead, dissociative mechanisms, including numbing, become activated (Fonagy, 2003). In general, numbing is thought to be uniquely protective and adaptive in the short term (Jones, 2002; Punamäki, 2009), while traumatic events are taking place or shortly thereafter. Under such extreme circumstances, youth's capacities to grapple with traumatic experiences, and with the meanings and implications of their own and others' actions, are severely compromised; numbing helps them to blunt or evade those meanings and implications and minimize distress (Rousseau & Measham, 2007). In the longer term, however, numbing is linked to problematic developmental consequences when these strategies persist over time, manifest themselves in extreme ways (e.g., dissociation), or become generalized into an overall interpersonal style. Indeed, when such tendencies effect the blunting of normative emotional responses to events, they are likely to result in acquired (or "secondary") psychopathic characteristics, lack of empathy or remorse, or a blunted interpersonal style that contributes to antisocial behavior (Kerig, Bennett, Thompson, & Becker, 2012; Punamäki, 2009). But even when these patterns of psychological and emotional numbing are circumscribed to youths' understandings of their war-related experiences, they may nevertheless interfere in significant ways with youths' abilities to reconcile such events with their broader understandings of themselves, and thus thwart recovery. In these respects, such disruptions of a process fundamental to meaning-making may partially explain why emotional and psychological numbing are ultimately linked to dysregulated, aggressive behavior, and poor psychosocial adjustment (Fonagy, 2003; Wainryb, Komolova, & Florsheim, 2010).

The relation between numbing and moral thinking is not yet fully understood. It is not yet clear whether numbing of agency reflects a relatively passive blunting of psychological experience or a more active attempt to avoid exploring the psychological implications of experiences. Nevertheless, given that numbing does not permit narrators to reconcile their own violent actions with their moral beliefs, it is plausible that if maintained over the long term, this way of constructing a sense of their own moral agency might result in youths developing a view of the world in which they cease to notice the ways in which their own actions, and perhaps also other people's actions, have moral relevance (Posada & Wainryb, 2008; Wainryb et al., 2010).

4.4 Searching for, but Failing to Find, Meaning in War

The stories and findings described in previous sections suggest that, for many youth, exposure to war-related violence results in polarized, imbalanced, or essentialized forms of meaning-making, or in the numbing of meaning—all due to the ways in which violence distorts or interferes with the processes underlying the narrative construction of meaning. In many cases, however, youth attempt to make sense of their war-related experiences but fail to find or create sensible or intelligible meanings. As Bonanno (2011, p. 12) argued, "The sobering fact is that there are limits to human endurance. When adversity is relentless, when we are confronted with repeated casualties, repeated emergencies, endless streams of bad news, our ability to respond does begin to break down." And yet, to call this a breakdown or failure may be a misnomer: by definition, traumatic events are those that shake the foundations of people's belief systems about themselves and the world. Senselessness and absurdity are thus at the core of traumatic experiences, and the recognition of this fact—that no sensible or intelligible meaning can be made of such events—may be necessary for recovery (Rousseau & Measham, 2007). Consider the following two accounts, one by a young woman who retells an experience she had 5 years earlier, when she was 16 years old, in a forest in Sierra Leone (Human Rights Watch, 2003, pp. 28–29); the second by a Bosnian teenager describing his recollection of the beginning of the war (Weine, Klebic, Celik, & Bicic, 2009, pp. 272–273):

> *I was hiding in the bush with my parents and two older women when the RUF found our hiding place. I was the only young woman and the RUF accused me of having an SLA husband. I was still a virgin. I had only just started my periods … There were ten rebels, including four child soldiers armed with two RPGs and AK-47s. The rebels wore ski masks so only their eyes were visible. They said that they wanted to take me away. My mother pleaded with them, saying that I was her only child. The rebels said that 'If we don't take your daughter, we will rape or kill her.' The rebels ordered my parents and the two other women to move away. Then they told me to undress. I was raped by the ten rebels, one after the other. They lined up, waiting for their turn and watched while I was being raped vaginally and in my anus. One was about 12 years old, the three other about 15. They threatened to kill me if I cried. My parents, who could hear what was happening, cried but could do nothing to protect me. I was bleeding a lot from my vagina and anus and was in so much pain. My mother washed me in warm water and salt but I bled for three days. I can no longer control my bladder or bowels as I was torn below. … Before I got a catheter in 2001 I had no friends, I smelled too bad. I am still in pain, I also have nightmares.*

> *When the war started we were too young to understand what was going on and why, but not too young to feel pain, to be scared and hopeless. Maybe we were not too young to understand but we did not have anyone to teach us more about our neighbors, about history, about who we are. My Serbian classmates, kids that I grew up with, were carrying weapons. In one day they became complete strangers. In some ways I became a stranger to myself, too. My life and the lives of my family members were in danger because of our names and religion. I never knew those things mattered, which means that I did not know many things about myself, too.*

It is hard to imagine how a 16 year old, or anyone, might make sense of the experience of being gang-raped, her body savagely mutilated, while her parents are watching but unable to protect her. Evidence is beginning to accumulate that some forms of meaning-making of traumatic experiences, especially those that are overly positive or redemptive, may be maladaptive (Bonanno, 2013; Lilgendahl et al., 2013). Indeed, at least under some circumstances, "it may be more adaptive to simply move forward and assume one can change the future rather than to try to make sense of a past that may simply be senseless" (Sales, Merrill, & Fivush, 2013, p. 106). Yet, having a constant reminder of past horrors may make it impossible, or exceptionally difficult, to simply move forward. How does a young girl unlearn that her body (and by extension, everyone's body) can be savaged? What is she to do with the knowledge that people—that other *children*—are capable of torture; that despite their power and love, parents cannot necessarily keep their children safe; that any form of violence that can be imagined can be committed? Although grasping the fundamental senselessness of some experiences may be the most adaptive way for youth to begin moving forward, it may also be unfeasible to leave such gruesome experiences squarely in the past, particularly when consequences linger.

The second account is representative of the type of failure in meaning-making reported to be prevalent among Bosnian and Serbian youth (Jones, 2002). In comparison to, for example, Israeli-Jewish and Palestinian youth, who could rely on a coherent historical and ideological discourse to make meaning of their war-experiences, Bosnian and Serbian youth felt alienated from politics, had few opportunities for meaningful participation in the conflict, and often expressed a sense of bewilderment and powerlessness in the face of the violent events that disrupted their lives. Unsurprisingly, therefore, when these youth tried to come to grips with their war-experiences and interrogated the implications of these experiences for themselves and their worlds, they reached few adequate answers.

Whereas acknowledging, and ultimately coming to terms with, the senselessness of some events may constitute a necessary first step away from the grips of trauma, the realization that some experiences are meaningless or inexplicable is also likely to carry additional consequences. Research has shown that youth who fail to construct meanings out of their war-experiences are at particular risk for experiencing lower well-being and higher distress (Jones, 2002). Each of the above accounts conveys a palpable sense of distress—one that may be, at least in part, accounted for by the fact that these youth experience the violent events they depict not only as disturbing and terrifying, but as ultimately inconsistent with the ways in which they have previously understood themselves and the world. In addition, if the world is experienced as senseless, youth may feel ambivalent about making future moral commitments; their trust in others—and perhaps in themselves—is fundamentally compromised. This may be especially acute when the sense of unintelligibility, unpredictability, and powerlessness arise, as is sometimes the case, not in relation to the experience of having been victimized, but in relation to the experience of having victimized others. Indeed, many former child soldiers exhibit such a sense of their own constrained and helpless agency. Consider the following account by a 15-year-old girl, about her experience as a former combatant in one of the Colombian armed groups (Wainryb, 2011).

> *One night they sent me and Renato, and the mission was—I had never killed anybody, never, and so the comandante said "Your mission is to kill these people who've been collaborating with the military." And I um I thought—kill them? I didn't even know what to do because y'know I had never even seen a dead person. And so, we walked like two days, we walked, we walked, we walked. When we got to that place—there were four people, three men and one woman. That woman, she had kids of all sizes, like this and like this and like this [shows different heights]. And it was raining, like pouring rain, pouring. And we get to their house and Renato asked to see their IDs. And we told them to come with us to the river … And then Renato said to me "You stay there with this woman". And I said ok because I was in a panic, I felt like a panic, here, my heart was beating so loud. And then, it was like an hour, and suddenly I hear the first shots, and I—my nerves, I was—I felt, I was so scared, so so so so scared, and the shots—I saw that one of the guys had escaped and he was running. And the woman she says to me "Why is he running?" And I shot her. Right here (points to her ear). Because obviously she was gonna run away too, and so I shot her here (points again). I don't know, I took the gun and I shot her and I didn't think, I mean, I didn't think, I forgot everything, everything, and I shot her, and I killed her right away, and there was no way back. I—I almost died. I was—I was—I left her there, dead. And Renato comes back and he asks about the woman. And I said, I—she's dead. And I started crying, I cried, I touched her blood like this, like I—I—I felt such remorse, such regret suddenly, I wanted to kill myself. To have taken her life, and she had all these kids, so many kids. Who will make sure they study, I started thinking, who? All these thoughts suddenly came to my mind, who will watch the kids? And I still think of her, I see her image when I shower, I can never wash my hair, I can't stand under the shower because her image comes to me, it always comes when I'm in the shower.*

This account is not numb; this girl richly describes her confused feelings and thoughts. Yet, in so doing, she constructs a sense of her own agency in this event as severely constrained. At first, the constraint appears to be external: she was ordered to find and kill these people. But the core of her account pivots on her sense of being out of control: she is confused, uncertain, terrified. The sudden act of shooting this woman—the four words, *And I shot her*—constitutes a startling, unexpected, and shocking turn of events. And, importantly, it appears as though it is not just us, the readers, who are shocked and bewildered. The narrator seems to have profoundly stunned herself: *I don't know, I took the gun and I shot her and I didn't think, I mean, I didn't think, I forgot everything, everything.* This story is remarkably troubling, when compared to the other examples discussed in this section, precisely because the sense of incoherence, incomprehensibility, and helplessness arises vis-à-vis the narrator's own actions: it is her own actions, rather than those of others, that she does not foresee, control, or understand. In spite of the poignant sense of self-loathing at the closing of the event and in its aftermath, an essentialized construction of her own agency is somewhat undermined by the lingering sense of powerlessness and diminished agency.

The sense of diminished agency and helplessness that grows from youths' failed attempts at making sense of their war-experiences has important developmental implications that are distinct from those described in relation to the avoidance of meaning-making. Whereas numbing and avoidance lead youth to not consider the implications of their experiences, the pattern described in the present section—one where youth *are* actively considering connections between their self-understandings and their war-experiences, but failing to make sense of them—may result in a sense of passive victimhood and weakened control. If youth develop a pervasive sense of themselves as victims of either the senseless aggressive actions of others or of uncontrollable circumstances, in the long term this interpretive style may result in an impoverished understanding of their own capacity for choice and action and, perhaps, in the selective blaming of others for conflicts or their consequences (Wainryb & Pasupathi, 2010; Wainryb & Recchia, 2015).

5. ON WAR-EXPOSURE, AND THE INTRACTABILITY OF PSYCHOLOGICAL INEQUITIES: CONCLUDING THOUGHTS

Regardless of youths' vast capacities for adaptation, war and violence are not optimal conditions for developing and thriving, and youths' potential for resilience—in spite of its immensely seductive appeal—does not undo the very real and grave horrors of war. In this chapter we have discussed the multiple, complex, and enduring inequities that war creates in children's and adolescents' broad ecology, resulting in widespread and pervasive imbalances in terms of their education, health, and safety. We have also discussed the ample and unequivocal evidence for the short-term and long-term consequences of war-exposure on child and adolescent mental health; these consequences, we argued, constitute a distinct source of additional inequities, as a considerable proportion of the world's youth population is severely traumatized, exhibiting persistent distress symptoms, disrupted interpersonal relationships, and functional impairment, and many more—and their own children, down the line—remain at increased risk for future vulnerability. And, finally, we turned to a much less understood set of inequities created by war—those involving disrupted moral capacities. In this respect, we have argued that war alters youths' moral development pathways in significant, and perhaps at times irrevocable, ways. As children and adolescents attempt to make sense of and come to grips with gruesome and disturbing war-experiences, and with their own actions and other people's actions in war-contexts, they are often forced into less than optimal ways of thinking and meaning-making about themselves and others as moral agents, and about justice and goodness in general. These suboptimal adaptations—at times protective and at times less so—in turn constrain the moral decisions these youth will likely be capable of in the future, including in postconflict settings where they are called on to participate in and contribute to civil society. As we have outlined in earlier sections, these ways of constructing moral agency may fuel into cycles of violence and revenge; may contribute to overwhelming and dysfunctional feelings of guilt and shame and to stunted growth, and curtail youths' potential to reimagine themselves as moral beings unshackled from their narrow war-bound self-views; may numb youths' awareness of the moral dimensions of life; or create a sense of meaninglessness and despair that thwarts their motivation to engage in the complexities of a moral life. And as these youths become adults living around the world, their ideas about themselves and others as having the potential to live a moral life, and their ideas about conflict and justice, revenge and forgiveness, become—or should become—meaningful for all of us who share a planet with them.

Immense and worthwhile efforts have been made by humanitarian agencies to address the psychosocial and emotional needs of war-affected youth. And given the grim statistics with which we opened this chapter concerning the extraordinary inequities affecting populations living in the midst of wars, much more still needs to be done to address their needs for health and nutrition, security, education and job-training, and mental health. The inequities created by war-exposure that pertain to the development of youth's moral capacities have remained comparatively understudied. The scarce attention given to these issues may in part be due to the fact that most research undertaken with war-affected youth has, realistically, had to accommodate competing and very pressing priorities, such as conducting concrete assessments of youth psychosocial needs or their PTSD levels, all of which could directly inform recovery efforts. In part, the dearth of knowledge about the moral capacities of war-exposed youth may also be due to the fact that the moral development community has been slow to adapt its conceptual and empirical tools to ascertain, not just how war-exposed youth reason about hypothetical moral scenarios, but how they make sense of their everyday experiences with war and violence in light of their moral concepts.

It may also be important to consider the possibility that the interest and investment in the disruption in the development of youths' moral capacities have been somewhat dampened or muted due to the perceived intractability and recalcitrance of these effects, and by the potential implications that such information may have for how war-affected youth are broadly perceived. Scholars in the field of human rights advocacy (Carpenter, 2010) have noted that advocacy agendas are often determined by not only the actual merit of humanitarian problems but coalitional politics of transnational networks. Thus, humanitarian agencies and human rights advocates often make strategic decisions about where to place resources and attention—decisions that are informed by the political context, their estimation of the probability of success, and other concerns shaped by the ways in which governments, the media, academia, and local players frame a problem. This type of strategic decision-making can work against or dull the articulation of a specific set of problems or issues, especially when such issues are perceived as threatening other issues on the advocacy agenda, or when advocates estimate that advocacy around certain issues might actually lead to worse outcomes for the population of concern. Therefore, what becomes a focus of concern and attention—what comes on the agenda—is often the result of a political negotiation, with certain issues coexisting on the agenda more easily than others. Humanitarian groups working with war-affected youth must understandably, and ethically, be concerned with not doing harm. In turn, the injunction to do no harm may be construed, in part, as involving the need to avoid or steer clear of stigmatizing war-affected youth or presenting them as so "damaged" that they are no longer palatable to funding agencies. In other words, the articulation of what these youths need—of what is "wrong" with them—becomes a function of, or becomes at least in part contingent on, what we think we can give them. The psychological sciences must remain alert, however, so that these understandable goals do not result in the overlooking of some forms of inequities created by war, or in the denial of long-term vulnerabilities of war-affected youth. Even when children are at the foreground of everyone's concern, the manner in which they are represented may mitigate against taking some of their needs and vulnerabilities seriously.

REFERENCES

Agadjanian, V., & Prata, N. (2003). Civil war and child health: Regional and ethnic dimensions of child immunization and malnutrition in Angola. *Social Science & Medicine, 56*, 2515–2527. http://dx.doi.org/10.1016/S0277-9536(02)00286-1.

Avery, L. (2004). A return to life: The right to identity and the right to identify Argentina's "living disappeared" *Harvard Women's Law Journal, 27*, 235–272.

Barenbaum, J., Ruchkin, V., & Schwab-Stone, M. (2004). The psychosocial aspects of children exposed to war. *Journal of Child Psychology & Psychiatry, 45*, 41–62. http://dx.doi.org/10.1046/j.0021-9630.2003.00304.x.

Bar-Tal, D. (2007). Sociopsychological foundations of intractable conflicts. *American Behavioral Scientist, 50*, 1430–1453. http://dx.doi.org/10.1177/0002764207302462.

Betancourt, T. (2015). The intergenerational effect of war. *JAMA Psychiatry, 72*, 199–200. http://dx.doi.org/10.1001/jamapsychiatry.2014.2669.

Betancourt, T., Borisova, I., Williams, T., Brennan, R., et al. (2010). Sierra Leone's former child soldiers: A follow-up study of psychosocial adjustment and community reintegration. *Child Development, 81*, 1077–1095. http://dx.doi.org/10.1111/j.1467-8624.2010.01455.x.

Betancourt, T., & Khan, K. (2008). The mental health of children affected by armed conflict: Protective processes and pathways to resilience. *International Review of Psychiatry, 20*, 317–328. http://dx.doi.org/10.1080/09540260802090363.

Bonanno, G. (2011). Japan: Too much trauma. *Newsweek*. Retrieved from, http://www.newsweek.com/japan-too-much-trauma-66545.

Bonanno, G. (2013). Meaning-making, adversity, and regulatory flexibility. *Memory, 21*, 150–156. http://dx.doi.org/10.1080/09658211.2012.745572.

Borisova, I., Betancourt, T., & Willett, J. (2013). Reintegration of former child soldiers in Sierra Leone: The role of caregivers and their awareness of the violence adolescents experienced during the war. *Journal of Aggression, Maltreatment & Trauma, 22*, 803–828. http://dx.doi.org/10.1080/10926771.2013.824059.

Carpenter, R. (2010). *Forgetting children born of war: Setting the human rights agenda in Bosnia and beyond*. New York: Columbia University Press.

Denov, M. (2010). *Child soldiers: Sierra Leone's Revolutionary United Front*. Cambridge: Cambridge University Press.

Derluyn, I., Broekaert, E., Schuyten, G., & De Temmerman, E. (2004). Post-traumatic stress in former Ugandan child soldiers. *Lancet, 363*(9412), 861–863.

Ellison, M. (2012). Female child soldiers with the Lord's Resistance Army struggle to return to normal. *Toronto Star*. Retrieved from, http://www.thestar.com/news/world/2012/05/19/female_child_soldiers_with_the_lords_resistance_army_struggle_to_return_to_normal.html.

Feldman, R., & Vengrober, A. (2011). Posttraumatic stress disorder in infants and young children exposed to war-related trauma. *Journal of the American Academy of Child & Adolescent Psychiatry, 50*, 645–658. http://dx.doi.org/10.1016/j.jaac.2011.03.001.

Fonagy, P. (2003). The developmental roots of violence in the failure of mentalization. In F. Pfäfflin (Ed.), *A matter of security: The application of attachment theory to forensic psychiatry and psychotherapy* (pp. 13–56). London: Kingsley.

Freud, A., & Burlingham, D. (1943). *War and children.* New York: Medical War Books.
Garbarino, J. (2008). *Children and the dark side of human experience: Confronting global realities and rethinking child development.* New York: Springer.
Hammack, P. (2011). *Narrative and the politics of identity: The cultural psychology of Israeli and Palestinian youth.* New York: Oxford University Press.
Human Rights Watch (2003). *"We'll kill you if you cry": Sexual violence in the Sierra Leone conflict.* Human Rights Watch. Retrieved from, https://www.hrw.org/sites/default/files/reports/sierleon0103.pdf.
Human Rights Watch (2012). *No place for children: Child recruitment, forced marriage, and attacks on schools in Somalia.* Human Rights Watch. Retrieved from, https://www.hrw.org/sites/default/files/reports/somalia0212ForUpload_0.pdf.
Jones, L. (2002). Adolescent understandings of political violence and psychological well-being: A qualitative study from Bosnia Herzegovina. *Social Science & Medicine, 55,* 1351–1371. http://dx.doi.org/10.1016/S0277-9536(01)00275-1.
Kerig, P. K., Bennett, D. C., Thompson, M., & Becker, S. P. (2012). "Nothing really matters": Emotional numbing as a link between trauma exposure and callousness in delinquent youth. *Journal of Traumatic Stress, 25,* 272–279.
Kerig, P., & Wainryb, C. (Eds.), (2014). *Trauma, psychopathology, and resilience among child soldiers around the world.* New York: Routledge.
Kuterovac-Jagodic, G. (2003). Posttraumatic stress symptoms in Croatian children exposed to war. *Journal of Clinical Psychology, 59,* 9–25.
Lacocque, J., Bergreen, B., Fitoussi, R. (Producers), & Severson, J. (Director). (2010). A perfect soldier [Motion picture]. Cinema Guild.
Lilgendahl, J., McLean, K., & Mansfield, C. (2013). When is meaning making unhealthy for the self? The roles of neuroticism, implicit theories, and memory telling in trauma and transgression memories. *Memory, 21,* 79–96. http://dx.doi.org/10.1080/09658211.2012.706615.
Litz, B., Stein, N., Delaney, E., Lebowitz, L., Nash, W., Silva, C., et al. (2009). Moral injury and moral repair in war veterans. *Clinical Psychology Review, 29,* 695–706. http://dx.doi.org/10.1016/j.cpr.2009.07.003.
MacNair, R. (2002). *Perpetration-induced traumatic stress: The psychological consequences of killing.* Westport, CT: Praeger.
McKay, S., Robinson, M., Gonsalves, M., & Worthen, M. (2006). *Girls formerly associated with fighting forces and their children: Returned and neglected.* London: Coalition to Stop the Use of Child Soldiers. Retrieved from, http://www.africafiles.org/article.asp?ID=11134.
Organization for Economic Cooperation and Development. (2014). *Fragile states 2014: Domestic revenue mobilization in fragile states.* Retrieved from, http://www.oecd.org/dac/governance-peace/conflictandfragilitybe/docs/FSR-2014.pdf.
Palosaari, E., Punamäki, R., Qouta, S., & Diab, M. (2013). Intergenerational effects of war trauma among Palestinian families mediated via psychological maltreatment. *Child Abuse & Neglect, 37,* 955–968. http://dx.doi.org/10.1016/j.chiabu.2013.04.006.
Pals, J. (2006). Constructing the 'springboard effect': Causal connections, self-making, and growth within the life story. In D. McAdams, R. Josselson, & A. Lieblich (Eds.), *Identity and story: Creating self in narrative* (pp. 175–199). Washington, DC: APA.
Posada, R., & Wainryb, C. (2008). Moral development in a violent society: Colombian children's judgments in the context of survival and revenge. *Child Development, 79,* 882–898. http://dx.doi.org/10.1111/j.1467-8624.2008.01165.x.
Punamäki, R. (2009). War, military violence, and aggressive development: Child, family, and social preconditions. In B. Barber (Ed.), *Adolescents and war* (pp. 62–80). New York: Oxford University Press.

Qobil, R. (2010). The sexually abused dancing boys of Afghanistan. BBC World Service, 7 Sept.; 'The Dancing Boys of Afghanistan', PBS FRONTLINE TV documentary, 20 April. http://www.bbc.com/news/world-south-asia-11217772.

Recchia, H., Wainryb, C., & Posada, R. (in preparation). Links between exposure to violence and youths' ideas about revenge. Concordia University.

Rotabi, K. (2012). Child adoption and war: 'Living disappeared' children and the social worker's post-conflict role in El Salvador and Argentina. *International Social Work*, *57*, 169–180. http://dx.doi.org/10.1177/0020872812454314.

Rousseau, C., & Measham, T. (2007). Posttraumatic suffering as a source of transformation: A clinical perspective. In L. Kirmayer, R. Lemelson, & M. Barad (Eds.), *Understanding trauma: Integrating biological, clinical, and cultural perspectives* (pp. 275–293). New York: Cambridge University Press.

Ruffins, E. (2010). Cambodian man clears land mines he set decades ago. *CNN*. Retrieved from, http://www.cnn.com/2010/WORLD/asiapcf/07/29/cnnheroes.cambodia.demining/index.html.

Saile, R., Ertl, V., Neuner, F., & Catani, C. (2014). Does war contribute to family violence against children? Findings from a two-generational multi-informant study in Northern Uganda. *Child Abuse & Neglect*, *38*, 135–146. http://dx.doi.org/10.1016/j.chiabu.2013.10.007.

Sales, J., Merrill, N., & Fivush, R. (2013). Does making meaning make it better? Narrative meaning-making and well-being in at-risk African-American adolescent females. *Memory*, *21*, 97–110. http://dx.doi.org/10.1080/09658211.2012.706614.

Save the Children. (2013). *Attacks on education: The impact of conflict and grave violations on children's futures.* Retrieved from, https://www.savethechildren.net/sites/default/files/Attacks%20on%20Education_0.pdf#overlay-context=.

UNICEF. (2009). *Machel study 10-year strategic review: Children and conflict in a changing world.* Retrieved from, http://www.unicef.org/publications/files/Machel_Study_10_Year_Strategic_Review_EN_030909.pdf.

United Nations Development Programme. (1990). *Human development report 1990.* New York: Oxford University Press.

United Nations Development Programme. (2005). *Human development report 2005: International cooperation at a crossroads.* Retrieved from, http://hdr.undp.org/sites/default/files/reports/266/hdr05_complete.pdf.

Wainryb, C. (2011). 'And so they ordered me to kill a person': Conceptualizing the impacts of child soldiering on the development of moral agency. *Human Development*, *54*, 273–300. http://dx.doi.org/10.1159/000331482.

Wainryb, C., & Kerig, P. (2013). The person and the social context: Future directions for research on the traumatic effects of child soldiering around the world. *Journal of Aggression, Maltreatment & Trauma*, *22*, 887–895. http://dx.doi.org/10.1080/10926771.2013.823592.

Wainryb, C., Komolova, M., & Florsheim, P. (2010). How violent youth offenders and typically developing adolescents construct moral agency in narratives about doing harm. In K. McLean & M. Pasupathi (Eds.), *Narrative development in adolescence: Creating the storied self* (pp. 185–206). New York: Springer.

Wainryb, C., & Pasupathi, M. (2010). Political violence and disruptions in the development of moral agency. *Child Development Perspectives*, *4*, 48–54. http://dx.doi.org/10.1111/j.1750-8606.2009.00117.x.

Wainryb, C., & Recchia, H. (2015). Youths' constructions of meanings about experiences with political conflict: Implications for processes of identity development. In K. McLean & M. Syed (Eds.), *The Oxford handbook of identity development* (pp. 369–386). New York: Oxford University Press.

Weine, S., Klebic, A., Celik, A., & Bicic, M. (2009). Tasting the world: Life after wartime for Bosnian teens in Chicago. In B. Barber (Ed.), *Adolescents and war* (pp. 255–280). New York: Oxford University Press.

Wessells, M. (2006). *Child soldiers: From violence to protection*. London: Harvard University Press.

Wiessner, P., & Tumu, A. (1998). *Historical vines: Enga networks of exchange, ritual, and warfare in Papua New Guinea*. Washington, DC: Smithsonian.

World Bank. (2006). *World development report 2006: Equity and development*. New York: Oxford University Press.

World Bank. (2011). *World development report 2011: Conflict, security, and development*. Retrieved from, http://siteresources.worldbank.org/INTWDRS/Resources/WDR2011_ Full_Text.pdf.

CHAPTER TEN

Global Equity and Justice Issues for Young People During the First Three Decades of Life

Anne Petersen*,†,1, Silvia H. Koller‡, Frosso Motti-Stefanidi§, Suman Verma¶

*CHGD, University of Michigan, Ann Arbor, MI, United States
†Global Philanthropy Alliance, St. Joseph, MI, United States
‡Instituto de Psicologia, Universidade Federal do Rio Grande do Sul, Porto Alegre, Brazil
§National and Kapodistrian University of Athens, Athens, Greece
¶Panjab University, Chandigarh, India
[1]Corresponding author: e-mail address: annepete@umich.edu

Contents

Abstract

This chapter takes a global perspective on equity and justice during development from childhood into adulthood. Globally, the population of young people is booming with the most rapid growth among young people in the poorest countries. While already faced with significant issues related to development and thriving, this population boom

Equity and Justice in Developmental Science: Implications for Young People, Families, and Communities (S.S. Horn, M.D. Ruck & L.S. Liben, Eds.)
Advances in Child Development and Behavior (J.B. Benson, Series Ed.), Vol. 51
ISSN 0065-2407 http://dx.doi.org/10.1016/bs.acdb.2016.05.006

also exacerbates equity and justice for these children. Given this urgent situation, this chapter builds from the large body of minority world research, as well as the emergent majority world research, to argue that in order to turn the youth bulge into a demographic dividend, researchers must utilize a positive development framing rather than the more dominant problem-focused framing in studying these issues. The structural challenges confronting young people growing up in contexts marked by poverty; weak systems and institutions, especially those serving education, health, and justice; weak political and governance systems; and continual conflict must also be addressed by global and national governmental bodies. This chapter will emphasize the strengths and opportunities of the majority world, highlighting some of the strong, emergent examples of programs that support and develop the strengths of young people. We conclude with a discussion of appropriate support required from the minority and majority worlds that would further strengthen young people globally and enable them to become leaders of a more just, equitable world.

1. INTRODUCTION

More than half the world's population is now under age 30 years (UNESCO, 2013). If these young people lived in a more equitable and just world, they would have a more promising future. Instead, we currently have a world in which violence, greed, and corruption are rampant, and in which demagogues prey on the fears of people. Those who are weaker always suffer more under these conditions. Globally, children are particularly at risk because they lack the necessary support and protection from families, communities, and nations to become healthy, contributing adults. Because of this, equity and justice for children globally has never been more important, as both a scholarly topic and as a focus for advocacy.

Children and youth represent the future of any nation and their development should be nurtured so that they can become productive and healthy citizens. While there is little global research on the extent to which children are valued, we can infer value from data on the risks to children through child maltreatment (Lansford, Deater-Deckard, Bornstein, Putnick, & Bradley, 2014; UNICEF, 2015d) and child mortality. Data from UNICEF (2015a) demonstrate that child mortality is strongly related to poverty. The World Health Organization (WHO) for the first time in 2009 provided youth mortality data and noted that, like child mortality, most causes of mortality (such as malnutrition, poor health care, and violence) are preventable. The World Economic Forum identified widening economic inequality as the second most important worldwide trend of global concern, related especially to level of education and access to improved water and sanitation services (Pan American Health Organization, 2013).

Data on the status of children and youth are difficult to find. Population projections place the world population at 10 billion people by 2050, with 2.4 billion under 17 years of age (UNICEF, 2015a). Population growth is not uniform, as the poorest countries are growing the fastest, especially African and South Asian countries (UNFPA, 2014). What is also clear is that the benefits of economic advance are unfairly distributed globally, with the rich getting richer and poor falling further behind. UNICEF (Diers, 2013), like many other global organizations (e.g., USAID, 2012; World Bank, 2015c), argues that the only way to change the current trajectory of increasing economic inequality is to capitalize on the youth bulge by engaging youth in finding solutions. Inspiring biographies and autobiographies of courageous young people who not only survive incredible challenges such as war and violence, but also go on to thrive support this point and also supplement the meager data that exists regarding young people globally. Much can be learned from biographies of young people such as the "lost boys" of Sudan (Baker, 2008; Loming & Tabb, 2012) as well as Malala Yousafzai (Yousafzai & Lamb, 2013), the girl who championed education in Pakistan and was recognized with a Nobel Prize.

This chapter focuses on global equity and justice for children and youth. While equity and justice issues exist in any single nation, whether in the minority or majority world, a global perspective is different because it takes into account forces that have transnational effects. Transnational effects such as the global marketplace, for example, affect young people across nations by providing job opportunities for youth anywhere. Similarly, we are learning in powerful and sometimes tragic ways that health can no longer be considered only from a national perspective; epidemics are transmitted globally at rapid speed, much faster than our health-care institutions are able to treat them. These two examples—jobs and health care—make it clear that the key issue globally is general infrastructure, and more specifically, infrastructure for economic activity and institutions for education, health care, and other essential aspects of life. All of these affect children profoundly, and they are more likely to be inadequate in poorer countries. For example, an epidemic or disaster in a higher income country may mean injury but seldom death, whereas, in a poor country, death rates, especially for children, are often high following similar events.

In discussing equity and justice in the global context we use the terms minority and majority worlds (World Bank, 2015a), terms that have replaced developed/developing or other more pejorative terms used to refer to regions of the world. Using the World Banks economic classification system, the minority world is the higher income world—less than 15% of the global population—and includes the United States and Canada (North America), most countries of Europe, South Korea, and Japan (Asia), with Australia, New Zealand, and Chile the only higher income countries in the global south. The majority world encompasses the remaining 85% of the global population.

In this chapter we identify the challenges to achieving equity and justice that confront children and youth globally. Although challenges exist in most of the minority world as well as the majority world, the lack of much research on these topics in the majority world (Verma & Petersen, 2015) has contributed to the neglect of some of the most important factors facing young people globally. We then discuss the opportunities for children and youth. Although poverty and conflict provide formidable challenges, opportunities for children and youth in countries facing these issues exist through the implementation of effective programs as well as through the increasing access to information through the internet. Finally, we provide examples of effective programs globally and regionally that help support strong beginnings for children and youth to achieve more equity and perhaps justice. We conclude the chapter with thoughts on additional efforts required to support children and youth so they can play significant roles in the future of their families, countries, and the world.

The chapter authors believe that it is appropriate to focus on children and youth, up to the age of attaining adult roles (which we have arbitrarily set at 30 years). While this choice is defensible developmentally, it complicates our use of data. Global data are generally missing on adolescence, and even data on children are complicated, with much health data focused on age 5 and under. The age of majority (based on legal definitions) varies from age 15 for a few countries to age 21 for many. So despite the many ways to define the category of young people, we focus on the first three decades of life.

2. SETTING THE CONTEXT

2.1 Rights of Children

Child rights have been addressed globally, through the Convention on the Rights of the Child (CRC, United Nations, Office of the High

Commissioner on Human Rights, 1989). The CRC was adopted in 1989 and is now ratified by 194 countries, including every member of the United Nations, except for Somalia and the United States. This special convention focuses particularly on the rights of people under the age of 18 years, and gives children the same basic human rights as adults. The rationale for the CRC is that unlike most adults, children need special care and protection because of their greater vulnerability due to size, strength, and generally incomplete developmental status. The CRC also responded to issues of child maltreatment and abuse through neglect, violence, or exploitation. Children were recognized, as being especially vulnerable to poor living conditions, such as poverty, inadequate health care, poor nutrition, unsafe water, poor housing, and environmental pollution. Disease, malnutrition, and poverty threaten the future of children and therefore the future of the societies in which they live.

According to the Convention, children have the right to survive and thrive, to learn and grow, to make their voices heard, and to reach their full potential. These rights imply that children have access (at a minimum) to: (a) food, clean water, and sanitation facilities; (b) primary health care; and (c) education. Furthermore, they have the right to be protected from all forms of child abuse, neglect, exploitation, and cruelty, including the right to special protection in times of war and protection from abuse in the criminal justice system. These rights need to be protected and promoted without discrimination of any kind, regardless of where in the world they live—the minority or the majority world, or who they are—independent of their gender, their parents' social status, race, ethnicity, religion, political affiliation, or any other status.

2.2 Child Justice

According to UNICEF (2013), millions of children worldwide are subjected to violence, abuse, and exploitation. This means that despite the CRC, children are not yet fully protected. In addition to the millions of children who have already become victims, millions more are at risk because they are not adequately protected against violence. Children with disabilities, those who live or work on the street, those in residential care or detention, and ethnic minorities are at elevated risk. Social service systems, which have flaws in the minority world, are nonexistent in many parts of the majority world. Juvenile justice systems, again often flawed in the minority world, fall far short of international standards in most of the majority world. For example, children arrested for petty offenses are often placed in "protective custody" by administrative bodies outside the justice system, with limited legal safeguards. While parental care is not always safe for children, it is typically better than the alternatives. Yet in Central/Eastern Europe, for example, 1.3 million children live in family substitute care, with half of these in residential care without much support or caring environments (UNICEF, 2013).

Goldson and Muncie (2012) argue that the existence of global agreements on child rights is the necessary precursor for child justice but there are important limitations currently. They note that despite the establishment of an international monitoring body that meets three times a year to comment on specific areas of child rights (e.g., education, HIV/AIDS) as well as to review signatory compliance with the CRC no formal sanctions for noncompliance exist. This makes the CRC both the most ratified as well as the most violated of all international human rights instruments, particularly with juvenile justice. Thus for both the minority and majority worlds, the inadequacy of both local systems of juvenile justice and shared principles of equity and justice more generally make implementation of global policy impossible. Further, globalization has made injustices to poor children—such as child trafficking—even easier. At the same time, Goldson and Muncie (2012) argue that the principles of the CRC could serve to protect children if we identified more effective ways to require compliance. Despite the lofty goals of the CRC, the lack of child justice just outlined represents the first of the challenges to equity and justice for children and youth globally.

3. GLOBAL CHALLENGES TO EQUITY AND JUSTICE FOR CHILDREN AND YOUTH

Children are developing organisms, and their adaptation and development emerge from interactions with their social contexts and broader environments (Lerner, 2006). Over the course of individual development, behavior and adaptation are influenced by past and current interactions between a child and other people as well as the supportive vs threatening conditions of their environment. Thus, children's experiences during development have far-reaching consequences on their adaptation and mental health well into adulthood (Cicchetti & Rogosch, 2002; Keating, 2016).

Societies and more proximal contexts (e.g., family, school, peers, neighborhood) that protect and support children's survival and positive development contribute to the development of healthier, better-adjusted, and productive adults, thus serving the interests of both individuals and society

(Masten, 2014a). However, there are significant and very large differences both between and within societies in the degree to which they provide experiences that promote positive development and well-being in children (Verma & Petersen, 2015).

In spite of some worldwide improvements in the situation of children, great inequities in child survival, development, and protection are still recorded across the world (Verma & Petersen, 2015). The world is failing to provide equally to all children the elements necessary for positive development and the protection from adverse and traumatic circumstances to which they are entitled. Societal attitudes, customs and practices, as well as inefficient or indifferent governments may explain the frequency of violations of children's rights. However, our failures to provide safe and good-enough environments for children's healthy development are expected to have deleterious consequences for their current and long-term functioning, adaptation, and psychological well-being, and likely contribute to the reproduction of disadvantage. For example, not obtaining an education may contribute to the continuation of the cycle of poverty and make young people vulnerable to preventable diseases such as HIV (UNICEF, 2015c).

Three primary factors represent key challenges to a just world and to equitable development for children: geographic location of residence, poverty, and gender (UNICEF, 2010). These factors are most important for the most basic needs such as birth registration, surviving the first few years of life, having access to primary health care, and attending school. These factors are often highly interconnected, creating disparities within disparities. For example, girls living in the majority world are more disadvantaged than boys in terms of access to education. The underlying causal factors of national (and sometimes local) leadership and governance, with their associated structures of education, health, and justice are also key systems affecting the lives of young people (Bronfenbrenner, 1979). Globalization is thought to have weakened all national and local systems (e.g., Banai, Ronzoni, & Schemmel, 2011), which adversely affects especially those who contribute little economically such as children and the elderly. Thus, geographical location both in terms of global region and residential location within a region should be considered indicators or "social addresses" for explaining living conditions and challenges to equitable development.

3.1 Geographic Location

The region of the world where the child lives is an important factor connected to disparities in equity and justice in child survival, development, and protection (UNICEF, 2010). Inequities in meeting children's needs and respecting their rights are observed when comparing different regions of the world but also different geographical areas within these regions. Sub-Saharan Africa and South Asia are the poorest in terms of child survival and development (UNICEF, 2010). The population in these regions has the lowest rates of access to basic health care, safe drinking water, and basic sanitation as well as the highest rates of child mortality. Half of the 8.8 million deaths of children worldwide under 5 years of age recorded in 2008 occurred in sub-Saharan Africa alone. These two regions also have the highest percentage of out-of-school children, accounting for more than three quarters of the 100 million primary school children worldwide who currently do not attend school. In addition, 80% of young people 15–24 years old worldwide living with HIV reside in sub-Saharan Africa. South Asia also has the highest rate of child marriage, a practice that impacts risk for young people for several reasons. First, the child bride's formal education is often abandoned. Second, the girls become socially isolated because they may be forbidden to have contact with their own relatives and old friends. Coupled with their young age and powerlessness, these factors make them more vulnerable to domestic violence and sexual abuse. Finally, adolescent pregnancy and motherhood is an additional risk factor for both the mother's and the child's well-being (UNICEF, 2015c).

In addition to these regional differences, the specific geographical location of the family's residence is also connected to significant disparities as it may impede access to essential services. An urban–rural divide is particularly pronounced in the case of access to clean drinking water and sanitation facilities. For example, of the 884 million people worldwide who still do not have access to clean drinking water, 84% live in rural areas. However, disparities are also observed within urban areas where the urban poor have considerably lower access to clean water and sanitation facilities. Similarly, data from 43 countries of the majority world show that 86% of urban children vs only 72% or rural children attend primary school (UNICEF, 2010).

3.2 Poverty

Poverty often deprives children of their most basic human rights. It is connected, among other things, to higher child mortality, stunting, higher probability of not attending primary school, and higher probability that girls will marry before 18 (UNICEF, 2010). Surprisingly, in many countries around the world, a reduction of under-five mortality has been accompanied by increasing inequality (e.g., Save the Children, 2015). Thus, in 18 of 26 majority world countries that saw a 10% decline in under-five mortality, the inequality between the poorest 20% of households and the richest 20% of households either increased, in some cases by 10% points, or stayed the same. Another example of the effects of poverty is stunting, which is an indicator of chronic under nutrition. In the majority world, children whose families are in the bottom 20% of the socioeconomic ladder are twice as likely to be stunted compared to children growing up in the richest families of the same country. In terms of access to education, according to data from 43 countries of the majority world, children from the poorest families are less likely to attend primary school compared to children from the richest families. Finally, even though the prevalence of child marriage in the majority world has decreased, overall this improvement has been mainly restricted to wealthier women (UNICEF, 2010). This pattern of increasing inequality has led to efforts to ensure global solutions, such as the Sustainable Development Goals (discussed later) require goals for all income groups, thus decreasing the likelihood of pursuit of "quick wins" which turn out to advantage higher income groups (Save the Children, 2015).

The global financial crisis that started in 2008 in the United States and soon spread around the world exacerbated differences between countries and between people within countries. In Europe, for example, *Southern European countries*, such as Greece, Cyprus, Italy, Portugal, Spain, as well as Croatia, and Ireland were among the worst hit by this economic recession. The number of children whose families were considered *income-poor* (*below the poverty line*) increased significantly between 2008 and 2012 in Southern European countries, the Baltic States, Iceland, and Ireland (e.g., Iceland from 11.2% to 31.6% and in Greece from 23% to 40.5%). Furthermore, the number of families who were *severely materially deprived* (e.g., cannot afford to pay rent, to heat their home, to eat meat or proteins regularly) doubled during this period in countries like Greece (from 10.4% to 20.9%) and Italy (from 9% to 18%) (UNICEF, 2014). Within these countries, even though everyone was affected to some degree, the economic crisis hit hardest the poor and most vulnerable. Families with children, migrant and single-parent families, low socioeconomic status families, and large households were among the hardest hit, some being unable to cover even the basic needs of their children, revealing that the minority world is not immune to inequities in protecting children's rights.

3.3 Gender Inequality

Gender inequality is one of the most pervasive forms of inequality worldwide, posing several challenges in the areas of human rights, educational and economic opportunities, maternal mortality, access to resources, academic achievement, occupational aspirations, social relationships, domestic roles, and sexuality and sexual prejudice (Jones, Holmes, & Espey, 2008; Russell, Kosciw, Horn, & Saewyc, 2010). Many aspects of gender disadvantage have already been discussed—especially those accruing to girls such as less access to education and the set of disadvantages related to the practice of early marriage for girls. Education for girls is especially important because of the correlation with later marriage, lower maternal mortality, healthier babies, and more children in school, thus influencing future generations (UNESCO, 2015).

Evidence suggests high rates of gender discrimination experiences among children and youth even in countries with clear legal statutes that prohibit it (Brown & Bigler, 2005). Killen, Rutland, and Ruckk (2011) report that in North America, despite stringent laws, gender exclusion is still widespread, resulting in negative social and academic outcomes for females (Gillen-O'Neel, Ruble, & Fuligni, 2011). In addition, gender stereotypes and societal expectations regarding gender and sexual orientation are a part of the social milieu of children and adolescents (Horn, 2006) often leading to denial of equity and justice for young people who do not adhere to these expectations (e.g., sexual minority youth; Killen et al., 2011). Globally, this is even more strongly the case for children/youth whose gender identity differs from their sex assigned at birth (Grant et al., 2011; International Commission of Jurists, 2009; Kollman & Waites, 2009; United Nations, Office of the High Commissioner on Human Rights, 2012).

To summarize, factors such as poverty and unequal power reinforced by societal structures lead to gender discrimination, most often against girls but also other gender and sexual minorities and contribute to gender inequality globally. Greater gender equality requires a systemic framework that links empowerment, rights, and gender equity in all social sectors (Bryan & Varat, 2008). A strong economic base cannot be built without strengthening girls' and vulnerable youth's social and economic assets to break the chain of intergenerational poverty. Women who have control of their assets are more likely than men to invest in the health and education of their children and other family members. Investing in girls is not simply a question of economic justice, but economic effectiveness (Population Council, 2009).

3.4 Additional Factors

Over and above these primary inequities, some children face what have been termed "especially difficult circumstances" (UNICEF, 2009). These include different types of violence against children, including female genital mutilation/cutting, child trafficking, child sexual exploitation and abuse involvement in armed conflict and child prostitution, as well as migration, child labor, and involvement with justice systems. Such outright violations of children's rights may be encountered both in the minority and the majority worlds. These experiences pose a direct threat to children's positive adaptation, development, and psychological well-being (Masten, 2014b; see chapter "'And I Shot Her': On War, and the Creation of Inequities in the Development of Youths' Moral Capacities" by Wainryb and Bourne, this volume).

Another widespread global phenomenon is migration. Migrant children face the stress related to leaving their home country and moving into a new country, and the challenges of dealing with acculturation, discrimination, and the often low socioeconomic status of their families (Motti-Stefanidi, Berry, Chryssochoou, Sam, & Phinney, 2012). However, in spite of these challenges, most immigrant children are often highly motivated to succeed in their new country and after an initial period of difficulties following migration, adapt, and do well. Thus, even though migration is grouped together with the experiences considered as "especially difficult circumstances," it bears significant differences from rare and unusually hard experiences like child trafficking or child prostitution.

4. GLOBAL OPPORTUNITIES FOR EQUITY AND JUSTICE FOR CHILDREN AND YOUTH

In the prior section we identified many formidable challenges to achieving equity and justice globally: largely, poverty amplified by inadequate infrastructure in key systems such as health, education, and justice. In such limited contexts what could possibly provide opportunity? We identify three global opportunities: (1) the youth bulge in the majority world, demographic shifts providing demographic opportunity; (2) capitalizing on aspects of globalization; and (3) using a positive theoretical frame to design effective interventions for children and youth. We discuss each of these in turn, recognizing that without conscious strategic actions, each of these factors could make the current situation much worse.

4.1 Youth Bulge

By 2025 the global population of children will increase by 4%, with the majority of growth in the global south (You & Anthony, 2012). The share and number of children living in the world's poorest regions and countries will continue to grow rapidly. In particular, by mid-century, one-third of all children under age 18 will be African. At the same time, old-age dependency will continue to increase, globally, and quite sharply in China, threatening resources available for children.

The youth bulge will increase the working age population over the same period of time, with the most dramatic increases in Africa and declines in Europe and China (Lam & Liebbrandt, 2013). The opportunity with the youth bulge is that if these young people are provided with education and training leading to employment, the youth will constitute an economic dividend (Diers, 2013). Providing these opportunities within the countries with the highest youth bulge such as in sub-Saharan African countries and other countries in the global south will also provide an economic boost to these countries. Investment in the development of youth and economic opportunities in their countries must be made. Some efforts to accomplish these goals are already beginning, and are discussed in the next section on programs.

Another approach to capitalizing on the youth bulge is for higher income countries to facilitate in-migration to balance their net losses in the work force (World Bank, 2015b). This has happened to a small degree with the recent massive migrations from Syria and other countries in the Middle East, but most of the immigrants have moved to other lower-income or middle-income countries.

All reports are consistent in emphasizing that the youth bulge and broader demographic shifts constitute an opportunity in which wealthier nations and related development organizations should invest. Conversely, not capitalizing on and preparing for this demographic shift will be costly not only financially but also with tremendous human costs.

4.2 Capitalizing on Globalization

Globalization has changed markets and the flow of information, and it has significant effects on children and youth (e.g., Silbereisen & Chen, 2010; Thompson, 2012). While it has contributed to some problems for child equity and justice, such as with the ease of human trafficking due to rapidly changing and unregulated global markets, there are also opportunities for youth in these same global markets and more open flow of information, especially important for youth who were previously more isolated. Thus, it is essential to leverage globalization to create more opportunities. Young people, especially in the minority world, already exploit the knowledge available on the Internet to develop and pursue interests leading to future educational and occupational opportunity. Currently social media is being developed for educational purposes in the minority world, largely by universities. Increasingly young people in the minority world are using social media for many purposes but access to the Internet is available to only one-third of the majority world, primarily due to lack of reliable power. The growth of Internet resources as well as applications to use them effectively, however, will continue to increase exponentially (International Telecommunications Union, 2015). While these new opportunities are important, they must be accompanied by global policy to protect children from harm. UNICEF is already working on guidelines for positive use of information and communication technology for children (Livingstone & Bulger, 2014).

4.3 Positive Development Framing

Along with the youth bulge and opportunities for access to knowledge and resources through the Internet, effective efforts must capitalize on strengths of young people. Researchers in the minority world (e.g., Larson, 2000; Lerner, 2004) have developed a theoretical framework termed "positive youth development (PYD)" that focuses on strengths of young people rather than their problems, and views development from the contextual perspective of Bronfenbrenner (1979, 2005). Minority world research has found that youth who live in contexts that support their positive academic, social, and psychological development feel better about themselves and their contexts (e.g., families, peers) and both the young people and their meaningful social groups benefit from these (Jelicic, Bobek, Phelps, Lerner, & Lerner, 2007). The concept of PYD was quickly taken up in the United States for programs and policy as well as research. A major review of programs intending to benefit youth (Catalano, Berglund, Ryan, Lonczak, & Hawkins, 2004) concluded that youth programs and interventions that utilize a positive development framework achieve the best results for youth. More recently, a review of effective global programs (Catalano et al., 2012) concluded that PYD programs are also highly effective globally. While majority world research has used this perspective less frequently, papers from a 2014 conference on PYD demonstrate the viability of the concepts for developmental processes and for interventions targeted at for young people from diverse contexts globally (Petersen, Koller, Motti-Stefanidi, & Verma, 2016). Finally, UNICEF (2015c) identified young people themselves as a key strategy for addressing our increasingly unequitable world; young people who recognize and use their assets will be best prepared to play this role.

5. EFFECTIVE PROGRAMS AND INTERVENTIONS

To address the challenges of achieving equity and justice for children and youth globally, it is important to have effective programs or interventions. As with research generally, intervention research has been primarily with minority world populations. For example, in the 1990s, US developmental scientists and prevention researchers aligned with practitioners and policy makers to identify evidence-based positive developmental outcomes for young people in programs and research (Catalano et al., 2004; Catalano, Gavin, & Markham, 2010). One compelling quote by Karen Pittman (Pittman & Fleming, 1991) was that "problem-free is not fully prepared," capturing the shift from a problem focus to one focused on developmental opportunities for youth in programs and interventions.

By the early 2000s, intervention research methods also advanced tremendously. Starting with medical intervention research, randomized controlled trials became the recognized best practice research design globally and this trend has grown to include educational and community-based interventions. Previously, researchers made a distinction between intervention and prevention, the former being for treatment of problems and the latter for reducing risk factors or supporting protective factors for problem behavior or illness. Preventive interventions have been preferred globally for broad-scale reductions of health problems, for example, and are usually integrated with a developmental perspective (e.g., Catalano et al., 2012). Now, and especially with the introduction of positive frameworks (e.g., Catalano et al., 2004), prevention and intervention are usually merged into intervention science (Petersen et al., 2014; Weurmli, Tubbs, Petersen, & Aber, 2015). In this chapter, we follow that convention.

5.1 Global Policy Initiatives

For decades, global multinational organizations (e.g., WHO, World Bank) have launched systematic efforts to improve human development (e.g., Catalano et al., 2012), becoming the primary source of program effectiveness information for the majority world, often focusing on low- and middle-income countries (Verma & Petersen, 2015). Increasingly, these programs have integrated developmental science with intervention science (Weurmli et al., 2015). We note that these global policy initiatives use the term "development" to refer to human development in the context of nations, regions, and globally. Whereas previously, global development meant primarily economic development for nations, it now includes human development as a central component.

5.1.1 Millennium Development Goals

Unlike the CRC discussed earlier, which issued the statement that human rights extend to children, the Millennium Development Goals (MDGs) constituted the first global intervention aimed at improving life conditions for people globally. In September 2000, at the Millennium Summit—the largest ever gathering of its kind—world leaders adopted the UN Millennium Declaration, committing their nations to a new global partnership to reduce extreme poverty. The advantage of the UN Millennium Declaration over the CRC was time-bound targets, known as the MDGs which concluded with 2015. MDGs ranged from halving extreme poverty rates to halting the spread of HIV/AIDS and providing universal primary education (UNICEF, 2010). The Millennium Declaration also explicitly addressed the need to protect children from conflict, violence, abuse, and exploitation. MDGs galvanized unprecedented efforts to meet the needs of the world's poorest and most vulnerable (United Nations, Department of Economic & Social Affairs, 2007).

As with other United Nations conferences and summits, the Millennium Summit generated global consensus on a shared vision for development based on a participatory process. This comprehensive set of developmental goals, of which the MDGs are an integral part, is referred to as the UN Development Agenda. It served as the internationally shared framework for development, with clear expectations for action at the global, regional, and country levels. The agenda covered interlinked issues ranging from poverty, gender equality, social integration, health, population, employment, and education to human rights, the environment, sustainable development, finance, and governance.

This initiative by the UN not only drew attention to issues of equity and social justice for all human beings and as citizens but also fostered the spirit of partnership. The UN's participatory nature of the deliberation process engaged all the key stakeholders: governments, UN system organizations, other intergovernmental and nongovernmental organizations, civil society, and the private sector. This process produced a global partnership for development, with a framework for mutual accountability (United Nations, Department of Economic & Social Affairs, 2007). Resources for the MDGs came from multinational, national, and private foundation funds. While many global frameworks have been adopted, the MDGs were the first to include goals with accountability expectations, thus becoming an unprecedented global intervention.

The MDGs provided the global developmental framework for the past 15 years. The MDG's 2015 Report (United Nations, 2015) reviewed the progress made toward the goals. The data and analysis presented in this report prove that with targeted interventions, sound strategies, adequate resources, and political will even the poorest countries can make unprecedented progress. In brief, the MDGs helped lift more than 1 billion people out of extreme poverty, made inroads against hunger, improved school enrollment rates, and protected the planet. The MDG process created new partnerships, improved public opinion about such global development processes, and demonstrated the value of setting ambitious goals. In the following sections, we review MDG results that improved the lives of children and youth aged 0–30 years. Except when we specify regions, the results apply globally.

MDG 1 aimed to eradicate extreme poverty and hunger. While this MDG did not specifically target children, young people around the world are disproportionately poor. Over the past two decades, there was a significant decline in extreme poverty. In 1990, nearly 50% of the population in the developing world lived on less than $1.25 a day; that proportion dropped to 14% in 2015, far exceeding the targeted goal.

MDG 2 aimed to achieve universal primary education. The primary school net enrollment rate in the developing region reached 91% by 2015, up from 83% in 2000. The number of primary school-age children not in school fell by almost half worldwide, to an estimated 57 million in 2015, down from 100 million in 2000. Similarly, the literacy rate among youth aged 15–24 increased from 83% to 91% between 1990 and 2015, with the gap between women and men narrowed. While this goal of universal enrollment in primary education was not achieved, progress in this area was significant.

MDG 3 focused on promoting gender equity and women's empowerment. School enrollment of girls increased across the developing region. In

Southern Asia in 2015, 103 girls enrolled in school for every 100 boys compared to 74 girls for every 100 boys in 1990. Significant gains were also seen in the employment and status of women, important for positive outcomes for children.

MDG 4 aimed at reducing child mortality. The global under-five mortality rate declined by more than half, dropping from 90 to 43 deaths per 1000 live births between 1990 and 2015. In sub-Saharan Africa, the annual rate of reduction of under-five mortality was over five times faster during 2005–2013 than it was during 1990–1995. Measles vaccination helped prevent nearly 15.6 million deaths between 2000 and 2013, and the number of measles cases declined by 67% for the same period.

MDG 5 aimed to improve maternal health, highly relevant to children. Since 1990, the maternal mortality rate declined by 45%. In Southern Asia, the maternal mortality ratio declined by 64% between 1990 and 2013, and in sub-Saharan Africa, it fell by 49%. Globally, more than 71% of births were assisted by skilled personnel in 2014, an increase from 59% in 1990. In Northern Africa, the proportion of pregnant women who received four or more antenatal visits increased from 50% to 89% between 1990 and 2014. Contraceptive prevalence among women aged 15–49, married or in a union, increased from 55% in 1990 to 64% in 2015.

MDG 6 focused on combating HIV/AIDS, malaria, and other diseases, all of which affect children disproportionately. New HIV infections fell by approximately 40% between 2000 and 2013, from an estimated 3.5 million cases to 2.1 million. By 2014, 13.6 million people living with HIV were receiving antiretroviral therapy (ART). ART averted 7.6 million deaths from AIDS between 1995 and 2013. Over 6.2 million malaria deaths were averted between 2000 and 2015, primarily for children under-five years of age in sub-Saharan Africa. The global malaria incidence rate fell by an estimated 37% and the mortality rate by 58% (United Nations, 2015).

The MDG's Report 2015 (United Nations, 2015) not only highlighted the significant achievements made on many of the MDG targets worldwide but also pointed to the uneven progress across regions and countries and significant areas for further continued action. Despite these advances, millions of people are still being left behind, especially the poorest and those disadvantaged because of their sex, age, disability, ethnicity, or geographical location. Targeted efforts are needed to reach the most vulnerable groups. The review of progress on the MDGs also concluded that data for evidence-based decision making and accountability will be crucial for the post-2015 development agenda (United Nations, 2015).

5.1.2 Global Sustainable Development Goals

In September 2015, world leaders adopted a universal and transformative agenda for sustainable development, with a set of sustainable goals at its core. The Global Sustainable Development Report (United Nations, Department of Economic & Social Affairs, 2015) establishes the 2030 Agenda for Sustainable Development, building from the successes of and learning from the MDGs. An important lesson from the MDGs was that many countries and regions achieved progress by targeting those who were better off, thus exacerbating the status of the poorest and most vulnerable groups. The 17 Global Sustainable Development Goals (GSDGs) and 169 targets demonstrate the scale and ambition of this new global agenda. They seek to realize the human rights of all and achieve global equality. The goals balance the three dimensions of sustainable development: economic, social, and environmental. Alongside continuing development priorities such as poverty eradication, health, education, and food security and nutrition, the GSDGs include a wide range of economic, social, and environmental objectives along with efforts to build more peaceful and inclusive societies. A central feature of the GSDGs is the insistence on attention to both boys and girls.

Perhaps the most important goal for children and youth is goal 3, providing for inclusive and equitable quality education at all levels (i.e., lifelong learning); importantly developmental scientists were significantly involved in the development of that goal. The goals states that all people, regardless of sex, age, race, ethnicity, as well as people with disabilities, migrants, indigenous peoples, especially children and youth in vulnerable situations should have access to lifelong learning opportunities that help them acquire the knowledge and skills needed to take advantage of opportunities and to participate fully in society. The goal aims to provide children and youth with nurturing environments (e.g., safe schools and cohesive communities and families) for full realization of their rights and capabilities, thus helping countries to reap the demographic dividend of youth. Implementation of the GSDGs began on January 1, 2016. Counties will implement the agenda taking into account their national realities, capacities, and resources while respecting national policies and priorities (United Nations, Department of Economic & Social Affairs, 2015).

In addition to the MDGs and the new GSDGs, multinational government organizations also have global initiatives. For UN organizations, these are largely aligned with global goals. UNICEF is most relevant to the focus of this chapter though UNESCO also has some education programs. In alignment with the CRC, all UNICEF programs take a human rights-based approach to programming (UNICEF, 2015b). This means that the conceptual framework for all UNICEF programs aims to enhance developmental processes based on international human rights standards and focused on promoting and protecting human rights. UNICEF programs seek to analyze inequalities at the heart of developmental problems and redress discriminatory practices and unjust power distributions that impede developmental progress. UNICEF has several initiatives such as the #ENDviolence against children initiative in the *Child Protection and Social Exclusion* focus area and the Out-of-School Children Initiative in the *Education* focus area. This initiative addresses the needs of the nearly 125 million children globally who are excluded from school. UNICEF initiatives and programs are generally conducted with specific partner countries or regions.

5.2 National and Topical Interventions

Most countries of the majority world, except perhaps for the poorest, participate in multinational interventions beyond those mentioned earlier. In addition, interventions focused on specific topics such as education or health are launched at the national level. Integrated interventions (e.g., Black & Dewey, 2014) may cover more than one service sector in order to address a need or problem of children. Integrated interventions have become especially popular with early childhood education by offering both nutrition and child development services in the same program, thus targeting the key risk factors that make children susceptible to stunting and impaired development. For example, the colocation of services enables families to access both nutrition and development resources in one setting and the coordination of messages provides families with appropriate, reinforcing information. Furthermore, children with the most disadvantages often experience the greatest gains from these integrated interventions (Black & Dewey, 2014). The Integrated Child Development Services Scheme (ICDS) in India is one such example (http://www.childlineindia.org.in/Integrated-Child-Development-Scheme-ICDS.htm).

Several recent meta-analyses of international early childhood intervention programs (Engle et al., 2007; Nores & Barnett, 2009) found long-term benefits on child development. High-quality and high-intensity programs that provide family support and direct learning experiences to families with young children over a long period of time are effective in improving early childhood outcomes (Britto & Ulkuer, 2012). A widely cited example is the

Turkish Early Enrichment Project (Kagitcibasi, Sunar, & Bekman, 2001), a caregiver-focused structured intervention consisting of a home visitor working with the key caregiver on a range of early childhood skills, including literacy, language, and problem solving. This project has achieved long-term impact on children's higher school attainment, better primary school grades, and strong vocabulary scores.

In India, the five-year Global Education First Initiative (GEFI) was launched in September 2012 to accelerate progress toward the Education for All goals and the education-related MDGs (http://www.un.org.in/task-teams/global-education-first-initiative). The India program led to a global campaign initiative launched in December 2014 to raise children's and youth's awareness of disabilities and inclusion. The *DrawDisability* campaign, led by United Nations GEFI, in partnership with the Global Observatory for Inclusion, and the GEFI Youth Advocacy Group, invited children and youth to reflect on the lives of persons with disabilities through drawings, thus becoming a narrative tool for social change toward greater equity.

5.3 Community-Engaged Interventions

Community-engaged interventions represent another type of initiative aimed at improving conditions for young people worldwide. Community-engaged interventions that have significant educational components are widely regarded as the most effective way to assure that cultural norms and practices are observed in interventions (Weurmli et al., 2015). A primary ethical issue in much intervention work, especially in the majority world, is the lack of engagement of the intended beneficiaries in the design and implementation of interventions. It is unethical to impose intervention designs created elsewhere, with implementation conducted by foreign scientists, without consultation with and participation from those intended to benefit from the intervention (e.g., Miller, Goyal, & Wice, 2015; Tchombe, Nsamenang, Keller, & Fulop, 2013). Engaging community groups and, more broadly, those whom an intervention is intended to benefit is the most ethical way to approach intervention research (Taylor-Ide & Taylor, 2002). Community-engaged approaches to intervention have proven to be effective in many countries in the minority world (Eccles & Gootman, 2002). For example, the US government has engaged these approaches for health promotion generally, providing resources on a website: http://www.healthypeople.gov/2020/About-Healthy-People. These approaches, however, are less common in the majority world (Verma & Konantambigi, 2010). In this section, we will highlight some of the few community-based interventions from the majority world.

5.3.1 Early Childhood

In the Asia region, community-engaged programs for early childhood development empower caregivers to create stimulating environments to promote the well-rounded development of children to 6 years of age. A review of such programs in Bangladesh and India (Jabeen & Karkara, 2005) identified parents as a strategic group for implementation of the Convention of the Rights of Children. The focus of the programs was on strengthening parental involvement and creating awareness around child participation, gender sensitization, and violence against children, and this program provided services related to health, education, and nutrition for children along with protection of child rights against child abuse and neglect, and violence.

5.3.2 Disadvantaged Children and Youth

Community-engaged programs ensuring healthy development for children and youth often shift the focus of the work to prevention and early intervention. An evaluation of one such program in Ireland and Northern Ireland (Paulsell, Grosso, & Dynarski, 2009) examined the extent to which program activities influenced government policy, provider practice, university research, and advocacy efforts targeted at disadvantaged children, youth, and parents. The findings suggest that the Disadvantaged Children and Youth program has been a catalyst for change in encouraging government investment in evidence-based prevention and early intervention, promoting evidence-based practice among service providers, and engaging the academic sector in policy-oriented research. Such collaborative efforts are receiving strong support from the community and represent a model for effective practice.

5.3.3 Street Children

Another area in which community-engaged interventions have been particularly promising has been work regarding street children, a disadvantaged group that has drawn worldwide attention and that is visible across the urban landscape in many regions of the world. Street children are the extreme manifestation of deteriorating social capital and social exclusion. While the immediate factors responsible for their condition are unique for each child, they generally represent some combination of low family income, lack of housing, failure in school, familial abuse and neglect, armed conflicts, and natural disasters. A World Bank report (Volpi, 2002) evaluated 18 interventions for street children from Brazil, Bulgaria, Columbia, Ghana, Italy, Kenya, Mexico, the Philippines, Portugal, Romania, and United States. Selection preference was given to development-oriented initiatives, aimed at increasing children's opportunities to be integrated in school, family, and labor market. The existence of evaluation and evidence of replicability were also used as selection criteria. Most interventions were implemented by NGOs, but a few were cooperative ventures by NGOs and local governments in which program activities for street children were integrated into municipal development programs. The programs provided services directed primarily at the children and those that involve schools, family, and community. Some also included advocacy and social mobilization. Interventions also varied with the age of the target group. Those geared to young children concentrated on basic assistance and school and family reintegration, while activities aimed at adolescents also included job training, legal defense, housing, and sexual health. Some of the emerging factors for effective program implementation with this population were: use of trained professionals, a development-related focus, reaching children where they were, individualized attention and need-based services, children's participation, inclusion of physical and mental care, involving family and community, lobbying and advocacy, integration of services, networking, and institutional cooperation. The program evaluation highlights the need for preventive programs and policies for street children that will strengthen the connection with their family, school, and the community.

What emerges from the above intervention evaluations is the need for programs to be based on sound research and to be a good fit with the local culture, the existing service delivery system, and the needs and interests of affected families, children, and youth. As an exemplar of this we cite a cross-cultural study undertaken with street children that informs effective intervention design. An international collaborative research team (Verma, Santa Maria, & Morojele, 2011) conducted a cross-cultural multimethod study on pathways of risk, protection, and well-being among street children in four developing countries: India, Indonesia, the Philippines, and South Africa. Within the child rights framework and a comparative theoretical model guided by theory and research on risk, protection, and resilience, the study examined the similarities and differences in the sociocultural contexts (e.g., street-, home-, or shelter-based) organizing street children's development.

Participants included 488 street children aged 11–18 years who comprised three categories of street children: *family-based* (children working on the streets and living with their families), *street-based* (children living on the streets with no family contact), and *shelter-based* (children living in shelters or institutions). Results revealed that the street-based kids were most vulnerable and an "at-risk" group when compared to the other two groups. Family or significant others support was protective in India but not in the other three countries. Positive school climate reduced engagement by children in risky behaviors across the countries. Self-efficacy and peer support were strong predictors for problem solving orientation. Girls experienced greater family support and perceived school climate as more favorable than boys. For the family-based children, parents and community safety nets regulated work. For the street-based children, the role of the peers was paramount. For the shelter-based children, quality of care and monitoring was crucial for engagement in nonrisk activities. Across the four countries, risk factors were: victimization, impaired parental relationships, lack of time to attend school, police and shelter abuse, negative gang pressure, engagement in petty crimes, drugs, and survival sex. Protective factors were parental support, schooling, sense of efficacy, supportive street community, participation in community activities, skill development, and access to jobs (Sharma & Verma, 2009). These results suggest that interventions enhancing protective factors are likely to help this vulnerable population.

The street girls reported both perceptions of self-efficacy and feelings of depression and mental health-related problems. Girls, compared to boys on the street, were more likely to internalize violence and were at a greater risk of continuous abuse (Sharma & Verma, 2013). Street girls need to be considered as a special group for policy makers, with programs formulated differently than those for the male street children; in addition, they must be considered for placements in safe shelters when they are completely on their own.

5.3.4 University–Community Partnerships

Universities also sponsor community-engaged programs in the majority world. This example from Brazil is of an intervention that fostered positive development in low-income youth aged 12–14 years. *Youth in Scene* was a social program founded by the Federal University in Porto Alegre, Brazil, and funded by the Brazilian Ministry of Education. A group of students and professors worked with low-income youth participants from social welfare programs. The program purpose was to expand and improve the youth's knowledge and to promote their rights. Education on rights and promotion of participatory action, serving as a protagonist, and learning leadership were the main topics of the sessions. The intention was for the youth to solve not only current problems but also those they might experience through their life cycle. The intervention team used the bioecological theory of development (Bronfenbrenner, 1979, 2005) and the four pillars of education (Delors, 1998): Learning to know, Learning to do, Learning to live together, and Learning to be. Three program components were developed: (1) Theoretical and practical approaches to rights, solidarity, and The Four Pillars Approach; (2) Participatory action/protagonist/leadership roles applied to the Youth in Scene microsystem created at the university; and (3) Participatory action/protagonist/leadership roles applied to the community where the youth come from, especially focused on social and political action (Souza, Dutra-Thomé, Schiró, Aquino-Morais, & Koller, 2011).

The main focus of the program was to raise awareness of human rights and to combat violations of rights, such as juvenile labor exploitation and violence. Learning about their rights and effective strategies enabled the youth to cope with their challenges and helped create protective factors in their lives, thus enabling the youth to shape a better life and plan for the future. Monthly meetings at the university and weekly meetings in their own communities focused on topics such as solidarity, optimism, well-being, life projects, cooperation, responsibility, and other positive factors. The intervention team encouraged a major shift in the vision that such young people have of themselves, promoting their role as change agents and protagonists in the exercise of citizenship, strengthening their self-esteem and self-efficacy, and enabling nonviolent struggle for their rights.

From the very beginning program planners sought to give voice to youth and to match the activities and the objectives of the program to the participants' needs. Activities were planned and carried out in groups with adolescents and work team members. Team members recorded in field diaries their experiences in the program. The participants were exposed to new situations, and unforeseen moments, to which they then had to respond, sometimes requiring improvisation. They were expected to join groups with different people and confront different situations. Often they had to modify their own concepts and ways of expression to be better understood by the group. Novel activities and situations required new roles and behaviors, and helped them accept each other and together, solve daily problems. They also learned teamwork, made contact with diverse institutions and groups of people, and shared with others their progress toward a common objective—a better future.

The program evaluation revealed many effective program components including the number of new activities engaged and topics addressed, staff effectiveness, new learning about rights and responsibilities, and growth of friendship networks within the group. After completion of the second and third program components, organizers observed increased actions in the communities including youth participation in events such as conferences, youth meetings, and lectures at schools, church, and community associations. The youth also reported increased community participation. Some specific examples deserve mention. In one community, youth participants were mediators in the municipality as community board members. One girl was National Representative of the State at a Brazilian Conference of Children's Rights in Brasilia (the capital of Brazil).

Overall, participants achieved a good knowledge of their rights and the rights of others. The participatory action/protagonist/leadership model changed their lives and their roles in their communities and families. Reports from participants revealed many positive aspects of the program and social practice of the youth members of *Youth in Scene*.

5.4 Strategic Interventions

We also want to mention the category of strategic interventions, interventions designed to create systemic change over interconnected systems. This perspective emerges from organizational development efforts originating from the theories of Lewin (1958) and broadly promoted by Senge (2006) among others. While typically only partially successful, these massive interventions achieve some change or at least forward momentum because they focus on what can be rather than getting caught in the vicious cycle of the status quo (e.g., Sanders, 1998). A key feature are feedback loops that continually improve processes, and strategic philanthropy has especially embraced this perspective (e.g., Kania, Kramer, & Russell, 2014).

6. CONCLUSIONS

What we hope has become clear in this chapter is the importance of taking a global perspective to issues of equity and justice for young people. The global demographics alone—dramatically increasing youth bulge primarily in the poorest countries—compel our attention to supporting productive futures for children and youth. The challenge is primarily one of providing equity and justice for these young people. As many global institutions have articulated, this potential demographic disaster must be turned into a demographic dividend. We concur with UNICEF and others that a major strategy must be to engage young people in identifying and implementing solutions. This engagement strategy is the only one likely to be effective while being implemented on a large scale.

While we know quite a lot about the current status of children/youth in the minority world as well as what kinds of interventions have proven effective to improve their development and health, there is still much to learn, especially about the interventions and social structures required to achieve equity and justice in the majority world. As we frequently note, many of the differences between the minority and majority worlds involve the severity of conditions overall. For example, sheer survival through childhood to adulthood is much less likely in the majority world, primarily because of weak or nonexistent supportive infrastructure (e.g., health systems) to help with daily life and especially to respond to natural (e.g., earthquakes, drought, floods) and human disasters (e.g., conflict). This level of intervention must be undertaken by global and national institutions.

The work we have discussed has made clear the importance of including children and youth in global equity and justice efforts. Too often, especially with globalization, less powerful groups like children and youth are left out of broader equity and justice considerations. Yet, they are the future for any nation and must be engaged for sustainable communities and nations. On a global level, the MDGs made significant headway toward addressing these considerations, and the new Sustainable Development Goals should create even greater progress. But these programs target specific problems such as child survival and literacy. Much more is needed to provide opportunity for young people. A major area for philanthropy is youth social entrepreneurship (e.g., IYF, iyfnet.org; Global Philanthropy Alliance, globalphilanthopyalliance.org), but these programs are small and poorly evaluated. We note, however, that some majority world countries are beginning to provide funding to youth, such as Kenya (youthfund.go.ke).

We have also frequently noted that there is too little research from the majority world. Some researchers from the minority world have noticed this gap and engaged in extractive research from these parts of the world. Like the analogy from mineral or other natural resource extraction, simply gathering data from the majority world is neither equitable nor just. A better approach for the near term is for minority world researchers to partner with those from the majority world with agreements for data to remain in country and with explicit efforts for all researchers to learn from the research process, including those yet in training. Increasingly majority world researchers are working without such assistance, or sometimes partnering with researchers from other majority world countries. This chapter includes many such examples. Some challenges continue for majority world researchers such as equitable access to publication outlets: both journals and books. Research infrastructure is rapidly being aided by the Internet; what remains to be addressed is equitable access to reliable power, connectivity, and person-dependent resources such as the example of publication outlets.

We have included program research in our discussion of research but policy research is too infrequent globally, in both the minority and majority worlds (e.g., Petersen, 2009, 2011). While the specifics of current challenges depend on features of the place, increasingly problems are now global—whether from migration, health epidemics, or global climate change. There are some emergent efforts to tackle these policy questions—for example, the International Consortium of Developmental Science Societies (http://www.srcd.org/advancing-field/srcd-initiatives/international-consortium-developmental-science-organizations)—but much more is needed. We also recognize many important calls emphasizing child/youth development in achieving global equity, justice, and peace (e.g., Christie et al., 2014; Hamburg & Hamburg, 2004).

REFERENCES

Baker, M. (2008). *The lost boys of Sudan: An American story of the refugee experience.* Athens, GA: University of Georgia Press.

Banai, A., Ronzoni, M., & Schemmel, C. (Eds.), (2011). *Social justice, global dynamics: Theoretical and empirical perspectives.* London: Routledge.

Black, M. M., & Dewey, K. G. (2014). Promoting equity through integrated early child development and nutrition interventions. *Annals of the New York Academy of Sciences, 1308*, 1–10.

Britto, P. R., & Ulkuer, N. (2012). Child development in developing countries: Child rights and policy implications. *Child Development, 83*(1), 92–103.

Bronfenbrenner, U. (1979). *The ecology of human development.* Cambridge: Harvard University Press.

Bronfenbrenner, U. (2005). The bioecological theory of human development. In U. Bronfenbrenner (Ed.), *Making human beings humans* (pp. 3–15). Thousand Oaks: SAGE.

Brown, C. S., & Bigler, R. (2005). Children's perceptions of discrimination: A developmental model. *Child Development, 76*, 533–553.

Bryan, E., & Varat, J. (2008). *Strategies for promoting gender equity in developing countries: Lessons, challenges, and opportunities.* Retrieved July 23, 2015, from www.wilsoncenter.org.

Catalano, R. F., Berglund, M. L., Ryan, J. A. M., Lonczak, H. S., & Hawkins, J. D. (2004). Positive youth development in the United States: Research findings on evaluations of positive youth development programs. *The Annals of the American Academy of Political and Social Science, 591*(1), 98–124.

Catalano, R. F., Fagan, A. A., Gavin, L. E., Greenberg, M. T., Irwin, C. E., Jr., Ross, D. A., et al. (2012). Worldwide application of prevention science in adolescent health. *Lancet, 379*(9826), 1653–1664.

Catalano, R. F., Gavin, L. E., & Markham, C. M. (2010). Future directions for positive youth development programs that promote adolescent sexual and reproductive health. *Journal of Adolescent Health, 46*, 592–596.

Christie, D. J., Panter-Brick, C., Behrman, J. R., Cochrane, J. R., Dawes, A., Goth, K., et al. (2014). Health human development as a path to peace. In J. F. Leckman, C. Panter-Brick, & R. Salah (Eds.), *Pathways to peace: The transformative power of children and families: Vol. 15* (pp. 273–302). Cambridge, MA: MIT Press.

Cicchetti, D., & Rogosch, F. A. (2002). A developmental psychopathology perspective on adolescence. *Journal of Consulting and Clinical Psychology, 70*, 6–20.

Delors, J. (Ed.), (1998). *Educação: Um tesouro a descobrir. Education: A treasure to be discovered* São Paulo, Cortez/Brasília: UNESCO International Commission Report for the XXI siglo. MEC/UNESCO.

Diers, J. (2013). Why the world needs to get serious about adolescents: A view from UNICEF. *Journal of Research on Adolescence, 23*(2), 214–222.

Eccles, J., & Gootman, J. (2002). *Community programs to promote youth development.* Washington, DC: National Academy Press.

Engle, P. L., Black, M. M., Behrman, J. R., Cabral de Mello, M., Gertler, P. J., Kapirini, L., et al. (2007). Strategies to avoid the loss of developmental potential in more than 200 million children in the developing world. *Lancet, 369*, 229–242.

Gillen-O'Neel, C., Ruble, D., & Fuligni, A. (2011). Ethnic stigma, academic anxiety, and intrinsic motivation in middle childhood. *Child Development, 82*, 1470–1485.

Goldson, B., & Muncie, J. (2012). Toward a global "child friendly" juvenile justice? *International Journal of Law, Crime and Justice, 40*, 47–64.

Grant, J. M., Mottet, L. A., Tanis, J., Harrison, J., Herman, J. L., & Keisling, M. (2011). *Injustice at every turn: A report of the national transgender discrimination survey.* Washington, DC: National Center for Transgender Equality and National Gay and Lesbian Task Force.

Hamburg, D. A., & Hamburg, B. A. (2004). *Learning to live together: Preventing hatred and violence in child and adolescent development.* New York: Oxford University Press.

Horn, S. S. (2006). Group status, group bias, and adolescents' reasoning about the treatment of others in school contexts. *International Journal of Behavioral Development, 30*, 208–218.

International Commission of Jurists (2009). *Sexual orientation, gender identity and international human rights law.* (practitioners guide no. 4). Geneva, Switzerland: Author.

International Telecommunications Union (2015). *ICT facts and figures 2015. http://www.itu.int/en/ITU-D/Statistics/Documents/facts/ICTFactsFigures2015.pdf. Accessed 01.13.16.*

Jabeen, F., & Karkara, R. (2005). *Government support to parenting in Bangladesh and India.* Stockholm: Save the Children Sweden.

Jelicic, H., Bobek, D., Phelps, E. D., Lerner, J. V., & Lerner, R. M. (2007). Using positive youth development to predict contribution and risk behaviors in early adolescence: Findings from the first two waves of the 4-H study of positive youth development. *International Journal of Behavioral Development, 31*(3), 263–273.

Jones, N., Holmes, R., & Espey, J. (2008). *Gender and the MDGs: A gender lens is vital for pro-poor results.* London: Overseas Development Institute.

Kagitcibasi, C., Sunar, D., & Bekman, S. (2001). Long-term effects of early intervention: Turkish low-income mothers and children. *Journal of Applied Developmental Psychology, 22*, 333–361.

Kania, J., Kramer, M., & Russell, P. (2014). Strategic philanthropy for a complex world. *Stanford Social Innovation Review, Summer.* Retrieved September 1, 2015, from http://ssir.org/up_for_debate/article/strategic_philanthropy.

Keating, D. P. (2016). *The stress gene: The lifelong impact of early life adversity—And how to break the cycle.* New York: St. Martin's Press.

Killen, M., Rutland, A., & Ruck, M. D. (2011). Promoting equity, tolerance, and justice in childhood. *Social Policy Report, 25*(4), 3–25.

Kollman, K., & Waites, M. (2009). The global politics of lesbian, gay, bisexual, and transgender human rights: An introduction. *Contemporary Politics Special Issue: The Global Politics of LGBT Human Rights, 15*(1), 1–17.

Lam, D., & Liebbrandt, M. (2013). *Post-2015 UN MDG development agenda employment and economic growth: Global demographic trends and their implications for employment.* Retrieved December 2015, from http://www.post2015hlp.org/wp-content/uploads/2013/05/Lam-Leibbrandt_Global-Demographic-Trends-and-their-Implications-for-Employment.pdf.

Lansford, J. E., Deater-Deckard, K., Bornstein, M. H., Putnick, D. L., & Bradley, R. H. (2014). Attitudes justifying punishment and physical and psychological aggression towards children: A study in 25 low- and middle-income countries. *The Journal of Pediatrics, 164*, 1208–1213.

Larson, R. W. (2000). Towards a psychology of positive youth development. *American Psychologist, 55*, 170–183.

Lerner, R. M. (2004). *Liberty: Thriving and civic engagement among American youth.* Thousand Oaks, CA: Sage.

Lerner, R. M. (2006). Developmental science, developmental systems, and contemporary theories. In R. M. Lerner (Ed.), *Handbook of child psychology: Vol. 1. Theoretical models of human development* (pp. 1–17). Hoboken, NJ: Wiley.

Lewin, K. (1958). *Group decision and social change.* New York: Holt, Rinehart, and Winston.

Livingstone, S., & Bulger, M. (2014). A global research agenda for children's rights in the digital age. *Journal of Children and Media, 8*(4), 317–335.

Loming, L., & Tabb, M. (2012). *Running for my life: One lost boy's journey from the killing fields of Sudan to the Olympic Games.* Nashville, TN: Nelson Thomas.

Masten, A. S. (2014a). *Ordinary magic: Resilience in development.* New York: Guilford Press.

Masten, A. S. (2014b). Global perspectives on resilience in children and youth. *Child Development, 85*(1), 6–20.

Miller, J. G., Goyal, N., & Wice, M. (2015). Ethical considerations in research on human development and culture. In L. Jensen (Ed.), *The Oxford handbook of human development and culture: An interdisciplinary perspective* (pp. 14–27). New York: Oxford University Press.

Motti-Stefanidi, F., Berry, J., Chryssochoou, X., Sam, D. L., & Phinney, J. (2012). Positive immigrant youth adaptation in context: Developmental, acculturation, and social psychological perspectives. In A. S. Masten, K. Liebkind, & D. J. Hernandez (Eds.), *Realizing the potential of immigrant youth* (pp. 117–158). Cambridge: Cambridge University Press.

Nores, M., & Barnett, W. S. (2009). Benefits of early childhood interventions across the world: (Under) investing in the very young. *Economics of Education Review, 29*, 271–282.

Pan American Health Organization, Washington, United States of America. (2013). *Outlook on the global agenda 2014.* Geneva: World Economic Forum. Retrieved April 13, 2014, from http://www.weforum.org/reports/outlook-globalagenda-2014.

Paulsell, D., Grosso, P. D., & Dynarski, M. (2009). *The Atlantic Philanthropies' disadvantaged children and youth program in Ireland and Northern Ireland: Overview of program evaluation findings.* Retrieved November 21, 2015, from https://www.mathematica-mpr.com/our-publications-and-findings/publications/the-atlantic-philanthropies-disadvantaged-children-and-youth-program-in-ireland-and-northern-ireland-overview-of-program-evaluation-findings.

Petersen, A. C. (2009). Inconvenient truths: Behavioral research and social policy. In M. A. G. vanAken, R. E. Tremblay, & W. Koops (Eds.), *Development of behavior problems* (pp. 229–245). New York: Psychology Press.

Petersen, A. C. (2011). Global issues in research and social policy. *Bulletin of the International Society for the Study of Behavioral Development, 2*(60), 20–22.

Petersen, A. C., Joseph, J., Feit, M., & Committee on Child Maltreatment Research, Policy, and Practice for the Next Decade: Phase II, Board on Children, Youth, and Families (Eds.), (2014). *New directions in child abuse and neglect research.* Washington, DC: National Academies Press.

Petersen, A. C., Koller, S. H., Motti-Stefanidi, F., & Verma, S. (2016). *Positive youth development in global contexts of social and economic change.* New York: Routledge (in press).

Pittman, K. J., & Fleming, W. E. (1991). *A new vision: Promoting youth development. Testimony of Karen J. Pittman before the house select committee on children, youth and families.* Washington, DC: Academy for Educational Development.

Population Council. (2009). *The adolescent experience in-depth: Using data to identify and reach the most vulnerable young people: India 2005/06.* New York: The Population Council.

Russell, S. T., Kosciw, J., Horn, S. S., & Saewyc, E. (2010). Safe schools policy for LGBTQ students. *Social Policy Report, 24*, 1–24.

Sanders, T. I. (1998). *Strategic thinking and the new science: Planning in the midst of chaos, complexity, and change.* New York: The Free Press.

Save the Children. (2015). *The lottery of birth.* Retrieved January 11, 2016, from https://www.savethechildren.net/sites/default/files/STC_The_Lottery_of_Birth_Final-EVERYONE%20COVER.PDF.

Senge, P. M. (2006). *The fifth discipline* (2nd ed.). New York: Doubleday/Currency.

Sharma, D., & Verma, S. (2009). Typologies of protection in a risky world: Narratives by marginalized street children. *The Indian Journal of Home Science, 28*(1), 64–77.

Sharma, D., & Verma, S. (2013). Street girls and their fight for survival across four developing countries. *Psychological Studies, 58*(4), 365–373.

Silbereisen, R. K., & Chen, X. (Eds.), (2010). *Social change and human development: Concepts and results.* Thousand Oaks, CA: Sage.

Souza, A. P. L., Dutra-Thomé, L., Schiró, E. D. B., Aquino-Morais, C., & Koller, S. H. (2011). Criando contextos ecológicos de desenvolvimento e direitos humanos para adolescentes [Building ecological context for human rights and development for adolescents]. *Paidéia, 21*, 273–278.

Taylor-Ide, D., & Taylor, C. E. (2002). *Just and lasting change: When communities own their future.* Baltimore, MD: John Hopkins University Press.

Tchombe, T. M. S., Nsamenang, A. B., Keller, H., & Fulop, M. (Eds.), (2013). *Cross-cultural psychology: An Afrocentric perspective.* Limbe, Cameroon: Design House.

Thompson, R. (2012). Changing societies, changing childhood: Studying the impact of globalization on child development. *Child Development Perspectives, 6*, 187–192.

UNESCO. (2013). *Statistics on youth.* Retrieved December 8, 2015, from http://www.unesco.org/new/en/unesco/events/prizes-and-celebrations/celebrations/international-days/world-radio-day-2013/statistics-on-youth/on.

UNESCO. (2015). *Education for all global monitoring report 2015.* Retrieved August 4, 2015, from http://en.unesco.org/gem-report/report/2015/education-all-2000-2015-achievements-and-challenges.

UNFPA (2014). *The power of 1.8 billion: Adolescents, youth and the transformation of the future.* Retrieved May 31, 2016. http://eeca.unfpa.org/publications/state-world-population-2014-report.

UNICEF. (2009). *Progress for children 2009.* Retrieved March 28, 2016, from www.unicef.org/publications/files/Progress_for_children.

UNICEF. (2010). *Progress for children achieving the MDGs with equity.* New York: Author (no. 9).

UNICEF. (2013). *Child protection.* Retrieved December 8, 2015, from http://www.unicef.org/ceecis/protection_1174.html.

UNICEF. (2014). *Innocenti report card 12, children of the recession: The impact of the economic crisis on child well-being in rich countries.* Florence, Italy: UNICEF.

UNICEF. (2015a). *Progress for children 2015.* Retrieved July 18, 2015, from http://www.unicef.org/lac/Progress_for_Children_No._11_22June15.pdf.

UNICEF. (2015b). *Human rights-based approach to programming.* Retrieved December 2015, from http://www.unicef.org/policyanalysis/rights/.

UNICEF. (2015c). *The state of the world's children: Reimagining the future.* Retrieved January 2016, from http://sowc2015.unicef.org/on.

UNICEF. (2015d). *Multiple Indicator Cluster Survey (MICS).* Retrieved March 28, 2016, from http://www.unicef.org/statistics/index_24302.html.

United Nations. (2015). *The Millennium Development Goals Report 2015.* Retrieved August 20, 2015, from http://www.un.org/millenniumgoals/2015_MDG_Report/pdf/MDG%25202015%2520PR%2520Global.pdf.

United Nations, Department of Economic & Social Affairs. (2007). *United Nations development agenda: Development for all.* Retrieved August 22, 2015, from http://www.un.org/esa/devagenda/UNDA1.pdf.

United Nations, Department of Economic & Social Affairs. (2015). *Transforming our world: The 2030 agenda for sustainable development.* Retrieved December 17, 2015, from https://sustainabledevelopment.un.org/post2015/transformingourworld.

United Nations, Office of the High Commissioner on Human Rights. (1989). *Convention on the Rights of the Child.* Retrieved August 24, 2015, from http://www.ohchr.org/en/professionalinterest/pages/crc.aspx.

United Nations, Office of the High Commissioner on Human Rights. (2012). *Born free and equal: Sexual orientation and gender identity in international human rights law* (HR/PUB/12/06). New York: Office of the United Nations High Commissioner for Human Rights.

USAID. (2012). *Youth in development: Realizing the demographic opportunity.* Washington, DC: US Agency for International Development.

Verma, S., & Konantambigi, R. (2010). Interventions for development of social skills among children in developing countries. In P. K. Smith & C. H. Hart (Eds.), *The Wiley-Blackwell handbook of childhood social development* (2nd ed., pp. 646–661). Singapore: John Wiley.

Verma, S., & Petersen, A. C. (2015). Global concerns with adolescent health with a case study of India. In L. A. Jensen (Ed.), *The Oxford handbook of human development and culture: An interdisciplinary perspective.* New York: Oxford University Press. http://dx.doi.org/10.1093/oxfordhb/9780199948550.013.22.

Verma, S., Santa Maria, M., & Morojele, N. (2011). A cross-cultural view to the study of resilience among street children. *ISSBD Bulletin, 1*(59), 11–14.

Volpi, E. (2002). *Street children: Promising practices and approaches.* Washington, DC: World Bank Institute.

Weurmli, A. J., Tubbs, C. C., Petersen, A. C., & Aber, J. L. (2015). Children and youth in low- and middle-income countries: Toward an integrated developmental and intervention science. *Child Development Perspectives, 9*(1), 1–6. http://dx.doi.org/10.1111/cdep.12108.

World Bank. (2015a). *Updated income classifications.* Retrieved August 15, 2015, from http://data.worldbank.org/news/2015-country-classifications.

World Bank. (2015b). *Human development indicators 2015*. Washington, DC: World Bank. Retrieved March 28, 2015, from http://data.worldbank.org/data-catalog/world-development-indicators.

World Bank. (2015c). *World undergoing major population shift with far-reaching implications for migration, poverty, development: WB/IMF report*. Retrieved March 28, 2015, from http://www.worldbank.org/en/publication/global-monitoring-report.

You, D., & Anthony, D. (2012). *Generation 2025 and beyond* (occasional papers no. 1). New York: UNICEF. Retrieved December 9, 2015, from http://www.unicef.org/media/files/Generation_2015_and_beyond_15_Nov2012_e_version.pdf.

Yousafzai, M., & Lamb, C. (2013). *I am Malala: The story of the girl who stood up for education and was shot by the Taliban*. New York: Little, Brown and Company.

AUTHOR INDEX

Note: Page numbers followed by "*f*" indicate figures, and "*t*" indicate tables.

C

D

G

H

I

J

K

M

Q

R

S

T

U

V

SUBJECT INDEX

Note: Page numbers followed by "*f*" indicate figures, and "*t*" indicate tables.

V

W

Y

CONTENTS OF PREVIOUS VOLUMES

VOLUME 5

VOLUME 6

VOLUME 7

VOLUME 8

VOLUME 9

VOLUME 10

VOLUME 11

VOLUME 12

VOLUME 13

VOLUME 14

VOLUME 15

VOLUME 16

VOLUME 17

VOLUME 18

VOLUME 19

VOLUME 20

VOLUME 21

VOLUME 22

VOLUME 23

VOLUME 24

VOLUME 25

VOLUME 26

VOLUME 27

VOLUME 28

VOLUME 32

VOLUME 33

VOLUME 34

VOLUME 35

VOLUME 36

VOLUME 37

VOLUME 38

VOLUME 39

VOLUME 40

VOLUME 41

VOLUME 42

VOLUME 43

VOLUME 44

VOLUME 45

VOLUME 46

VOLUME 47

VOLUME 48

VOLUME 49

VOLUME 50

FSC
www.fsc.org
MIX
Papier | Fördert
gute Waldnutzung
FSC® C083411

Kolibri 360 GmbH
Ferdinand-Jühlke-Straße 7
99095 Erfurt, Deutschland
produktsicherheit@kolibri360.de